The Labor of Lunch

CALIFORNIA STUDIES IN FOOD AND CULTURE
Darra Goldstein, Editor

The Labor of Lunch

WHY WE NEED REAL FOOD
AND REAL JOBS
IN AMERICAN PUBLIC SCHOOLS

Jennifer E. Gaddis

UNIVERSITY OF CALIFORNIA PRESS

University of California Press, one of the most distinguished university presses in the United States, enriches lives around the world by advancing scholarship in the humanities, social sciences, and natural sciences. Its activities are supported by the UC Press Foundation and by philanthropic contributions from individuals and institutions. For more information, visit www.ucpress.edu.

University of California Press
Oakland, California

© 2019 by Jennifer E. Gaddis

Library of Congress Cataloging-in-Publication Data

Names: Gaddis, Jennifer E., 1985– author.
Title: The labor of lunch : why we need real food and real jobs in American public schools / Jennifer E. Gaddis.
Other titles: California studies in food and culture ; 70.
Description: Oakland, California : University of California Press, [2019] | Series: California studies in food and culture ; 70 | Includes bibliographical references and index.
Identifiers: LCCN 2019017211 (print) | LCCN 2019022225 (ebook) | ISBN 9780520300026 (cloth : alk. paper) | ISBN 9780520300033 (pbk. : alk. paper)
Subjects: LCSH: National School Lunch Program (U.S.) | School children—Food—United States. | School children—Food—Government policy—United States. | School children—Nutrition—Government policy—United States.
Classification: LCC LB3479. U6 G37 2019 (print) | LCC LB3479.U6 (ebook) | DDC 371.7/160973—dc23
LC record available at https://lccn.loc.gov/2019017211
LC ebook record available at https://lccn.loc.gov/2019022225

Manufactured in the United States of America

27 26 25 24 23 22 21 20 19
10 9 8 7 6 5 4 3 2 1

To all the school lunch workers, past, present, and future

CONTENTS

List of Illustrations ix
Acknowledgements xi

Introduction: Why We Need to Fix the Food and the Jobs 1

1 · The Radical Roots of School Lunch 16

2 · The Fight for Food Justice 52

3 · From Big Food to Real Food Lite 96

4 · Cafeteria Workers in the "Prison of Love" 134

5 · Building a Real Food Economy 174

Conclusion: Organizing a New Economy of Care 215

Notes 229
Bibliography 255
Index 279

ILLUSTRATIONS

1. Workers making prepack sandwiches in a central kitchen 4
2. Free lunch in Washington, DC, kindergarten, 1942 6
3. UNITE HERE real-food, real-jobs protest, Chicago, 2012 9
4. Workers preparing lunches in Boston's New England Kitchen 27
5. Poster, US School Garden Army, WWI 36
6. Work schedule for a 1930s high school cafeteria 40
7. Surplus food distribution for free school lunches in California, 1939 43
8. Worker feeding children lunch in Virginia schoolroom, 1942 44
9. Industry representative showing how to reheat frozen airline-type lunches 70
10. Coca-Cola sign outside rural Arkansas school cafeteria, 1950s 79
11. Supervisor of urban school lunch program oversees production in a high school kitchen, Connecticut 82
12. Prepack assembly line in a central kitchen 85
13. Worker slicing commodity meat in a central kitchen 101
14. School poster celebrating the Arkansas poultry industry 102
15. Worker with quick-scratch individual pizzas 124
16. Worker baking muffins for 750 students, Maryland, 1947 156
17. Sign from 1950s student protest of cafeteria conditions 158
18. Workers preparing lunch in a Maryland high school, 1947 163
19. Arkansas school lunch managers learning bread-making techniques, 1948 165

20. Cooks preparing lunch in a small-town Wisconsin school, 1954 *168*
21. UNITE HERE "No More Frozen Food" protest, Chicago, 2012 *173*
22. High school production-kitchen staff, Minneapolis *182*
23. Minnesota farm-to-school farmer *193*
24. Minnesota carrot farmers at farm-to-school celebration *207*
25. Food truck at farm-to-school barbecue, Minneapolis *209*

ACKNOWLEDGMENTS

A great many people and organizations have helped bring this book into being. I could never have written it without the hundreds of people on the front lines of school foodservice who assisted me along the way. I'm humbled by the work they do to feed the nation's children and by the trust they put in me to tell this story. While I interviewed many more people and visited many more schools than appear in this book, I learned something new from each encounter.

I'm grateful to school districts across the country and to the School Nutrition Association for granting me permission to conduct research with their staff and members. I'd also like to thank Jeffrey Boyce and the staff at the Institute of Child Nutrition for assisting me with the collections housed at the Child Nutrition Archives.

While I was at Yale, this project benefitted from the mentorship of Karen Hébert, Juliet Schor, Maria Trumpler, and John Wargo. At the University of Wisconsin–Madison, I grew tremendously from the mentorships of Erik Olin Wright, Jane Collins, and Nan Enstad. Erik helped me find a footing within emancipatory social science and pushed me to think more deeply about how the National School Lunch Program could become a "real utopia." Jane's work on economic value, commodity chains, and gendered labor continues to inspire me. Nan's advice on how to enliven my historical writing helped to make this a much better book, as did her insightful recommendations for improving earlier versions of this manuscript. The food studies networks at both Yale and the University of Wisconsin–Madison provided valuable opportunities to workshop this book, as did a First Book Workshop facilitated by the UW–Madison Center for the Humanities. I specifically thank Jennifer Klein, Amy Bentley, Nan Enstad, Jane Collins, Rima Apple,

Michael Apple, Jack Kloppenburg, and Connie Flanagan for the many helpful suggestions they made during the workshop.

I owe a tremendous debt of gratitude to my early readers, who were by my side as this book evolved from an initial idea into a full-fledged manuscript. Top on this list are Amy Coplen, Emily Gaddis, and Liz Hennessy. Amy pointed me to academic conversations that strengthened the book's theoretical frame, while always encouraging me to foreground the activist side of my scholarship. She read multiple drafts of several chapters with a generous spirit, always helping draw out the best in my writing and scholarship. Emily is the best cook I know, a zero-waste trash hacker, and a feminist who spends her free time fighting alongside her neighbors for environmental justice. I am extremely lucky to call her my big sister. She was the perfect test audience for this book's wider appeal, and I thank her for the helpful input, on-demand advice, and constant cheerleading. Liz offered invaluable input at so many critical moments. Her friendship and supportive presence during writing dates always helped me get words on the page.

I credit my grandma, Patsie Ruth, for my love of food and thank her for the gift of her time and spirit. I thank my mom for teaching me to be a lifelong learner, feeding me "real" food, and encouraging me in all my pursuits, and I thank my dad for emphasizing the importance of service to community as an important life goal. Thanks also to Alexia Ferracuti and Kate Whitacre for the friendship and encouragement they've given me over the years. My partner, James Pyecroft, kept my spirits high during the ups and downs of book writing with his sweet nature, silly sense of humor, and home cooking (he's the second-best cook I know). I appreciate that he has always believed in me and coached me to be kinder to myself.

I also wish to thank my colleagues in the Department of Civil Society and Community Studies, especially Carolina Sarmiento, for their support. Several students assisted me with this research and provided feedback on the book manuscript, including Claire Barrett, Amina Maamouri, Liz Schnee, Kelly Weldon, Maddie Wilinksi, and Julia Machgan. Labor organizer Cristina Cruz-Uribe brought me into the real-food, real-jobs movement and has long been an invaluable interlocutor, pushing me to stay relevant and helping me refine my research and writing on the labor of lunch. My fellow school lunch researchers Amy Rosenthal, Janette Byrd, and Andrew Ruis all provided helpful feedback on earlier drafts of this manuscript, as did farm-to-school regional coordinator Andrea Northup.

Kate Marshall, my editor at the University of California Press, was an early champion of this project. Her thoughtful editorial guidance, unwavering support, and commitment to action-oriented scholarship made this a better book. My thanks to Kate, Bradley Depew, Enrique Ochoa-Kaup, and the team at UC Press who ushered this book through the publication process. I'm grateful to Janet Poppendieck, Amy Bentley, and Josée Johnston, who provided feedback that substantially strengthened the book, and to an anonymous historian who pushed me to dig deeper into the history of school lunch. I owe a tremendous thanks to Megan Pugh, who vastly improved the narrative structure and argumentation of this book through her patient, skilled, and attentive developmental editing, and to Susan Paton for her skilled and efficient help with preparing the notes and bibliography.

Lastly, this book would not be what it is today without the support I received from the National Science Foundation, the Robert and Patricia Switzer Foundation, the Meta Schroeder Beckner Endowment, the Baldwin Wisconsin Idea Endowment, and the UW–Madison Institute for Research in the Humanities. Support for this research was also provided by the University of Wisconsin–Madison Office of the Vice Chancellor for Research and Graduate Education with funding from the Wisconsin Alumni Research Foundation.

Introduction

WHY WE NEED TO FIX THE FOOD AND THE JOBS

In 2004, after a long day at work, Lisa, a forty-eight-year-old assistant cook in New Haven, Connecticut, took off her apron and joined a delegation of workers to give her carefully planned testimony to a packed school board meeting.[1] "Good evening, distinguished board members and all in the room who have an ethical obligation to our children," she began. "I see some faces whose children I have had the honor of personally feeding. I use the word *honor* because it is the highest trust a parent can give, letting someone else care and nurture their children," she continued. Even though Lisa was in a union, UNITE HERE Local 217, she worried that speaking before the board of education might result in workplace retaliation.[2] But, as she later told me, she felt morally obligated to draw attention to the district's cost-cutting measures.

Aramark, the for-profit company tasked with managing New Haven's school lunch program, had slashed workers' wages and benefits and lowered the quality of the food they served. Lisa had lived in the city her entire life, raised children who attended the city's public schools, and worked for sixteen years as a "lunch lady" in the city's foodservice department. "Maybe many aren't aware things are not good," Lisa surmised, "because my coworkers and I, at immense personal cost, have attempted to maintain standards and keep the children from being affected, including working extra hours without pay." But, she explained, "We are wearing down quickly under a corporate management mentality, with wages that are not in keeping with the cost of even getting to work, let alone feeding our own families." What's more, workers had been instructed to hawk unhealthy "new and enticing extras" to children who could afford to pay for brand-name chips, drinks, and candy, while kids in the free and reduced-price lunch program received food Lisa said was not always of "decent quality."

The expectation that cafeteria staff work harder and faster made it increasingly difficult for them to find the time to "wipe a child's nose, tie a shoe, or take a moment to ask, 'Why aren't you eating that, sweetie? Well, maybe I have a minute to help you with that.'" If the board of education stayed the course, Lisa warned, "The once caring, nurturing, smiling lunch lady will be a thing of the past."

With the rise of a modern-day food movement, attempts to "fix" school lunch abound, but too often, they fail to engage, learn from, and respect the nation's lunch ladies. High-profile champions like Michelle Obama, Alice Waters, and Jamie Oliver have helped to popularize school gardens and scratch-cooked lunches. Meanwhile, parents, social entrepreneurs, nonprofits, academics, policymakers, and even some major food companies have worked to make school lunches healthier, more equitable, and more sustainable. But these initiatives will be limited in impact if frontline school kitchen and cafeteria workers are not valued for the care they provide to America's children. Workers like Lisa are not a cost to minimize, but rather a force for positive social change. This is a core argument of *The Labor of Lunch* and a missing link in most theories of change that inform contemporary school lunch activism.

The coalition of New Haven cafeteria workers, activists, and allies fighting to cut ties with Aramark knew that the most meaningful reforms to school lunch programs allow space for workers to lead. Lisa's 2004 speech was part of a multiyear campaign that finally convinced the board of education, in 2008, to bring management back in house.[3] It was a victory for workers, who wanted, and won, a greater role in determining lunch policies and priorities.[4] It was also a victory for the public, improving the quality of food and care for tens of thousands of children. Lisa had written out her speech on a stack of 3 × 5 notecards, which she hung onto for years. In 2012, during one of my many visits to the city's central kitchen, she pressed the stack into my hands and told me she wanted me to understand what she had helped to accomplish.

I now understand that the struggles Lisa and her allies faced at the local level were a microcosm of challenges faced at the national level. The New Haven school lunch program is part of the US National School Lunch Program (NSLP), which was created in 1946 with the goal of uplifting the health of the nation's children and supporting the American food and farm economy. For over seventy years, however, the NSLP has failed to escape the trap of "cheapness." *Cheap,* in the way I use the term, isn't just a synonym for low-cost.[5] Rather, it is the guiding political and economic philosophy, business strategy, and consumer expectation that shapes our everyday lives—one that has had disastrous effects on the healthfulness of school lunches and the wider world. The cheap, factory-farmed, and industrially manufactured foods that make up the core of the "standard American diet" are making us sick—so much so that treating preventable dietary diseases has become a multibillion dollar industry.[6] Cheap production practices contribute to climate change, which threatens our very survival on the planet. And cheap pay traps millions of families in poverty—including those of many school food-service workers who struggle to make ends meet.

The NSLP operates within a political climate of austerity in which cheapness reigns supreme and care is assigned little economic value.[7] The nation's 56.6 million elementary and secondary students (50.7 million of whom attend public schools) all qualify for subsidized school lunches, whether they purchase them at "full price" or receive free or reduced-price lunches.[8] The majority of the 32 million children who participate in the NSLP come from low-income households and are disproportionately students of color and children of either single mothers or married mothers who work outside the home.[9] Another 20 million school-aged children opt out of the NSLP, instead bringing packed lunches from home; purchasing food from their school's à la carte line, a nearby restaurant, or a corner store; or simply skipping lunch altogether.[10]

The federal government determines subsidies through a formula that dispenses cash funds and an allotment of agricultural commodities (physical food) per child served. Yet the NSLP's $13.6 billion budget doesn't stretch very far. During the 2018–2019 school year, the maximum federal reimbursement for a "free" school lunch in the contiguous states was $3.54, and $0.45 for a "full price" lunch.[11] After schools paid for labor, administration, equipment, facilities, and ongoing utility costs, they typically had just $1.50–$1.75 to spend on each tray of food.

Local school food authorities, who are typically hired by a district superintendent or school board, are pressured to make public care cheaper. Squeezing school kitchen and cafeteria workers by reducing their benefits, hours, and wages is one tactic. Purchasing cheap industrially processed food, serving it in dingy, dark school basements, and making do with outdated, inadequate equipment are others. The effects of this cost cutting reverberate across the fields, factories, and warehouses that form the supply chain of the NSLP's cheap food economy and the 21.5 million workers employed across the US food chain.[12]

Keeping the NSLP locked into this model of cheap food cuts against the basic premise of food justice, a process that, as Rasheed Hislop puts it,

FIGURE 1. Workers making prepack sandwiches in a central kitchen facility. Records of the Office of the Secretary of Agriculture, 1974–ca. 2003, National Archives and Records Administration.

encompasses "the struggle against racism, exploitation, and oppression taking place within the food system that addresses inequality's root causes both within and beyond the food chain."[13] A better school lunch program isn't a silver bullet for achieving food justice, but it is an ideal place to begin making a national commitment to shift toward healthy and sustainable diets that support community well-being.[14]

The NSLP operates largely as a social welfare program for low-income families and a public subsidy for large-scale factory farms and processed-food companies. Since the 1970s and the widespread embrace of neoliberal political and economic projects, the pursuit of cheap food, cheap labor, and cheap care has pushed millions of middle- and upper-middle-class families out of the NSLP.[15] They pursue seemingly "better" alternatives for their own children, but in so doing they fail to hold Congress, the US Department of Agriculture (USDA), and Big Food companies accountable for the quality of the NSLP. For these tens of millions of Americans, packing school lunches is part of the morning ritual. Yet it adds to the mental load and list of domestic chores performed by individual caregivers—often women—and inadvertently reduces political will to invest in an NSLP that provides high-quality food and care for all children and families.[16]

Antigone Books

411 N 4th Ave
Tucson, AZ 85705
(520) 792-3715

Transaction #:0001695S
Station:Stayon 2, 2, Gen STAT! DH2
Saturday, Oct 01 26, 2019   4:02 PM

SALES:
1 @ 27.95 9780203030033   29.95
  The Labor of Lunch: Why We Nerd Real Food
SUBTOTAL   29.95

TAX:
SalesTax   @8.7000%   2.61
TOTAL TAX   2.61
GRAND TOTAL   32.56

TENDER:
Cash   40.56
TOTAL TENDER   40.56
CASH CHANGE   8.00

Thank you for shopping at
Antigone Books! Returns for store
credit only.

Please visit us at www.antigonebooks.com

0001695S
0001695S

Antigone Books

411 N. 4th Ave.
Tucson, AZ 85705
(520) 792-3715

Transaction #:00016955
Station:Station 2, 2 Clerk:STATION2
Saturday, October 26 2019   4:02 PM

SALES:
1@ 29.95 9780520300033		29.95
The Labor of Lunch: Why We Need Real Foo		
SUBTOTAL		29.95

TAX:
Sales Tax	@8.7000%	2.61
TOTAL TAX		2.61
GRAND TOTAL		32.56

TENDER:
Cash	40.56
TOTAL TENDER	40.56
CASH CHANGE	$8.00

Thank you for shopping at Antigone Books! Returns for store credit only.

Please visit us at www.antigonebooks.com

00016955
00016955

Sorting children into "free," "reduced price," and "paid" categories diminishes the political will that is so desperately needed to advance food justice in our nation's schools. Sociologist Amy Best reminds us that failing to treat the food that young people consume as a public good exacerbates class inequalities and devalues the unwaged and low-waged care work disproportionately undertaken by women. "It is in this context that private markets step in," she argues, "capitalizing on this disconnect and in the process both undermining our ability to envision food as a public responsibility and part of a public and widely accessible system of care, and accelerating our drive toward increasing privatization and devaluation of public goods."[17]

Ultimately, school lunch is about community. It's also about the conflicts between civil society, the government, and the private sector over what children should be fed, whose responsibility it is to feed them, who should do the work of feeding them, and what, exactly, this work should entail. More often than not, food for children to eat at school is prepared by a woman—a child's caregiver, a private sector factory worker, or a public sector lunch lady—for free or for poverty wages. Let me pause for a moment to explain how debates about school lunch are fundamentally about care: what it means to care well, how much care is worth, and whether caring for public goods like children and the environment should be the private responsibility of individuals in the home or a public responsibility that is collectivized and shared.

Care isn't just about personal relationships, families, or even communities—we're interconnected in a globalized world that demands we care for distant others and our shared environmental commons, if we are to care well. Scholars Berenice Fisher and Joan Tronto define care as a "species activity that includes everything we do to maintain, continue, and repair our world so that we may live in it as well as possible."[18] When we understand care in this way, we begin to see how questioning the social organization of care strikes at the heart of how economies work. And when we recognize that homes, schools, and commercial food production spaces are all part of a broad, political economy of care, we can better situate our personal struggles and desires within political discussions about the future of the NSLP.[19]

School lunch workers are all part of a larger political economy of care that currently depends on (mostly) women's unpaid and low-wage labor in order to function. Care work, also known as reproductive labor, encompasses the mental, manual, and emotional work required to sustain life and provide for the next generation.[20] It has long been cast as "women's work," and therefore assigned little economic value within the patriarchal institutions and

FIGURE 2. School lunch worker serves free lunches to children in a Washington, DC, kindergarten in 1942. Library of Congress Prints and Photographs Division.

capitalist economies that depend on the ability to access a ready supply of cheap (if not free) reproductive labor. Doing the laundry, feeding the family, helping the children with their homework, managing their logistical and transportation needs, and worrying about their futures are just a few examples of the unpaid care work that happens in American homes every day. Such care work is often done out of love and duty when unpaid, but when it moves into the market, those who perform this labor (e.g., domestic workers, home healthcare workers, daycare workers, K–12 teachers) struggle to escape the societal expectation that care should be cheap.

School cafeteria workers care for the nation's children, yet they cannot afford to adequately care for themselves or their families on the paychecks they bring home.[21] They face precarious employment conditions that demand self-sacrifice as an integral part of striving to care well for students. We cannot fix school lunch without fixing these jobs. School cafeteria workers are among the lowest paid public sector workers, and their rate of unionization lags far behind that of K–12 teachers. Racial equity is also a problem: white women and men are more likely to be in supervisory positions and to hold the advanced degrees that child nutrition departments now require of new foodservice directors in school districts with more than 2,500 students as part of the Healthy, Hunger-Free Kids Act of 2010.[22] This formal requirement makes it difficult for frontline foodservice workers to climb their way up the school lunch job ladder, since as of 2008, only about 24 percent of frontline K–12 cafeteria workers had ever been to college and only 3 percent had earned a bachelor's or higher degree.[23]

The School Nutrition Association (SNA), a national nonprofit association with 58,000 members employed in school nutrition programs, doesn't publish detailed statistics on the demographics of the NSLP workforce. However, US Census data suggests that frontline cafeteria workers' race and ethnicity largely mirrors the population of the states where they live.[24] My own anecdotal observations suggest that racial and ethnic minorities are disproportionately clustered in the lowest rungs of the child nutrition profession, which is common in other types of food chain labor and care work.[25]

Even more significant than the poverty-level wages these frontline school foodservice workers earn is the lack of full-time work in schools that have outsourced the labor of cooking to faraway factories. The average K–12 cafeteria employee worked twenty-five hours a week for forty weeks in 2008, earning an annual median income of just $9,300. These extremely low wages pushed over one-third of the nation's 420,000 school cafeteria workers to participate in at least one public assistance program designed to address food insecurity or child and family poverty.[26] These workers can and should be lifted out of poverty, while school districts transition to "from-scratch" preparation using locally grown and sustainably sourced ingredients, if the NSLP is to ever reach its full potential as a beacon of food justice and community health.

A NEW FUTURE FOR SCHOOL LUNCH ACTIVISM

In December 2018, the Trump administration rolled back hard-won updates to the NSLP's nutritional standards—including restrictions on refined grains, salt, and flavored milk—which was a blow to school lunch activists.

Playing defense and preventing further erosion to the integrity of the NSLP is vital, but not sufficient.[27] It's time to go on the offensive and to create the program we want to see. To do so, we will need to cultivate a transformative school lunch politics that is responsive to escalating concerns about climate change, environmental justice, and racial justice. We will need to make new connections between school lunch and feminist food politics, while tapping into the growing strength of the food justice movement and the emergence of a new generation of worker-led campaigns for economic justice. Through it all, we'll need the active support of parents—including both upper-middle-class parents whose children bring lunches from home and working-class parents who cannot afford to refuse the financial subsidy provided by the NSLP. We'll need the support of all parents who want schools to serve minimally processed lunches made with nutritious ingredients—what I call "real food"—instead of highly processed, industrial factory food that looks as if it could have been pulled from the freezer section of the local supermarket or purchased at a fast food restaurant.

We can make school lunches reflect American families' needs and desires for a healthier, tastier, more ecologically sustainable and socially just food system, but not without the help of school kitchen and cafeteria workers.[28] The quality of their jobs and the quality of the food they serve are interlinked. More often than not, K–12 lunch ladies work multiple low-wage, part-time jobs and still struggle to put food on the table and a roof over their own children's heads. Yet there are plenty of lunch ladies who are school lunch activists in their own right. Some bend the rules slightly—serving a second helping to a child they know is hungry—while others rise up together to demand high-quality lunches for the children they feed (fig. 3).

Lisa's union, UNITE HERE, has emerged as a national leader in bringing the food and labor movements together in a holistic campaign for real food and real jobs. The union defines real food as "food that is cooked from fresh ingredients rather than processed items, is sourced locally and ethically, and utilizes production methods that are humane and respect our environment." This definition and the priorities it outlines are likely familiar to many readers who identify as foodies or food activists, but the notion of what constitutes a real job, especially in the context of school foodservice, is fuzzier. The union defines real jobs as those that "pay a living wage (with health and retirement benefits), that allow workers to disclose food safety or quality issues, and to form a union through a legal and democratic process of their own choosing without threats and intimidation."[29]

FIGURE 3. UNITE HERE Local 1 workers gather in protest outside Chicago Public Schools headquarters in April 2012 as part of a series of actions in their real-food, real-jobs campaign. Courtesy UNITE HERE.

When real food and real jobs go hand in hand, school kitchen and cafeteria workers are far more likely to be hired into full-time jobs, which allow them to invest more of themselves into caring for children.[30] Their work is far more important than most people realize. School cafeteria workers attend to children's physical and emotional needs in a host of ways: serving food; providing pureed meals to children with special needs; opening milk cartons for very young children; knowing children's names, life situations, food preferences, allergies, and dietary restrictions; following food safety procedures; tweaking menu items to make them tastier and more visually appealing; lobbying for schools to serve healthier meals; assisting families in completing the paperwork for free and reduced-price lunch applications; and in some cases, personally paying for children's lunch fees when they don't have enough money.

School cafeteria workers also oversee the environment where many children experience hundreds of meals each year, from which many develop lifelong food and dining habits. They maintain the physical spaces where children eat: preventing cross-contamination, ensuring that food is stored at safe temperatures, washing lunch trays and tables, restocking napkins and utensils, cleaning the serving line and cafeteria floors, disposing of food waste, decorating the cafeteria for holidays, posting signs or pictures with nutritional information around the cafeteria, and translating signs and other information from English into another language.

School lunch workers typically live in the communities where they work. It's not uncommon for them to have friends or acquaintances among the parents, aunts, uncles, and neighbors of the children they are feeding, just like Lisa in New Haven. This makes cafeteria workers especially well suited to what some feminist scholars call community mothering, or "weaving and reweaving the social fabric."[31] When it comes to the public work of feeding children at school, community mothering involves fostering children's relationships and social connections both intra- and intergenerationally; it means knowing which children are friends, whether they are related to each other, and how they are connected to older generations. In schools with gardens or farm-to-school programs, it may also include connecting students to the people who grow their food by reminding them of the food's origins and the labor behind it.

Community mothering also encompasses the mental, manual, and emotional labor required to model respectful interpersonal behavior, mediate interactions between unruly children, and encourage cliques to be more accepting of difference. It includes caring enough about children to notice when they are coming late to school, making time to listen to them about what might be going on at home or in other areas of their lives, and talking to parents about their concerns. Launching community campaigns and applying for grants to send food-insecure children home on Fridays with backpacks of food for the weekend and advocating for healthier, fresher foods are other manifestations of community mothering that help to build a new economy of care in American public schools. In New Haven community mothering continues to motivate Lisa and her coworkers to use their collective power to fight for high-road reforms.

The social organization of care is an evolving social, cultural, political, and economic process secured through what feminist geographer Cindi Katz refers to as a "shifting constellation of sources," including the household, the state, markets, and civil society.[32] So when I use the language of care to discuss the intimate and daily routine of feeding children, I am doing so in order to uncover larger structural questions about which institutions, people, and practices should be used to accomplish concrete caring tasks and to what ends.[33] How we choose to organize and reward the care work within the NSLP impacts children's health and well-being, the lives and livelihoods of food chain workers, and the food and agricultural systems that feed us.

What exactly this "constellation of sources" should look like when it comes to feeding and caring for children during the school day has been a major point of contention among government agencies, civil society activists, and powerful agriculture and food companies for well over one hundred years. It wasn't until after a half century of civil society activism and experimentation at the local level that the federal government created what we now know as the NSLP. While there was never an organized social movement that called itself the "nonprofit school lunch movement," I use this notably ahistorical term in the first two chapters of this book in order to provide continuity across the multiple generations of school lunch activism that led to the NSLP's creation and stabilization.

Looking backwards helps us to recast the long history of the NSLP as a social movement dedicated to creating a new economy of care and reshaping the nation's public infrastructure for care provisioning. The successes and failures of the women (and their allies) who worked together to create public school kitchens and cafeterias during the Progressive Era (1890s–1920s) provide not only inspiration for the future, but also a needed reminder of how the NSLP was shaped by patriarchal views about the value of care work and how it should be organized. Likewise, the activists of the 1960s and 1970s who organized against the various forms of institutionalized racism and classism within the NSLP but failed to challenge the basic premise that food, labor, and ultimately care should be cheap offer a cautionary tale to the many real food activists looking to revolutionize how school lunches are sourced and prepared.

To learn about this history, I delved into stacks of trade magazines and how-to books written by well-known "lunch ladies," and sorted through boxes of letters, training manuals, pamphlets, and photographs at the National Child Nutrition Archives in Oxford, Mississippi.[34] I read every issue of the monthly journal of the American School Food Service Association (ASFSA, now the SNA), from 1957 to 1981, as well as a collection of over 180 oral histories of child nutrition professionals collected through the National Child Nutrition Archives Oral History Project. This helped me better understand the breadth and commonality of experiences among school foodservice directors, managers, and frontline staff over the course of the NSLP's long history. But why, I continued to ask myself, have multiple generations of school kitchen and cafeteria workers faced such an uphill battle when striving to care well for the children they feed?

Some of the information I found aligned with the chronology of school lunch activism I'd learned about from historian Susan Levine's and sociologist Janet Poppendieck's excellent histories of the NSLP.[35] I did, however, uncover episodes of resistance and reinvention during my archival research that surprised me, including a (failed) campaign to make the NSLP free for all children and the resurgence of school gardens to combat rising food and energy costs in the 1970s. Such initiatives diverge from the trend toward privatization and commercialization that defined school lunch for generations of children attending school between the 1970s and early 2000s. Grappling with the trade-offs, missed opportunities, and partial successes of these earlier waves of school lunch organizing can help today's activists make strategic, informed decisions about when to make compromises and when to push for deeper, structural reforms.

To better understand what this might take, I traveled the country from 2011 to 2016, visiting over two dozen school districts, some for just a day and others for a week or more, in five states spanning the Midwest, New England, and the Southeast. I conducted semistructured interviews with over sixty school foodservice workers—ranging from dishwashers to cooks to citywide directors of child nutrition programs—and spoke informally with many more. I visited schools in rural, suburban, and urban districts with varying demographic profiles, but the field sites I chose for this project are by no means a nationally representative sample of the NSLP. Wherever I went, local foodservice directors often cautioned me to remember that every school is different and every community is unique. While I feel confident that I have assembled a picture that speaks to many common experiences within the NSLP, there are sure to be variations that I missed and important issues that I leave unexplored.

My daily ritual of reading the SNA's Smart Brief email newsletter, along with newspaper and magazine articles about school lunch and farm-to-school programs, helped me make sense of my own fieldwork within the broader national context. So, too, did the time I spent talking to dozens of Big Food sales representatives at the food shows linked to the SNA's annual national conferences in 2012 and 2016. Participating in legislative lobbying alongside child nutrition professionals at the SNA's 2012 legislative action conference, attending state and regional school food shows, and touring factories where industrial cooking equipment and USDA commodity foods are manufactured provided yet other windows into the NSLP. Stepping outside of these mainstream school lunch circles, I also attended conferences put on by prominent national nonprofits, including School Food Focus and the National Farm to School Network.[36]

Along the way I grew more critical of the strategies that for-profit companies are using to adapt to, and in some cases circumvent, the real food movement. The new generation of "clean label" and "like-scratch" premade foods these companies are manufacturing does have its virtues—fewer artificial additives and preservatives, for example—but it also has significant drawbacks. Namely, it continues to yield control of the NSLP to powerful players in the processed food industry and keeps frontline school kitchen and cafeteria workers trapped in part-time jobs that make it difficult to care well for themselves, let alone the children they feed at school. By following this industry-led approach—which I call "real food lite"—schools are inadvertently weakening the transformative potential of the real food movement to build healthy, ecologically sustainable, socially just community economies.[37]

There's another way to build a better meal on the lunch tray, and that's to invest in the labor of lunch: revaluing the care work done by lunch ladies and providing them with the skills, time, and infrastructure necessary to prepare healthy meals from scratch (i.e., increasing what I call "culinary capacity"). Unlike real food lite, this high-road strategy has the potential to create better quality jobs for school foodservice workers, many of whom are the mothers and grandmothers of the children they feed. It also has the potential to help reverse the cheapening of the American food system, shifting power away from Big Food corporations to local communities and food chain workers. To achieve such a dramatic realignment, we must first identify and build "way stations," or feasible social changes that create a path toward more emancipatory possibilities.[38]

A major goal of this book is to help readers envision what these way stations might be through case studies of leading districts like Minneapolis Public Schools and others that are investing in real food and real jobs. I hope the book offers inspiration and concrete ideas for cocreating a better future rooted in a revolutionary politics of sustainability—one in which labor isn't exploited, but valued; where care work isn't denigrated, but esteemed; and where the natural world isn't plundered, but preserved.[39]

Lisa and the rest of New Haven's school cafeteria workers are already well on their way to building the collective power necessary to push for change. They weathered the financial crisis of 2007–2009 by refusing to negotiate a new contract with the city. They were terrified by all the givebacks that teachers and paraprofessionals were forced to make during their contract negotiations. But in late 2012, they geared up for a contract fight. Cristina Cruz-Uribe, the Local 217 organizer, recruited an organizing committee of workers who made a commitment to lead the campaign. They surveyed their coworkers to determine what the negotiating priorities should be, and the hundred-plus surveys all told the same story: workers wanted to be able to care well for themselves and "their kids," both at home and at school. They went on community radio, spoke at events, and protested outside the mayor's office—and eventually it paid off. Their 2013 labor contract expanded the number of full-time cook positions in the schools by thirty-two, while securing full labor rights for the most vulnerable group of substitute workers, raises across the board, and a commitment from the district to pilot new strategies for serving fresh and local food in the schools.

During the spring of 2013, I volunteered, with Local 217 organizer Cristina Cruz-Uribe, to help write a report based on the workers' vision for school lunch in New Haven.[40] By then, I had been doing ethnographic research in the New Haven school lunch program for two years. As my research progressed, I found myself spending more and more time in the city's kitchens and cafeterias and at union meetings, talking with workers. I realized their perspectives were practically nonexistent in academic work on the NSLP and largely absent from activists' discussions about school lunch reform. Many of the workers told me they were used to folks like me from Yale University who came to the schools to do plate-waste studies, taste tests, and other forms of nutrition "interventions." But these visitors had never really expressed much interest in them or their jobs, other than to ask for their assistance in whatever the academic study, taste test, or nutrition intervention might be. But the more time I spent in the kitchens, the more the workers shared stories with me, brought in old photographs, and introduced me to retired colleagues. I credit them for teaching me just how central labor is to the story of school lunch.

Public institutions like the NSLP are part of both the economy and our shared infrastructure for meeting the real and concrete need to care for ourselves and one another. School lunch activists have known this for well over a century yet struggled to overcome powerful political and economic forces that make their dreams hard to realize. *The Labor of Lunch* examines this long history of conflict, building on a rich body of academic and activist literature on school lunch reforms and uncovering hidden ties to feminist politics and labor struggles that extend far beyond the lunchroom. I hope my analysis will help readers recognize how gender and labor justice are intimately interconnected to the ecological, public health, and social justice goals that animate contemporary school lunch activism. And perhaps more importantly, I hope it will help the movement weave them together into a powerful coalition politics.

There is much to be gained by providing high-quality, sustainably sourced, freshly cooked, universally free school lunches to all children. Likewise, there is much to be gained by creating high-quality jobs for school kitchen and cafeteria workers. And the foundation for coordinated collective action is already in place. Roughly 95 percent of public and nonprofit private schools in the United States currently participate in the NSLP. This means nearly every community in the country has at least one public, charter, or private school that participates in the NSLP, and many schools also offer breakfast, snack, and dinner to students through federal child nutrition programs administered by the USDA. If we organize together for a better future, we can leverage these public programs to advance food justice and a new economy of care in American public schools. Making such changes might seem daunting, but when we form coalitions—of youth, workers, families, activists, and scholars—we have the strength to remake the labor of lunch as we know it.

ONE

The Radical Roots of School Lunch

Free lunches for all. School gardens. Cooking classes. Canning and food preservation workshops. Health, nutrition, and biology classes that spark children's curiosity and widen their ability to think across disciplines through the experiential study of food and agriculture. Children participating in the labor of lunch, learning from and building relationships with well-trained, adequately compensated adults in a community economy of care. Family and neighborhood engagement. This was all part of Emma Smedley's vision for a nonprofit school lunch program that would operate not as "a mere appendage of the educational system" but rather as "one of the arteries through which the active blood of co-operation runs."[1] While these lofty aspirations sound like the goals of today's school lunch advocates, Smedley, one of the most influential leaders of the nonprofit school lunch movement, was writing about them back in 1920.

Smedley's name has been lost to history, yet her vision is remarkably modern. She'd fit right in with Alice Waters, the famed chef, author, and sustainable-food activist who launched an online pledge for public education at the beginning of the 2018 school year. On the webpage announcing the pledge, Waters describes cafeterias as "the heart of our schools."[2] It's almost as if Waters is calling forth the ghost of Emma Smedley, heart metaphor and all, to urge the American public to recognize and elevate the status of the National School Lunch Program (NSLP). The campaign asks individuals and organizations to promote the values of nourishment, stewardship, and community by pledging their support for free, sustainable lunches made with food purchased directly from farmers and ranchers who take care of the land and their workers.[3]

Transforming the NSLP in the way Waters proposes offers a path to begin living out a democratic ethos of care that extends beyond the walls of our public schools to the farms, ranches, and fisheries that turn "nature" into food. But if Smedley and her compatriots were unsuccessful a century ago, when opposition from ingrained political interests and Big Food companies was much less severe, what hope do present-day activists have in finally realizing the full power and potential of public school lunch programs?

I, for one, am optimistic. The time I've spent over the last seven years learning from leaders working to create a new economy of care within the NSLP has left me with a strong sense of just how widespread the desire for change actually is. This isn't a "fringe" movement. Thousands of dedicated parents, school lunch workers, public health advocates, local food activists, and nonprofit organizations are already engaged in this work. Their school lunch reform agendas span a range of interrelated topics, including public health, racial justice, economic development, workers' rights, and environmental sustainability. These issues are also bound up within what feminist scholars call "social reproduction," defined by Giovanna Di Chiro as the "intersecting complex of political-economic, socio-cultural, and material-environmental processes required to maintain everyday life and to sustain human cultures and communities on a daily basis and intergenerationally."[4] That includes care work, a form of reproductive labor that keeps people clothed, sheltered, and fed. Without it, daily life wouldn't be possible.

How the reproductive labor necessary for social reproduction should be organized (who should do it and how much it's worth) and the desirability of "cheap food" economies have long been debated. For well over a century, the premise that social reproduction should be cheap, if not free, has driven down standards of care and limited the power and possibility of public school lunch programs. It's meant that the workers (mostly women) who care for children are paid poverty wages in districts that aren't unionized. And it has allowed school lunch to remain semiprivatized, while the "educational" side of public schools is paid for collectively. Math, English, and a host of other academic subjects are offered to children free of charge, but when they walk through the cafeteria doors, any façade of egalitarianism fades. No one expects a math teacher to collect children's fees at the classroom door. Cafeteria workers, on the other hand, must sort children according to their eligibility for free, reduced-price, or paid lunches and charge them accordingly.

In many ways, the history of school lunch in America reflects the gender, racial, urban, and class politics of the twentieth century. Any strategy for reforming school lunch will necessarily be limited if we do not take the time to first understand the intersectionality of social problems that allowed the

NSLP's cheap-food economy to arise in the first place. Learning about the history of school lunch activism—and what the labor of lunch looked like at various points in school lunch history—can help today's generation of school lunch activists identify the root causes of injustice within the NSLP and organize for a better future.

THE PROGRESSIVE ORIGINS OF THE NSLP

While not always recognized as such, the NSLP is the product of generations of women's activism. It didn't spontaneously arise in 1946, with the passage of the National School Lunch Act, as a beneficent social service for American schoolchildren. It has a history—and a feminist one at that. For over a hundred years, reformers—most of them women—have fought to decommercialize childhood and establish new forms of public caregiving as an alternative to the for-profit vendors and private households that would otherwise supply the labor of lunch.[5] In many ways, the school lunch debates of the Progressive Era were an ideological battleground over the appropriate role of government in family life and, relatedly, the position of women in society vis-à-vis their responsibility for performing unpaid care work in the home.

Early school lunch reformers like Emma Smedley did not always self-identify as feminists or conceptualize themselves as belonging to a larger "nonprofit school lunch movement," as I refer to it, but that's what their efforts amounted to. They worked for the greater good in a spirit of shared enterprise to reimagine the labor of lunch—and care more broadly—not as a private, gendered responsibility, but as a public necessity. The movement began in the 1890s, when reformers created charitable lunch programs for the extremely poor. The "penny lunch" programs that followed served even more children, and by the end of World War I, nonprofit lunch programs were flourishing across the nation. This expansion of public care was a concrete result of Progressive Era activism that historians call "maternalist," because it was led by women and focused on traditionally female spheres of influence: home and family.[6] Shrouded in the respectability of maternalism, these same reformers led bold campaigns for a more caring state, calling on governments at all levels to protect workers, families, and the environment from the destructive forces of unregulated capitalism.[7]

Feeding children was but one piece of a much larger economy of care that they aimed to renegotiate by altering and innovating the material infrastructure involved in satisfying real and concrete caring tasks. Public kitchens and laundries, cooperative housekeeping, kindergartens, and public school lunch programs were, for these reformers, tactics for addressing the economic and spatial issues that made homes, neighborhoods, and cities oppressive for women and unhealthy for everyone. Urban historian Dolores Hayden situates this activism within a longer lineage of material feminist activism stretching from the end of the Civil War to the onset of the Great Depression.[8] Key to the material feminists' theory of social change was the belief that housewives should be recognized as workers within the capitalist system— just like the many working-class women who toiled in sweatshops, canneries, and slaughterhouses—even though their labor happens to be unpaid and in the home. The women who put in long hours caring for their families— tending to the needs of children and husbands, regenerating their bodies, minds, and souls for a new day at school or work—should be the ones to decide how concrete activities of care are organized. In making such a claim, material feminists brought the language and goals of labor organizing and trade unionism to individual women's homes.

They organized together to build a more just, caring, and healthy society. Their stories offer not only a history of the present—teaching us how the "status quo" came into being—but also a warning to never lose sight of the feminist potential of school lunch. Take Ellen Swallow Richards, the first woman to graduate from the Massachusetts Institute of Technology, for example. Her many claims to fame include founding the field of home economics in the early 1900s and earning a place in 1951 as a "Wonder Woman of History" in the DC Comics franchise. She was the brains behind America's first nonprofit school lunch program. In 1894, the Boston School Committee hired Richards and her nutritionist-friend Mary Hinman Abel to supply school lunches for several of the city's neediest schools. They oversaw production at the New England Kitchen, which they'd founded in 1890 as a public laboratory kitchen and takeaway shop designed to use the latest technology and scientific knowledge to provide healthy, safe, affordable meals for the masses. They met those goals. Thrifty purchasing, streamlined menu planning, energy-efficient cooking, and centralized production kept costs low. But simply making food affordable and available doesn't mean everyone will actually want to eat it. By all accounts, the New England Kitchen's bland, institutional meals were a tough sell.

Even "Wonder Women" stumble. The patronizing, ethnocentric undertone of "bringing good food to others" that haunts the contemporary food movement has roots extending at least as far as Richards and Abel's community kitchen.[9] The working-class immigrants they had originally hoped to feed didn't have much appetite for the "Yankee" foods served at the New England Kitchen.[10] So Richards and Abel jumped at the opportunity to serve a new, younger, and perhaps more impressionable group of eaters in the local schools. If they could get immigrant children to like these foods, new attitudes toward their "scientific" way of eating might just trickle up to their parents. And if not, at least they would be protecting kids from profit-seeking street vendors who sold goods laden with copious amounts of salt, fat, sugar, and germs.

In an early precursor to the type of school wellness policies now mandated by the federal government, Richards and other members of the Boston School Committee crafted a policy in 1894 stipulating that "only such food as was approved by them should be sold in the city school houses."[11] Scientifically nutritious, sanitary, affordable foods that could be eaten quickly and digested easily—the New England Kitchen's specialty—were precisely what the committee was looking for. Best of all, the city wouldn't need to build kitchens in the schools since all the food could be prepared offsite in the New England Kitchen and transported to the schools. And since the whole operation was run as a not-for-profit, the kids could get higher quality food at a cheaper price.

This phenomenon of educated women inserting themselves in city politics to fight for new forms of public provisioning had a name: "municipal housekeeping." Drawing on maternalist political discourse, so-called municipal housekeepers argued that the ability for mothers to protect their homes and care well for their families required them to exercise their moral authority in the public sphere.[12] Universal education, pure food, clean water, fresh air, and sanitary streets were necessary for their ability to survive well, and they should not be viewed as somehow disconnected from the home or the "women's sphere," the thinking went.[13] What's more, they turned women's status as caretakers for children, husbands, and the elderly into a badge of honor that rendered them uniquely suited for "keeping house" at the city scale.

For women—even the relatively privileged white women from the upper and middle classes—such a political undertaking would be doomed at the onset unless they built collective power. They didn't yet have the right to vote, yet there they were, making demands on the city and state officials in charge of public works.[14] Luckily, they knew better than to go it alone. Tens of thousands of women joined clubs, aid societies, and parent-teacher associations.

Together they experimented with new forms of care infrastructure that would make homes, neighborhoods, and cities healthier and more enjoyable for everyone. The public parks, public libraries, community kitchens, public baths, public laundries, nonprofit public school lunch programs, cooperative purchasing clubs, kindergartens, and settlement houses that opened their doors in American cities were the result of their efforts.

At the same time, Progressive Era activists pursued legal protections for women and child workers who toiled on farms and in factories. Their efforts to secure children's access to free public education worked: from 1890 to 1920, while the number of school-aged children in the United States increased by 49 percent, school enrollments increased by 70 percent.[15] Compulsory education promised not only to protect children from the grit and vice of city life but also to mold them into adults capable of participating in a society undergoing extreme technological and social change. The whole idea of what it meant to be a child—and the special status designated to childhood as a unique period of life—was already changing irreversibly from what sociologist Viviana Zelizer calls the "economically useful" child of the 1870s into an "economically useless but emotionally priceless" recipient of adult care.[16]

Mothers were, in most cases, expected to take responsibility for ensuring the health and well-being of their "priceless" children as they navigated life between home and school. Public health reformers, physicians, and other experts stressed the importance of protecting children from all sorts of foodborne pathogens and toxic chemicals that might poison their bodies and weaken their minds. This was easier said than done. Ingredient labels were practically nonexistent. And unscrupulous profit-seekers might add sawdust, chalk, clay dust, or other "extenders" to bulk up the weight and profitability of flour, bread, crackers, cookies, and the like.[17]

Shopping one's way to safety wasn't an option even for the well-to-do. Risk was systemic. There weren't any national regulations preventing food companies from using whatever production practices they saw fit until Upton Sinclair's 1906 book, *The Jungle*, catapulted food safety to the top of the national policy agenda. As an active member of the Socialist Party, Sinclair hoped that his heartbreaking tale of immigrant families ruthlessly abused by employers, landlords, and other profit-seekers in and around Chicago's stockyards would cause his readers to rethink the brutality of industrial capitalism. Stories of rancid meat laced with chemicals to mask the telltale signs of spoilage, dead rats ground into sausage filling, and a worker who was accidentally killed, boiled, and turned into lard captivated the public.

Women took action. The General Federation of Women's Clubs, often considered the "voice of organized womanhood," pushed the government to pass legislation that would ensure they had access to pure and unadulterated foods.[18] This legislation, the Pure Food and Drug Act of 1906, while a step in the right direction, ultimately did little to ensure food safety or mitigate labor abuses. Some women's groups took it upon themselves to create their own certification systems and labeling mechanisms for food purity and ethical production practices. By screening food and other consumer goods and purposely selecting those that fit their standards, they were engaging in what scholar Norah MacKendrick calls "precautionary consumption."[19]

School lunch offered a logical mechanism through which to scale up precautionary consumption to the neighborhood level since children were already gathered in one place. Plus, as one mother wrote in a 1906 issue of *Harpers' Bazaar,* "Of all the work a mother has to do for her children, none is more monotonous, more troublesome, than the putting up of lunches day after day, with a due regard for variety and wholesomeness and for the fickle and often unreasonable taste of the child."[20] For many women, outsourcing the labor of lunch to professionals like Richards and Abel seemed a winning idea. The pressure to embody a split identity, "part nutritionist, part psychologist, part chef, and part entertainer," to borrow historian Andrew Ruis's lovely turn of phrase, was something they could do without.[21] Besides, the public health workers and teachers who peered into their children's lunch baskets could be remarkably judgmental about the food and unkind in their assessments of mothers who failed to meet their standards.[22]

Poor and working-class women had a hard time living up to these ideals. Long hours and grueling labor conditions in sweatshops and domestic service left little time or energy to attend to the immediate needs of their children, let alone engage in the careful food sourcing and preparation expected of upper- and middle-class mothers. Wages were low in the factories and stockyards. It wasn't uncommon for married working-class women and children—despite changing norms about their rights to a protected existence—to spend hours in wage labor just to help their families survive.[23] Spending hours in the morning putting together safe, nutritious, and attractive school lunches was not often an option. They might be able to spare a few pennies for their children's lunches, but in the absence of public lunch programs like the one Richards and Abel started in Boston, the only place for children to spend their lunch money was at the for-profit concession stands run by school janitors (and their wives) or nearby street vendors. Their stores of cheap, handheld foods laden with sugar, salt, and starch were a delight to many sweet-toothed children and an abomination to the municipal housekeepers who judged them to be both unsanitary and unhealthy.[24]

Mothers had little control over what their children actually ate when they gave them lunch money. The US Office of Home Economics warned in a 1916 pamphlet that "pickles and pies, or, at best, only starchy foods and sweets are likely to make up the bill of fare" when children made their own food choices.[25] Muckraking journalist John Spargo took a more sensationalist tone in his 1906 book *The Bitter Cry of the Children,* declaring that city kids whose mothers gave them lunch money could be found on the streets, gambling, stuffing their faces with pickles and cream puffs, and buying packets of cigarettes to suppress their appetites. Not a great situation. According to Mary Swartz Rose, then a leading expert on child nutrition, taxpayer money was wasted on public education if the children in the nation's classrooms were "listless from hunger" and "befogged by indigestible food."[26] Without proper nourishment, how could children be expected to learn?

No child should go hungry in the "richest nation on Earth." This—along with the argument that public dollars were being wasted on children who were physically unable to learn due to malnutrition—became a key talking point in the ideological fight for nonprofit school lunch programs. Tugging at people's heartstrings and appealing to their economic sensibilities took nonprofit school lunch advocates only so far. Financial, political, legal, and ideological obstacles existed at every level, from the macropolitics of the state's legal authority over the educational system to the micropolitics of selecting which (if any) children were "deserving" of charitable assistance. The idea of providing free school lunches to all children was especially controversial. The conservative men who held the majority of seats on local school boards and in state legislatures believed free school lunches stunk of "socialism." Instituting such a policy would, undoubtedly, have the unintended consequence of "pauperizing" children and eroding parents' work ethic, they warned.[27] Two could play at having the moral upper hand. Besides, they had their own economic trump card: using tax dollars to build school kitchens and cafeterias was an unnecessary expense for urban school authorities to absorb when children could simply bring food from home or purchase something from a vendor.[28] In other words, education dollars should be used to hire more teachers, reduce class sizes, and improve instructional quality, not to feed children cheap (let alone free) school lunches.

School lunch reformers saw things differently. They wanted a collective solution that would help mothers from all social classes care well for their children. The middle-class women active in the social clubs and charities of the municipal housekeeping movement understood home and community were inextricably bound together. They believed concerns once identified as the responsibilities of individual housewives and mothers—like packing a "perfect" school lunch basket—were in actuality public and political. Many of them were tired of women's care work being undervalued not just by individual men but by society at large. When the 1900 US government census classified married women as "dependents," implying that—along with infants, young children, the infirm, and the elderly—these women required economic subsidy from men, New England Kitchen cofounder Mary Hinman Abel fought back.[29] "Suppose housewives went on a strike and refused to do housework," she asked. "How would it impact an individual family's income? The profitability of a company? Or the total economic output of the country?" Through consciousness-raising discussions like this, Progressive Era feminists developed a counternarrative: patriarchal capitalism would implode without women's unpaid (or low-paid) care work, so really their husbands (and the economic system they were serving) were dependent on *them*.

The burgeoning new field of home economics sought to elevate women's status by imbuing feminized care work with scientific authority and teaching women about the social significance of the wealth they controlled. At the turn of the nineteenth century, the pioneers of home economics, including Abel and her New England Kitchen compatriot, Ellen Swallow Richards, believed that teaching women scientific approaches to home management would not only improve the household's health and well-being but also streamline the number of hours women needed to spend on unpaid domestic labor.[30] In theory, this would free them to spend more time engaged in social, political, and environmental activism, which would benefit the "social whole."[31]

This version of home economics education is a far cry from the stereotypical midcentury "stitch and stir" classes in which young girls were indoctrinated into a deskilled, corporate domesticity, and there was a strong politics behind it.[32] Caroline Hunt, one of the field's most influential early philosophers, played a key role in articulating this politics through her public writing and academic teaching. She is a local legend at my home institution, the University of Wisconsin–Madison. She was the School of Human Ecology's first professor back in 1903, when it was called the Department of Home Economics, and the only woman to hold a full-time instructional position at the university. She was also its lowest-paid professor.

Yet the curriculum she developed was cutting-edge, even by today's standards. She did action-oriented scholarship, community-based teaching, and citizen science long before the terms were invented. Hunt's full-time students pursued a rigorous education in the physical sciences, biological sciences, social sciences, and humanities that was grounded in real world problems. Field trips and applied projects helped them learn to think across disciplines and with an eye toward social justice. When it came to food, Hunt's students learned to scrutinize quality, measuring caloric and vitamin content in laboratories, and the conditions under which the food was grown, processed, and packaged. Purchasing ready-made processed foods might hold a certain time-saving appeal, but as Hunt wrote in a 1903 essay, the "waste of life and productive power" brought about by child labor, inadequate pay, and unsanitary work environments should give women pause. If they refused to purchase such "cheap" products and instead redirected their purchasing power to ethical food companies, they could "determine to a large extent what shall be made and under what conditions it shall be made."[33]

Of course, for Caroline Hunt, individual acts of ethical consumption were not a replacement for collective action. She urged women to organize together in a "spirit of cooperation and mutual aid" that crossed lines of race, class, age, ethnicity, and citizenship.[34] She advocated a strategic blend of consumer activism, support for labor organizing, and issue-based campaigns to pass new forms of legislation to protect the dignity of workers. She even enlisted farm women from across the state who attended her 1908 "Housekeepers Conference" to monitor industrial pollution in Wisconsin's waterways and recruited them to participate in a campaign for pure food. Eventually, Hunt's emphasis on collectivizing and politicizing care work proved too radical for the university's board of regents. They wanted her to focus on manual-skills education—sewing and cooking—divorced from the political economic critique and social justice organizing she held dear.

It's unclear whether she was fired or quit, but Caroline Hunt's career as a home economics professor was over. However, her influence on school lunch was just beginning. After it opened in 1915, the US Office of Home Economics hired Hunt to write several publications on the topic of the "lunch problem." How to pack the best home lunches? How to start a lunch program in a one-room schoolhouse? How to organize a school lunch program for large, city schools? Caroline Hunt had answers. And thanks to the hundreds of middle-class women reformers who pressured the federal government to form new social welfare agencies, she had a government-sponsored platform for dispensing advice to women across the country. The municipal housekeepers who had initially targeted their reform efforts closer to home—at the neighborhood and city scales—had begun to shift their focus to the national scale around 1910. They had the organizational infrastructure to demand real change. The General Federation of Women's Clubs alone boasted a national membership of 800,000 women who were organized into state federations.[35] They, along with home economists and other women professionals, convinced the federal government to create the Children's Bureau in 1912 and the Office of Home Economics in 1915.[36] These agencies gave women like Hunt a place from which to pursue scientific research and public education campaigns directed at improving the quality of life for children and their mothers.

Back in Boston, the New England Kitchen was pioneering an approach to school lunch delivery that relied on exactly the "spirit of cooperation and mutual aid" that Caroline Hunt had hoped to impart to her home economics students. In 1907, the Women's Educational and Industrial Union (WEIU) had taken over the daily logistics and operation of the nonprofit lunch program, which served over seventeen high schools. WEIU workers repurposed industrial laundry baskets into communal lunch baskets, carefully lined each one with paper and filled it with all the components for a nutritious lunch, and shipped them off to the schools (fig. 4). They became national experts on the labor of lunch, providing hands-on, experiential training to women who traveled to the New England Kitchen to learn how to operate lunch programs in their own communities. Between 1916 and 1926 alone, these visitors came from thirty-one different states.[37]

The New England Kitchen operated under what is now called a "central kitchen" model, in which food is prepared in one large production facility and transported to the school cafeterias where children eat. This wasn't the only system in place, however. In 1910, the Boston Committee on Hygiene of the Home and School Association—a group of some twenty parents' associations and teachers—sponsored a program for elementary students in which school lunches were prepared in on-site kitchens.[38] It charged a penny per lunch in schools that had domestic science teachers and students take on the labor of lunch, and two pennies if the labor was hired out.[39] In both models—centralized and decentralized production—minimizing the cost of labor was the key to keeping safe, nutritious lunches affordable.

The ability to claim improved nutrition, taste, purity, and variety was crucial if reformers hoped to make the case for increased public investment in nonprofit school lunch programs. At the very least, they had to promise to

FIGURE 4. Workers employed by the Women's Educational and Industrial Union prepare lunches in the New England Kitchen. Courtesy Schlesinger Library, Radcliffe Institute, Harvard University.

provide cheap care in order to convince nonbelievers to give their programs a shot. Emma Smedley, for example, assured the Philadelphia school board in 1909 that an experimental lunch program based on "sound food principles" would quickly pay for itself. The board agreed to pay for the initial equipment, space, heat, light, gas, and steam for cooking. All other costs—food, labor, administration, and Smedley's salary—would have to be paid for by lunch sales or private donations. Smedley proved herself up to the challenge. By 1920 she was managing a staff of three hundred workers who fed fifty thousand children per day in 46 schools—an impressive achievement, though another 184 of the city's schools still lacked what she considered to be "proper" lunch service.[40]

The rapid growth of Philadelphia's nonprofit school lunch program transformed Smedley into a school lunch celebrity. She received so many letters requesting details about Philadelphia's lunch program that she wrote a 165-page book on the subject. By the time the book was published in 1920, she'd come to think of school lunch as a "business enterprise ... with a scientific and social aspect."[41] In other words, she knew that balancing the books had to be priority number one. Her own experience dealing with school administrators, coupled with cautionary tales from other cities, had taught her how important it was to focus on controlling costs and attracting "customers." It was much easier to deflect criticism, when it came, if the program was on solid financial footing.

Smedley, unlike some of her contemporaries, experienced the legitimacy of being recognized as the head of an official department within the public school system. She did her best to build a positive reputation for the department, knowing that winning support from principals, teachers, parents, and students was vital. In her book *The School Lunch: Its Organization and Management in Philadelphia,* she instructed those planning to embark on the "cooperative venture" of starting a lunch program to take the time to meet with students and "invite their cooperation" and explain how they could "help to keep down labor costs."[42] By teaching students about the nonprofit model—which was key to providing safe, healthy food at the lowest possible cost—school lunch reformers could, Smedley argued, increase students' willingness to "cooperate" in their experimental programs as paying customers.

A few pennies could buy students a balanced lunch prepared in a sanitary kitchen under the supervision of a dietitian, generally an educated woman with a home economics degree or equivalent work experience. The labor of lunch was distributed across school buildings—each with its own kitchen (though Smedley did explore the viability of a central kitchen model)—and coordinated via a centralized administrative office staffed by a secretary, two clerical assistants, two general assistants (one for elementary, the other for high schools), and Smedley herself. When hiring dietitians for the schools, Smedley looked for women who viewed school lunch as a vocational calling, not a job of last resort.[43] Only true believers—women dedicated to the mission, vision, and values of the movement—made the cut. At least that's what Smedley told her readers in *The School Lunch,* though it's hard to know for sure with the limited data available. We do know, however, that once hired, they exuded absolute professionalism in their appearance. Dressed entirely in white, from the caps atop their heads to the stockings and shoes adorning their feet, Philadelphia's school dietitians distanced themselves and their nonprofit school lunchrooms from "dirty" street vendors and profit-seeking concessionaires.[44]

But it was more than appearance, or even gender, that separated the dietitians from their school lunch competition. They were public employees who earned the same salary as the elementary school domestic science teachers. Many considered themselves to be an integral part of the school community. After all, they were working at the schools at least eight hours per day, five days a week. They were multitaskers who not only did managerial tasks like food ordering, staff scheduling, and record keeping but also stepped in to do manual labor like preparing, cooking, and serving lunches. They also worked the cashier station. Things might have changed a bit seasonally based on the menus they planned and ingredient availability, but most days followed an expected rhythm. Once a month, the dietitians emerged from the insular world of their own school kitchens and cafeterias to gather together at what Smedley called their "family council." These meetings gave all the dietitians employed by the Philadelphia school lunch department a time and place to meet one another, exchange ideas, and uplift the "spirit and stimulus of the work."[45]

Family council was really a form of ongoing professional education for dietitians and a way to expand the nonprofit school lunch movement in new directions. They listened to academic lectures on pertinent topics, invited folks to demonstrate how to use new food products and labor-saving equipment, and went on field trips to visit other spaces of bulk food production like factories, hotel restaurants, and hospital cafeterias. They also had the opportunity to connect their work in Philadelphia's schools to that of women reformers in other parts of the country. Whenever Emma Smedley or one of her assistants attended a home economics conference or visited a school lunch program in another city, the "family" got to hear about it.

This all helped elevate Philadelphia, like Boston, into one of the premier training grounds for women who wanted to work in public school lunch programs. Smedley even institutionalized a five- to ten-month apprenticeship that gave recent home economics graduates practical training in school lunch management. This ensured that Philadelphia schools would have a ready reserve of well-trained workers should any vacancies arise. It also helped spread Smedley's school lunch philosophy to other cities that hired her trained student-dietitians after their apprenticeships were completed and socialized a new generation of women to embody the culture of the nonprofit school lunch movement.

The professionalism and sense of purpose they aimed to cultivate extended, at least in Smedley's Philadelphia school kitchens, to the "women helpers" who assisted dietitians in the school kitchens and cafeterias. Most of these workers were older women from the surrounding neighborhoods who were "not fitted for factory work" on account of their age.[46] These women did, however, have ample experience caring for themselves and others, and with close supervision by trained dietitians, they could be "thoroughly imbued with the spirit of the lunchroom" in no time.[47] They certainly looked professional in their uniforms: white shirtwaists, black skirts, and white serving aprons. During the day they worked side by side with the dietitian and her assistant, rotating tasks to increase interest and reduce the strain of repetitive motion on their bodies. All told, they worked between four and eight hours each school day, depending on the staffing needs of each school, and received overtime pay for any hours worked in the evenings or on Saturdays. They also had paid holidays and a schedule for regular wage increases based on their work performance and duration of employment.

Being a "woman helper" in one of Philadelphia's school kitchens or cafeterias was, by Progressive Era standards, a decent job. The work environment was certainly more pleasant, sanitary, and safe than the average textile mill, cannery, or factory. This was by design. Emma Smedley and other home economists of her generation were committed to elevating the status of "domestic" work, while simultaneously improving women's lives and livelihoods in concrete ways. That said, it was a constant struggle to secure the financial resources necessary to treat workers fairly since school lunches had to be cheap enough for working-class students to afford. But Smedley was not willing to sacrifice the economic well-being of her women helpers just to deepen the financial subsidy that the nonprofit model already provided.

Instead, Smedley invited students to "cooperate" in the labor of lunch. She hired students to help serve lunches in exchange for a small wage. Just like their adult coworkers, they were expected to look professional while on the job: white coats for boys and white aprons for girls. She also brokered a pilot program in which a girls' domestic cookery class in one of the high schools canned a variety of goods for the school lunch program. The domestic science students benefitted from access to free food and canning supplies—which dramatically increased the range of food preservation techniques they were able to practice—and the school lunch department saved money on labor costs.[48] Smedley didn't want to stop there. Like the Progressive educator John Dewey, she believed that school gardens could connect children to nature and foster a spirit of inquiry that cut across academic subjects.[49] She dreamed of integrating food across the curriculum, but her vision required teachers and administrators to see the educational value of food and make space in their curriculum, and she struggled to get them all on board.

Elevating care work—and the labor of lunch more specifically—to the pinnacle of the educational hierarchy flew in the face of prevailing conventions. The federal government had invested money in home economics education in public schools with the passage of the 1914 Smith-Lever Act, but the idea of placing food at the center of academic life for all students—not just girls—was a far more radical proposition. With the responsibility for feeding children still firmly rooted in the "woman's sphere," and public school boards still dominated by conservative men, the integration of experiential food-based learning into the school day remained piecemeal at best. Progressive Era reformers like Smedley had to scale back their visions and settle for the permission to simply exist as a nonprofit addendum to existing school activities.

Even when nonprofit school lunch programs were successful, they might be shut down. Take, for example, the Women's School Alliance of Wisconsin. In 1904, it organized the state's first "penny lunch" program for children in two working-class Milwaukee neighborhoods that were known for having lots of mothers who worked outside the home. Children's fees and donations from private individuals, churches, societies, and clubs covered the cost of the penny lunch program. The home kitchens of women who lived near the schools were used to prepare the lunches. This helped minimize start-up costs for the alliance's new experiment in charitable food assistance. The model worked well enough. In 1910, when the alliance was poised to begin penny lunch programs in additional schools, they brought six additional home kitchens into their production network. Like many experimental school lunch programs initiated by women's clubs, the alliance ran on volunteer labor, with the hope that public authorities would later assume responsibility for the service. It wanted the type of institutionalized support that Emma Smedley had in Philadelphia. Instead, when the alliance failed to convince the county board to take on ownership, its whole penny lunch experiment was disbanded.[50]

Even school boards that seemed ready to make a nonprofit school lunch program a permanent part of the educational system could reverse course. In 1921 the Chicago Board of Education opted to outsource what had been a successful nonprofit school lunch program run by domestic science teachers to for-profit concessionaires in an attempt to cut costs, ignoring the many letters of protest from the Women's City Club of Chicago. In New York City, the nonprofit school lunch program launched by home economist Mabel Hyde Kittredge suffered a similar fate. In 1909, Kittredge and a coalition of like-minded home economists, educators, physicians, and philanthropists in the School Lunch Committee (SLC) had initiated a penny lunch program in several of New York City's poorest neighborhoods. The SLC was funded by revenue from food sales and private charity. Some of America's best known capitalists, including John D. Rockefeller, Andrew Carnegie, and J. P. Morgan—whose reliance on cheap labor made it difficult for working-class parents to care well for their children on their own—made contributions to the SLC.[51]

Like nonprofits today, the SLC was expected to maximize the amount of funding it channeled into direct service: feeding kids. This meant keeping the cost of labor and infrastructure to a minimum. The SLC put stock in what we might now call "satellite kitchens" to accomplish this objective. In May 1914, when the popular ladies' magazine *The Modern Priscilla* heralded the New York City lunch program as an inspiration to the nation, the SLC was poised to begin using what it called "group kitchens."[52] Each of these group kitchens would function as a central production site and distribution hub for schools within a given radius. Switching to the New England Kitchen production model—instead of continuing with on-site production at every school like Smedley was doing in Philadelphia—seemed to the SLC like the best course of action.

Parents across New York City's bureaus wanted their children to have access to the SLC lunch program. It had been an enormous boon for working-class families: in 1915, the SLC served 550,000 penny lunches and another 300,000 free lunches to poor students who couldn't afford to pay. Parents and their allies pushed the New York City Board of Education to take over responsibility for the SLC lunch program and replicate its efforts across the city's schools. Their activism worked. In 1918, the board of education took control of the SLC's school lunch dominion. But this transfer of ownership turned out not to be the panacea for food justice that activists had hoped. The labor of lunch proved a sticking point. The board balked at the idea of allowing city funds to cover anything other than the cost of food and equipment, arguing that the $50,000 bond approved by the city's board of aldermen would amount to nothing if schools were allowed to use these funds to pay workers' salaries.[53] In the end, the SLC's nonprofit lunch program was, according to historian Andrew Ruis, "mostly replaced by a for-profit concessionaire system with no public health or educational mandate, no nutritional requirements, no reduced-price or free meals for poor children, and virtually no oversight of any kind."[54]

Not even widespread community support, national acclaim for its nonprofit school lunch model, or years of hard work invested in building a new infrastructure for care was enough to keep the SLC's "experiment" from being scrapped. The SLC lacked formal decision-making power over educational priorities and resources—a reality that became even more acute when the board of education assumed ownership of the nonprofit school lunch program the SLC had incubated. When the SLC had been in charge, however, it had managed to avoid latching itself to the ethnocentric project of "Americanization" that so many other Progressive Era reformers (including Ellen Swallow Richards and Emma Smedley) had embraced in order to gain support for their school lunch programs.[55] Instead of trying to indoctrinate students into a bland "American" way of eating, typified by Yankee white sauce, Mabel Hyde Kittredge and her team looked for ways to apply the lessons of scientific nutrition to immigrant foodways. Hoping to "beat the pushcart man at his own game," the SLC sold copycat street foods that were made with pure (unadulterated) and sometimes healthier ingredients.[56] The SLC also hired women whose social backgrounds matched those of the children they were feeding. The cultural knowledge these workers brought to the labor of lunch helped the SLC ensure it was accounting for ethnic tastes and religious requirements when designing school lunch menus.[57]

However, not all school lunch reformers were so broad-minded about the need to take direction from students and their families. Like many other Progressive Era reform efforts, penny lunch programs reflected and in some cases perpetuated unequal power dynamics related to race and class.[58] The inability of many professional home economists, in particular, to organize across lines of difference—to embrace the "spirit of cooperation and mutual aid" that Caroline Hunt preached—limited the power of the movement as a feminist project. The Progressive Era nonprofit school lunch movement was led by northern white women concerned with how industrialization was affecting city life. The lack of racial and ethnic diversity in key leadership positions was directly related to the advantages that middle-class, white, American-born women had when it came to accessing higher education and devoting time to volunteer activities.[59] When these relatively privileged women turned their attentions to the labor of lunch, they often tried to impose their own values on the marginalized populations they purported to serve.

The "savior complex" was omnipresent among the college-educated white women trained in fields like social work, public health, industrial medicine, urban sociology, and home economics. They wanted to use their academic training to address real social problems and created their own institutions from which to do this work.[60] Some, like Nobel Peace Prize–winner Jane Addams, whose Chicago Hull House was a beacon in the US settlement house movement, were careful to take a participatory approach to community-based research and action that valued the perspectives and contributions of those they sought to help. Others, like Florence Kelley, a renowned labor justice advocate and social justice feminist, helped build new organizational infrastructure for protecting civil rights. Kelley, for instance, served as the general director of the National Consumers' League and a founding board member of the National Association for the Advancement of Colored People (NAACP). Unfortunately, her approach was more the exception than the rule, especially at the level of local women's clubs, which were typically segregated.

White women reformers, who were sufficiently privileged to envision the government as a force for public good, lobbied for federal, state, and local governments to institutionalize their efforts at "municipal housekeeping." They largely ignored the South, where about 90 percent of African Americans lived in 1890. Of course, African American women have long participated in networks of mutual dependence and cooperative assistance, but they often found themselves fighting a different set of battles, to combat lynching and ensure that African Americans be treated and protected as full citizens.[61] Black women had less leisure time in which to join women's clubs and pursue organized charitable work: in 1890, for example, 23 percent of married black women worked outside the home, compared with only 3 percent of white women.[62] Even so, by 1910, the creation of African American women's clubs outpaced that of white women's clubs per capita.[63] This trend was fueled by African American migration from the rural South to the urban North where the women's club movement was much stronger. Over fifty thousand women were active club members of one of the thousand-plus chapters of the National Association of Colored Women by 1914.[64] They, like members of white women's clubs, sought to advance social and political reforms that would benefit their communities.

The club women of the Progressive Era delivered concrete social reforms with immediate impact, but this wasn't their end goal: they wanted to carve out a space for women in national politics. The high degree of coordination and cooperation they had built within their own organizations strengthened their belief in democracy.[65] This, in turn, convinced them to target large social organizations—like state and federal governments—that played an outsized role in the political and economic systems that shaped their everyday lives. But the confrontational politics they so carefully disguised in a cloak of maternalism proved too radical to survive the conservative backlash following the 1917 Bolshevik victory in the Soviet Union and ensuing Red Scare of 1919–1920 in the United States. Even moderate women's groups like the General Federation of Women's Clubs were subjected to antifeminist "witch hunts."[66]

The US War Department, conservative media outlets, and right-wing women's organizations accused individual women, their "progressive" organizations, and even the Federal Children's Bureau of supporting an international socialist agenda. The collective spirit of the day was effectively crushed, but the municipal housekeepers, home economists, and other social reformers organizing at the turn of the twentieth century managed to leave behind a national landscape dotted with hundreds of experimental models of nonprofit school lunch programs and other forms of public care.

Their vision for a community economy of care had contradicted the belief that feeding children was women's work, to be performed in private. Yet conservative politicians were reluctant to provide funding for nonprofit school lunch programs, fearing that too much official assistance would invite communism into the hearts and minds of young Americans. Even as municipal governments and school boards began to recognize child nutrition as a matter of national concern—as they did during World War I, when surveys showed widespread malnutrition among new military recruits—there was debate about how much the government should intervene. To increase the supply of healthful foods available to children, the US Department of War called on citizens to join the "school garden army" (fig. 5) and succeeded in recruiting two million urban and suburban youth to serve as "soldiers of the soil."[67]

Meanwhile, the norms governing middle-class motherhood and women's social activism were shifting. Progressive Era women reformers had focused on the needs of the "social whole," but by the 1920s, mothers were increasingly focused on satisfying the needs of their own children, family, and immediate community.[68] The concern for social justice and charitable work on behalf of the poor that had defined the Progressive Era all but evaporated during the Roaring Twenties. Home economics curriculums in colleges and high schools increasingly prioritized manual skills and largely ignored the philosophical questions of political economy that had motivated many of the field's early founders.[69]

These broader changes in American society altered the character of the nonprofit school lunch movement. Most of the new programs created in the 1920s were organized by groups of mothers for the benefit of their own children's schools. They were still working collectively, but for a different purpose. The poor students and working-class neighborhoods that had been the central focus of social settlement house workers, home economists, and women's clubs a generation earlier were no longer the ones to benefit most from the efforts of the nonprofit school lunch movement. What's more, it would become ever

FIGURE 5. School garden promotional poster from World War I. Special Collections, USDA National Agricultural Library.

harder for parents with limited economic resources to provide the capital necessary to create a penny lunch program in their children's schools as a new norm of public-private partnership solidified within the movement.

In some ways, public-private partnerships had always been part of the picture. For the first few decades of school lunch organizing, advocates had looked to their own social networks for financial donations, volunteer labor, and even privately owned buildings—such as women's home kitchens—to get their experimental programs off the ground. This was a financial and hopefully temporary compromise. Unfortunately, the practice of relying on a mix of private charity, children's fees, and limited public investment became so widespread that alternatives were rarely mentioned. As early as 1916, in a pamphlet for the US Department of Agriculture's Office of Home Economics, Caroline Hunt asserted that it was "almost universally agreed" that nonprofit school lunch programs could be financially self-sustaining under such a model. Ideally, the initial cost of equipment and facilities would be covered by the school board or another source of public funding. So, too, would the salary of a program supervisor well versed in home economics. The cost of food and labor could then be covered by soliciting private donations and charging parents a small fee for their children's lunches.[70] In this model, it was important to make use of volunteer and student labor, centralized production, and self-service in order to minimize the costs of the operation and ultimately feed more children, especially those too poor to pay for their own lunches.

This "almost universally agreed upon" model shaped the trajectory of the nonprofit school lunch movement during a critical phase of expansion in the 1920s and 1930s. When possible, professionally trained women sought to improve the nonprofit school lunch programs started by teachers and mothers who lacked formal training in nutrition science, sanitation, and bulk food preparation.[71] The US Bureau of Home Economics, then the largest employer of women scientists in the nation, continued to conduct research that directly informed the menu design, culinary techniques, and personnel management of school lunch programs. At the same time, Cooperative Extension (a federal-state partnership tied to land-grant universities) hired home economists to work with communities in rural areas to establish hot lunch programs and school gardens.[72]

The nonprofit school lunch movement had arrived. It was no longer just an urban phenomenon, but a national project. When Dr. Mary de Garmo Bryan, then chair of the department of institutional management at Columbia University's Teachers College, published *The School Cafeteria* in 1936, she wrote approvingly of "the change from the lunchroom, limited in size, and tucked away in basement or dark waste spaces, to the well-planned cafeteria, kitchen, and storage rooms, well-lighted and well-ventilated."[73] According to government estimates, there were 64,500 full-service school cafeterias nationwide, with another 7,500 projected to open each year.[74] This didn't include the thousands of rural schools that served a single hot dish, using systems like the heat-and-serve "pint-jar" method that required no specialized kitchen or cafeteria facilities.[75]

The practical information compiled in *The School Cafeteria* was an invaluable resource for this growing network of public school lunch programs. Anything a would-be school lunch director needed to know about kitchen and cafeteria design, equipment selection, personnel management, or record keeping could be found in the bulky volume, which included nearly four hundred pages on the topic of food purchasing alone. Sample menus and food specification tables helped novice school lunch directors understand the options available on the market, while strategies for judging product quality helped them make wise purchasing decisions. In short, the book taught a new generation of school lunch professionals to clearly communicate with vendors about their needs and instructed them to never accept the inferior products or services pushed by unscrupulous salesmen.

The School Cafeteria also provided the nonprofit school lunch movement with a snapshot of itself—summarizing four decades of local experiments led by the women reformers of the Progressive Era and presenting the results of former SLC leader Mabel Hyde Kittredge's 1926 nationwide survey of school lunch programs. By looking at this data in aggregate and combing through all of the academic articles written about school lunch, Bryan was able to distill four commonly held beliefs. First and foremost, the labor of lunch is a public responsibility in communities where children cannot return home for a noonday meal. In such cases, it falls to the board of education to ensure students have access to school lunches. Second, the program must be self-sustaining and operate according to principles of good business management. Third, trained dietitians should be in charge of school lunch programs to "ensure the service of nourishing, palatable food at the lowest possible prices." And lastly, communities ought to incorporate into their school lunch programs the rich and diverse educational opportunities that school kitchens and cafeterias offer (e.g., gardening, cooking, nutrition, sanitation, food preservation, and etiquette classes).[76]

The basic assumptions about nonprofit school lunch programs in 1930s America looked much the same as they did in the Progressive Era when Emma Smedley published *The School Lunch*. So, too, did nonprofit school lunch activists' ongoing fight to kick for-profit vendors out of the nation's schools. They wanted nonprofit programs run by the district (i.e., self-operated) and denounced the practice of "outsourcing" the labor of lunch to for-profit vendors. By the mid-1930s, it was common for the school boards of large cities in the North and Midwest to control their school lunch programs directly. This was often not the case in newly built suburbs and rural areas where nonprofit school lunch programs, if they existed, were still under the purview of parent groups or private for-profit caterers. In an outsourced program, the board of education granted permission to another party to sell food to children on school premises with the expectation that the caterer would turn a profit.

Children had only so much to spend on their school lunches, so for-profit vendors looked for ways to cut costs, including lowering standards for food quality and nutritional value. Vendors also pushed "the sales of candies, cakes, cheap bottled drinks, and similar items on which the profit is largest."[77] Nonprofit reformers saw this as a surefire recipe for malnourishment and hyperactivity. They also saw outsourcing as a terrible use of public resources. First of all, according to Dr. Mary de Garmo Bryan, vendors were "using public property for private business without fair compensation." Most schools charged for-profit vendors a nominal rent or none at all. And, hypothetically speaking, if schools had made for-profit vendors pay rent commensurate with the value of the space plus the cost of heat, light, cleaning, and replacement of equipment, the high rent would have forced the vendors to jack up the prices of menu items in order to make a profit.[78] If the main goal of school lunch programs was to provide children with healthy, affordable food, nonprofit was the only logical way to go.

The data Bryan and her colleagues collected from schools around the country told a consistent story: Under the commercial model, the nutritional value, quality, and variety of food was inferior, and meals were more expensive. Nonprofit school lunch programs had a track record of delivering better, cheaper food. Cheap labor was the key to their success. In 1929, the 212 self-operated nonprofit school lunch programs Mabel Hyde Kittredge surveyed spent about 2.3 times as much on food as they did on labor. Home economists' principles of scientific management helped school lunch directors figure out novel ways to maximize their meals per labor hour (fig. 6). But it was labor market discrimination that allowed nonprofit school lunch programs to stretch their dollars even further. Married women who were effectively barred from pre–World War II labor markets made up a cross-class and multiracial/multiethnic pool of underutilized cheap women workers for school kitchens and cafeterias.[79] Men of "equal abilities" were not usually available at the wages paid, according to Mary de Garmo Bryan, but women workers, "if properly chosen" were apt to be "orderly, painstaking, cleanly workers, who are interested in the children and anxious to do their jobs well."[80]

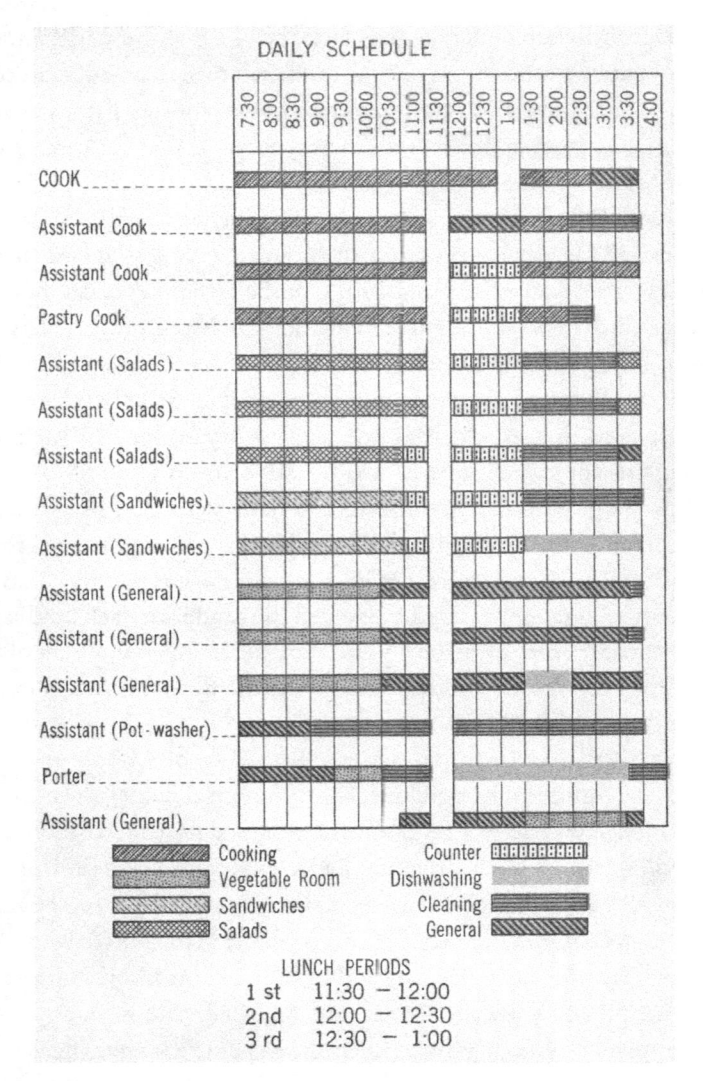

FIGURE 6. Work schedule for a high school cafeteria serving 1,000 meals per day in the 1930s. Nearly all jobs were for eight hours a day in larger cafeterias because tasks included food preparation, service, and clean up. Reprinted from Mary de Garmo Bryan, *The School Cafeteria*.

Professional home economists like Bryan prided themselves on their ability to offer school lunch workers a higher minimum hourly wage and better package of benefits than nearby restaurants.[81] They could push the envelope only so far, however, since they were expected to run self-sustaining "businesses" that charged the lowest possible price to child customers. Their only sources of revenue—food sales and private donations—had to cover the cost of wages for all school lunch employees (except the director's salary if it was paid by the school board), replacement of small equipment, ice and refrigeration, paper and cleaning supplies, laundry and uniform service, fuel, equipment repair, and other miscellaneous expenses. In this sense, not much had changed since Caroline Hunt's 1916 report. Neither, really, had the vision of an *ideal* school lunch program that Emma Smedley laid out in 1920.[82] What was beginning to change, however, was the federal government's relationship to the nonprofit school lunch movement. Uncle Sam was finally poised to take action on the "lunch problem."

THE NATIONALIZATION OF SCHOOL LUNCH

During the Great Depression, working-class and middle-class housewives staged coordinated public actions to demand public assistance and price controls so they could afford to feed their families. Their activism reignited the attempts of Progressive Era housewives and emerging professionals to politicize the links between the supposedly separate private and public spheres of economic life.[83] New Deal programs responded in kind: the federal government sought to care for its citizens—including hungry children at school. By 1941, nonprofit school lunch programs had become such a popular wing of the new welfare state that securing the future of these programs was "every citizen's concern." That's what Druzilla Kent, director of teacher training at the University of Tennessee, Knoxville, wrote in an article for *School Life,* the official journal of the Office of Education, urging the federal government to invest in the nonprofit school lunch movement. It wasn't just food or nutrition at stake but also the democratic core of American society. That's why, Kent argued, the federal government needed to defend the public character of school lunch from the forces of commercialization and privatization.[84]

Kent wanted the federal government to uphold the support for nonprofit school lunch programs that it had provided during the Great Depression. In 1931, under the Hoover administration, the President's Organization on

Unemployment Relief encouraged communities to mitigate the effects of poverty on children and families by ensuring that all students received a nourishing noonday meal with "no outward distinction between those able to pay and those not able to pay."[85] Then, in 1932, the Reconstruction Finance Corporation provided the first federal aid to school lunch programs in Missouri. This turned out to be a drop in the bucket compared with the federal efforts under President Franklin D. Roosevelt's New Deal.[86] Nonprofit school lunch programs became the beneficiaries of both free food and free labor, courtesy of Uncle Sam.

Under the New Deal's Agricultural Adjustment Act, the US Department of Agriculture (USDA) sought to stabilize free-falling agricultural prices by manipulating supply and demand. But destroying government-owned stores of crops and livestock and paying farmers not to grow food provoked a moral outrage that motivated even traditionally conservative members of American society to question the rationality and desirability of a capitalist economy prone to boom-and-bust cycles.[87] To mitigate this growing crisis, the USDA and the Roosevelt administration needed a socially and politically acceptable outlet for the "surplus" crops and livestock they removed from the market. Nonprofit school lunch programs fit the bill. In 1933, the Federal Surplus Relief Corporation began donating these commodities to nonprofit school lunch programs (fig. 7). Donations varied from year to year and were based on the calculations of USDA economists tasked with stabilizing prices for agricultural producers. The donations were not always aligned with children's taste preferences, but financially prudent school food directors did their best to make efficient use of whatever they were given.[88]

This model of food assistance proved popular and was subsequently expanded in 1935. Any school with a nonprofit school lunch program was eligible to receive donated food from the USDA as long as the program director followed USDA reporting guidelines, agreed to provide free lunches to children who couldn't afford to purchase their own, and promised not to reduce purchases of locally available foods. Then, in 1939, when escalating European hostilities began to threaten agricultural export markets, the USDA ramped up its efforts to help communities expand access to subsidized school lunches.

While increasing the domestic market for US agricultural products was in many ways the top priority for federal school lunch policy, nutrition mattered too. In what the War Food Administration labeled a "national tragedy," roughly one-third of the five million young men who were rejected as unfit

FIGURE 7. Workers employed by the Bureau of Commodity Distribution with surplus food to send to a Pasadena, CA, elementary school's free lunch program on December 6, 1939. *Los Angeles Herald Examiner* Collection, Los Angeles Public Library.

for military service during the World War II draft suffered from physical conditions caused or at least exacerbated by childhood malnutrition.[89]

"Defense nutrition" became a rallying cry for the creation of a permanent national school lunch program.[90] Throughout the 1930s and early 1940s, the federal government provided free labor to help communities feed poor children a nutritious school lunch. Ellen Woodward, assistant administrator of the Works Progress Administration (WPA), summed up the purpose of the program in a 1935 speech: "The WPA is making it possible for many underprivileged children of the present to grow into useful, healthy citizens of the future . . . through the daily service of warm, nourishing food, prepared by qualified, needy women workers."[91] In other words, by investing public money in the labor of lunch, the WPA was helping poor children and creating jobs for working-class women who would otherwise be unemployed.[92] At the time, the WPA employed about 7,400 school lunch workers in thirty-nine states. A related New Deal agency, the National Youth Association, hired another 16,000 unemployed youth ages 16–25 to work in school lunch programs.

FIGURE 8. Worker employed by the Works Progress Administration serves lunches in an East Lexington, VA, school in April 1942. Records of the Office of the Secretary of Agriculture 1900–1959, Child Nutrition Archives.

School lunch programs blossomed. By March 1941, the WPA employed over 64,000 school lunch workers. Stationed in over 95,000 schools, spread across all fifty states, the District of Columbia, and Puerto Rico, Uncle Sam's school lunch recruits prepared and served six million lunches per day during the 1941–1942 school year (fig. 8).[93] All told, their labor accounted for between one-quarter and one-third of typical school lunch budgets.[94] These jobs were good for schools, children, and the workers who held them.

Professional home economists, experienced school lunch managers, and old-guard school lunch reformers stepped into leadership roles within the fledgling national school lunch program. They helped prepare WPA workers, many of whom had never before worked in a restaurant or cafeteria, for their new jobs. They worked with the USDA and state agencies to develop and circulate WPA work manuals to build culinary capacity. And they converted their cafeterias into regional training centers that provided WPA workers with practical experience preparing school lunch recipes for hundreds of children using bulk production techniques.[95] In addition to scaling up their home-cooking skills, the WPA workers needed to learn how to plan scientifically nutritious menus and substitute ingredients in order to make use of USDA surplus foods.[96] To make the WPA school lunch work a bit easier, the WPA canned over ten million quarts of USDA commodity foods and dried another two million pounds every year from 1935 to 1942.[97] This minimal preprocessing cut down the time required for food preparation and allowed rural schools without adequate refrigeration to benefit from the USDA commodity program.

At its peak, the WPA fed one in four school-aged children. My grandmother, Patsie Ruth, a Dust Bowl baby who migrated from Oklahoma to California, was among them. But unfortunately for poor children like her, the WPA hot lunch program was disbanded in 1943. Unemployment was no longer a pressing social problem. Millions of men had been shipped off to war and the defense industry needed women workers. Still, children needed to be fed, and mothers with jobs outside the home needed help caring for their children. However, need didn't exactly translate into federal aid. The USDA commodity donations schools received dropped from a high of 454 million pounds in 1942 to 93 million pounds in 1944.[98] Food was increasingly shipped overseas to US soldiers and allied countries instead of public school kitchens. There were no more surpluses. School administrators began to fear that federal donations would stop entirely, making it exponentially more difficult for their nonprofit school lunch programs to be financially self-sustaining, especially if they continued to serve free lunches to poor children.

Their fears weren't unfounded. During wartime, the War Food Administration (WFA) took over as the main federal agency in charge of boosting the nonprofit school lunch movement. The WFA billed its Community Lunch Program as a cooperative, patriotic venture for parents and neighbors to support the health of the nation, but in reality the WFA offered more rhetoric than resources. The WFA encouraged communities (and especially women) to supply in-kind donations of labor, food, and supplies to make their community lunch programs viable. A 1945 WFA pamphlet, for example, suggested that women preserve local vegetables during the summer, assist with food preparation and service during the school year, and host card parties, minstrel shows, special dinners, and bazaars to raise money.[99] Men, for their part, could use their carpentry skills to build tables and benches for cafeteria seating and hunt wild game to donate to the lunch program.

This type of self-provisioning helped to bolster the domestic food supply during World War II—a good reminder of how quickly food systems can change when mass numbers of people are mobilized around a common objective. By 1943, just two years into the war, a network of roughly twenty million Victory Gardens produced 40 percent of the fresh produce consumed by the civilian population.[100] The USDA and WFA actively encouraged communities to plant Victory Gardens for school lunch programs. These could be small and distributed or large and centralized. High schoolers in Redlands, California, for example, cultivated a small 125- by 130-foot plot. The teen gardeners grew vegetables for their own school lunches and produced enough surplus to feed the rest of their 1,300 classmates. They also grew seedlings that were planted in six elementary school gardens for younger students to cultivate and harvest. In Jeff Davis County, Georgia, the Victory Garden initiative looked entirely different: Local school officials and civil society organizations built an 11-acre countywide consolidated garden. They also operated a community cannery, which was a "direct out-growth" of their prior efforts to can food for school lunches. In time, this became a shared community asset that anyone could use free of charge to preserve perishable products—vegetables, meat, and chicken—with the help of a trained Home Demonstration Club agent.[101]

These Victory Gardens and community canning facilities were right in line with the visions that Progressive Era reformers like John Dewey and Emma Smedley held decades earlier. During World War I, several cities had used their school kitchens as community canning and cooked food centers when classes weren't in session.[102] But during World War II, such cooperative efforts shifted from niche to mainstream. Fruit and vegetable consumption soared, even during the winter months, since three out of four families canned their own produce.[103] By the end of the war, class-based disparities in dietary quality (as measured by vital nutrient consumption) were nearly eliminated by these self-provisioning efforts and government food rationing.[104]

That said, the shift in federal support away from school lunch and toward the war effort had dealt a major blow to the nonprofit school lunch movement. Only 3.8 million children in thirty thousand schools around the country participated in the WFA school lunch program during the 1944–45 school year. In contrast, 6 million children had participated in the WPA program just three years prior. Why the sudden drop? Schools that depended on federal contributions of free labor and donated food to balance their budgets were squeezed out under the WFA model, which required them to apply for cash reimbursements after nearly a month of operation.[105] Schools that couldn't float the operating expenses lost out on the federal subsidies available through the WFA Community Lunch Program. What's more, the reimbursement dollars came with strings attached: schools could not outsource their lunch programs, and the reimbursement money could be used only to purchase food and pay the salary of a trained nutritionist. These stipulations were intended to bolster the communal character and nutritional integrity of school lunch, but most states exploited a loophole in the law. They hired only one professional to cover the entire state, which did little to guarantee the quality, fairness, or efficiency of the Community Lunch Program.[106]

This lack of public investment exacerbated existing racial inequalities within the nonprofit school lunch movement. During the Great Depression, white Americans disproportionately benefitted from New Deal policies and programs, including school lunch subsidies. Almost every state received some level of financial support from the Reconstruction Finance Corporation to subsidize the cost of cafeteria space and equipment, but it fell to local officials to decide how these resources should be distributed within their states and communities. Perhaps not surprisingly, they awarded white students a disproportionate share of federal aid.[107] This injustice was worst in the Jim Crow South, where black schools were generally overseen by white administrators who systematically limited their educational opportunities and access to financial resources.[108]

Thelma Flanagan, often referred to as Florida's First Lady of school lunch, collected reports from around the state that demonstrate this type of institutional racism.[109] In 1945, Mrs. Crawford, the director of a school lunch program at a white school in Pensacola, reported to the WFA that her school kitchen had been outfitted with a "large restaurant range, a steam table, and other modern mass feeding equipment" through a mix of private donations and federal funding. In contrast, many of Florida's rural agricultural communities were miles away from ice, milk routes, and electricity. Throughout the 1930s, teachers in the black schools in Florida's Leon County, then the "hog and hominy, cotton and tobacco" part of the state, cooked the community lunch—often a pot of soup and corn bread prepared on top of the stove that furnished heat for the school. It wasn't until 1944 that these schools were outfitted with cabinets, ranges, work tables, and other equipment necessary to prepare more varied lunches. This isn't to say that the upgrade in kitchen infrastructure made it easy for them to participate in the WFA Community Lunch Program like Mrs. Crawford's white Pensacola school did. Black schools were much less likely to have the financial cushion necessary to apply for the cash subsidy of the WFA Community Lunch Program.[110]

By the end of the war, the majority of the American public wanted the federal government to make a larger, permanent investment in the labor of lunch, despite the troubles the WFA model had inflicted on the national network of nonprofit school lunch programs. A bipartisan coalition of thirty-two national groups—including farmers, child welfare advocates, professional groups, women's clubs, and all the major educational, civic, medical, and labor organizations—asked Congress to enact a bill that would guarantee federal support for nonprofit school lunch programs.[111] Letters of support poured into Congressional offices from the homes, schools, and civic clubs of constituents in every voting district, but it was the USDA and macroeconomic concerns that elevated school lunch to the top of the legislative agenda.

Farm leaders knew, based on the events following World War I, that prices for agricultural commodities were likely to collapse after World War II ended. Hoping to prevent the nation from slipping into another economic depression, Congress devised a two-year grace period that would provide farmers with federal price supports for their commodity crops.[112] This legislation, passed in 1941, all but guaranteed the USDA would once again need a politically and morally acceptable outlet for "surplus" food. The USDA worked behind the scenes to build a powerful lobbying network: the Coordinating Committee on School Lunches (CCSL). The CCSL helped key stakeholders—nutritionists, home economists, nonprofit organizations, government agencies, farm lobbyists, commercial food industry representatives, teachers, and parents—harness their collective energy into the singular goal of passing a school lunch bill.[113]

Their efforts culminated in the introduction of two Senate bills, one of which became the National School Lunch Act of 1946 (NSLA).[114] It thus became the official policy of Congress "as a matter of national security, to safeguard the health and well-being of the Nation's children and to encourage the domestic consumption of nutritious agricultural commodities and other food, by assisting the States, through grants-in-aid and other means, in providing an adequate supply of food and other facilities for the establishment, maintenance, operation and expansion of nonprofit school lunch programs."[115] At face value, this legislation seems to be Emma Smedley's dream fulfilled. The devil is in the details.

Congressional debates over school lunch legislation had dragged on for nearly two years, evolving into a litmus test for states' rights and federal intervention in "local" affairs.[116] Conservative Republicans, mainly from the Northeast and Midwest, saw federal support for the labor of lunch—a private family responsibility, in their view—as a dangerous step toward communism. Legislators in the Jim Crow South, on the other hand, had no issue with the public nature of school lunch programs, but they feared the legislation might be some sort of Trojan horse for African American civil rights.[117] Lastly, representatives from farming states were adamant that the legislation include a provision that would benefit their constituents by extending USDA price supports for commodity crops. These competing concerns and priorities shaped the resulting legislation, arguably more so than the desires of the Progressive Era women reformers who came before them or even the CCSL coalition.

Prioritizing the demands of women who had frontline experience within the nonprofit school lunch movement would have launched the NSLP in a fundamentally different direction. First and foremost, they wanted the Office of Education, not the Department of Agriculture, to be the administrative home for the program.[118] They also wanted nonprofit school lunch programs to be woven into the basic fabric of public schooling and for nutrition education to be integrated into K–12 curriculum. They lost both battles. Congress granted the USDA jurisdiction over the NSLP and refused to provide legal or financial support for nutrition education within the National School Lunch Act of 1946. What little funding legislators had earmarked to assist schools with purchasing culinary and cafeteria equipment was axed from the federal budget after the first year. And despite heavy opposition from liberal women's organizations, labor unions, civil rights activists, and child welfare advocates, the NSLA required that state and municipal school food authorities contribute $3 for every $1 the federal government supplied to local school lunch budgets. The women who had worked in the WPA and WFA lunch programs throughout the 1930s and early 1940s knew this would yield a fractured economy of care excluding many poor communities from participating in the NSLP.

Congress refused to change the NSLA's funding formula. Instead, the bill's primary architect, Senator Richard Russell (D-Georgia), doubled down, praising the NSLA's ability to "protect the rights of all children . . . whatever race, color, or creed."[119] In theory, it was inclusive of poor children. Any school that wanted to participate in the NSLP—and gain access to federal cash assistance and USDA surplus commodities—had to promise to serve "needy" children free school lunches that met the minimum nutritional standards set by the US secretary of agriculture. But this was an ambiguous task at best. The NSLA didn't provide any financial guidelines for what constitutes "needy" or designate any special funding to help schools offset the cost of free lunches.

At the NSLA signing, President Truman shared his hope that "all state and local authorities will cooperate fully" in helping the nonprofit school lunch movement reach "every possible community."[120] Such rhetoric conjures an image of American egalitarianism that obscures the unequal ability of working-class communities and communities of color to access this shared public financing. In truth, the NSLA relied on private donations and tax revenue sourced from states and communities with very different tax bases for funding public infrastructure. This set up an economy of care that increasingly benefitted the white, middle-class Americans who were already poised to prosper during the postwar era. "Cooperating" with the federal government to reorganize the labor of lunch just wasn't an option for those who couldn't afford to do so.

While this first wave of nonprofit school lunch organizing—spanning from the 1890s to the 1940s—failed to deliver a postcapitalist model for collectivizing care, present-day activists would do well to keep the "radical" roots of the NSLP in mind. Reimagining school lunch is an inherently feminist project, and it will continue to be so as long as people who identify as women perform a disproportionate share of reproductive labor. When we understand the historical context of the nonprofit school lunch movement as inseparable from a broader set of feminist struggles over the political economy of everyday life, the importance of school lunch reform in the twenty-first century begins to look quite different. It's not just children's health and well-being that is at stake but also the way in which we as a society choose to allocate and value the concrete tasks of caring for others and our shared environment.

Paradoxically, by agreeing to operate financially self-sustaining "businesses," Progressive Era school lunch reformers legitimized the notion that feeding children was less important than other school activities and not really part of the public educational enterprise. They may not have had much of an alternative, given the patriarchal nature of government and business at the time. But if Ellen Swallow Richards, Emma Smedley, Caroline Hunt, and their material feminist sisters had had more power to shape the policies and priorities of the movement they launched, we would be in a very different place today. Likewise, if the many women involved in the WPA and WFA school lunch programs had been the ones to craft a school lunch bill, today's school lunch activists might not find themselves fighting for universal free lunches, "real" food, school gardens, nutrition education, and the like.

This history of the radical roots of school lunch may read as a frustrating story—and to some extent it should—but I hope it also offers inspiration for how we might, collectively, reimagine and ultimately fight for a school lunch program that meets our highest ideals. Likewise, the next wave of coordinated school lunch organizing, which occurred in the 1960s and early 1970s, has much to teach us about racial injustice and the role of powerful corporate players—let's call them "Big Food" for short—in cheapening school lunch. Understanding how Big Food corporations exploited economic, racial, and ecological crises of the 1960s and 1970s for their own gains is a useful exercise for today's real food activists operating in a neoliberal era that pushes public-private partnerships as the solution to complex social problems. This next chapter of school lunch history is about more than just the arrival of Big Food, however. It's also about the struggles for food justice led by women and communities of color who argued that school lunch was a universal right.

TWO

The Fight for Food Justice

The 1960s and 1970s brought tremendous social change to all corners of American society—school lunch included—that shaped what the National School Lunch Program (NSLP) looks like today. These changes, which helped feed millions of poor, hungry children, were the product of widespread community organizing and coalition building. However, unintended consequences stemming from heavy private sector involvement and political inaction caused both food and job quality to suffer. Activists were split on their priorities, but one thing was sure: poverty was hard to ignore, despite all the Cold War rhetoric proclaiming America as the "richest nation on Earth."

Lunch ladies helped to draw attention to how poverty affected the children in their care. For example, in the mid-1960s, about two decades after Congress created the NSLP, a cafeteria director at a Georgia elementary school revealed that hungry students still weren't getting enough to eat. Some were so desperate that they pilfered discarded leftovers from the dumpster. Lunch in her school cost only 20 cents (about $1.50 in today's money), but this was more than many families could afford. Of the seven hundred students at her school, she estimated that one hundred were sufficiently "needy" to qualify for free lunches, yet there was only enough money in the school lunch budget to feed thirty-two of them. Speaking to *New York Post* education reporter Bernard Bard for his 1968 book *The School Lunchroom: A Time of Trial* under the condition of anonymity, Mrs. X—as Bard called her—worried that publicly blaming the local school board could get her fired.[1]

Mrs. X was fed up. She had witnessed for far too long the effects of child poverty and malnutrition on the young people she so desperately wanted to feed. Like other frontline school lunch workers from the Progressive Era on, she tried to stretch the school lunch budget, but there never seemed to be enough money to feed all the nation's needy children. In Mrs. X's case, the board of education had demanded she "stay out of the red" and operate a financially self-sustaining school lunch program. Complying meant denying free lunches to children whose need was obvious. Some of these children would sneak down to the basement of the school, where the kitchen and cafeteria were located, and beg Mrs. X to "give them some little chore to pay for their lunch." So she let them sweep floors, empty garbage pails, carry milk containers, and wash dishes during their lunch period. For these hungry children, enduring the stigma attached to working in the school cafeteria to earn a free lunch was worth it: they needed to eat.

Officially, Mrs. X's school was supposed to provide free lunches to all these needy children since it was participating in the NSLP. She wanted to follow the law, but her hands were tied. Local and state policymakers were the ones who decided how much public funding would trickle down to her school cafeteria. Without sufficient funding from government sources, Mrs. X and others like her looked to philanthropic clubs, religious organizations, and prominent members of the local business community for donations. They urged these charitable "sponsors" to feed the poor, hungry children in their communities. This model worked decently well in the suburbs, where middle-class families lived, but not in urban and rural schools where poor children tended to cluster.

In the two decades after the National School Lunch Act (NSLA) was passed in 1946, suburbanization exacerbated the inequalities inherent in the legislation's funding structure. Residential construction boomed in the 1950s, and after the 1954 Supreme Court ruling *Brown v. Board of Education,* white flight—the exodus of white families avoiding integration—increasingly siphoned wealth from city school systems to the suburbs. And even though the federal government poured tax dollars into building airports, highways, hydropower plants, irrigation projects, hospitals, and other forms of public infrastructure, it was then—as now—primarily the responsibility of state and local governments to finance the construction, maintenance, and renovation of public K–12 schools, including their kitchens and cafeterias. While urban schoolchildren could walk home for lunch, saving schools the hassle and cost of running a lunch program, children in car-dependent suburbs weren't seen as having that option. So when state and local governments financed the construction of new suburban schools, including a functional kitchen and cafeteria was standard practice.

The timing of this school construction played a major role in the suburbanization of the nonprofit school lunch movement. By 1965, a majority of

Americans resided in the suburbs.[2] To accommodate the demographic influx of people from cities and rural areas, suburbs built new K–12 schools. And by this point, nonprofit school lunch programs were no longer "experimental," as they had been in the 1920s, when urban education underwent a major expansion. Kitchen and cafeteria facilities became a standard feature for suburban schools and newly consolidated rural schools built in the 1950s and 1960s. According to one national survey, nine out of ten newly constructed schools included such facilities in their building plans by the mid-1960s.[3] Urban schools lagged behind, stuck in an anemic economy of care that denied subsidized school lunches to millions of American children.

Public school facilities, kitchens and cafeterias included, were further strained by the massive number of young baby boomers who entered their doors. Overcrowding was commonplace. Schools tried to make do by feeding children in their classrooms and shrinking lunch periods to as little as twenty minutes. The federal government, for its part, made a bad situation worse by not increasing the school lunch budget to keep up with the changing population: per-student contributions dwindled from 31.1 percent of the total school lunch budget in 1947 to 22.5 percent by 1960.[4] What funding schools did receive often ran out in January or February if they had high participation.[5] Scrambling to balance their budgets, foodservice directors weighed the pros and cons of raising school lunch prices. It wasn't a straightforward proposition: raising prices to offset the loss in federal subsidy could put the NSLP out of reach for some families, and any decline in revenue from paying students would chip away at the economies of scale that schools depended on to keep lunch cheap for everyone and free for a select number of needy students.

Without designated federal or state funding for free lunches, nonprofit school lunch programs depended on what insiders called the "bite tax" to create a pseudopublic form of fundraising at the local level. In this model, school lunch professionals set aside a portion (roughly one-tenth) of the revenue from the fees charged to paying students to pay for needy children's free lunches.[6] But the bite tax depended upon the ratio of ten paying customers for each child in need of a free lunch. Some districts, fearing that the bite tax might raise prices too high for families who could barely afford school lunch fees, rejected the practice altogether.

Despite the clear need for more public resources, many states dodged even the most basic cost-sharing responsibility outlined in the NSLA. They reclassified private money—charitable donations, sales revenue, and bite taxes collected by cashiers—as public funding that satisfied the requirement that

$3 be contributed by state and local sources for every $1 of federal school lunch aid.[7] State and local governments exploited this loophole in the law, but it was the US Department of Agriculture (USDA) that decided to allow charitable gifts and children's payments to count in the first place. This continued the long tradition of hybrid public-private provisioning begun in the Progressive Era and delayed the expansion of the NSLP into poor communities, which is exactly what those on the frontlines of the nonprofit school lunch movement had predicted. The American School Food Service Association (ASFSA; a professional association formed in 1946 after a merger of the Food Service Directors Conference and the National School Cafeteria Association) sent Congress a report in 1947 that clearly illustrated how discrepancies in state-level investment had allowed some school lunch programs to flourish during World War II while others had floundered or declined to participate in the War Food Administration's Community Lunch Program.[8] They feared the NSLP might be afflicted by the same problem, but neither Congress nor the USDA made any effort to heed their concerns.

As a result, the national rollout of the NSLP was much slower than activists had hoped. By 1960, only half of public and private K–12 schools had opted into the NSLP. These 64,000 schools fed 14 million students, an impressive number, but a mere third of the total student population.[9] As of 1963, nearly 70 percent of the 8.5 million children whose schools did not participate in the NSLP were concentrated in counties and metropolitan areas with a population of one hundred thousand or more.[10] That urban and poor rural schools were underserved by the NSLP was a product of institutional racism. State and local school food authorities had near total discretion over how federal funding was distributed at the level of school districts and even individual school buildings.[11] Racism was endemic.

Congress did not address racial discrimination within the NSLP in the early 1960s outright, but it did take some initial steps to address inequities when it modified the NSLA in 1962. The federal school lunch appropriation formula was revised to account for the participation rate and relative poverty of each state. Special Assistance funding for free and reduced-price meals was also added to the NSLA at this time, but the provision went entirely unfunded until fiscal year 1966.[12] Congress also instructed the USDA to enforce the 1946 provision that required schools participating in the NSLP to provide free lunches to needy children. However, this congressional mandate, like the unfunded Special Assistance Program, did little to improve conditions for poor children. The USDA deemed its sole mechanism of enforcement too politically unpopular to actually use: if state or municipal officials were found guilty of not providing meals to needy children, the USDA's only recourse was to withhold cash appropriations and commodities to the entire state.[13] Punishing state and local governments who refused to comply with the free lunch provision could actually result in more unfed needy children, so the USDA chose not to act.

Local incentives for identifying and feeding these children changed during President Lyndon B. Johnson's first term in office, when Congress passed a flurry of new legislation that expanded the government's role in caring for children, the poor, and the elderly. The Food Stamp Act of 1964 and the Economic Opportunity Act of 1964 allocated federal money for food assistance and community-based antipoverty programs. The 1965 Elementary and Secondary Education Act provided significant federal funding for schools with high concentrations of children from low-income families. The Older Americans Act of 1965 provided federal funding for home-delivered and community-based meals for low-income senior citizens. And the Child Nutrition Act of 1966 (CNA) required schools participating in the NSLP to provide every poor child with a free school lunch. This was all part of a broader set of federal policy initiatives, legislation, and programs dubbed the "Great Society."[14] Yet progress was slow to take hold: the NSLA's free lunch provision remained unfunded until 1968, and no uniform eligibility standards were issued until 1970.

Grassroots activists demanded change. Frustrated parents, local labor unions, church groups, and a suite of national organizations—including the NAACP, Community Nutrition Institute, Children's Foundation, Food Research and Action Center, Public Voice, and the National Council on Hunger and Malnutrition—took legal action against municipal governments and school boards.[15] In 1967, for example, the Arkansas Council of Human Relations filed a lawsuit against the rural Palestine School District alleging misuse of federal funds.[16] Parents of students at the local black school accused the district of intentionally misdirecting federal money from the 1966 Child Nutrition Act that had been earmarked for free lunches. According to the plaintiffs, this was only the latest in a series of discriminatory decisions about how to allocate federal school lunch funding in the seven-hundred-person town. Technically speaking, both schools were participating in the NSLP, but the benefits white and black families gained from Palestine's school lunch program were separate and unequal. The black school didn't have a kitchen or cafeteria; the white school had both. The black children's lunches were prepared at the white school, then packed into the back of a pickup truck for a bumpy journey on the dirt road that connected the schools. These lunches couldn't be reheated with the "corroded" and "unusable" equipment the district had provided, the parents claimed, which meant their children never had a hot lunch.

Parents across the country told similar stories. So when a network of middle-class women's organizations set out to document discriminatory practices within the NSLP, they found a pattern of injustice.[17] Coalitions of activists demanded that the federal government take responsibility for providing meaningful, equitable care to all children through the NSLP, and ASFSA, the professional organization for school food workers, followed their lead. Congress responded by issuing new legal protections for children and guaranteed funding for free and reduced-price lunches. At the same time, however, the USDA flung open the doors of public school cafeterias to private companies that sold cheap precooked food, snacks, and soft drinks. This cheapening of school lunch through privatization and commercialization was billed as a cost-effective, expedient strategy for rectifying the institutional racism of the NSLP. But, as many activists knew, children and workers deserved better.

RIGHT TO LUNCH ACTIVISTS DEMAND BETTER

School lunch activism in the late 1960s and early 1970s was amplified by a group of women partnering to advance positive social change. Between October 1967 and March 1968, local members of the Committee on School Lunch Participation (CSLP) worked with Jean Fairfax, a staff member at the National Association for the Advancement of Colored People (NAACP), to design and implement a nationwide survey of school lunch programs. The CSLP united five national women's organizations across lines of race and religion to tackle the problem of food justice in the NSLP. The National Council of Catholic Women, the National Council of Jewish Women, the National Council of Negro Women, Church Women United, and the Young Women's Christian Association engaged their network of women volunteers in what we might now call an action-oriented, community-based research project. Under the umbrella of the CSLP, they interviewed roughly 1,500 people—including administrators, teachers, cafeteria staff, and parents—and accumulated a body of rich, heartfelt stories and concrete statistics to share with policymakers and the public.[18]

The entire administrative and legal structure of the NSLA was biased against poor people and communities of color. That was the CSLP's main finding. The committee's final report, *Their Daily Bread,* first published in April 1968, applauded the efforts of the hardworking, dedicated, and cooperative school lunch personnel who tried their best to feed children a nutritious, affordable lunch. They were in no way blaming lunch ladies or their direct supervisors for the systemic failings of the NSLP. Rather, they blamed higher-ups within school districts and local policymaking circles who held the power to decide whether needy children had access to free school lunches without discrimination. Paternalistic and at times prejudicial treatment of low-income children had persisted even after the enactment of the Child Nutrition Act of 1966. For example, one administrator required children to be deloused before they could have a free lunch.[19] Others required poor kids to scrub dishes, serve meals, or help with record keeping in exchange for free lunches, just as Mrs. X did in her cafeteria.[20]

The USDA had failed to "safeguard the health and well-being" of these children, a primary goal of the NSLP, so another federal agency stepped in to fill the void. Joseph Califano, head of the newly created Department of Health, Education, and Welfare, encouraged communities to use funds from the 1965 Elementary and Secondary Education Act (ESEA) to start "emergency" free lunch programs that operated outside USDA purview in areas where the NSLP was not yet operating.[21] From its interviews, the CSLP learned that the segregated all-black schools in South Carolina relied solely on ESEA funds for lunches, while the all-white schools received NSLP funding.[22] In Little Rock, Arkansas, the committee found ESEA funds provided nearly all the free lunches.[23] And in Minneapolis, Minnesota, it discovered that three thousand free lunches were served each day using ESEA funding, while only eighty-seven free lunches were served using NSLP funding.[24] By gathering such stories and printing them in *Their Daily Bread,* the CSLP provided authoritative evidence for a broad-based school lunch movement that coalesced as the civil rights and antipoverty movements intensified during the summer of 1968.[25]

Their Daily Bread demanded that the federal government solve the problems plaguing the NSLP. The CSLP recommended that Congress convert the NSLP into a universally free program, but if this proved financially unworkable, it should at least issue uniform free-lunch-eligibility standards and guarantee reimbursements for all the free lunches schools served. The CSLP activists had a clear vision for a new economy of care in American public schools, but they also knew their proposal for a universal free school lunch program was a long shot given the escalating costs of the Vietnam War, the strain Great Society programs placed on the federal budget, and the historical reluctance of the US government to fully fund nonprofit school lunch programs. Congress went with the second, cheaper option of focusing reform efforts and federal dollars on poor children, effectively turning the NSLP into a means-tested social welfare program. And this was only after the "right-to-lunch" movement, to borrow a phrase from historian Susan Levine, had exerted enough political pressure to force the issue.

During the right-to-lunch movement, civil rights organizations leveraged the data and recommendations of *Their Daily Bread* to motivate both lawsuits and mass street protests that went far beyond the polite politics of cooperation that members of the "respectable" CSLP usually preferred. "One of the major demands that came out of the race riots of the late 1960s was for school nutrition programs," ASFSA executive director Dr. John Perryman recalled years later. Perryman had been attending an ASFSA industry seminar when the director of a large city's school lunch program lamented that inadequate infrastructure kept him from doing his job: "I still have more than one hundred schools without any foodservice, but there is nothing I can do about it at this time because there are absolutely no facilities." At that moment, as Perryman recalled, a civil rights activist arose from the audience and said, very calmly, "When we bring legal action against you, you will find a way."[26]

The threat of legal action and the court orders handed down in cases that went before a federal judge helped expand the NSLP, especially in urban school districts, but such tactics were generally used only after right-to-lunch activists staged direct actions, organized petitions, and sent delegations to speak with local officials. At times, they coordinated their efforts. In 1969, for example, parents, major civil rights organizations, and the National Council on Hunger and Malnutrition organized a nationwide boycott of the NSLP. Their goal was to focus political pressure on local school boards that were refusing to provide free lunches, and they chose dates with excellent optics: October 12–17, National School Lunch Week. President John F. Kennedy had established this designation in 1962 in order to encourage "citizens and civic groups to extend every effort in support of the school lunch program," and for these activists, that meant fighting for justice.[27] John Kramer, the executive director of the National Council on Hunger and Malnutrition, urged parents to keep their children home, or at the very least, to withdraw them in the middle of the day if their schools did not offer free lunches. Local community organizations would instead provide free lunches to these children and record the names of parents who were willing to bring lawsuits against their school boards.[28] Dozens of cities participated and eventually pursued legal action to secure poor children's right to lunch.

That same year, in New York City, a delegation of poor Puerto Rican mothers and their allies, United Bronx Parents, went so far as to dump "full plastic garbage bags of food collected from school trash bins after lunch at a federal government building in downtown Manhattan."[29] These parent-activists launched the first sustained, grassroots campaign to improve school lunch in the South Bronx. In 1969 and 1970, the shared project of claiming their children's right to a free school lunch "mobilized and politically empowered hundreds of people who, because of poverty, language barriers, and often, relative newcomer status to the United States, were unaccustomed to making demands on the city's institutions of power," according to historian Lana Dee Povitz.[30] Their community organizing yielded concrete results: They not only secured their children's right to lunch but also took partial control over the labor of lunch in 1971 as the administrators of New York City's free federally funded summer meal program.

On the national stage, the Poor People's Campaign (PPC) for economic justice, organized by Dr. Martin Luther King Jr. and the Southern Christian Leadership Conference in 1968, called on the federal government to provide all poor children with free school lunches. A month after Dr. King was assassinated, three thousand people occupied Washington Mall for six consecutive weeks, forming a protest camp called Resurrection City from May 21 to June 24, 1968. This multiracial group of activists forced policymakers to witness the struggles of poor families and protested outside of Congress, the USDA, and other federal agencies that had excluded people of color from accessing the same benefits as white Americans. Activists within the National Welfare Rights Organization (NWRO), one of the organizations at the forefront of the PPC, spoke of the unique challenges that black women, and especially single mothers, faced when trying to care well for themselves and their families. The NWRO pushed back against politicians who viewed women who had children out of wedlock as "undeserving" of government assistance and fought for their children's right to high-quality education, housing, clothing, food, and healthcare.

The NWRO turned reproductive politics on its head. It questioned why women should be held individually responsible for caring for their children, rather than reshaping society to make caring well a collective, public responsibility. And why, when raising children is a form of work, should they be expected to do this work for free? As more women asked themselves these questions, the NWRO grew from 130 affiliated locals in 1966 to 800 in 1971. At the height of the welfare rights movement, in the summer of 1969, national membership exceeded 25,000 people, most of whom were African American women. They "brought with them just about all that they had," including a love for their children "so strong that they were willing to take on the local, state, and federal government with their bare hands, and their bodies and their brains," recalled Beulah Sanders, a black welfare recipient and NWRO leader.[31]

NWRO mothers met with policymakers and staged popular education events designed to empower other poor mothers. And at times they resorted to more confrontational tactics: filing lawsuits and organizing their own random checks to ensure schools were in compliance with federal law.[32] They simply wanted their children to be treated with dignity and not singled out as "poor students." In Cook County, Illinois, over 1,100 people signed a petition to the superintendent of Chicago Public Schools to end the "humiliating requirements" that families were forced to endure to qualify for free school lunches.[33] Through publications like their 1969 pamphlet "The New School Lunch Program Bill of Rights," the NWRO educated poor mothers across the country about their children's rights and what to do if these rights were violated.[34]

Around the same time, the Black Panther Party (BPP), founded in 1966, began feeding children free meals as part of a broader suite of programs designed to collectivize social reproduction and further a revolutionary politics of black liberation. The BPP ran twenty community-based "survival programs," the most celebrated of which was the Free Breakfast for Children Program (FBCP). In September 1968, a group of neighborhood mothers who were active in their local parent-teacher association helped the Panthers start the first FBCP.[35] The FBCP quickly spread from its original location in St. Augustine's Church in Oakland, California, to forty-five cities across the country. BPP leaders played a significant role in fueling this expansion when, in late 1969, they ordered all chapters to start an FBCP in their communities.[36]

The children the Panthers were feeding had been systematically excluded from the NSLP, just as their parents had been a generation prior. But through the FBCP, at a time when Congress and the USDA continued to disregard the needs of poor black families, the Panthers were able to model a loving approach to providing children with emotional and physical sustenance through an economy of care rooted in mutual aid and community self-determination. Notably, both women and men were involved in the daily operation of the FBCP, which some former BPP leaders credit with opening up space to challenge the group's notoriously patriarchal gender relations.[37] In this way, care work became a necessary facet of revolutionary politics, worthy of everyone's contribution regardless of gender.

Mainstream media stories about the BPP feeding tens of thousands of poor black children exposed millions of Americans to a working example of how social reproduction could be collectivized at the neighborhood scale in a truly egalitarian fashion. The BPP survival programs embarrassed and threatened the Johnson administration and the legacy of its Great Society initiatives. The FBCP, in particular, shed light on how the US government was still failing to meet its citizens' most basic needs for sustenance.

At the height of the Cold War, exposing the continual injustice of life in capitalist America was a politically dangerous course of action. It made the BPP and other "radical" activists a target for the Federal Bureau of Investigation's (FBI) covert counterintelligence program, COINTELPRO, which was designed to infiltrate, disrupt, and ultimately destroy domestic political organizations deemed "subversive." The bureau's director, J. Edgar Hoover, actually went so far as to call the BPP the "greatest threat to the internal security of the country."[38] None of the BPP's survival programs worried the FBI more than the FBCP, which was universally popular among party members and nonmembers alike. The BPP, which was often pictured in national media as a group of dangerous men walking around with guns, was recast in a positive, if not heroic light, when its members began caring for children through the FBCP. It offered a way to build community and movement strength, which is precisely why the FBI viewed it as such a threat. David Hilliard, a former BPP leader, put it this way: "Food serves a double purpose, providing sustenance but also functioning as an organizing tool; people enter the office when they come by, take some leaflets, sit in on an elementary PE (political education) class, talk to cadre, and exchange ideas."[39]

Yet there were critics within the BPP who disagreed about the political potency of the FBCP and other community-based survival programs, disparaging them as "reformist" and not revolutionary.[40] BPP cofounder Bobby Seale urged people to understand mutual aid programs as the lifeblood of a radical politics. "A revolutionary program is one set forth by revolutionaries, by those who want to change the existing system to a better system," he explained. "A reform program is set up by the existing exploitive system as an appeasing handout to fool the people and keep them quiet."[41] What the BPP offered through its community-based free breakfast program was, in this sense, a revolutionary program that catalyzed a series of new government-sponsored reform programs.

In the spring of 1968, just as the FBCP was taking off at the national scale, Congress began funneling money to many of the same low-income communities that the NWRO, the BPP, and others were organizing into a powerful political movement that included right-to-lunch activism. Congress appropriated $32 million of the NSLP budget to expand lunch service to impoverished areas with "a high concentration of working mothers or mothers enrolled in job training programs," but total federal school lunch funding remained flat for the 1968–1969 school year.[42] The following year, Congress increased the NSLP budget by $50 million and earmarked an additional $5 million for free lunches. This uptick in funding signaled a series of much more significant changes to the federal child nutrition landscape that would occur during the Nixon administration (January 1969–August 1974).

The social organization of care—how children are fed, why, and by whom—has real political consequences. By 1975, in addition to massively expanding its free lunch program into urban communities, the USDA had fully coopted the Panthers' free breakfast program, dishing out food—but no servings of revolutionary politics—in the same low-income communities the BPP had served.[43] The expansion of the USDA's pilot school breakfast program during the late 1960s and its subsequent promotion into a permanent federal food assistance program in 1975 can, on the one hand, be seen as a positive attempt to address the problem of child hunger. But it was also a strategic way for the federal government to curtail the BPP's growing political influence.[44] The example of Ronald Reagan illustrates this well. As governor of California—home to the BPP's central headquarters in Oakland—Reagan led his state's efforts to expand the USDA's school breakfast program, which had begun as a small pilot program in 1966. Yet when Reagan became president, he pushed through draconian budget cuts to federal child nutrition and food assistance programs.

Whatever politicians' motivations might have been, by the end of the 1960s they knew they needed to respond to public outrage about the inequities and inadequacies of the NSLP. In December 1969, President Nixon hosted the White House Conference on Food, Nutrition, and Health in Washington, DC. The three thousand delegates from the public and private sectors who attended this multiday strategy session were tasked with gathering data from their states and whatever communities they happened to represent. At the opening plenary, Nixon told the delegates it was time for the federal government to "claim responsibility" for solving the problems of hunger and malnourishment that afflicted "millions of Americans, too young, too old, or too hurt by life to do without [their] help."[45] After several days of deliberation, the conference delegates prepared a report outlining several high-priority policy proposals, including passing legislation that would create a universally free school breakfast and lunch program.[46] The government's hand-selected advisory panel came to the same conclusion as the CSLP women's clubs who authored *Their Daily Bread:* providing free school meals for all children was the best way forward.

This was just the beginning for activists who dreamed of enacting a rights-based framework for child health and nutrition. Jean Fairfax—the director of the Division of Legal Information and Community Service for the NAACP Legal Defense and Education Fund who had coordinating the CSLP's data-gathering project back in 1968—believed the delegates to the 1969 White House Conference on Food, Nutrition, and Health had not gone far enough. Their final report framed children's right to food squarely in terms of their ability to access "nutritional resources" for optimal health. In 1971, Fairfax outlined an alternative moral and legal framework that would guarantee to all children

1. The right to have their nutritional needs identified.
2. The right to knowledge about what their bodies require so that they will eventually make wise nutritional choices.
3. The right to be in a dependable food delivery system which will assure that their total nutritional needs are met.
4. The right to be fed in an environment which is psychologically wholesome and under conditions which enhance dignity and move them to experience joy.
5. The right to be children, that is, to have society concerned about them until they reach maturity and to intervene actively on their behalf in matters relating to their nutritional welfare.[47]

Legally promising these rights to children would transform the NSLP into a far more caring institution. Individual caloric needs, religious restrictions, allergies, food intolerances, and the ability to chew and digest foods would be respected. Children would be taught why certain foods are healthy and would be fed those same foods in the school cafeteria. The power to decide what kitchens and cafeterias look like, how they are equipped, and what atmosphere they create would necessarily shift to accommodate the perspective of children and the frontline kitchen and cafeteria workers who feed them.

In Fairfax's vision, the NSLP would foreground children's rights and help to foster a new economy of care. Democratic Congressman William Clay, an influential black civil rights advocate from Missouri, shared her optimism and penchant for community organizing. In his 1969 keynote address to attendees of the ASFSA Core City Seminar, Clay called out ASFSA's 35,000 members for hiding out on the sidelines of the right-to-lunch movement and being unwilling to call out Congress for "spending more than $200 million just to get one rocket to the launching pad, but only $550 [million] for the entire school lunch program."[48] As a professional organization, ASFSA had never been particularly confrontational or imaginative when it came to politics. Clay urged them to get political and to think big. "Whoever said that school lunchrooms should be frequented only by students? Why couldn't adults get food there?" he asked. "Why should a lunchroom be closed at 2 pm?" A school kitchen is publicly owned by taxpayers and therefore should be operated as a public kitchen, he noted, emphasizing that "it is a valuable facility, large enough to gather people, teach people, as well as feed people."[49] School kitchens and cafeterias could become vibrant public spaces for social justice organizing if ASFSA members were willing to knock on doors, speak to community groups, and lobby politicians to enlist support.

Congressman Clay's vision for turning school kitchens and cafeterias into public spaces that collectivize care work and enrich community life remains elusive. That's not to say ASFSA ignored his call to action: They adopted the tagline "Feed Them All" for the 1970 national conference and National School Lunch Week theme.[50] They followed this up with a multiyear campaign in which ASFSA members lobbied Congress and the USDA to create a universal free school lunch program. The USDA would seem like a natural ally for the cause since the agency's budget and influence would grow if more children participated in the program. But the USDA refused to support ASFSA's campaign. In October 1971, ASFSA executive director Dr. John Perryman wrote an open letter to Assistant Secretary of Agriculture Richard Lyng, expressing deep frustration that had been building within the nonprofit school lunch movement for decades. "Never, while school foodservice must continually fight for its survival, must continually fight for its place in education, must continually fight for its presence on school campuses, must continually be faced with a shifting foundation of support; never, while school foodservice is relegated to a ticket-taker sideshow, can the program develop its rightful potential," Perryman wrote.[51] Lyng responded with a firm dismissal. "As much as I appreciate the role of proper nutrition in child development," he wrote, "I feel that the federal government should not take over that responsibility from parents who have ample resources to carry it out themselves."[52]

Lyng and the USDA increasingly viewed the NSLP as a social safety net for poor families and clung to the belief that the labor of lunch was, at heart, a family responsibility. Attempting to force the USDA's hand, ASFSA's Legislative Committee devised a bill, H.R. 5291, which would create a universally free school lunch program, and recruited a congressional sponsor to champion the proposed legislation.[53] To bolster their case, Perryman marshalled evidence from countries with universally free school lunch programs and proposed innovative changes to tax policy that would raise the funds necessary to serve all lunches for "free" at the point of service. If costs were collected behind the scenes through tax returns, there would be no need for cashiers to maintain "economic segregation" by sorting children into three camps—full-price, reduced-price, and free lunches. This practice, Perryman argued, wasted taxpayer money on administrative overhead and weakened the democratic ethos of public schools. "There is no economic means test in the social security program," he lamented. "There is none in Medicare, there is none in the use of public highways or the postal system, there is none in the balance of education, only an archaic, lingering feeling that for food at school we must separate the economic classes."[54]

So why was school lunch treated so differently? Perryman didn't say so, but one answer is clear: gender. Feeding children, unlike transportation or healthcare, had long been considered a "woman's responsibility." The premise of a universally free school lunch program struck an ideological nerve in the 1970s, just as the very idea of experimental penny-lunch programs had done in the early 1900s. During both eras, feminist activists were gaining strength in numbers and challenging the assumptions of patriarchal capitalism. In its official publications, ASFSA never explicitly linked its proposal for a universally free school lunch program with the concerns of second wave feminism. If enacted, the legislation would most certainly have lessened the burden of unpaid care work for all women with school-aged children. But the white middle-class mothers who played such an important role in pressuring Congress to pass the NSLA back in 1946 didn't take up the fight for a universally free school lunch program. Instead, many of them fled the NSLP altogether as food quality declined, prices rose, and school lunch became stigmatized as "welfare" food. Middle-class mothers who could afford to take on the labor of lunch increasingly opted to send their children to school with a packed lunch.

As scholar Joan Tronto's work makes clear, this shift—from outward-looking, collective care to inward-looking concern for one's own family—is the logical outcome of seeking to care well in a patriarchal capitalist society that favors competition over collaboration. The construct of what Tronto calls "competitive caring" pushes parents who support equal opportunity in the abstract to organize their lives in ways that ensure their children have special advantages over other children. This, in turn, generates an empathy gap, or what Tronto describes as "unsympathetic disregard" for poor children, whose families are seen as immoral or deficient for their inability to care for their own children.[55] In the case of school lunch, this socially ingrained competitive care dynamic helped parents, mostly mothers, justify their decisions to pack lunches for their own children when a government-subsidized alternative was available.

A severe conservative backlash following the race riots of the late 1960s widened this empathy gap even further. Then, as the country slipped into a full-blown recession from 1974 to 1976, the prices of food and other basic necessities soared. Even middle-class families felt the pinch as consumer demand flattened and unemployment rates climbed. Economists invented a new word, *stagflation,* to describe what was happening. This macroeconomic shift and the challenges it posed to middle-class families became a key talking point in ASFSA's ongoing campaign to create a universally free school lunch program. After all, the federal government had stepped up to provide free lunches to all poor children, so why not extend a helping hand to all struggling families? The Nixon administration had already passed legislation to provide free and reduced-price meals to children from the poorest ten million families, but ASFSA wanted the government to help an additional thirty million middle-class families who were "trying to meet their obligations, pay their bills, pay their taxes, keep up with inflation, and help pay for the food of those children less fortunate than their own."[56] The appeal was unsuccessful.

Congress didn't budge on the issue of universal free school lunches. The NSLP, it seemed, was already on the upswing. More schools were participating than ever: 88,900 in 1975, up from 74,900 in 1969. During that time, the federal school lunch budget rose from $582.5 million to more than $1.9 billion per year. This increase in funding helped an additional 5 million children gain access to the NSLP, bringing average daily participation up from 19.4 million to 24.9 million children. And with the Nixon administration's focus on helping the needy instead of subsidizing rich and poor alike, the percentage of lunches served for free or at reduced-price had jumped from 15.1 percent in 1969 to 40 percent in 1975.[57] The overall focus of federal food policy during this time was to help poor people across the lifespan—very young children, single mothers, and the elderly—through the creation of new federal nutrition programs including the Special Supplemental Food Program for Women, Infants, and Children (WIC) and the Elderly Nutrition Program. School lunch was just one piece of an increasingly costly care puzzle.

ASFSA executive director Perryman blamed this "new competition" for drawing public funding and attention away from the NSLP. "When the NSLA was passed in 1946, it had the field to itself. Now there's competition from the WIC program, the day care program, summer feeding program, elderly feeding program, and food stamp program," he explained to the ASFSA membership in November 1976.[58] Perryman's assertion that ASFSA's bid for a universally free school lunch program was unsuccessful because these other programs had become "the darlings of the liberal groups who once supported the school lunch program" suggests a limiting belief that the government's capacity to support public care is a finite, zero-sum game.[59] What if instead—as right-to-lunch activists like Jean Fairfax and Congressman Clay had hoped would happen—ASFSA had seized the opportunity to rewrite the rules of the game?

School kitchens and cafeterias could have become the central hub for coordinating multiple, interrelated public food programs in a new economy of care. This would have stretched federal dollars, while meeting community needs. Some forward-thinking schools proved this by running experimental programs that fed children and the elderly using kitchen and cafeteria infrastructure first developed exclusively for the NSLP.[60] For most school lunch directors, however, simply complying with the NSLP's free lunch mandate was a big enough challenge. Pursuing a universal free school lunch program, let alone dreaming up new ways to care for multiple constituencies, were luxuries they couldn't afford. This was especially true in urban and rural areas where low-income people of all ages were clustered. Securing funding for kitchen and cafeteria infrastructure was priority number one for schools that were joining the NSLP for the first time. And, perhaps unintentionally, it was this drive to expand care to poor children in schools without adequate facilities that provided Big Food manufacturers and for-profit management companies with the perfect cover to invade not-for-profit school kitchens and cafeterias.

THE PRIVATIZATION OF THE NSLP

When the National School Lunch Act was passed in 1946, Congress stipulated that participating schools could not outsource the management of their programs to for-profit private contractors. But in the late 1960s, for-profit management companies and other private sector experts argued that they could provide better and cheaper care than the lunch ladies in charge of the nation's schools could.[61] Together, they lobbied Congress to lift the restrictions and allow them to bring the talents of the private sector to bear on the problem of feeding children in urban schools without kitchens.[62] The National Restaurant Association even went so far as to publish a position statement in 1969 that claimed the USDA's ban violated basic civil liberties by preventing schools from accessing the benefits of "professional handling."[63] Others in the pro-industry camp tried to pin the blame on ASFSA, accusing it of denying millions of children access to food by clinging to the outmoded notion that private for-profit companies had no place in the NSLP.[64] Tactically, this was a brilliant move. Accusing ASFSA of putting its own economic interests and ideological concerns over the needs of children undercut the organization's moral authority. Suddenly it was no longer the hero of the school lunch story, but rather the villain to be overcome.

Industry lobbyists argued that privatization was the best way forward. A vocal coalition of ASFSA leadership, parent groups, and labor unions disagreed. They feared what might happen if for-profit companies were allowed to control the country's vast network of public school kitchens and cafeterias. Despite their concerns about these companies not having children's best interests at heart, the USDA sided with industry lobbyists and overturned the rule in March 1970.[65] The USDA was, to be sure, the direct catalyst for this change, but ASFSA—and the American public at large—had helped to lay the groundwork by embracing new convenience foods throughout the 1950s and 1960s and "outsourcing" at least a portion of the labor involved in food preparation to private companies.[66]

School lunch was privatized and commercialized in other ways too. Manufacturers offered all sorts of plug-and-chug solutions to help schools cope with rising labor costs and the new federal free lunch mandate. Schools

FIGURE 9. Morton Frozen Foods consultant training foodservice worker to "rethermalize" frozen airline-type meals. Courtesy Bridgeport Public Schools.

with working production kitchens could rely on bulk convenience foods—such as frozen, prebreaded chicken patties; frozen hot dogs; frozen pizza; and dehydrated mashed potato pearls—to cut labor costs. Likewise, schools without working production kitchens could turn to preplated lunches or "airline-type" meal packs, reheated in portable ovens tucked inside a janitor's closet, multipurpose room, hallway, or any other available space (fig. 9). This would not only cut labor costs but also eliminate the need to build costly cafeterias in poor communities. Through these strategies, the frozen and convenience food industries did help schools feed more children with a limited budget. But the cheapening of school lunch came at a cost: poor food quality, a deskilled labor force, and a shift to speedy, transactional service devoid of meaningful interactions between children and the workers who feed them.

There were upsides and downsides to allowing corporations to colonize school cafeterias—and this wasn't lost on ASFSA. In a 1970 issue of the organization's flagship publication, the *School Foodservice Journal* (known prior to 1971 as the *School Lunch Journal*), ASFSA executive director Perryman weighed in on the debate. "If the choice is between the appetizing aroma of cooking food permeating school corridors, loving and lovely ladies in white, starched uniforms and a sparkling food service facility on one hand and the more limited menu, more limited appeal and limited charm of transported food on the other, then the choice for the former is easily made." But if the choice is the "limited menu, limited appeal and limited charm" of frozen preplated lunches or no lunch at all, the decision should be a no-brainer: convenience foods all the way.[67]

At the local level, school cooks had been slowly incorporating convenience foods into their repertoire for decades. There were tradeoffs, however, and Earnestine Camp—a school lunch area supervisor for the Arkansas Department of Education—knew this, so she devised a series of questions managers could ask themselves when deciding whether to purchase "efficiency foods"—or as she liked to call them, "e-foods."[68] If they chose to go the route of convenience, she warned, school cooks would need to use their creativity to "enliven" the flattened tastes and textures of industrial foods by adding a "whisper of garlic," a "flutter of a well-chosen herb," or a "swish of spices."[69]

Adding some local flavor to industrially produced e-foods could improve their palatability and attractiveness, but even the most talented cook was powerless when it came to sprucing up single-serving prepackaged lunches that were reheated and served to children without ever being opened by a school lunch worker. The public took note. As more and more school lunch programs gravitated toward reheating frozen food, reconstituting dehydrated mixtures, and generally outsourcing the work of cooking to industrial manufacturers, the NSLP's reputation as a purveyor of affordable, mostly "home-cooked" food declined. "Let's face it," wrote a reader of the *Bridgeport Post* in a 1972 op-ed after the district began serving airline-type frozen lunches, "it's a TV dinner with a fancy new name.... Each child is handed his tray of weighed, measured, sealed, heated food and that is it!"[70] Thomas Farley, the foodservice director of Milwaukee Public Schools, had more pointed criticism, telling the *New York Times* restaurant critic Mimi Sheraton, "Why, that meal pack stuff could gag a maggot."[71] Sheraton went into detail: "The instant mashed potatoes are caked into the compartments like library paste, carrots are waterlogged, shriveled peas are often burned black, the corn kernels are almost empty, the string beans are brownish and the baked beans are mushy."[72] Clearly, cheapness had a price.

Poor taste, unpredictable texture, and unappetizing appearance weren't the only shortcomings. The factory-made frozen meal packs that many poor children ate during the late 1960s and early 1970s were often deficient in basic nutrients like iron, calcium, magnesium, and vitamins. The USDA had never set minimum standards for these micronutrients, so nothing about this nutritional lapse was illegal.[73] Protein was a different story: each reimbursable school lunch was required to contain a minimum of two ounces, but independent studies and government probes revealed frozen preplated lunches to be short on protein.[74] A two-year audit of New York City public schools, for instance, found that one-third of the frozen airline-type meals it served to children did not meet the USDA's minimum protein requirements.[75] This pointed to a national problem since schools across the country purchased frozen preplated lunches from the same four companies—Intercontinental Foods Industries, National Portion Control, Mass Feeding, and Morton Frozen Foods—that had been authorized to handle donated USDA commodities on behalf of schools.

Skimping on protein, the most expensive part of a school lunch, helped industry skim profits from the NSLP. "An ounce of protein costs about fourteen to sixteen cents," Thomas Carroll, the foodservice director of Bridgeport Public Schools and an early champion of the frozen airline-type lunch, explained in a local newspaper. "If you have just a quarter of an ounce off thousands and thousands of meals, you're talking about a lot of money."[76] Shrinking a burger patty or a slice of meatloaf wasn't the only way to cheapen protein. School lunch officials and convenience food manufacturers also experimented with synthesizing new sources of protein.

The USDA fast-tracked approval for novel proteins made from oil seeds and beans to be used as "extenders" in school lunch staples like hamburgers and chicken patties in a ratio not to exceed 30 parts to 70 parts on the basis of weight.[77] Agrifood giants including Archer-Daniels-Midland, Cargill,

Central Soya, Pfizer, General Mills, Ralston Purina, Griffith Laboratories, Miles Laboratories, and Swift Chemical got in on the game. Through advertising campaigns and public relations efforts, they promoted these newfangled proteins as both economical and ecologically responsible. Their methods worked. New York City school lunch officials "opted to cut back on meat portions and integrate less costly substitute proteins in order to combat rising food prices and nationwide food shortages," the *New York Times* reported.[78]

Not everyone within the school lunch community was eager to accept these cheaper "meat" products, even atop kid favorites like cheese pizza. ASFSA executive director Dr. John Perryman used his monthly column to remind the rank and file to keep their eyes on the prize. "Our purpose is to get the greatest quantity of the best nutrients possible inside the child for the money we have available," Perryman wrote. "Let us give engineered foods a chance to prove themselves just as synthetic fabrics have!"[79] Ironically, though, the more ASFSA members attempted to "hold the price line" by serving cheap, industrially fortified creations, the less credible they seemed when seeking public support for a universal free school lunch program. In 1974, for instance, a twenty-five-member panel chaired by Ronald Pollack, executive director of the nonprofit Food Research and Action Center (FRAC), delivered a report to the Senate Select Committee on Nutrition and Human Needs opposing ASFSA's proposed universally free school lunch program.[80] The report had harsh words for both the ASFSA and USDA, arguing that neither should be trusted with the labor of lunch. Pollack chided the USDA for pushing schools to use new processing technologies and industrial foods that, in the committee's view, had not undergone adequate long-term tests for potential side effects on children's health. It would be better, the committee concluded, to allocate federal resources to nutrition assistance programs dedicated to feeding the very young, the elderly, and poor adults.[81]

Pollack had good reasons to be critical. USDA officials were alarmingly cozy with Big Agriculture and Big Food. After World War II, USDA policies and financial subsidies encouraged farmers to adopt high-yield production practices reliant on chemical fertilizers, synthetic pest control, and mechanization. Factory-produced food became the gold standard of economic efficiency—an ideology that spilled over into the NSLP during Orville Freeman's (1961–1969) tenure as head of the USDA. The next two USDA secretaries, Clifford Hardin (1969–1971) and Earl Butz (1971–1976), left even more of a mark on the NSLP and the future of the American food system. Hardin, a former professor of agricultural economics, stayed for only two years before exiting the USDA's revolving door to join Ralston Purina Corporation, where his successor was also a board member. Both men were extremely proindustry, but Butz was the more influential of the two. He is to blame for what the writer Michael Pollan calls the "cornification" of the American food system.[82]

Secretary Butz oversaw the USDA during a critical period of transition for the NSLP and other public food programs. He saw himself as a friend to Big Ag and Big Food and resented the public assistance programs he was tasked with administering. Senator George McGovern, a Democrat who served as chair of the Senate Select Committee on Nutrition and Human Needs from 1968 to 1977, even called out Butz in an interview with the *New York Times* for holding his own agency's food assistance programs in contempt.[83] The high percentage of departmental resources "taken up" by food stamps, school lunches, and other nutrition and social programs, were, according to McGovern, the secretary's "greatest source of unhappiness" as director of the USDA. Butz had been a controversial pick from the start. His brash demeanor and ties to industry didn't go over well with everyone, and he barely made it through his Senate confirmation hearings. But once he cleared that hurdle, he didn't hold back. He accused environmentalists and organic farmers of condemning "hundreds of millions of people to a lingering death by malnutrition and starvation."[84] He advised small family farmers to "get big" or "get out" and railed against the "phony consumerists" who warned people to avoid the chemical additives in packaged, highly processed foods.

By the summer of 1976, Secretary Butz had earned a spot on the Center for Science in the Public Interest's "terrible ten" list of persons and institutions.[85] However, his hostility toward consumer advocates and the environmental movement wasn't enough to get him fired. It took getting publicly outed as a racist to render him unfit for his cabinet position. Under pressure, he resigned his post on October 4, 1976, after *Rolling Stone* printed a comment he had made while on a private plane after attending the Republican National Convention. When asked why the Republican Party was struggling to attract black voters, Butz had offered up his own theory: "I'll tell you what coloreds want. It's three things: first, a tight pussy; second, loose shoes; and third, a warm place to shit. That's all!"[86] He tried to walk back the statement, to no avail. The American public didn't believe him when he claimed that his use of "a bad racial commentary" in no way reflected his real attitude.

Notably, Butz had stepped into the position of secretary of agriculture right after grassroots activists had succeeded in forcing a mass expansion of the NSLP to provide free lunches to poor children, many of whom attended predominantly African American schools. The successes of this second wave of national school lunch activism deserve celebration, especially in light of the tremendous amount of lingering prejudice—not just personal, but institutional—that they were up against. As secretary of agriculture, Earl Butz had the freedom to set USDA policy priorities and a platform from which to lobby the government to provide additional funding for the NSLP or even to pass the legislation ASFSA had proposed for a universally free school lunch program. Instead, he worked to ensure that Big Agriculture and Big Food could cheapen the American food supply and increase their own profits. In so doing, he oiled the gears of a machine that was bigger than his own making—one that, in many ways, had already been set into motion.

That's not to say the NSLP's shift toward cheap industrial foods in the early 1970s was inevitable. Nor—as Ronald Pollack and other antihunger advocates pointed out—was it politically neutral. The USDA—and for that matter, the ASFSA—could have championed the causes of poor children, public health, and equity more robustly. Instead, the USDA did away with the legal protectionism that had helped insulate the NSLP from the capitalist profit seeking of private management firms and Big Food processing companies. The situation became even worse in the late 1970s and early 1980s when the political revolution of neoliberalism pushed governments at all levels to slash public expenditures on schools, social welfare programs, and environmental protection in order to keep corporate profits high and taxes low.[87] By shrinking government in this way, neoliberal policy changes devolved concrete caring responsibilities that had been collectivized through government programs back onto individual families and civil society. But the quality of care provided by the NSLP had entered a downward spiral long before neoliberalism took over the national psyche.

Many of the battles the first generation of nonprofit school lunch activists fought during the Progressive Era over the privatization and commercialization of school lunch were revisited anew after the NSLA was passed—only this time the opposition was much more powerful, sophisticated, and coordinated. Big Food and Big Soda weren't about to pass up the chance to use school cafeterias to shape a generation of children's food preferences and brand loyalties. Their "spatial colonization" of the school food environment, to borrow a term from scholar Anthony Winson, was several decades in the making.[88] Building on the introduction of e-foods to the NSLP in the 1950s, public-private partnerships launched in the 1960s helped Big Food gain a stronger footing in school cafeterias. Congress, the USDA, and charitable foundations sponsored pilot projects designed to test novel ways for delivering nutritious, space-saving, sanitary lunches faster and more cheaply to inner city schools. Often, these projects included direct partnerships with for-profit corporations, either in the design and delivery of school lunch operations or the contribution of "expert" advice.

New York City Public Schools (NYCPS) launched one of the most influential of these experiments during the 1965–66 school year with the help of a $75,000 grant from Educational Facilities Laboratories, an independent research subsidiary of the Ford Foundation. Two cafeterias were selected for a pilot "frozen food" program, which penny-pinching district administrators immediately deemed a success. Eugene Hult, head of the New York City Office of School Buildings, favored expanding the model across the district since, as he put it, "a frozen-food kitchen takes up one-third of the space, and costs one-half the dollars of a conventional kitchen."[89] If NYCPS were to replicate the model, limited resources could be stretched to cover the cost of starting lunch programs in school buildings that didn't have kitchen facilities.

The 45- × 35-foot kitchen pumped out 925 frozen preplated lunches per day.[90] A conventional kitchen of the same size would have been able to serve only 350 school lunches. Visitors from nearby states and as far away as Britain and the Netherlands traveled to view New York City's "kitchen of the future" for themselves. The New York City Department of Education also took notice of the frozen lunch experiment and, in November 1968, appropriated $1 million to install such kitchens in 367 elementary schools without existing kitchen facilities.[91] The trade journal *Merchandising* heralded the decision as a "dramatic breakthrough" for the processed food industry.[92]

Frozen food made the labor of lunch more compact, while giving school lunch a space-age makeover. The sleek new equipment used to "rethermalize" the frozen lunches made countertop stoves and bulky cooking equipment look messy and old-fashioned, just as the futuristic look and feel of preplated lunches wrapped in aluminum foil made ceramic plates and melamine lunch trays seem humdrum. Indeed, the whole system appeared to liberate lunch ladies from the drudgery of cooking from scratch and washing dishes, just like the millions of American housewives the convenience food industry hoped to save from the drudgery of domestic labor.

National publications, including ASFSA's flagship journal, lauded districts that partnered with the private sector to bring innovative thinking to school lunch. Soon, the frozen food manufacturers who were initially reluctant to invest significant money in R & D began competing for lucrative school lunch contracts.[93] To separate themselves from the pack, they offered a suite of services. For example, Banquet Frozen Foods, a popular supplier of TV dinners to American homes, provided on-call specialists who could deliver presentations to school board meetings and PTA gatherings, tailor the "Banquet Plan" to specific requirements, and provide in-service training for staff. Each company tried to outcompete. Many relied on endorsements from school food professionals to drum up business. Some went so far as to sponsor, or even author, feature-length photo essays and case studies that featured their products in operation in various school districts.

By the mid 1970s about 70 percent of urban school districts had at least experimented with serving frozen lunches, thanks in part to a USDA policy that restricted how eligible schools with high concentrations of low-income children were allowed to use their Special Assistance Funds. Once again, policymakers treated the labor of lunch as a private, rather than public, concern. Schools were allowed to use the extra funding they received to purchase food and equipment but not to pay for labor or building kitchen and cafeteria infrastructure. Investing in frontline kitchen and cafeteria workers and production kitchens was not allowed. Yet purchasing equipment—like a rethermalizing oven and wire baskets to hold prepack lunches—was perfectly in compliance with how these funds could be used. So, too, was purchasing food, including premade lunches with "built-in" labor.[94] For the poor school districts that relied on this federal cash transfusion to make expanding the NSLP possible, purchasing frozen preplated lunches or making their own preplated lunches on a semiautomated assembly line seemed to make the most financial sense. So that's what the majority of urban school districts did, at least in some capacity, in the buildings that didn't have kitchen facilities. But these lunches were never really that popular once the initial excitement of getting a lunch program wore off.

In 1977, when the USDA held a series of public hearings in eight major US cities, the bulk of public criticism centered on the interlinked issues of poor food quality, excessive waste, and the commercialization of school lunch.[95] This proved to be the final nail in the coffin for ASFSA's universal free school lunch campaign. Kids were throwing away massive amounts of uneaten food, which posed a major public relations problem for the NSLP and created a new opportunity for Big Food companies to sell schools fast-food knockoffs "fortified" with micronutrients like vitamins and minerals.[96] ASFSA published position pieces in its journal that were written by influential food scientists and nutritionists who believed this industry techno-fix was the best way forward. Dr. Paul Lachance, a professor of food science at Rutgers University, was one of them. His argument was simple: the average kid is more likely to eat a fortified cookie than a serving of steamed spinach and more likely to participate in the NSLP if the main entrée is a familiar hamburger (engineered for maximum nutritional content) instead of an unfamiliar creamed chicken casserole.[97]

If kids could get all of their necessary macro- and micronutrients from a fortified Super Donut or Tater Tots, why not update school lunches for a new generation of eaters? Len Frederick, a retired supermarket executive turned director of Las Vegas's school lunch program, chose to do exactly that in the early 1970s. His full-throttle drive to transform Las Vegas's school lunch program into a fast-food-style operation selling fortified milk shakes, burgers, and fries attracted national attention for its astounding success in cutting costs while increasing average daily participation to roughly 90 percent of Las Vegas public school students.[98] However, children weren't choosing balanced meals: soda, cookies, cinnamon buns, and fortified milkshakes had tremendous amounts of sugar. Frederick claimed that the reimbursable combo meals he marketed to kids were healthy, but nutritional analyses proved otherwise. Still, no one could deny that he'd taken a school lunch program that was operating at a loss and transformed it into a revenue-generating machine in less than six years.[99]

At the national scale, the nutritional and economic integrity of the NSLP had been under strain for years. In 1972 the National Soft Drink Association had convinced Congress and the USDA to drop restrictions on "competitive foods" and allow schools to have vending machines in their cafeterias.[100] ASFSA executive director Dr. John Perryman was so outraged that he sent a letter to every single member of Congress, blaming them for "open[ing] the door to the sale of ANY food item to ANY child of ANY age in ANY school location at ANY time."[101] He feared giving Big Soda and Big Food companies free rein in the school lunchroom would subject school food authorities to "never ending pressures" to generate financial revenue to cover their own operations and supplement other aspects of the school lunch budget by selling branded food and drinks in direct competition with the NSLP (fig. 10). This was a valid concern—and an accurate prediction—but Perryman's outrage over the USDA's decision to allow competitive foods in schools downplays the ASFSA's role in bringing about this transformation in the first place.

FIGURE 10. Commercial branding in the school food environment of a rural Arkansas school in the 1950s. Earnestine Camp Photo Collection, Child Nutrition Archives.

Of course, it was Congress and the USDA, not the ASFSA, that set school lunch policy and invited for-profit industries to "partner" with the public sector to feed the nation's children. But ASFSA leadership—along with the home economists who founded the very first nonprofit school lunch programs in the early 1900s—all bought into the ideals of economic efficiency, scientific rationality, and cheapness above all. Their task, as ASFSA's president Helen Crane put it in 1951, was to provide children with lunches of "maximum nutritive value, prepared under the most sanitary conditions" at "minimum cost." Achieving this objective required each school lunch worker to "do her job in the most efficient manner possible."[102] Over the next two decades, ASFSA led the charge in helping schools identify ways to make labor more efficient. This, in turn, would help the nonprofit school lunch movement better achieve its mission of feeding all children an affordable, if not free, lunch. Unfortunately, in a phenomenon all too familiar within the care sector, this pitted the needs of caregivers against the needs of care receivers. The economic needs of school lunch employees were sacrificed for the "greater good" of feeding children. This, paradoxically, drove down standards of care even further as schools relied more and more on factory-made food to increase their labor efficiency. Children and workers suffered the consequences.

ASFSA, the organization that could, in theory, have pushed back against this anemic economy of care had an alarmingly codependent relationship with the food industry. Back in 1946 when a group of committed nonprofit school lunch leaders had formed the ASFSA, they had to purchase food and equipment just like a for-profit company. Some of the nation's leading lunch ladies, including Emma Smedley, had relied on corporate sponsors to finance their publications. ASFSA also relied on advertising revenue and other forms of corporate sponsorship to finance its monthly black-and-white newsletter, which soon evolved into a full-color glossy magazine called the *School Lunch Journal*. Since Congress did not allocate funds in the NSLA for worker training, these publications were a vital and cheap training medium for thousands of independent school lunch supervisors.

ASFSA took charge of publicizing training opportunities around the country and offering its own training courses for school lunch managers and directors to attend. For those who couldn't afford to travel to such in-person trainings, ASFSA's publications were a godsend. Women in even the most isolated rural school kitchens could read case studies of exemplary school lunch programs and access a treasure trove of hard-learned practical advice. Nonprofit school lunch elders authored tutorials on equipment purchasing, advice on writing competitive contracts, versatile recipes with step-by-step photographs, work simplification techniques, and other tricks of the trade. USDA employees and members of allied organizations like the American Dietetic Association, the American Home Economics Association, and the Parent Teacher Association also contributed to these publications, which were a vital source of news related to the NSLP. Annual congressional appropriations, projected changes to the availability of USDA commodity foods, and the latest statistics on participation rates in the NSLP were all gathered by ASFSA and reported back to the membership so that individuals knew how they fit within a larger whole. It wasn't long, though, before the codependent relationship between home economists and the processed food industry left its mark on ASFSA and the NSLP.[103]

Soon after the ASFSA launched an annual food show in 1947, the *School Lunch Journal (SLJ)* praised the vendors who'd rented space: they weren't just salespeople with a pitch, but educators and allies who could triage problems, suggest creative ways to use USDA commodities, diagnose culinary mishaps, and provide novel marketing ideas to attract more children to the cafeteria.[104] The names of these "trusted" companies were shared with all ASFSA members—not just those who attended the national food show—in a special feature in the *SLJ*. Then, in 1953, the *SLJ* began selling advertising space to a "select group" of carefully vetted companies.[105] "The nicest way we can say THANK YOU to our advertisers is in purchasing their products wherever they meet a need," ASFSA president Anne Maley reminded her members in a 1959 column.[106]

Industry advertisements targeted to school lunch directors typically featured labor-saving equipment, ready-made convenience foods, and shortcut ingredients that made meal preparation easier. They needed to convince the old-fashioned guardians of the lunch tray who rejected "modern" food trends and methods to give their products a shot. Industry touted the labor-saving potential of its "heat-and-serve" products and disparaged the culinary skill of the NSLP's frontline workers. A series of advertisements and industry-sponsored articles sought to rebrand frontline workers as "inexperienced housewives," which may have been true in some cases, but that didn't mean they couldn't be trained to be useful employees. Besides, unpaid care work in the home is itself a form of "experience" that is directly applicable to caring for children in public school cafeterias.

Yet by the end of the 1950s the subtle and sometimes not-so-subtle messaging about the superiority of what industry called "built-in labor" spilled over from advertisements into the articles written by leading child nutrition professionals and industry specialists. One June 1958 article promoting the exciting new world of packaged ready-made foods went so far as to ask, "Isn't it a shame that someone doesn't introduce half as many new and 'easy-to-use employees' on the market per month?"[107]

Such disregard for frontline employees increased as the NSLP grew in size and complexity from what the trade journal *Volume Feeding Management* described as a "cracker-barrel, backwoods business" into a "billion dollar industry."[108] This evolution brought with it an influx of white men to back-of-the-house positions at the top of the school lunch job hierarchy (fig. 11). In order to recruit these men to the labor of lunch, superintendents of large Midwestern school districts were starting to offer salaries competitive with what men in the private sector were earning, according to ASFSA Midwest Regional Director Wade Bash. He saw this as a good thing. "We are at a point that our management must be concerned with fractional cent savings applied to every lunch in order to keep costs more nearly balanced with income," he wrote in the April 1963 issue of the *SLJ*.[109] That's why, in his view, men with private sector experience in food manufacturing or retail were better suited than women trained in home economics to running large school lunch programs.

FIGURE 11. Men from the private sector food industry, including Thomas Carroll of Bridgeport, CT, joined the ranks of the NSLP in greater numbers during the 1960s and 1970s as supervisors of urban school lunch programs. Courtesy of Bridgeport Public Schools.

Some high-powered officials took exception to this idea that school lunch should be treated as a business like any other, gender-based discrimination and all. Rodney Ashby, the Utah state director of school lunch programs, feared this new style of management would fundamentally alter the character of the NSLP as a form of public care performed for the benefit of children and families. Yet, as a state-level administrator, he was hard-pressed to defend what he observed to be inefficient and inconsistent use of donated USDA commodities. The NSLP needed public investment and stronger worker training programs in order to maximize its public value, not men with food service management experience, he argued in an April 1961 issue of the *SLJ*.[110] But neither Congress nor the USDA provided schools with dedicated funding for worker training. It was up to individual states, local governments, and even individual school lunch departments to decide how much, if anything, to invest in training workers.

Deskilling the labor of lunch seemed like the path of least resistance. It had worked for popular fast food companies like McDonald's, so why not the NSLP? The exponential growth of fast food chains in the 1950s and 1960s was like a cultural upheaval for the food industry, which quickly shifted to prioritize routinization, standardization, and automation above all else. The fast food industry's technological innovations and managerial tactics altered industry standards for meals per labor hour. This put pressure on cash-strapped school lunch programs to keep up or risk looking inefficient in the eyes of Congress and the American public. An individual school district couldn't control food prices or dictate federal reimbursement rates, but it could choose to adopt management and production techniques that cut labor costs.[111] ASFSA increasingly encouraged schools to do so in 1964 after it gained a foothold in the National Restaurant Association, the world's largest trade association of restaurant owners and institutional foodservice operators. In 1965, ASFSA even partnered with the National Restaurant Association to offer an educational seminar on the strategies fast food restaurants used to maximize labor efficiency, despite high turnover among their "untrained" and "indifferent" workers.[112]

By the late 1960s, ASFSA's ongoing flirtation with the fast food industry was partly out of necessity. Labor costs were slated to go through the roof because of a 1966 amendment to the Fair Labor Standards Act, which increased the federal minimum wage by $0.15 per year from the 1967 minimum of $1.00 until it reached $1.60 in February 1971.[113] In theory, ASFSA leadership loved the idea of wage increases for the lowest paid workers in school kitchens and cafeterias. But they knew school lunch programs were already struggling to cover labor costs, which typically accounted for one-third of the budget. Pushing labor costs higher without raising the price of school lunch would mean they'd have to either find ways to purchase cheaper food or illegally scale back their free lunch programs, since Congress did not earmark any funding to help the NSLP account for the sudden salary bump. ASFSA president Marion Cronon addressed the issue head on at the association's 1967 national conference, telling the crowd, "As wages increase, either the efficiency of the worker must be correspondingly increased or new systems must be introduced."[114]

A cadre of nonprofit organizations and allied professional associations coached ASFSA and the NSLP down the path of worker deskilling forged by the fast food industry. In 1968, a subsidiary of the Ford Foundation published an influential report, *20 Million for Lunch,* which recommended that school administrators "carefully evaluate any ideas or proposals from suppliers, which may lessen the labor cost burden on his program."[115] Likewise, *A Guide for Financing School Food and Nutrition Services,* jointly published in 1970 by ASFSA and the Association of School Business Officials, advised administrators to build their school lunch programs around items that are "partially or completely prepared by the processor."[116] The USDA articulated a similar stance through its policy decisions and a series of position pieces published in ASFSA's monthly journal. USDA Assistant Secretary for Marketing and Consumer Services Richard Lyng, a former Big Ag executive, maintained an ongoing dialogue with ASFSA from his appointment in March 1969 until he left his post to become the president of the American Meat Institute in January 1973. Lyng advised ASFSA to trust in the "astounding research and development work . . . done by the food industry both for the space program and the modern commercial market."[117] The message resonated.

Advertisements promising to help schools "hold the price line" flooded the pages of ASFSA's publications. Modern marvels like Pure-Pak disposable milk and juice cartons, foam trays, the Spork (patent pending!), single-serving Nabisco graham crackers wrapped in plastic cellophane, and Kellogg's Frosted Flakes in "grab-and-go" prepack plastic bowls offered schools new ways to reduce labor costs. The built-in labor that was once restricted to food preparation could help with food portioning, service, and even clean up. Purchasing "disposables," as they were called, meant schools didn't need to install dishwashers or hire folks to do dishes. Likewise, purchasing food pre-portioned in single-serving containers eliminated the need to pay frontline

FIGURE 12. Workers filling prepack lunch trays in a central kitchen facility. Records of the Office of the Secretary of Agriculture, 1974–ca. 2003, National Archives and Records Administration.

cafeteria workers to portion meal components onto children's lunch trays. Perhaps most importantly, these modern commercial innovations helped to make school lunch easily portable and scalable. Schools could, therefore, solve two of the NSLP's most pressing problems—rising labor costs and unequal food access—with a single, convenient solution: built-in labor.

Large urban school districts gravitated toward this overall strategy of cost reduction, while looking for ways to cut out the for-profit middleman. The Senate tasked the USDA with researching how mechanized production in central kitchens might help expand the NSLP to underserved urban schools as early as 1962. By manufacturing their own airline-type preplated lunches in district-owned-and-operated central kitchens (fig. 12), urban districts could still increase meals per labor hour without funneling additional school lunch funds into corporate profits. Thomas Carroll, the school foodservice director of Bridgeport Public Schools—one of the earliest and most vocal advocates of airline-type lunches—explained this to the *Hartford Courant* in 1976, just as the district was about to open a central commissary with the capacity to produce twenty thousand preplated meals per day: "It's far cheaper to do it this way and provides jobs for Bridgeport residents and business for local companies instead of out-of-state conglomerates."[118]

This decision to invest in its own production facility allowed Bridgeport to take advantage of equipment subsidies tied to congressional support for high-tech feeding systems. At the time, the USDA's philosophy of "productionism" was fundamentally reshaping agriculture and food policy, the labor of lunch included.[119] In the late 1960s, Assistant Secretary Richard Lyng advised ASFSA to partner with industry to concentrate their combined "nutrition, technological, and management know-how on the development of large-scale food commissaries that convert raw food into attractive meals in well-controlled, high-speed production facilities."[120] Like Bridgeport, Minneapolis Public Schools took this route. Under the leadership of a former food industry executive, Gary Krimmel, the district opened a $5 million central nutrition center in December 1975. The goal was to increase production speed from an average of fourteen meals per labor hour at the district's on-site kitchens to forty meals per labor hour in the semiautomated central kitchen.[121]

The school foodservice departments in Bridgeport and Minneapolis oversaw production of their own airline-type lunches, and the USDA encouraged all K–12 schools to take the wisdom of the private sector to heart. Yet there were ASFSA members who openly defied this guidance. They believed the desire for efficient labor should not eclipse other priorities like the quality of care provided by the NSLP. Gwen Chegwidden, a school foodservice director in Murrysville, Pennsylvania, felt so strongly about the topic that she wrote a letter to the editor of the *School Foodservice Journal,* asserting that the "talents of workers who are concerned for children should not be wasted on some assembly line assignment." She cited data that documented a decline in school lunch participation when on-site production kitchens were converted into receiving kitchens that reheated and served preplated lunches shipped from a central kitchen. "How can we justify a delivery system that has low participation as a known factor?" she asked. The smarter strategy, in her view, was to focus on increasing participation since economies of scale help keep labor costs in check.[122]

Welcoming with open arms the private-sector innovations for cheapening school lunch that the USDA supported had the unintended consequence of undercutting the public value of the NSLP. The signs were all there. Paying middle-class "customers" were fleeing the program, and rampant food waste had become a national problem. Clearly the nation's school lunch leadership was failing to meet the goals of the NSLP to "safeguard the health and well-being of the Nation's children and to encourage the domestic consumption of nutritious agricultural commodities and other food." But as far as Congress, the USDA, and many local administrators were concerned, they'd done their duty by responding to the right-to-lunch movement's demand that poor children have access to free school lunches. Guaranteeing all children's right to food and nutrition in the way that Jean Fairfax imagined was never part of the equation. Neither was democratizing care by ensuring it is performed throughout society, instead of by low-wage workers marginalized on the basis of their citizenship, race, ethnicity, gender, and class.

The NSLP was built on the premise of cheap care, and cheap care required cheap labor. Local school boards typically employed school lunch staff directly, but their compensation packages were meager in comparison with other public sector employees. Teachers, nurses, bus drivers, and custodians all had higher wages and were much more likely to have full-time jobs than school kitchen and cafeteria workers. For decades, ASFSA had struggled to translate the social and economic value of the labor of lunch into a sizable paycheck for its members. As a professional association ASFSA was supposed to represent all ranks of school lunch professionals from part-time dishwashers to district-level administrators. Yet it was extremely top-heavy with managers and directors whose social class, educational attainment, job security, and race/ethnicity separated them from their frontline hourly employees. Recruiting school cooks, cashiers, and dishwashers was a perennial struggle for ASFSA. Marjorie Ellis, a cafeteria manager from New Hampshire, wrote an open letter to ASFSA leaders suggesting that these workers would "gladly become members if they could be truly convinced of the active concern of the ASFSA with their economic status—especially salary-wise, pensions, and other advantages conceded custodians and other school personnel."[123]

A small group of ASFSA leaders were already embroiled in exactly this fight, including Thelma Flanagan, a former ASFSA president, who testified before the House and Education Labor Committee in May 1968. "There is no other group in our school family who is more dedicated to serving children, who is more underpaid, and who is sometimes less appreciated, except by the children, than the school foodservice workers," she argued. "The child has never been expected or required to pay the salary of the bus driver or the custodian, but he is required to pay the school food service worker's salary."[124] This economic exceptionalism implied that the labor of lunch was somehow different—and less important—than other forms of work needed to care for and educate children. The resemblance to mothering, the most widespread and undervalued form of unpaid care work that exists, didn't help matters.

Frontline workers were expected to become "second mothers," who, in the words of ASFSA president-elect Ruth Cutter, might be "called upon to watch over and tend the sick child, to administer first aid and to comfort the child with little hurts and bruises." This ability to connect with and care for the kids was, in her view, the most important ingredient for a successful school lunch program. "A mediocre cook who can enlist the love, respect, and admiration of the children may scorch the soup or burn the meat and be forgiven, whereas the superb cook without love for, and of, the children she serves would not only be unforgiven, but would lose customers and probably put the program in the red," she wrote in the December 1959 issue of the *School Lunch Journal*.[125] By the end of her one-year term in office, she was convinced that ASFSA needed to address the unjust employment status of school lunch workers head on. "I hope that in the immediate future it may become, if not the single most important, at least one of the chief concerns of our own association," she wrote in the June 1961 issue of the *SLJ*.[126]

During the 1960s, as large numbers of other public sector workers joined unions, ASFSA remained relatively silent on the issue, perhaps because they were preoccupied with the challenge of meeting the NSLP's free lunch mandate without adequate funding. But in the 1970s, as that struggle died down, ASFSA published a series of letters to the editor of the *School Foodservice Journal* that debated unionization. The pro-unionization camp within ASFSA argued that local districts should pursue the path of public sector unionization because it would not only increase their bargaining power at the local level but also elevate their influence on the national political stage. Others disagreed, claiming unionization would enable "freeloaders" to shirk their job duties and still be paid the same under a union contract, or worse, attract new employees who didn't really care about the children and just wanted a union job with decent wages, benefits, and job security.

One member, whose name and school district ASFSA withheld upon her request, called out the faction within the nonprofit school lunch community who believed "collective action by employees is inconsistent with effective service to the child." Only by demanding that school lunch workers get what she called "good jobs" with equitable salaries and fringe benefits, could they hope to create the conditions for high-quality caregiving.[127] Whether the labor of lunch was revalued by "forward-looking action of communities and school boards" or brought about by the "collective, and on occasion, militant, action" of public sector employees wishing to unionize was, for this ASFSA member, "rather beside the point."[128] She saw the fate of children and cafeteria workers as interlinked within a single economy of care.

Virginia Dehn, a high school cafeteria manager from Atlantic City, New Jersey, agreed, and took aim at ASFSA for sitting out the fight while other professional associations had actively supported their members' unionization drives. "Here, in New Jersey, the Education Association is constantly battling for higher wages, less students per class, more free periods and health benefits," she wrote. "You name it, and they solidly fight for it, and they are supported by the National Education Association." School lunch was different, Dehn pointed out with two simple questions: "When have you ever read of a state school foodservice association supporting cafeteria workers for higher wages, better working conditions and, in some situations, a safe place to work? When have you ever read where the American School Food Service Association has been outspoken about the low wages so customary in school foodservice?"[129]

Even though some ASFSA leaders cared passionately about this issue and tried to lobby on behalf of school lunch workers, their lack of success stunk of indifference to Virginia Dehn and others on the outside of their inner circle. So, too, did ASFSA's decision to not pursue a national strategy of sector-based unionizing that would encompass all school lunch workers from the lowest-paid dishwasher to the highest-paid district supervisor. Instead, if school lunch workers wanted to unionize, they would have to decide to do so in individual school districts without formal leadership or financial support from the association. Some people found local unionization efforts risky. Jack Ninemeier, chief consultant for the Wisconsin Department of Public Instruction, weighed in on ASFSA's unionization debate in a 1972 letter to the editor. He urged any district contemplating a unionization drive to heed the example of his home state, which had developed strong public sector unions in the 1960s.[130]

The school cafeteria workers who voted to unionize "won the battle" of securing higher wages, but in doing so nearly "lost the war," according to Ninemeier. As labor costs went up after the union contract went into effect, district administrators began looking for ways to cut hours by outsourcing whatever aspects of the labor of lunch they could to cheaper sources. Kitchens equipped for scratch cooking were downgraded to "warming kitchens," and workers' hours were cut since they were needed only to reheat food prepared off-site with cheaper labor. Ninemeier wrote that the unionized workers nearly lost their jobs. But "losing the war" wasn't the only possible outcome.

ASFSA was a membership-based professional organization and advocacy group—not a union—but it would have been well positioned to lead the fight for unionizing the NSLP workforce. Instead, ASFSA decided not to support unionization, effectively declaring that frontline workers didn't deserve a democratic workplace. Existing public and private sector unions—including UNITE HERE—failed cafeteria workers too, in part because sexism blinded them from seeing the real potential in organizing lunch ladies. A high density of unionized lunch ladies could have negotiated for better wages, benefits, and terms of employment, effectively remaking the NSLP to prioritize high-quality jobs and high-quality food. Instead, frontline workers continued to lack agency—a situation that had grave consequences for the NSLP.

The quality of food—and the labor conditions of those who created and served it—plummeted during the 1970s. Whether built into industrially produced foods or performed by kitchen and cafeteria staff, labor was a primary site of cost cutting for the NSLP. This cheapening had consequences for children's health. Frances Burrows, a school cook from Bridgeville, California, said as much after attending the California School Food Service Association's 1973 state conference. "I have no doubt the 109 prepared foods the exhibitors gave us came up to the specifications you require in nutrition, but the fillers, additives and preservatives made most foods tasteless and gluey," she wrote in a letter to the editor of ASFSA's journal. "The way things are being set up for the 'free lunch program,' only the truly starving child will benefit," she warned. "The middle-class child will continue to refuse warmed-over, filler-filled globs of unpalatable, but nutritious food."[131]

She was right. Middle-class children who could afford to opt out increasingly did so. By the mid-1970s, Americans had begun to judge the success of public programs just like any other consumer product.[132] Seen in this way, the NSLP fell short. Highly processed chicken nuggets, rehydrated mashed potato pearls, slices of frozen pizza, and strange concoctions like the Cup-a-Roni (a cake ice cream cone filled with what looks to be a scoop of macaroni with meat sauce) weren't worth paying for, let alone waiting in line, the thinking went. This is not to say that middle-class families weren't eating at fast food restaurants and reheating convenience foods at home—they were. Rather, it was the dual transformation of the NSLP into a racialized social welfare program coupled with the rapid cheapening of the food itself that caused some middle-class families to rethink whether school lunch was really "for" them.

By the end of the 1970s, the NSLP remained part of a stratified economy of care—far from ASFSA's ideal of a universal school lunch program. Millions of middle-class families reabsorbed the labor of lunch into their own households, privatizing care for their own children instead of fighting for better care for all. And while all this hurt the NSLP, it helped Big Food companies who profited from both the colonization of school cafeterias and time-strapped families who passed over the economic subsidy of school lunch in favor of purchasing what they considered to be "better" food for their children. But there were other paths that—if taken—might have improved the quality of the NSLP for all families and bolstered the nascent alternative food movement.

ALTERNATIVE VISIONS FOR SCHOOL LUNCH

For at least a decade, Americans had been seeking out alternatives to the industrial food system that the USDA had championed so wholeheartedly since World War II. Rachel Carson's 1962 book *Silent Spring* focused public attention on how pesticides and other agricultural chemicals damaged the environment.[133] Then, in the late 1960s and early 1970s, Dolores Huerta, Cesar Chavez, and the rank and file of the United Farm Workers union helped to launch the environmental justice movement by educating consumers about the harmful effects of pesticides on farmworkers' bodies and fighting for new legal protections.[134] Frances Moore Lappé's 1971 bestseller *Diet for a Small Planet* pushed Americans to think about the social and personal significance of the food they consumed. She illustrated how the standard American diet, which included large amounts of meat, hurt the environment and contributed to global food scarcity, and called on her readers to embrace a vegetarian diet. All the while, the 1960s counterculture had already begun experimenting with vegetarian and macrobiotic diets, food cooperatives, and organic agriculture, rooted in a back-to-the-land ethos.

What Big Food derided as "fad diets" gained new legitimacy from these public conversations about the moral and environmental dimensions of food. Objections to highly processed industrial foods were becoming increasingly mainstream—especially among upper-income consumers who had the resources to purchase fresh food and the time to prepare it themselves. To defend themselves against this culture shift—and its threat to their bottom line—highly capitalized food companies, along with their allied nonprofit and research enterprises, did their best to diminish and deflect the concerns of consumer advocates, environmentalists, and food-chain workers.[135] In response to the 1973 oil crisis, Big Food companies tried to market their newly engineered synthetic oil- and seed-based meat "extenders" as a cheap, convenient, ecologically responsible way to reduce overall meat consumption.

ASFSA covered these developments in the *School Foodservice Journal* and even featured the perspectives of people who spoke out against Big Food. For example, natural food advocate Paul Bragg was one of the leading figures in the food world whose thoughts on the USDA's school lunch program were featured in the September 1973 issue. "It's a cover-up, a fraud," he said. "Sure, a hot dog is classified as protein. But what kind of protein is that child getting? What kind of fruit? Is it soused with sugar?"[136] If he had his way, the NSLP would serve children meals consisting of salad, lean protein, and whole grains—more or less what the Healthy, Hunger-Free Kids Act of 2010 would later mandate. And ideally these foods would be organic, Bragg told ASFSA.

At that point, however, organic food was still associated with the hippie counterculture and dismissed as pseudoscientific by many food scientists. Thomas Jukes, a professor of nutritional science at the University of California, Berkeley, wrote a piece for the *School Foodservice Journal* saying as much. The blurb at the top of the article couldn't have been more polemical: "Are you or your friends being 'ripped off' at the health food stores by paying premium prices for supposedly 'pure foods' that are 'organically' grown? An eminent researcher, long acquainted with the truth about foods, sets the facts straight."[137] But the article itself had scientific tables, academic rigor, and an authoritative tone that was sorely lacking in the short pieces like Bragg's that advocated for organic food. While ASFSA did occasionally report findings from academic studies that were unfavorable to Big Food—as in January 1974, when it published a news brief about the possible link between hyperactivity and the consumption of artificial colors and flavors[138]—the vast majority of articles and advertisements took no issue with the conventional food system.

That said, ASFSA applauded local programs that managed to cook school lunches from scratch instead of reheating factory-made food. So did the national media. In 1976 *New York Times* food critic Mimi Sheraton called Milwaukee Public Schools a "school lunch utopia."[139] The district prioritized scratch cooking, which Sheraton believed to be "by far the best system in operation" after her three years of investigative fieldwork comparing different models of food preparation in urban school districts. The city's school foodservice director, Thomas Farley, was an outspoken advocate of cooking from scratch in on-site kitchens, hosting student advisory groups and involving community members whenever possible. The director of the school lunch program in Oakland, California, Frances McGlone, was a kindred spirit. She believed on-site production provided children with "better foods, better service, and a better atmosphere" and even ran an experiment to test this theory. In the early 1970s she transitioned one of the city's elementary schools that served preplated, mass-produced lunches to on-site cooking. Average daily participation jumped from 55 percent to 92 percent of the student population.[140]

Participation leaps like the one McGlone engendered were extraordinarily valuable for balancing the school lunch budget—since economies of scale help schools keep costs in check—and for the culture of the cafeteria. What we now call farm-to-school programs—which include local sourcing and school gardening—were another bright spot in the school lunch landscape that ASFSA celebrated. The March 1974 *School Foodservice Journal* ran a story about Frances Sanders, director of school lunch programs for Kingsport, Tennessee, who created her own supply chain by directly contracting agricultural land and farm labor to plant, cultivate, and harvest vegetables and fruits that were then processed during the summer for use throughout the school year.[141] Another issue reported on the efforts of Dr. Joe Crawford, school superintendent of Hazen, North Dakota, who launched what he called a "self-sufficiency" field-to-plate initiative that included milling local grain, purchasing beef from local ranchers, and starting student-run vegetable gardens on small tracts of land leased from local farmers. "Why should rural areas serve processed, artificially colored and flavored foods when we have the best food right out here in the country?" he asked. "Children want to eat good, fresh food so why can't we give it to them?"[142]

Such initiatives attracted national attention. In a June 1979 speech to the Parent Teacher Association's national gathering in Milwaukee, Carol Tucker Foreman, then assistant secretary of agriculture for food and consumer services, cited multiple examples of local sourcing and school gardening programs that she hoped might serve as inspiration for other school districts. The lunch program in Andover, Connecticut, for example, paid two students to grow food in a school garden. Impressively, their plot yielded nine hundred pounds of fresh produce, which was used to feed their classmates and local senior citizens, who could request home delivery of school-prepared lunches for fifty cents a plate.[143] It reflected what Foreman described as "a beautiful coming together of concerned parents, an innovative principal who uses instead of reviles available food programs, and food service personnel who care enough to serve the very best."[144]

Unlike the Victory Gardens of World War II, which were common in cities, the school gardens that ASFSA profiled in the 1970s tended to be in rural areas and large towns. Without the kitchen facilities to cook fresh ingredients from scratch, city schools with "closet kitchens" meant for reheating preplated lunches were hard-pressed to incorporate locally sourced ingredients or student-grown produce into their supply chains. Right-to-lunch-movement luminaries like Jean Fairfax and Congressman William Clay likely would have approved of the way in which communities like Andover were using their school kitchens and land to provide nutritious lunches to children and the elderly. But the low-income communities of color clustered in the nation's cities were largely told, implicitly and explicitly, to accept the changes the government and private industry put into place. It was, the story went, the only way to get their children fed, and there was no room for students, parents, or frontline cafeteria workers at the decision-making table.

Right-to-lunch activists succeeded in making free and affordable school lunches more widely available, but they weren't able to overcome the corporate interests that co-opted federal school lunch policy. The children these activists fought to protect deserved better than what the government ended up providing. So did the frontline kitchen and cafeteria workers who continued to care for them, while their own jobs became increasingly precarious.

There were viable high-road alternatives. Unionizing school cafeteria staff would have made school lunch programs more democratic. Building on-site kitchens and cafeterias instead of relying on airline-type meals and central kitchens would have allowed school cooks to be responsive to the dietary needs and preferences of their kids. Providing free lunches for all kids would have ensured that all families had a stake in fighting against the cheapening of the NSLP. Moreover, heeding the early warning calls of environmentalists like Rachel Carson and Frances Moore Lappé would have protected farmworkers and children from exposure to harmful chemicals and reduced the carbon footprint of the NSLP.

Instead, a commitment to "cheapness" ensured that nature would continue to be ransacked, that workers would continue to be exploited, and that children's care would continue to suffer. Without intersectional organizing that recognizes the connections between these problems, the true public value of the NSLP will never be realized. Only by embracing a revolutionary politics of sustainability—refusing to separate the food justice concerns of poor children from those of low-wage food chain workers and the health of the natural environment that makes all life possible—can today's activists expect a better outcome from their own organizing efforts.

THREE

From Big Food to Real Food Lite

"Have you ever *looked* at the list of ingredients on the back of a bottle of cheap maple-flavored pancake syrup?" Deb, a foodservice director in a suburban Minnesota town, poses this simple question to parents and administrators any time they question why—in spite of potentially higher ingredient and labor costs—she is so committed to serving real food in schools. Her deadpan delivery of the question hints that the sweet, golden-brown liquid is not a one-ingredient food sourced directly from a sugar maple tree. Aunt Jemima, a best-selling brand of maple-flavored syrup, contains corn syrup, high fructose corn syrup, water, cellulose gum, caramel color, salt, sodium benzoate and sorbic acid (preservatives), artificial and natural flavors, and sodium hexametaphosphate (an emulsifier and texturizer).[1]

Deb echoes the fears of a growing number of parents, public health advocates, and food movement activists who consider industrial food additives, including shelf-life extenders, taste stabilizers, artificial flavoring and coloring, and chemicals intended to speed and manage processing to be "ingredients of concern." The cheap maple syrup Deb points to is but one example of the hundreds, if not thousands, of highly processed food products that schools regularly serve through the NSLP.[2] Since people don't always understand how a diet made up of highly processed foods poses health risks beyond obesity, diabetes, and heart disease, Deb uses her own family history to illuminate the unseen risks of what some scholars refer to as the "neoliberal diet."[3] At PTA meetings and other community gatherings, she brings along her family photo album to use as a visual aid. One by one, she points out which of her extended family members have been diagnosed with cancer or other serious illnesses. Some died from diseases that she attributes to living in a farm community where chronic exposure to a mix of pesticides and other agricultural chemicals was treated as an unavoidable part of daily life. By the end, Deb has shown in a very personal and poignant way the hidden dangers of chemicals in the food system.

Environmental health advocates and scientists use the term "body burden" to describe the cumulative presence of harmful chemicals in an individual's body.[4] Chemicals are all around us—not just in the food we eat but also in the air we breathe, the personal-care products we apply to our skin, and most of the consumer goods we purchase—and some of these chemicals linger in the tissues and organs of our bodies. The chemicals and materials used to produce cheap industrial food have added hundreds, if not thousands of chemicals, including pesticides, bisphenol A (BPA), and phthalates, to the human body burden.

Navigating this landscape of chemical risk is challenging. For school food-service directors and dieticians, this means looking beyond allergens that cause an immediate, acute reaction in a specific child's body to synthetic chemicals that impact all children's bodies in much less straightforward ways over time.[5] Environmental toxins are often singled out as anomalous, but they are perfectly ordinary in the industrial food system: from the pesticides, herbicides, antibiotics, and hormones used to make crops and animals grow faster and fatter to the processing aids and additives that transform highly perishable agricultural products into shelf-stable goods. Some, like artificial colors, are relatively well-known and straightforward to decipher. Others are more obscure, like sorbates, a class of preservatives that prevents the growth of mold in a wide variety of school foods including cheese, syrups, jelly, cake, and dried fruits.[6]

What constitutes an "ingredient of concern," and to whom, is evolving. Schools committed to "cleaning" the NSLP supply chain typically rely on scientific evidence and medical research pointing to weight gain, reproductive disorders, or behavioral disorders in order to designate a specific ingredient as one of "concern." Recent insights from the field of environmental toxicology suggest that ingredients of concern—especially those that interfere with the endocrine system—can alter fat tissue development, disrupt appetite and metabolism, and heighten the risk of certain reproductive and behavioral disorders and cancers.[7] This knowledge fuels Deb's desire to change how school food is sourced and prepared. She even goes so far as to tell people in her community that it is her "moral responsibility" to prepare meals from scratch and carefully screen the labels of any processed foods served in the cafeterias she oversees.

For Deb, closely scrutinizing Big Food's high-tech concoctions is a core part of what it means to "safeguard" the children in her care. Having worked in school foodservice for three decades, she remembers what it was like in the 1980s and 1990s, when school cafeterias were first overrun with cheap, industrial food. At the time, Washington politicians, national business leaders, and people in communities all over the country were embracing what historian Bryant Simon describes as the "notion of cheap." Making food, labor, and public programs cheaper was, the thinking went, a fair and logical way to solve pressing problems like inflation, job loss, welfare dependence, and government inefficiency.[8]

THE NSLP'S CHEAP-FOOD ECONOMY

This emerging political-economic philosophy had its starkest effect on the NSLP in 1981, when the Reagan administration's Omnibus Budget Reconciliation Act slashed the federal school lunch budget by one-third, from $4.5 billion to $3 billion. Actually achieving this, while maintaining the nutritional standards for school lunches set by Congress, required creative reclassifications and a keen eye for analyzing meal components through the lens of scientific nutrition. The USDA convened a task force, overseen by a Reagan appointee, to put together a set of proposals to enable this herculean task of cost cutting. The task force came up with a variety of ideas—including using cheaper sources of protein like tofu and nut butters beloved by the 1970s counterculture—but the one that launched a media firestorm was a recommendation regarding tomato paste that was interpreted as a proposal to allow schools to serve ketchup (a condiment) in place of a traditional vegetable side dish. The whole ketchup-as-a-vegetable debacle was over within a matter of weeks. The White House withdrew the proposal after intense public backlash. However, while the ketchup affair certainly had the worst optics, it was only one of many proposed changes—many of which did take effect—that would intensify the NSLP's reliance on cheap, industrial food and cheap factory labor.[9] This cheap factory labor took even more of the "cooking" out of schools and replaced meals with snack-like foods.

Suddenly corn chips, pretzels, doughnuts, and pies could all pass as "bread" in the NSLP. At the same time, the USDA began to "modernize" its commodity distribution program, shifting more of the labor of lunch to Big Food factories. The USDA commodity program had been designed in the

1930s to remove surplus foods from the open market in order to protect farmers and agribusiness from fluctuations in supply and demand. USDA commodities were raw materials that required some form of labor to transform into an edible school lunch. Offie "Mama" Karnes recalled working with these foods in Virginia's Roanoke City Schools during the 1960s: "We got all kinds of vegetables and fruits, and we got ground beef, ground pork, and our chickens and turkeys, all those things back then; butter and cheese, even the flour for baking."[10] To extract value from these commodities, school lunch workers converted the donated food, which could be unwieldy to handle, into workable ingredients. An eight-cubic-foot block of commodity cheese might need to be broken into smaller, handheld quantities that could be shredded, sliced, or melted. A forty-pound case of unprocessed commodity chicken might need to be unpacked, thawed out, washed, cleaned (the fat and little feathers trimmed off), and eventually cooked—a sequence of events that could take two or even three days. Using a box cutter to open a cardboard box filled with bags of preshredded cheese or precooked frozen chicken products was much faster and cheaper for schools since less on-site labor was required. It was also less risky. Hundreds of children could get sick if cafeteria staff didn't follow food safety protocols when handling raw foods.

At the local level, schools contracted with for-profit companies to provide commodity processing support on an as-needed basis. For example, when, in 1960, Elizabeth Beavers, the foodservice director of Beaumont, Texas, Public Schools received a boxcar shipment filled with five hundred frozen lamb carcasses, she rented storage space at a local meat locker, where the lamb carcasses were "almost stacked to the ceiling," and paid a local butcher to process the lambs into butterfly chops, roasts, stew pieces, and ground lamb. The Beaumont school cooks were then able to prepare these minimally processed commodity lambs for two reasons: their schools had production kitchens, and Elizabeth Beavers was a firm believer in what she called "food production," which was not the same thing as "opening cans and heating the contents."[11]

Urban schools joining the NSLP for the first time in the late 1960s and early 1970s without such high levels of culinary capacity had an altogether different experience. As Betty Bender, the foodservice director of Dayton, Ohio, Public Schools during the early 1970s put it, the USDA commodities program really "drove preplate systems crazy." Kitchens designed to reheat food shipped in from a district central kitchen or commercial factory weren't equipped to handle the type of commodities that Elizabeth Beaver's staff cooked with in their production kitchens. If the Dayton central kitchen had wanted to prepare a preplated turkey lunch in its central kitchen, it would have needed to cook fifteen thousand pounds of USDA commodity turkeys and slice the meat into uniform pieces that fit neatly into its preplate containers. It just wasn't possible—the Dayton central kitchen didn't have the equipment, space, or labor to handle raw products on this scale. So Bender hired Ralston Purina, a multinational food company, to butcher, cook, preportion, and freeze the turkeys into a precooked protein that her staff could unbox and place into the preplate containers whizzing by on their semiautomated assembly line.[12]

By the end of the 1970s, school foodservice directors without the culinary capacity to make effective use of basic commodities shipped to their warehouses and storerooms in the form of ingredients began lobbying the USDA to send them finished products instead. They got their wish, and it didn't take long for schools with production kitchens to decide these easier-to-use commodities might be a better fit for their programs as well. Ruth Jonen, a former ASFSA president from the northwest suburbs of Chicago who had pushed for commodities modernization, praised the resulting system in her 2007 oral history: "You select the commodities that you want, and then you can say to the state, we want to divert so many dollars-worth of beef to this person, so many pounds of pork to this guy, so many pounds of eggs to this person and it comes back in the food product that is easier for us to prepare; the kids like it better."[13]

The USDA describes this practice of outsourcing the labor of turning commodities into ready-to-heat-and-eat menu items as a boon to the NSLP, stating that it "expands donated food use from a limited number of commodities to a broader array of nutritionally sound, popular items, while keeping labor costs to a minimum."[14] Each school food authority—typically a single department within a public school district or an administrative unit within a private school—chooses how their commodities dollars are spent. They can choose whether they'd like to receive USDA "brown box" commodities, which tend to be minimally processed foods used for scratch cooking, or divert their commodities to commercial processors. In the 2012 school year, approximately $1.3 billion worth of USDA commodity foods were made available to the NSLP, over half of which were diverted for further processing by one of the roughly 120 processors with a USDA commodity-processing contract. Over 80 percent of these processors holds a multistate or national contract, which can be quite lucrative, especially if large urban school districts opt to divert their commodities allocations.

FIGURE 13. Worker slicing USDA commodity precooked turkey ham in a central kitchen facility. Records of the Office of the Secretary of Agriculture, 1974–ca. 2003, National Archives and Records Administration.

To maximize the chances of this happening, manufacturers hire food brokers to represent their product portfolios. These brokers then shape NSLP supply chains by coaching schools to divert their commodities to the same Big Food manufacturers that make the frozen pizzas, hamburger patties, chicken nuggets, and other convenience foods they purchase on the open market. Doing so provides continuity of taste for the kids, who may get used to one brand and reject another. It also simplifies ordering and delivery logistics, which can help schools get lower prices from the manufacturers. Fair enough, but when cheapness is allowed to stand in as the most important indicator of value (as long as the products stay within the bounds of USDA's nutritional guidelines), much remains hidden.

Take Tyson Foods—a mainstay of the school lunch tray—as an example.[15] Billions, if not trillions, of cheap frozen precooked chicken nuggets and patties have entered the stomachs of children participating in the NSLP since the early 1970s, when Don Tyson, already a leader in the poultry industry, recognized the profit potential of processing chicken into hundreds of different product lines instead of simply selling whole or cut-up birds. The salt, fat, convenience, and cheapness were too much for the American public to resist. When the McDonald's chicken nugget was first unveiled in March 1980, over

FIGURE 14. Promotional poster for schools celebrating the Arkansas poultry industry. Earnestine Camp Photo Collection, Child Nutrition Archives.

80 percent of the chicken Americans purchased in stores and ate at restaurants was still in the form of a whole bird or pieces that were easily identifiable as specific parts of a chicken's body. Two decades later the opposite was true.[16] As more kids ate processed chicken products at home and at restaurants, school foodservice directors diverted more of their USDA commodity allocations to chicken processors like Tyson (fig. 14).

School lunch directors and menu planners accustomed to serving chicken wings, breasts, thighs, and drumsticks may have found it a bit wacky to serve chicken in the shape of rings, stars, flowers, or dinosaurs, but they joined the "fun-chicken" bandwagon for multiple reasons. First, these items were more popular among children, which not only drove up participation rates when these items were on the menu but also ensured that children were eating their full portion of chicken instead of pitching it in the trash. Second, reheating precooked chicken was considered much safer than preparing raw chicken from scratch, even in schools that had full cooking facilities. And third, outsourcing the labor of preparing chicken and other products from scratch allowed schools to decrease their foodservice labor costs since fewer full-time, skilled workers were required. How, though, if the NSLP operates as a not-for-profit enterprise, could labor be so much cheaper when outsourced to Tyson?

In helping to cultivate America's taste for processed chicken, Tyson, which introduced literally thousands of "value-added" chicken products in the 1980s and 1990s, created jobs so dangerous, strenuous, and low-paying that nearly three in four workers quit the company's processing plants within a year of being hired.[17] Tyson, like many of the other chicken companies implicated in the labor of lunch (in schools and out), was part of a tightly wound economic system that Bryant Simon calls "poultry capitalism." Ruthless competition between producers and manufacturers made the whole system of chicken production more dangerous for the environment, less healthy for consumers, and abusive of both the poultry workers and the animals they grew, caught, killed, processed, cooked, packaged, and shipped.

Many of the biggest names in industrial chicken (e.g., Tyson, Perdue, Chick-fil-A) were founded by ideologically conservative men who opposed government intervention in personal, social, and economic affairs. Ensuring that poultry farms and factories remained union-free, relying on vulnerable immigrant labor, setting up shop in poor communities, and shifting production to right-to-work states are just a few of the strategies that poultry capitalists have used to keep production cheap well into the twenty-first century. Yet it was the federal government's decision to roll back protections for workers and consumers in the late 1970s that facilitated the rise of poultry capitalism in the first place. After companies argued that cleaning fecal matter and other sources of diseases from birds one at a time was too laborious, for instance, the USDA approved a 1978 measure that allowed processors to wash broiler chickens in chemical baths, known to some—due to the amount of fecal matter suspended in the liquid during processing—as "fecal soup." The technique heightened the risk of *E. coli* poisoning from handling or consuming raw chicken, but it did make cheap chicken more profitable for processors. In another gift to poultry capitalists, the USDA allowed processors to ratchet up their assembly lines, from around seventy birds per minute to as many as one hundred birds per minute, which is brutally fast and dangerous for poultry workers.[18] In exchange, the cost of chicken would be cheaper for consumers, especially for the school and prison cafeterias where Uncle Sam picked up the tab.

As production of all sorts of cheap, chemical-laden foods—not just chicken—picked up in the 1970s and 1980s, school administrators ended up turning cafeterias into profitable outlets for powerful agribusiness companies. Public school budgets were strained by tax cuts that became tax revolts in some communities. With scant resources, local administrators were increasingly pressured to privatize their lunch programs and partner with soda and snack companies that offered cash, gym supplies, curricular materials, and other incentives for entering into exclusive contract agreements. Big Snack and Big Soda had maneuvered their vending machines into schools in the early 1970s, and in the mid-1990s, the USDA allowed fast food chains to follow. National chains—including Pizza Hut, Little Caesars, Domino's Pizza, Taco Bell, Subway, Chick-fil-A, McDonald's, Blimpie, and Arby's—jumped at the chance to reach some of the nation's youngest customers. Some of these companies formulated NSLP-compliant versions of popular products that schools could serve in subsidized school lunches and for-purchase through their à la carte lines. Other companies simply sold their standard products for cash, separate from the NSLP. They were competitors who could charge more without having to follow nutritional guidelines.[19]

THE REAL FOOD MOVEMENT

School lunch activists who want to reverse the harmful transformations brought about by this cheap food economy believe that children should eat "real food." Their desire—for food to undergo minimal processing, untainted by additives—has a long history, dating back to the pre–Civil War era and early natural foods capitalists like cereal king John Harvey Kellogg.[20] The commercial market for natural foods evolved alongside the nascent food movement for much of the twentieth century. This trend has only accelerated in the new millennium, with the rate of growth in the organic and natural food sectors far outpacing that of the conventional food sector. Both natural foods and organic foods fit under the broader umbrella of what the students, cafeteria workers, and food industry representatives I encountered during my five years of fieldwork call "real" food. One of the dietitians I interviewed put it this way: "We're really looking for real food, whole food, food that you can recognize ... understand the ingredients ... [and make] at home." In other words, natural food without industrial additives.

The resurgence of the natural food movement in the twenty-first century poses a potential threat to Big Food's profits, but the industry has invested billions of dollars to build up established brands and sensitize consumers to first accept, then actively crave the tastes and textures of industrial food.[21]

Sociologist Michael Carolan interviewed a number of Big Food scientists, advertisers, marketers, and executives to better understand the tactics they use to make industrial food seem benign, or even desirable, to consumers. Patty, a retired executive, told him about one of Big Food's primary strategies: the consumer veil. "Usually we'd want to keep how our food is raised and processed behind a giant veil," she said. "You never see an advertisement, ever, with an actual farm on it. I mean a real farm, where the animals come from—a factory farm." She explained why. "The general rule is that we don't want people thinking about that stuff. Let them think about how our food tastes, if it's nutritious, if feeding it to your family makes you a good parent."[22]

A faction within the child nutrition profession believes real food activists are unfairly targeting the processed food industry. Barry Sackin, a former lobbyist for the School Nutrition Association (SNA), has complained about the "group of people who think that the word *processed* makes [food] a terrible, horrible thing." To Sackin, this idea is a bit ludicrous. First off, schools don't have the labor required to prepare meals from scratch. Second, if a school decided to eliminate processed foods from its cafeterias, staples like bread and milk, both of which undergo some level of industrial processing before being packaged and shipped to schools, would have to be removed.[23] This was, more or less, the same perspective put forward by a high-ranking USDA official at the SNA's 2012 Legislative Action Conference. "Not everything needs to go back to scratch cooking. That's unrealistic. We need to reformulate," she told me and a room filled with foodservice directors and employees of SNA's industry partners. "The demon is not processed foods; it's what is in the foods."

But growing segments of the public are worried, and as they have identified new ingredients of concern on school lunch menus, more people have begun to lose trust in the government's ability to regulate the food industry effectively.[24] Against this backdrop of fear and confusion, new food blogs, books, and celebrity personalities have made it their mission to educate the public about the chemicals and low-quality ingredients that Big Food uses to maximize profit at the expense of human and environmental health. They fill an important niche, offering analysis, advice, and advocacy—often with the help of ad revenue or various forms of financial sponsorship—and with more polemics than science at times. But empowering consumers to make sense of an ever-evolving landscape of food production is slow going. With so many possible ingredients of concern, it can be hard to understand the health risks of consuming even a single product.[25]

"What's inside the twenty-six-ingredient school lunch burger?" This was the question Allison Aubrey, a National Public Radio (NPR) reporter, asked in April 2012, before dissecting a burger patty that had been served in Fairfax County, Virginia, until a parent-led organization, Real Food, Real Kids, pushed the district to source a less-processed burger with fewer artificial ingredients.[26] Even the NPR correspondents she spoke with had a hard time reading the words on the label. Lurking inside the twenty-six-ingredient school burger were multiple ingredients of concern, including caramel color, hydrolyzed soy protein, and disodium inosinate. Upon closer inspection—and consultation with a food scientist—some of the hardest to pronounce words like cyanocobalamin, riboflavin, and copper gluconate turned out to be part of the mix of vitamins and minerals added to the school burger to give it an extra nutritional punch. Nothing scary there, most folks would agree, but it takes a certain level of fluency in the vocabulary of industrial food additives and nutritional science to understand that cyanocobalamin is the man-made form of vitamin B-12. Even so, Real Food, Real Kids wanted the product and others like it booted from local schools. They won—at least in the case of the twenty-six-ingredient burger, which was replaced by a frozen 100-percent beef patty. All in the name of real food.

The NPR story was picked up by multiple media outlets including *Grist*, an online magazine specializing in environmental news and commentary, that repackaged it under a slightly more sensationalized headline: "What's Inside a School Lunch Burger? 26 Ingredients, and Only One Is Meat." The original NPR story involved a much deeper dive into the backstory of Real Food, Real Kids and a careful ingredient-by-ingredient analysis in a companion video. The *Grist* reporter called out NPR reporter Aubrey for ceding too much ground to a food scientist who "tries to justify this hideous progeny of a real hamburger and a Flintstones vitamin" using the familiar trope of enhanced nutrition for poor children whose parents can't afford to feed them a balanced diet. "But that doesn't explain the disodium inosinate, an MSG-like 'flavor enhancer,'" the reporter noted. Several people commented on the piece, including one person under the username "A Scientist," who sided firmly with the food scientist NPR interviewed for its piece. "Ok, those chemicals? They are VITAMINS, which exist in your free-range organic meat as well, they just aren't added," A Scientist wrote. "Get over your un-educated selves and realize that this product exists to make our kids healthier, especially since the area where this is served is relatively poor. If it's too hard to pronounce then learn how to read."[27] To be sure, some relatively innocuous or even beneficial ingredients may sound sinister even when they're not.

It's easy for people to assume the worst about strange-sounding ingredients—understandable even, given the federal government's track record when it comes to regulating the food industry. The modern globalized food system is incredibly complex. The FDA's current list of "Everything Added to Food in the United States" (EAFUS) covers over three thousand unique substances. Navigating the EAFUS database is challenging, and it includes only ingredients that are intentionally added to food. Thousands more are unintentionally added during processing, packaging, and storage, such as bisphenol A (BPA), exposure to which has been linked to hormonal, cardiovascular, and other health problems even at low doses. National media outlets and social media reporting on the health risks of BPA in 2010 spurred a consumer frenzy to avoid it and, shortly thereafter, a glut of reformulated disposable packaging proudly displaying the magical phrase "BPA-free." It's not to say that BPA-free alternatives are actually safer—researchers haven't yet applied the same level of scientific scrutiny to most of these substitutes—but the BPA substitutions certainly make average consumers think the problem has been solved even when it hasn't.

Environmental toxins abound and the government has limited authority to intervene. Dr. Richard Raymond, the USDA's former undersecretary of food safety, says that it would be challenging and largely impractical for the government to account for and label every substance in supermarket products.[28] Without this level of transparency, consumers must be able to trust that the FDA can take appropriate action behind the "consumer veil." However, the FDA lacks the funding and the scientific expertise to conduct its own independent reviews of food additives and processing agents, relying instead on industry-generated data to certify additives as "generally recognized as safe" (GRAS).[29] The GRAS list covers a wide range of processing aids and additives ranging from table salt to the ammonium hydroxide gas used to kill bacteria in Lean Finely Textured Beef (LFTB). Propyl paraben, a GRAS substance used as a preservative in baked goods, is also an endocrine disruptor that can accelerate the growth of breast cancer cells, impact fertility, and alter gene expressions. How can such a substance be "generally recognized as safe" to feed anyone, let alone children whose hormonal systems are rapidly developing? Because the companies doing the recognition can earn more money when they use it.

Many of the additives on the GRAS list are there simply by virtue of already being in food and other consumer products back in the 1950s when the FDA assumed that food was "safe" if there was no toxicological evidence proving otherwise. In 1958, Congress partially embraced the precautionary principle when it passed legislation that required the FDA to ban any new food additive that was found to cause cancer in laboratory animals. This same legislation grandfathered in a list of almost one thousand substances that were already widely used in processed foods and therefore generally recognized as safe. This move exempted almost all known additives from toxicological testing. Food companies were free to mix and match these additives in whatever combinations and concentrations they wished—precautionary principle be damned.[30] The GRAS list created an illusion of safety. What's more, it gave the upper hand to Big Food companies in public debates about food safety— if consumer advocates or natural food proponents questioned the safety of an additive, a Big Food public relations expert need only point to the GRAS designation as evidence that the additive was safe.

Members of the natural foods movement were critical of the FDA's actions, but they were outmatched by the industry-friendly academics, government officials, and Big Food companies that worked together to maintain the status quo. Nutritionists, dietitians, and home economists—some of whom were part of the movement for nonprofit school lunch programs— were, as sociologist Laura J. Miller put it, "eager to bolster their own professional credibility by defining health food as a fad and as a social problem."[31] Frederick J. Stare, head of Harvard University's Department of Nutrition, was perhaps the most visible example. He derided the natural food movement, defended industrial farming's heavy use of pesticides and herbicides, and promoted the use of chemical additives in processed foods as perfectly healthy and normal. Dr. Stare got his message out in multiple formats: Senate testimonials, expert witness statements in key court cases, and through his roles as the author of a nationally syndicated newspaper column and the editor of *Nutrition Reviews*. Dr. Stare was an academic, but *Nutrition Reviews* was published by the Nutrition Foundation, an organization of food and chemical producers that funded and publicized food-related research to strengthen Big Food's nutritional claims.[32]

Such public-private research enterprises, coupled with government support, bolstered a domestic food system built to deliver cheap, prepackaged, synthetic foods to every supermarket and corner store in the country. Yet by the end of the 1970s, citizen activists pointed to a growing body of evidence that bolstered their call for a new approach to food policy and dietary advice. And as the federal government worked on the first edition of *Dietary*

Guidelines for Americans (DGA), the debate intensified. Food journalist Patricia Wells described the situation in a May 1978 article for the *New York Times*. Industry was upset when it learned that a leaked document, *Guidelines for Food Purchasing in the United States*, meant to be released with the first *DGA*, suggested that "Americans could realize substantial savings on food bills if they avoided highly processed foods, bought more dried foods in bulk and more fresh foods, and made more purchases through cooperatives and farmers markets."

The *Guidelines for Food Purchasing* and the *DGA* were a hot-button political issue. As Wells reported: "On one side sits the powerful food industry lobby, on the other the advocates of a return to localized agriculture and a simpler, less processed food supply."[33] The whole thing became really political really fast. That's what pushed Nick Mottern, a staffer for the Senate Select Committee on Nutrition and Human Needs, who authored and leaked the *Guidelines for Food Purchasing* to take matters into his own hands. He told the *Washington Post* that several members of the Senate Agriculture Committee had expressed their opposition to the *DGA* and he didn't want them meddling with the purchasing guidelines he'd crafted for the benefit of American consumers.[34] After that, the Senate never formally released the *Guidelines for Food Purchasing*. Marshall Matz, special counsel for the Senate nutrition subcommittee (who, coincidentally, became the chief political lobbyist for ASFSA from the 1980s until shortly after the Healthy, Hunger-Free Kids Act went into effect) told the *New York Times* reporter Patricia Wells that Mottern's decision to release the draft "seriously prejudiced the possibility of our ever publishing it, since any changes we make, however minor, would be suspect."[35]

Two years later, however, when the USDA and the Department of Health and Human Services (HHS) issued the first *DGA*, it was clear from the industry-friendly modifications to the draft document that the "powerful food industry lobby" had emerged victorious in the struggle over the American diet. And as the scholar Marion Nestle has long pointed out, the *DGA*—updated every five years—continuously bows to the influence of the industrial food and farm sectors, rather than promoting healthy eating or ecological sustainability.[36] The most recent *DGA* advisory committee, composed of independent experts in the fields of nutrition, medicine, and public health, urged the USDA and HHS to include evidence-based recommendations on environmental sustainability and its relation to the American diet in the 2015–2020 *DGA*, and according to one national poll, three-quarters of US adults supported their inclusion. But industry was able to exert enough influence over the process that these ecological goals were dropped.[37]

At present, the USDA and HHS—whose combined power includes oversight of both the *DGA* and the NSLP—reinforce Big Food's influence over nutrition standards, reproduce health disparities along lines of race and class, and limit federal support for sustainable diets. The FDA has little power to push back. Even if the agency leadership has the political will to disrupt the status quo, it lacks the resources to prove that agrifood chemicals cause "actual harm" and should thus be removed or restricted. According to a 2013 report from the nonpartisan Pew Charitable Trusts, this leads to a situation in which the FDA focuses on lackluster public education initiatives or research carried out with voluntary industry cooperation.[38] The FDA released an updated GRAS rule in August 2016 after reaching a settlement agreement following a 2014 lawsuit filed by the Center for Food Safety. In a move that disappointed consumer advocacy groups—including the Center for Science in the Public Interest, the Consumer's Union, the Environmental Defense Fund, and the Environmental Working Group—the agency opted to continue allowing manufacturers to decide for themselves whether the additives they put on the market are GRAS without informing the FDA. Senator Ed Markey, a Democrat from Massachusetts, went so far as to equate the FDA's final rule to "a self-graded take home exam that the industry does not even have to hand in."[39]

A shift toward more aggressive government regulation of ingredients of concern behind the "consumer veil" or incorporation of ecological considerations into the *DGA* is unlikely under the Trump administration. On the campaign trail, President Trump made comments about getting rid of the "FDA food police" and pledged "agriculture will NOT be regulated based upon the latest trend on social media."[40] Given the hostile regulatory climate—which predated the Trump administration and has long cut across party lines—some pragmatists within the real food movement see shopping their way to safety as the most expedient course of action. By "voting" with their forks—or in the case of school lunch, their sporks—for the elimination of ingredients of concern, they hope to use a carrot instead of a stick to entice manufacturers to clean up their product formulations.

Pressuring the government to take on a more active role in regulating the industrial food system on an ingredient-by-ingredient basis has been successful in some instances. Consider the case of precooked hamburgers made with LFTB, or as critics on social media and TV named it, "pink slime." LFTB is made from beef "trimmings": the fat and connective tissue that is further away from a cow's muscles and closer to its skin and orifices (areas that are more likely to be contaminated with feces, dirt, and other sources of bacteria). The trimmings are heated to about 100°F and spun in a centrifuge to separate the solid proteins from the liquid fats. The lean beef is then compressed into blocks and exposed to a "puff" of ammonium hydroxide gas to kill food-borne bacteria like *E. coli* and salmonella. Since the ammonium hydroxide gas is a processing aid,[41] rather than an added ingredient, it does not have to be listed on product labels, even though research shows that LFTB contains three to four times more ammonia than untreated beef.[42]

At the peak of its use in 2009, LFTB was added to 70 percent of the US ground beef supply. Mixing LFTB into ground beef made it easy for food scientists to engineer particular fat ratios that consumers might be looking for at the grocery store (e.g., 90 percent lean). LFTB also cut the cost of the hamburger patties sold to fast food restaurants and institutional foodservice providers like schools and prisons. After a 2009 Pulitzer Prize-winning *New York Times* exposé revealed government tests had found that ground beef containing LFTB was four times more likely to contain salmonella than regular ground beef, many fast food restaurants voluntarily discontinued their use of LFTB.[43] The NSLP didn't. So in March 2012, Bettina Elias Siegel, a Harvard Law graduate who runs a blog on children and food policy called *The Lunch Tray,* launched a Change.org petition urging the USDA to stop purchasing LFTB for use in school meals.[44] To galvanize opposition against "pink slime," Siegel wrote that an ingredient "formerly used only for pet food and rendering" was unfit to feed the nation's children. She touched a nerve. "This pink slime is probably one of the most disgusting things I have ever heard of," commented a supporter from Indiana on the petition's webpage. "I am so angry that our government has no respect for US citizens. There is a trust that we put in you and I'm appalled at the things I have been learning about the food that we have been told is ok for us to eat and feed our children. How infuriating. CHANGE IT!"

Lifting the veil on pink slime generated sufficient consumer disgust and collective power to push the USDA to make a policy change to its commodities program. Over a quarter million people added their signatures to Siegel's petition, and several members of Congress rallied behind the cause. Less than two weeks after Siegel's pink slime petition was launched, the USDA announced it would allow schools to use their commodities dollars to purchase ground beef with or without LFTB.[45] Shortly thereafter, in June 2012, the commodity purchasing agents in all states except for Nebraska, Iowa, and South Dakota (all home, at the time, to LFTB processing facilities) had opted for the LFTB-free ground beef. This was a major win for real food activists, though it was only one ingredient of concern among many.[46] But almost as soon as Siegel's petition went live, Beef Products, Inc. (BPI), the largest manufacturer of LFTB, launched a website, beefisbeef.com, to help educate consumers about LFTB as a product consisting of "100 percent beef, no additives, no fillers."[47] By presenting LFTB as a "real" food that helps to reduce food waste and increase sustainable nose-to-tail consumption of resource-intensive animal products, BPI was, in effect, attempting to co-opt the language and concerns of real food advocates to legitimize its place within the food system—but the tide had already turned against it.

Such single-ingredient campaigns have become central to US food activism, as community groups and nonprofit organizations attempt to fill the holes left by a government without the resources or political will to guarantee the long-term safety of the food supply.[48] Strategically speaking, single-ingredient campaigns make good sense: it's much easier to publicly shame a company or group of companies into voluntarily eliminating the use of a single ingredient of concern than to ask for entirely "clean" labels, let alone an overhaul of the food industry. Other activists opt to work in collaboration with industry to help it become more responsive to the demands of the real food movement. Where lunch programs are concerned, that means building the type of public-private partnerships first instituted in the 1960s to feed urban and rural children in schools without lunch programs. This work typically happens at the district level or in coalitions of school districts aided by the nonprofit sector.

School Food Focus (Focus) and the Urban School Food Alliance (USFA) lead the two most prominent public-private partnerships working to make real food more accessible and affordable for all schools.[49] Together, the two coalitions leverage billions of dollars of combined purchasing power to push for a more aggressive timeline and agenda for what the USFA calls "innovative market solutions that are nutritionally wholesome, ecologically sound, economically viable, and socially responsible."[50] Both rely on market-based strategies, while creating a shared community of practice that helps foodservice directors from large urban schools connect with like-minded peers.[51] Of the two, Focus has been especially active in working with industry and child nutrition professionals to develop a shared set of parameters and expectations about how and when ingredients of concern should be eliminated from school food supply chains. In 2016, the organization released a procurement guide that identifies "unwanted ingredients" that manufacturers and school food procurement specialists should try to remove from the school food supply chain and places others on a "watch list" to carefully monitor and negotiate because their presence may impact food safety and nutritional quality.[52]

Some critics argue that public-private partnerships like these cede too much control to industry to define the parameters of change, rather than having public health experts and government officials impose stricter standards.[53] Others maintain that such voluntary agreements are the only way to move forward in the current regulatory environment. Both sides have a point. Organizations like Focus and the USFA lend long-term stability and clout to the real food movement, and public-private partnerships help individual school districts make meaningful progress. On the other hand, relying solely on market-based reforms means settling for relatively shallow changes, a path that I call "real food lite." Much like critical food scholar Julie Guthman's discussion of "organic lite," real food lite provides some concessions to the movement while simultaneously preserving some of the worst features of the cheap food economy.[54]

In many ways, real food lite is the logical manifestation of the food industry's response to consumer backlash against cheap industrial food. "For decades, you'd always hear some consumers talking about no artificial colors, no artificial flavor," Jeff Hamilton, the president of Nestle's prepared foods division, told a reporter in July 2015.[55] But only in the last couple of years has the momentum accelerated enough that Big Food has had to take action.[56] The scholar Nadia Berenstein writes that beginning "around 2010, and with increasing momentum, ingredient lists began to shrink, with fewer spooky chemical names." Some of the biggest names in Big Food have, in the past decade, "lined up to jettison artificial colors, flavors, and preservatives," while smaller upstarts "wield clean labels as a competitive weapon, angling for market share with ingredient lists so minimal they read like recipes."[57] In 2015, *Food Business News* declared clean labels the trend of the year.[58] Panera Bread, one of the largest fast casual chains in the United States, made headlines that May when it pledged to eliminate at least 150 artificial ingredients from its sandwiches, soups, salads, and bakery items.[59] Just one month later, Papa John's Pizza announced it would discontinue its use of fourteen ingredients of concern, including artificial flavors and colorings, by the end of 2016.[60] Real food lite had arrived.

BIG FOOD'S NEW PROFIT PLAY

The USDA created an organic standard in 2000, and fifteen years later, the FDA began soliciting public comments on a proposed rule for what constitutes "natural" food, but neither the government nor any third party has created a standard to judge whether food is "real" or "clean." So big companies are capitalizing on a common consumer feeling that ingredients with easily recognizable and pronounceable names are realer and cleaner than unfamiliar ingredients that sound like synthetic chemicals.[61] If companies can convince enough people that what they're selling is real, they can turn a powerful social movement into a passive and profitable market segment. Campbell's, for example, has enhanced its brand identity by positioning itself as a trusted leader in the business of "unprocessing" processed foods. The Campbell's website implies that the company's devotion to real food is so great that it will reinvent both itself and the entire industry: "It won't be easy, but we know it's the right thing to do for consumers, our company, our shareholders and our planet."[62]

Real food lite is a relatively recent trend, but Big Food has been capitalizing on the struggle to care well for decades. Oscar Mayer managed to find a lifeline for its struggling deli meats using exactly this strategy in the mid-1980s. According to the investigative journalist Michael Moss, it all began at the company's headquarters in Madison, Wisconsin, after cigarette giant Philip Morris acquired Oscar Mayer's parent company, General Foods.[63] Bob Drane, Oscar Mayer's vice president for new business strategy and development, was tasked with reversing the precipitously declining sales of bologna and other processed meats. Looking for leads, Drane conducted focus groups with the target clientele—women shoppers—to figure out why they weren't buying luncheon meat and what might make them buy more in the future. Their conversations yielded what Drane describes as "a gold mine of disappointments and problems." The moms wanted to provide healthy, tasty food for their kids, but the pressure of the second shift was an everyday struggle. "It's awful," the moms told Drane. "I am scrambling around. My kids are asking me for stuff. I'm trying to get myself ready to go to the office. I go to pack these lunches, and I don't know what I've got."[64] Even though preparing school lunches can be a source of joy for some women, it is a form of gendered labor. And just like any other form of labor, it can be a source of stress, particularly when the time and material resources to do the job well are hard to come by.[65]

Drane recognized that the time bind American families, especially mothers, were facing could be a new frontier for capitalism.[66] He responded by turning cheap Oscar Mayer cold cuts into Kraft Lunchables: a sandwich-like meal deconstructed into the plastic compartments of a sanitary sealed prepack container. When Lunchables first hit the US market in 1988, sales reached $218 million. Over the years, General Foods has rolled out more than sixty distinct varieties of Lunchables, from the classic Turkey and Cheddar Cracker Stackers to the enigmatic Pizza Kabobbles. The iconic Lunchables container has made room for a range of comarketed Big Food delights: Kool-Aid powder mixes, Capri Sun juice drink pouches, Cheez-Its crackers, Pringles chips, Reese's Peanut Butter Cups, Oreo and Chips Ahoy cookies, just to name a few. The amount of sugar, salt and fat in a Lunchable would make any nutritionist balk, but for busy mothers, Lunchables were a convenient time-saver with food their children would eat. And for a company whose processed deli meats had fallen out of fashion, Lunchables were an economic life preserver.[67]

Today, however, the standards of "good" middle-class care are evolving, and parents of means are seeking healthy children's food without the many ingredients of concern found in an average Lunchable. Advertisements and social media posts featuring stylish photos of children's school lunches or neatly arranged bento boxes can foster the impression that unless mothers pack healthy food for their children with creativity, joy, and devotion, they risk inadequacy. At the same time, the discourse of consumption frames the labor of lunch as a constant battle against the pocketbook, against finicky tastes, and against the limited time and energy that parents can devote to such a quotidian task. This extra work falls disproportionately on women's shoulders.[68] In a 2014 national survey, three-quarters of American women identified themselves as the person who usually prepares meals for the household.[69]

New businesses are rushing to turn that strain into profit. Revolution Foods and Applegate, for example, have launched their own organic and "real" prepackaged lunch kits as alternatives to Kraft Lunchables.[70] It's a smart move. The average American home cook spends only thirty-seven minutes per day on food preparation and cleanup.[71] That includes packing lunch for most of the 20 million kids who opt out of the NSLP and bring their own food to school. For parents facing both time crunches and the pressure to protect children from the harmful effects of the industrialized food system, buying a healthier Lunchable can seem like a saving grace.

The sociologist Norah MacKendrick calls such purchases "precautionary consumption" and frames them as a "calculated strategy of self-protection" against the forces that fail to "prioritize public health over industry profit."[72]

For families with sufficient means to try to raise an "organic child," complicated shopping routines can seem like another way to care well and to signal a commitment to real food.[73] In reality, providing slightly healthier options for a few children doesn't help poor kids and can even play into the psychology of competitive care. What's more, such consumption hardly threatens Big Food, especially when companies are able to charge a price premium and control the narrative of what makes food "real" or "clean" in the first place.

The USDA requires manufacturers to provide ingredient lists and basic nutritional information on packaged products, but most everything else a manufacturer may or may not want to disclose to consumers is purely voluntary. As a result, product labels and packaging claims have a near myopic focus on macro- and micronutrients, since this is nonnegotiable, and everything else is left unsaid unless the company thinks that sharing additional information will somehow make the product more attractive to potential consumers. This system of voluntary labeling offers scant insight into the question of what parents and schools are feeding children. Even Campbell's, which has been marketing its devotion to becoming "the most trusted food company in the world," is selective about what it reveals. In 2017, Campbell's launched a new website, whatsinmyfood.com, where people can discover the ingredients in each Campbell's product, from Pace Dip and Prego Sauce to Pepperidge Farm Goldfish crackers and Campbell's Tomato Soup. The site explains the purpose of each ingredient and identifies any that are genetically modified. In another statement on its Real Food Philosophy, Campbell's maintains that real food has roots in recognizable ingredients, is prepared with care for the environment, is affordable for all, and is delicious enough to feed family and friends.[74] Such values may sound right in line with alternative-food-movement activism, but what Campbell's fails to mention is that its version of real food continues to depend on resource-intensive industrial farms and low-wage labor. As long as shareholders insist that Campbell's maximizes profits, this is unlikely to change.

With real food lite, companies can market their commitments to real food without having to fully improve labor standards, phase out the use of antibiotics and pesticides, or reduce their reliance on Big Ag monocultures and feedlots. Still, even real food lite is more than some companies can muster. It is no small feat to manufacture cheap food without the ingredients of concern that are used to make highly processed foods look, taste, and store the way they currently do. Campbell's, despite my grumbling, is an industry leader in this space. Rolling out changes to a single product, let alone an entire portfolio of carefully formulated packaged goods, is an investment that requires a certain level of R & D prowess that not all companies have. Corporations' efforts to "go clean" depend on their ability to source or engineer the additives they need to make their products fit the constraints of the industrial food system without offending consumers' real food sensibilities. And when they are trying to meet the tight budgetary requirements of the NSLP, investing that extra effort can seem particularly daunting.

This was a prime topic of discussion at the SNA 2016 Annual National Conference. In a session on clean-label chemistry, food scientists and brand managers of commercial bakeries and deli meat companies spoke about the challenges they'd faced when trying to develop clean-label products for the NSLP. Deciding to "go clean" isn't for the faint of heart, they warned. It could take months or even years to launch a single clean-label product.[75] And once a product is developed, there's no guarantee it will be a commercial success. "Kids *like* the bold red of Frito-Lay's Flamin' Hot Cheetos," one presenter told the crowd. "They're used to the bright artificial colors of conventional products. Natural colors are much more subdued and far less fun." And then there's the issue of cost: natural ingredients are often more expensive than their synthetic counterparts (e.g., vanilla-bean extract versus synthetic vanillin). But it's the challenge of maintaining functionality while keeping ingredient labels short and easily understandable that causes the most headaches for food scientists. Multiple natural or clean ingredients may be needed to accomplish the work of a single ingredient of concern, and even then, the shelf life of the product might be significantly shorter.

At the same SNA conference session, the brand manager of the Jennie-O Turkey Store shared a case study from Jennie-O, which was targeting multiple ingredients for a clean-label makeover: sodium phosphate, caramel color, butylated hydroxyanisole, butylated hydroxytoluene, propyl gallate, modified food starch, sodium nitrites, sodium erythorbate, lactates, diacetates, and sodium. But each of these ingredients of concern plays a specific role in the conventional product's commercial success, so replacing them can be both daunting and risky. Sodium nitrite, the Jennie-O manager explained, does triple duty inside the turkey slice: it acts as a curing agent, flavor enhancer, and shelf-life extender. Likewise, sodium erythorbate accelerates the curing process, which speeds up production and makes the deli meat cheaper to produce.

Replacing ingredients of concern is sometimes easy and sometimes incredibly difficult. In the case of turkey, the Jennie-O rep at the SNA conference explained how celery juice powder and cherry powder can substitute for sodium nitrite and erythorbate. These look like natural ingredients on a product label, but not in the laboratories where they are made to exact specifications. Indeed, the world of industrial powders, juices, and extracts used in clean-label chemistry bear little resemblance to how an average consumer might imagine these substances. What appears natural to consumers on a label, as Nadia Berenstein notes, may actually be the result of an incredibly sophisticated chemistry experiment conducted in the R & D labs of "flavor companies, manufacturers of hydrocolloids, emulsifiers, dyes, and other staples of the industrial pantry."[76]

While natural additives are often highly refined to ensure purity, stability, consistency, and safety, there are some low-tech exceptions. For instance, regular white vinegar is a functional replacement for the acetates and diacetates that prevent listeria growth in Jennie-O's fresh turkey products. And baking soda, found in most home pantries, is a partial replacement for sodium phosphate, a compound used to adjust pH, bind moisture, and improve protein extraction.[77] That may sound straightforward, but in its revamped turkey products, Jennie-O boosts the functional power of the baking soda with an "all-natural" proprietary product the company will not divulge. It's a striking paradox: clean labels are meant to address the lack of transparency in the food system, but a secret, individualized edge might make for better profits.

Once a company has managed to take a conventional product "clean," it often charges a premium and uses the reformulated product in advertisements in order to strategically deflect attention from the poorer-quality foods in its product portfolios that make up a larger overall portion of its sales.[78] The Perdue Food Service flyer stuffed in the SNA conference welcome bags is a case in point. A photograph of a neatly arranged lunch tray featured Perdue chicken nuggets in the shape of what are either flowers or turtles, along with a serving of fresh fruits and vegetables. A pledge ran alongside the photo: "When we say no antibiotics ever, we mean it." What the flyer neglected to clarify, however, was that the pledge covered only its premium line of "no antibiotics ever" heat-and-serve chicken products. It didn't apply to the "classic conventional items" that make up the vast majority of sales to K–12 schools, where Perdue is one of the largest chicken suppliers.[79]

There is no reason to place blind faith in profitable industries' ability to regulate themselves.[80] As the government and the public decide how best to regulate and work with Big Food, Big Tobacco can serve as a cautionary tale. The scholars Kenneth Warner and Kelly Brownell have traced Big Tobacco's fifty-year effort to delay the implementation of stringent public health policies after numerous medical studies demonstrated that tobacco causes cancer.[81] Big Tobacco's first play, write Warner and Brownell, was to emphasize personal responsibility: People aren't forced to smoke, the argument went. They choose to do so and therefore must accept the health risks that go along with it. Tobacco companies also tried to spin the evidence of tobacco's dangers as "junk science" and funded their own scientists to conduct research questioning tobacco's links to disease. They tried to stifle government regulation through massive lobbying efforts and pledging to regulate themselves. And they introduced supposedly "safer" products—light, mild, and low-tar cigarettes—while simultaneously denying the addictive qualities of nicotine and continuing underhanded efforts to "hook" children.

Big Food has followed the same playbook and, in many ways, has had an easier time of it. Food is a more complex and varied product category than tobacco, and that helps industry manipulate public opinion, scientific uncertainty, and government regulation. As a result, children's diets continue to suffer. Public-private partnerships of the 1960s helped expand the NSLP to children who were systemically excluded. However, inadequate funding and regulatory oversight meant that the taste and nutritional quality of school lunch rapidly declined. More recently, the processed food industry—now even more consolidated and powerful than in the 1960s—has proven to be an unreliable partner in the national effort to improve children's diets. Big Food successfully lobbied Congress to change the 2010 Healthy, Hunger-Free Kids Act (HHFKA) to better align with its own profit motives.

The HHFKA—an effort to curb the child obesity epidemic—updated school nutrition standards to align with the *DGA* and placed limits on refined flour, starchy vegetables, salt, and other staples of the heat-and-serve economy. First Lady Michelle Obama was a vocal champion of both the HHFKA and the real food movement more broadly. Her Let's Move campaign encouraged chefs to work with their local school lunch programs to improve quality and get kids excited about cooking and eating healthy food. A bit of supplementary education would not threaten industry. But if schools could actually build capacity to shift away from the heat-and-serve paradigm and begin cooking with minimally processed ingredients, Big Food would lose billions of dollars and would have to relinquish its hold over the NSLP.[82] That could affect Big Food's profits outside of school, too: a revamped school lunch might "retune" children to favor fresh and natural options instead of the tastes and textures of industrial food.

In 2010 it seemed as if Let's Move was poised to confront Big Food for its role in fueling child obesity and malnutrition.[83] "We need you not just to tweak around the edges, but to entirely rethink the products that you're offering, the information that you provide about these products, and how you market those products to our children," the First Lady said in a speech to the Grocery Manufacturers Association. "That starts with revamping or ramping up your efforts to reformulate your products, particularly those aimed at kids, so that they have less fat, salt, and sugar, and more of the nutrients that our kids need."[84] By the time the HHFKA was poised to land in schools at the start of the 2012 academic year, however, the tenor of the Let's Move initiative had shifted from confrontation to cooperation with many of Big Food's worst offenders. Rather than push for concrete policy changes to food sold outside of schools and foods marketed to kids, the Obama White House eventually embraced a distinctly neoliberal approach to food-systems reform that continues to allow corporations to define their own parameters of change.[85]

Meanwhile, leaders of the School Nutrition Association and its industry "friends" were hard at work dismantling key aspects of the legislation that SNA members had helped pass just a few years prior.[86] In a campaign orchestrated by these vested interests, lawmakers inundated US Secretary of Agriculture Tom Vilsack with letters articulating their opposition to specific elements of the HHFKA standards that affected their industry constituents (especially the starchy vegetable and frozen pizza manufacturers that cornered the school lunch market in the 1970s).[87] Several industry heavyweights, including ConAgra and Schwan's Company, banded together to finance the Coalition for Sustainable School Meal Programs. It helped boost credibility for their claim that parents and school nutrition professionals thought the HHFKA regulations were too stringent.[88] Congress had gone "too far, too fast," they argued. "Choice" and "flexibility" were needed at the local level, not unyielding "Big Government" mandates.[89]

Conservative media pundits landed on this debate as part of a more expansive vendetta against the Obama administration and its so-called nanny-state approach to healthcare and food. Behind the scenes, industry continued to influence the legislative process through strategic lobbying and donations, but the SNA became the public face of the fight to retain the status quo. The SNA championed a waiver system that would exempt schools from meeting several of the HHFKA's updated nutritional requirements. SNA president Leah Schmidt told reporters that schools were "struggling with declining student participation, increased costs, and overly prescriptive requirements that stifle menu creativity and reduce the appeal of healthy school meals."[90] This position left the association politically isolated from many of its former HHFKA allies—including over two hundred civil society organizations, nineteen former SNA presidents, the First Lady, and Secretary of Agriculture Tom Vilsack—and reaffirmed the popular narrative that lunch ladies are happy to serve kids junk food on the public dime.[91] The whole episode is reminiscent of earlier ideological divides within the SNA during the 1960s and 1970s over the future of the NSLP, when members disagreed about whether to tie their fate to Big Food. But in this case, school foodservice directors in major cities around the country were largely united in their opposition to SNA's proposed waiver system and the industry influence contained within.

As all of the drama over the HHFKA was beginning to escalate in the summer of 2012 and demands for products with clean labels and short ingredient lists in and out of the lunchroom continued to grow, I had the opportunity to mingle with hundreds of school nutrition professionals at the SNA Annual National Conference. Was the HHFKA disrupting Big Food's hold on the school lunch market? Were public-private partnerships shifting the status quo? Were alternatives to industry reformulation, like cooking from scratch, gaining much traction in school kitchens? These were the questions at the forefront of my mind as I entered the SNA's exhibit hall—a giant food show that serves as ground zero of the NSLP's cheap-food economy.[92]

The SNA food show includes over eight hundred booths, so school foodservice directors, dieticians, and managers who attend the conference strategize in advance about where to go and how much to take in. It feels almost like a carnival, with signs and overhead displays competing for attention as each company tries to lure potential buyers toward its booths to taste foods and have their badges scanned so they can be sent additional product information and samples. The SNA's system of priority placement nudges buyers to visit the booths of the food show's biggest spenders, who have received priority points based on how many booths a company has purchased, whether it has attended the conference before, how robustly it participates in SNA corporate membership programs, and the total sum it spent on SNA sponsorship and advertising. More priority points translate into a better location on the showroom floor. This means that smaller companies, specialty vendors, and new entrepreneurs hoping to break into the nationwide K–12 market are at a disadvantage.[93]

I spent several hours watching people navigate the maze of over eight hundred brightly colored booths and stopped periodically to listen to the sales pitches and taste the samples. I walked all the aisles and chatted with child nutrition professionals from across the country about what types of products they were looking for and asked questions about what their programs were like back home. The major topic of the conference—the thing I heard so many people talking about in their informal conversations with each other, the hook that vendors used in their sales pitches, and the topic of so many of the conference sessions—was not scratch cooking or real food. It was the impending rollout of the HHFKA. At the end of the summer, when school resumed, they would all need to be ready to implement age-appropriate calorie limits, while serving a greater variety of vegetables and legumes, more whole grains, and less sodium. The collective anxiety was palpable.

Congress had required schools participating in the NSLP to make sweeping nutritional upgrades, but their budgets were slim. The maximum reimbursement rate in the contiguous states had been $3.15 for a free lunch, $2.75 for a reduced-price lunch, and $0.36 for a paid lunch. The HHFKA provided a mere six cents extra reimbursement per lunch. To comply with USDA regulations intended to ensure "free and open competition," schools participating in the NSLP must accept competitive bids for all purchases above a certain dollar amount called the "small purchasing threshold" ($150,000 as of March 2018).[94] Foodservice directors who lack the technical expertise or dedicated staff time to negotiate the bidding process and overhaul bid documents struggle to diversify their supply chains beyond the cheapest Big Food suppliers.

Bid documents can include a dizzying range of information for every product that schools source. The USDA procurement guide advises school food purchasing agents who prepare bid documents to carefully specify "things like name, federal grade, size information for container or product, bid unit, quality indicators (e.g., type, style, pack, syrup density, specific gravity, age, exact cutting instructions, weight range, composition, condition upon receipt of product, fat content, cut of meat used, market class, variety, degree of ripeness or maturity, geographical origin, temperature during delivery and upon receipt, sugar ratio, milk fat content, milk solids and bacteria count, brand names, trim or yield, preservation or processing method, trade association standards, chemical standards), packaging procedures, food testing procedures."[95] It's a lot to keep track of—so much that schools look for ways to simplify.

Industry, for its part, is eager to profit by providing plug-and-chug solutions like ready-made food guaranteed to meet the USDA's nutritional standards, with Child Nutrition (CN) labels to boot. When manufacturers get CN certification for their products and participate in the USDA's optional evaluation program for main dish products like burritos and pizza, they can guarantee that their factory-made foods will contain the appropriate, specified amount of protein, grains, dairy, vegetables, and fruit. Purchasing CN-labeled items saves schools from needing to test the nutritional value of food they might otherwise produce themselves, saving labor and eliminating liability risks. If a USDA audit found the CN-labeled food fell short, the company—not the school kitchen—would be responsible for paying the fines.

Some companies provide even more comprehensive options, such as complete monthly meal plans that conform to the HHFKA requirements. To the CEO of one for-profit school lunch provider—Justin Gagnon of California-based Choicelunch—the HHFKA would reinforce the NSLP's dependence on built-in labor and be a boon for industry. "If you're a cash strapped district, are you really going to put all of the effort and headache into a scratch program when it's so cumbersome to run, and food brokers are banging down your door with solutions that are cheaper and easier, and designed to check all of the boxes? The answer was 'no' even before the new regs, so I can't see how adding complexity to the regulations is going to lead to a wave of scratch cooking in our schools."[96] Predictions like Gagnon's were well founded but overlooked real changes happening on the ground, where thousands of school foodservice directors had already begun to try to serve more freshly prepared meals and real food in their cafeterias.

#REALSCHOOLFOOD VERSUS "REAL" FACTORY FOOD

In September 2015, the activist and "renegade lunch lady" Ann Cooper, along with celebrity chefs Alice Waters and Jamie Oliver, launched a social media campaign for #RealSchoolFood. "It is sad that we need a campaign to create awareness around the need for schools to serve REAL food that's cooked on-site with fresh ingredients. But the fact is, we do," a spokesperson for Cooper's nonprofit Chef Ann Foundation said in a kickoff statement.[97] Within a year, over 23 million people posted pictures of themselves holding up a #RealSchoolFood sign in order to express their support for the campaign.[98] Among the many tweets on the #RealSchoolFood Twitter feed is a picture of

FIGURE 15. Cook taking "quick-scratch" individual pizzas out of the oven. Records of the Office of the Secretary of Agriculture, 1974–ca. 2003, National Archives and Records Administration.

a lunch tray loaded with roasted diced sweet potatoes, kale salad with cranberries, orange wedges, a fish taco topped with cilantro, radishes, cabbage, and lime, and a carton of 1 percent unflavored milk. Underneath the picture is the caption: "R U ready for school? Leave the sack at home and trust your lunch lady!"

For many real food activists, "cooking from scratch with recipes based on fresh, whole ingredients"—as Ann Cooper put it in a 2016 press release—is the gold standard. Cooper pointed out that "Big Food companies are engineering processed products to meet federal guidelines, but a chicken nugget with whole-wheat breading and twenty other mystery ingredients does little to instill healthy eating habits." To "ensure that kids receive the nourishment they need today and a taste for real food that leads to a lifetime of healthy eating," she wrote, scratch cooking was key.[99]

Actually making this happen in schools without much culinary capacity is a challenge.[100] Real food pragmatists have embraced the logic of "speed scratch," which is certainly a step up from unbox-and-bake products in terms of taste, texture, and final appearance (fig. 15). Where a frozen factory-made burrito is wrapped in plastic and reheated at school, a speed-scratch burrito is freshly assembled from convenience components: precooked beef crumbles, premade refried beans, preshredded cheddar cheese, and a premade tortilla. There are hundreds if not thousands of unique speed-scratch recipes currently in use at cafeterias across the country. Some are simple, like making rice pudding by mixing a no. 10 can of commercial vanilla pudding with school-cooked brown rice. Others are more complex, like assembling premade dough, preshredded low-fat mozzarella cheese, presliced pepperoni, and premade pizza sauce into a carefully folded calzone and baking it in the oven. But all of them are easier and cheaper than true scratch cooking, which can require lengthy prep shifts and special equipment.

School foodservice directors looking to outsource the work of cooking real food have other options too. New entrepreneurs and custom processors have begun to compete with Big Food companies for market share in the real food space. Instead of bidding on a commercially available product that may or may not meet all specifications, schools can contract with a private processor to build a custom product around their exact specifications. Through such contracts, schools retain power over the ingredient specifications, sourcing, nutrition and taste profile of premade items they can use for speed-scratch recipes or reheat as-is.

Patty, a Southeastern food broker whom I met at the 2012 SNA conference works with both commercial and custom processors. She described herself as a "matchmaker" who connects food manufacturers and school foodservice directors. At the time, she was helping Tyson, a Big Food giant, develop a precooked whole muscle "chicken on the bone" to appeal to foodservice directors looking to serve real food. She was also consulting with a custom processing company in Louisiana that hoped to launch its own line of twelve "like scratch," CN-certified, fully cooked Creole entrées. Patty knew that getting CN certification would make school foodservice directors across the national market more likely to purchase the company's new line of Creole entrées. But the certification was especially important in Louisiana, where school foodservice directors were often already accustomed to making their own Creole dishes using quick-scratch or even full-blown scratch cooking. CN labels might convince them to replace their school-made versions with what the factory pumped out of a 300-gallon kettle.

When Patty invited me to shadow her for a week as she made her rounds in Louisiana, I jumped at the chance. During a visit to the headquarters of the custom processing company Patty represented, I watched a sales representative try to sell the new line of Creole dishes to a focus group of foodservice directors from the area. She began with a tour. After pulling on our protective hairnets, smocks, and booties, we walked through the facility, where she explained that "kettle cooking" produces food with minimal fat and maximum flavor. Industrial kettle cooking is much safer than scratch cooking in schools, she said, thanks to the company's "rigorous seven-level safety check," yet the process still yields "a rich flavor profile, as if you were making the recipe at home."

After the tour, we sampled the company's "like scratch" soups and sauces and provided our feedback on their standardized form. While we were busy tasting, the product representative reminisced about her days working as a manager in a nearby school cafeteria. "I remember it was really hard when people called out sick," she said. The room came alive with nodding heads and knowing sighs as she told a familiar story. One day, her school was supposed to serve King Cake, a Mardi Gras specialty, to eleven hundred people, but both of her bakers called out sick that morning. They were able to "pull it together," but not without a tremendous amount of stress. The beauty of "like scratch," she reminded us, is that this type of crisis could never happen. Relying on "built-in" labor—as the industry called it back in the 1950s, when serving commercially prepared convenience foods in schools was still controversial—eliminates the need for skilled labor in schools.

Like-scratch products, the sales rep told us, fit seamlessly into the existing model of reheating factory-made foods in school kitchens, reduce the likelihood of school's ever being held liable for food poisoning incidents, and cut costs. The plastic bags need only be submerged in boiling water until the temperature reaches 165°F. What's more, these like-scratch soups and sauces arrive ready to use in a lightweight plastic pouch, which eliminates the need to dispose of large volumes of food scraps, broken-down cardboard boxes, and empty metal cans at the end of the day. Soup-in-a-bag saves money on both labor and waste, which in turn frees up resources to purchase "real" food.

Across the country, in Oakland, California, RevFoods (short for Revolution Foods), relied on the same promises—providing hassle-free, like-scratch, preplated real food to schools—to transform from a start-up to a $100 million for-profit company in less than a decade.[101] According to the RevFoods' website, its mission is "to build lifelong healthy eaters by making kid-inspired, chef-crafted food accessible to all."[102] While staff at the Oakland headquarters do most of the recipe development, RevFoods produces its meals at facilities across the country that, as of October 2016, distributed to sixteen states and the District of Columbia. RevFoods builds its central production centers near metro areas with high concentrations of low-income children. This focus on underserved communities is core to RevFoods' identity as a social enterprise (and certified B Corporation).[103] It's also a sound business strategy.[104] The population density of the customer base is higher. So, too, is the likelihood that a large percentage of the kids qualify for free or reduced-price lunch.

RevFoods tells prospective clients that its school meals "focus on fresh, clean-label ingredients with an emphasis on fruits and vegetables." "No artificial colors, flavors, or sweeteners," the company promises. "Just the best ingredients, guaranteed." A *Time* magazine reporter who toured RevFood's California production facility in early 2010 affirmed that "the food was bright and fresh; no grease." But, he noted, "the scene didn't suggest home-cooked, slow-food purism. Fresh vegetables sometimes arrive already chopped. Produce isn't necessarily local. High-quality chicken shows up already baked and cut. A whiteboard reminded managers of the week's big number: the target MPLH, or meals per labor hour, measured to a tenth of a meal."[105] I saw the same process when I visited a RevFoods production facility in Louisiana in March 2013: workers were busy mixing, assembling, and packaging ingredients that mainly arrived prewashed, precut, and in some cases precooked. The process reminded me of what I'd already seen while doing fieldwork in district-owned central kitchens, except that here, the workers were employed by the private sector.

RevFoods centralizes labor in its production facilities to minimize cost and maximize speed and efficiency, and it employs nonunionized workers to further cut costs. Let's not sugarcoat the situation: this is factory labor and the workers RevFoods hires will not help build public schools' culinary capacity. And the profits RevFoods makes from its vending contracts will, by and large, go to investors, not workers' wages. Under a conventional vending contract, everything RevFoods delivers to the schools is preportioned and sealed in containers such that, as one company representative put it, "the office manager could actually serve lunch." It's the airline-type lunch of the 1970s updated for the real food era. To be fair, RevFoods is a leader in the "unprocessing" of commercially prepared school lunches, and it's possible that such efforts are helping to mainstream the very idea that real food is something an average consumer can expect from convenience food manufacturers.

At the same time, however, such companies—intentionally or not— undercut the power and possibility of a more robust real food movement. RevFoods' current business model, for example, does little to resolve the ecological externalities or economic injustices of cheap food. The company typically sources conventionally grown food that travels through Big Food's supply chains, preportions lunches in plastic single-use containers, and continues to deskill and devalue the labor of school-based kitchen and cafeteria staff. Concerns about union busting and food quality have arisen in some communities where RevFoods has set up shop.[106]

Companies like RevFoods do little to disrupt the NSLP's cheap food economy. Contrary to what promoters might say, these companies reinforce the basic labor structure of the cheap food economy, while keeping the conversation framed around ingredients, rather than larger issues like equity, labor, and infrastructure. Real food lite is not a path to sustainability or equity within the food system. For the NSLP to truly support real food in all of its power and potential, districts would need to build culinary capacity in nonprofit, publicly owned school kitchens. But for-profit food companies, trade associations, and social movement activists have been tightly connected in the labor of lunch for well over a century. That's why it would be a mistake to view industry efforts as "simple colonization" of cafeterias. Laura J. Miller writes that it's not just Big Food, but "rather the expansion of a receptive constituency that increases pressures on a movement to soften more radical expressions."[107] In other words, as the potential market for real food grows and the definition of what constitutes real food remains subjective, the lowest common denominator seems to win out.

When I went to the SNA Annual National Conference in 2016, signs of that market were everywhere. I spent two days making my rounds through the food show, stopping to chat with product representatives at many of the same booths I had visited four years earlier. Often I'd ask if they had any "clean-label" products—which seemed to be their preferred lingo over the colloquial "real" food—then nod my head as I listened to one of the inevitable three answers: a boilerplate set of justifications for why such foods aren't feasible for the school lunch market; a promise they were "working on it," though the product reformulations were difficult to get right; or a sales pitch peppered with buzzwords from the emerging real food lexicon. No artificial flavors or colors! No GMO ingredients! No preservatives! All natural! Whole muscle! Antibiotic-free! Nitrate-free! Gluten-free! Organic! Artisanal!

Between the many samples of pizza, chicken nuggets, mini hot dogs, French toast sticks, and sweet potato fries, I found some of the real food movement's major players, including School Food Focus, RevFoods, and the USDA Farm-to-School Program. I also found some of the same mainstream organic and natural brands that have become increasingly popular in grocery stores: Annie's Organics, Kind Snacks, Angie's BoomChickaPop, and Bolthouse Farms. At the outskirts of the show—recall the SNA system of priority points—I discovered several new companies that had never before attended an SNA Annual National Conference food show. The product reps at the Beyond Meat booth were serving a sausage pizza topped with vegetarian beef crumbles (made from pea protein) right next to the Humane Society's booth that promoted their Meatless Monday campaign. A few aisles over, a California start-up, Back to the Roots, had a colorful display of organic purple corn flakes and other cereal boxes alongside its DIY organic mushroom farms and classroom herb gardens.

Across the food show, vendors marketed real food novelties that could appeal to kids raised on the creations of Big Food and Big Snack while satisfying the requirements of the HHFKA: chewy dried raisins flavored with fruit juice and citric acid—like a Sour Patch Kid, but natural; crunchy baked chickpea snacks in multiple flavors—like convenience store corn nuts but legumes.[108] Both were sold by entrepreneurial boutique manufacturers who had built their business models around the perceived needs of the school lunch market in the real food era. Big Food companies that have enjoyed a robust forty-year monopoly on sales to school cafeterias and vending machines, on the other hand, must decide whether to stay the course or join the push for clean-label industrial food.

New, smaller companies are often leading the way. At the SNA 2016 food show, for example, several companies marketed clean-label, allergen-free premade sandwiches as an alternative to the ubiquitous Smucker's Uncrustables, a shelf-stable peanut butter and jelly sandwich filled with artificial ingredients and preservatives. My favorite of the wannabe Uncrustables consisted of two square slices of crustless white whole-wheat sandwich bread filled with sunflower-seed butter and jam inside a crinkly plastic package. The market for these very simple premade sandwiches is larger than might be expected. Making sandwiches and wrapping them takes time and money. Purchasing premade, individually wrapped grab-and-go sandwiches allows schools to outsource labor—deprofessionalizing and cheapening the cost of part-time lunch ladies—while making efficient use of commodity peanut butter and lower-cost factory labor. Smucker's had the market nearly cornered prior to the arrival of this new generation of clean-label sandwich makers—and the company wanted to keep it that way. About six months after the SNA food show, in February 2017, Smucker Foodservice sent out an email, promoting its "exciting K–12 resources and updates." "As part of our commitment to quality, we're making changes to keep you ahead of student preferences and parent expectations," the email read. "Beginning April 1, 2017, all Uncrustables Sandwiches will be made with no high fructose corn syrup and non-GMO ingredients."

There are good reasons to be skeptical about such voluntary clean-up efforts, particularly since Big Food continues to market unhealthy food to children. Questioning companies' motives—and the extent of their commitment to change—is completely logical given the continued existence of so-called copycat snacks in schools. As part of the HHFKA's broader suite of reforms, the USDA's Smart Snack rule, which went into effect in the 2014–2015 school year, was meant to improve the nutritional profile of the food children purchase through school vending machines and à la carte lines. Many of the mainstream real and natural food brands realized that their products were already Smart Snack compliant, so they jumped at the opportunity to enter a new marketplace and showcased their wares at the 2016 SNA food show. Big Snack companies had to reformulate if they wanted to defend their colonized terrain from these opportunistic invaders. So they did, rolling out "copycat," slightly healthier versions of their standard fare. There is nothing in the HHFKA or Smart Snack rules prohibiting Big Snack companies from comarketing their popular, unhealthy junk food brands in schools, as long as the product formulation meets the USDA's standards.

Critics argue this policy loophole undermines public efforts to improve children's health.[109] Big Food companies can use the same brand names, product names, logos, and spokes-characters for compliant snacks (sold to schools) and noncompliant snacks (sold to grocery stores, gas stations, and the like). Take TGI Fridays as an example. The brand encompasses a US-based fast casual restaurant chain and a wide variety of ready-to-eat consumer goods sold in the frozen food aisle and snack sections of grocery and convenience stores. TGI Fridays uses the same logo and branding for its Crunchy Fries, a Smart Snack sold only in K–12 schools, as the potato skins, onion rings, and other commercial products that don't meet the Smart Snack nutritional standards. I snagged a bag of Extreme Heat Crunchy Fries at the 2016 SNA food show and took it back to my hotel room for further "research." The text on the Crunchy Fries packaging checks a number of real food boxes: Baked, not fried. Smart Snack compliant. No artificial flavors. No artificial colors. No MSG. No preservatives. No gluten. No trans-fats. They're made from a mixture of whole-grain cornmeal, enriched cornmeal, and dehydrated potatoes, so they count as one bread-grain equivalent for the HHFKA meal pattern. After opening the bag, I was surprised to find the color far more muted than the picture on the package had suggested (paprika in place of red dye number 6, perhaps?). I popped a Crunchy Fry in my mouth. The texture—initially light and airy—became surprisingly dense as soon as I began to chew. The flavor was lightly spicy and not particularly salty. Overall, it tasted distinctly engineered, as if I could never approximate, let alone reproduce, the flavor or texture of corn-based "fries" using the tools in my home kitchen. Technically speaking, TGI Fridays Crunchy Fries are "clean," but most real food advocates, even those of a more pragmatic orientation, would balk at the idea of calling such a product real food.

Healthy ingredients matter, but eating clean-label TGI Fridays Crunchy Fries and Smucker's Uncrustables won't help children understand where their food comes from. Nor will it help them connect to the land and laborers responsible for feeding them. Instead, these handheld foods encourage children to eat "on the go" and reinforce the idea that healthful eating comes in the form of highly engineered packaged foods never touched by human hands. By focusing on ingredients of concern, Big Food and Big Ag respond only to the part of the real food movement that fits their industrial realities and profit motives. And when activists frame the problem in the same terms, they sacrifice a more holistic vision for the real food movement.[110] This brings us to the heart of the problem. Real food lite and much of the corporate real food lexicon focuses on the food alone—and its relationship to consumer health—while ignoring how capitalism's relentless pursuit of cheapness destroys lives, livelihoods, and the health of the environment.

The student activists leading the Real Food Challenge in college and university dining halls across the country have a far more expansive vision than companies like Campbell's and RevFoods. These young people see real food as the product of a "values-based food economy" that "truly nourishes producers, consumers, communities and the earth."[111] They are demanding that their schools source at least 20 percent Real Food annually by 2020; so far four statewide university systems and another forty-three colleges and universities have signed on to this Real Food Campus Commitment. Like the New Haven foodservice workers leading the UNITE HERE campaign for real food and real jobs, these student activists see human dignity, animal welfare, social justice, and ecological sustainability as a nonnegotiable set of priorities bound together in the notion of "real" food. The Real Food Challenge is organizing the collective power of youth activists to demand that the institutions that feed them are on the frontlines of building a new economy of care.

By naming and challenging the existing power structures of cheap food that make the world a less caring place, the Real Food Challenge is pursuing the type of confrontational food politics that real food lite threatens to circumvent.

In the conclusion of her book *Free for All: Fixing School Food in America*, Janet Poppendieck asks whether school food should be a mirror of the American food system or a leverage point for transforming it in a more just and sustainable direction.[112] Real food lite is the mirror, not the transformation. It selectively appropriates the concerns of the environmental and food movements while threatening to transfer even more regulatory control of the food system from the public to the private sector. It widens gaps in dietary quality between the rich and the poor.[113] And it focuses public attention on identifying and removing ingredients of concern without attending to the larger, systemic dangers that should cause just as much concern, if not more.

Big Food's consumer veil hides the realities of cheap labor and cheap food, enriching shareholders while harming the public. The US government has played into these companies' hands by ceding its regulatory power time and again. It's no wonder that so many food pundits and reformers champion self-provisioning—growing and cooking one's own food—as the safest path. Powerful leaders in the real food movement, including Michael Pollan and Mark Bittman, have suggested that the best way to reclaim power from Big Food and to care for ourselves, our families, and our environments is to cook our own food from scratch, using raw and minimally processed ingredients. But when real food activists encourage families to cook from scratch, they often discount the difficulty of consistently churning out home-cooked meals, a burden that, for centuries, has fallen on women.[114] It's easy to romanticize the meals prepared by our mothers, grandmothers, and great-grandmothers, but we shouldn't ignore the fact that many women had no choice but to perform this and other unpaid care work—or, in the case of many black and immigrant women, to do so while also performing paid care work for richer, typically white families.[115] Just like today's cheap-food economy, the "real" food of an earlier United States has a gendered, classed, and racialized history whose legacy is still with us.[116]

Individualized fixes simply cannot repair what is inherently a social problem. When middle- and upper-middle-class families decide to opt out of the NSLP and instead cook nutritious lunches for their own children, school lunch programs lose revenue they so desperately need to balance their budgets. Parents' competitive care ends up enlarging the nutrition gap, and poor children suffer. Packing a healthier lunch for one's own children is certainly a worthwhile activity and a meaningful expression of care, but it does nothing to improve the quality of the NSLP for children whose families can't afford to pack lunches. Nor does it help reduce the time bind of the second shift.

Today, as millions of women struggle to balance unpaid care work with outside employment, we need collective solutions. Consumer-based solutions like relying on home meal delivery kits with huge environmental footprints, purchasing clean-label Lunchables at the supermarket, or outsourcing whole lunch programs to for-profit companies who can hide their exploitative practices behind a consumer veil won't fix things. Nor will shaming busy mothers or scapegoating the low-wage, typically female workers on the frontlines of school foodservice.[117] As the most public faces of school lunch programs, these lunch ladies are frequent targets of criticism, despite the limited power they have over what or how the children in their care are fed. They want better systems too, and school lunch activists should work with them to transform the NSLP. Together, workers and activists can advance a revolutionary politics of sustainability that protects the environment, provides meaningful employment, and promotes the public health of whole communities.

FOUR

Cafeteria Workers in the "Prison of Love"

For the real food movement to advance food justice in American K–12 schools, kitchen and cafeteria workers must take center stage. Like the many women laboring away in home kitchens, their work often goes unnoticed and underappreciated, yet they provide tremendous value to society by raising and caring for children. Real food, as I've come to understand it, is about more than just ingredients. It's also about respect for those who grow, process, cook, and serve the food and the relationships children form with those who feed them. We have a long way to go. But the first step is learning about what it's actually like to be a lunch lady and what this job could be if we were to, in the words of my UNITE HERE colleagues, "respect the food" and "respect the lunch ladies."

One way to respect these workers is to create the conditions for them to care well. Too often, the National School Lunch Program's (NSLP) model of free, reduced-price, and full-price lunches causes workers to dole out care on a limited basis. Cafeteria workers use personal identification numbers to look up children's eligibility for free, reduced-price, and full-price school lunches and to check the balance of the personal accounts that children's caretakers fill with lunch money. During my fieldwork at an elementary school in Louisiana, a very small girl, probably in the first or second grade, walked past a cashier without paying. "Helloooo! Give me your number!" the cashier yelled after her. The little girl walked back to where she was sitting. "What is your number?" the cashier asked. The girl didn't answer. "What is your number?" The cashier asked again. Still no answer. "What is your number?" Again, no answer. Maybe the girl had forgotten the lunch identification number she had been assigned at the beginning of the year. Or maybe she didn't qualify for free lunch and knew she had accrued enough lunch debt to be denied a hot meal.

In many schools across the country, students with too much lunch debt are refused service entirely, given an identifiably inferior, stigmatized lunch—like a cold cheese sandwich—or subjected to the public humiliation of having their entire meal torn from their hands and dumped into the garbage. The practice, in its multiple forms, is known as "lunch shaming." The little girl in Louisiana was all too familiar with this policy for managing lunch debt. It's why she responded to the cashier's multiple requests for her identification number by keeping her head down, her mouth shut, and her hands clutched tightly on her tray. She was hoping for the best and, this time, she got it. After what felt to me like a minute of paralysis—and likely much longer to the little girl—the cashier sighed, said "All right," and let her take the tray of food without ever giving her identification number. The little girl never paid for the lunch. If it had been a manager, not just a university researcher observing this standoff, the sympathetic cashier would have been reprimanded—and possibly fired—for what technically amounts to stealing. Such harsh punishments are meted out in order to discourage frontline workers from shirking their duty to enforce the lunch-shaming policies set by their district supervisors.

This expectation that frontline workers deny food to children based on their financial standing detracts from the ethos of care and conviviality that many real food advocates hope to cultivate through garden and cooking classes. In the school I visited in Louisiana, for example, the real food initiatives sponsored by nonprofit organizations seemed to operate parallel to the NSLP. The nonprofit staff and volunteers provided experiential food- and garden-based education opportunities for the students and sought to elevate the culture of the cafeteria. During my visit in March 2013, student artwork decorated the walls of the cafeteria. A vase filled with fresh, student-grown flowers and brightly colored table linens added cheer to each table. But none of these efforts to "fix" school lunch changed the fact that the cashier—in a school foodservice operation outsourced to Aramark—was stuck serving cheap factory-made food and denying service to those who either didn't qualify for free lunches or couldn't afford to pay.

Frontline cafeteria workers like the Louisiana cashier put themselves at real personal risk, emotionally and financially, when attempting to care well for children by circumventing district lunch-shaming policies. This is not the story that Clayton Jones told in his widely syndicated 2017 political cartoon about lunch shaming, which features cafeteria workers as antagonists, not allies, to students who don't have the money to eat. The cartoon features two women—fat, aproned, scowling lunch ladies with giant breasts, large facial moles, and stray hairs—towering over a line of students carrying lunch trays filled with what appears to be a federally reimbursable meal of protein, milk, veggies, fruit, and grain. At the front of the line is one kid—different from the rest—whose tray is bare except for a small, pale, square-shaped cheese sandwich. "To remind your parents that you're in school-lunch debt," one of these workers explains as she draws the letter *L* on the student's forehead to remind him and his parents that they are all losers. The other lunch lady isn't any better. "Enjoy the cheese sandwich," she tells him. "Watch out for bullies."[1] It's not so much a warning as a prediction of what will happen to the child when he exits the lunch line.

A concern for these bullied children motivated Jones to use his cartooning skills to advocate for an end to lunch shaming. "I'm a dad. I know a lot of other dads and even mothers. I can't think of one who would be cool with a school employee writing on their children and branding them as a loser," he wrote in the text below the cartoon. "I know the current trend right now is to bully people, body-slam reporters, make fun of people who read, and degrade women by their appearance," he continued. "But can we not bully children? Can we stop adults from branding them as welfare kids?"[2] It's a great question and a worthy goal, but Jones's political commentary is off. A more instructive cartoon might feature government bureaucrats whose failure to adequately fund the NSLP results in some kids getting branded with an *L*. Or the economic pressures "near-poor" parents face when their income just exceeds the federal cutoff for free and reduced-price lunch eligibility. But those realities are harder to visualize—and far less familiar than the trope of lunch ladies as witches in hairnets.

Cafeteria workers, or lunch ladies, as they're generally called, are often portrayed as punch lines or scapegoats. It's politically convenient for anyone wishing to blame these workers for the systemic failings of the NSLP or the poor quality of "government programs." But it's not their fault. The budgets constraining school lunch programs are usually set by federal, state, and local policymakers who rarely, if ever, come face to face with the labor of lunch in school kitchens and cafeterias. The policymakers who decide what systems of public care should look like are disproportionately white, college-educated men.[3] From a position of what scholar Joan Tronto calls "privileged irresponsibility," policymakers both underestimate and devalue the extent of K–12 cafeteria workers' contributions to the NSLP.[4]

Across the country, school cafeteria workers struggle to care well under difficult conditions.[5] Far too often, cafeteria workers don't have the resources they need to provide for students or their own families. Many of the lowest-paid cafeteria workers hold down multiple part-time jobs just to survive and fear that if they end up earning too much, they'll be ineligible for the public welfare programs that make their finances workable. All of this is old hat for the NSLP—the labor of lunch has long been seen as women's work to be done cheaply or for free—but today there are many more jobs available to women than there were back in the early 1900s or even the 1970s. Recruiting and retaining frontline workers is much harder than it once was. As the foodservice director of one Midwestern district put it, "As soon as we get the bodies, we need to put them in a hairnet."

High turnover among frontline part-time employees fuels the cycle of deskilling, especially in districts without a union. It justifies the use of pre-cooked factory-made foods and makes real food lite seem like the only viable way to reduce children's consumption of ingredients of concern. But there is another way—one that could help lift thousands of women out of poverty while creating the foundation for a new economy of care in American communities. This alternative path relies on letting school kitchen and cafeteria workers cook for, not just police, children. Unfortunately, school lunch activists have been shortsighted, often paying attention to what children eat while ignoring the people who feed them. Public health advocates, farm-to-school champions, and other contemporary school lunch reformers deserve credit for working to improve children's health. They are chipping away at Big Food's power over the NSLP, but when their efforts minimize or ignore the need for real food *and* real jobs, the real food movement loses its transformative potential.

Farming, cooking, and eating are all relational acts that connect humans to each other and to the natural environment. These connections offer a space for what scholar Giovanna Di Chiro calls "living environmentalism" to flourish within the NSLP.[6] People's concerns about the maintenance and sustainability of everyday life made all the more difficult by economic and environmental exploitation are really about access to social reproduction, or the ability to care well for "individual bodies, particular communities, national cultures, and the earth itself," to borrow Di Chiro's phrasing.[7] The NSLP is a culturally, economically, and environmentally significant public institution that ordinary people can and should reclaim as part of a larger movement to build socially just, ecologically sustainable, democratically controlled solidarity economies. But this cannot happen until we assign greater value to care work that has remained invisible for far too long or, in the case of school lunch, ignored, stereotyped, racialized, feminized, papered over by a caricature, and pushed aside as a joke.[8]

Take, for example, the care worker featured in comedian Adam Sandler's 1993 song "Lunchlady Land." She wears brown orthopedic shoes and has visible gum disease—her body is rapidly decaying before the children's very eyes. And if it weren't for her trusty hairnet, the red wisps she keeps tied up might end up as unlucky surprises in the children's food. Not that it would make much of a difference in terms of quality—the food in Sandler's Lunchlady Land is sometimes burnt and, more often than not, disguised and repurposed into the next day's lunch. The food is so bad that it haunts the nameless lunch lady's unconscious. At night she dreams that a mob of angry cafeteria foods come to life, *Toy Story*–style, to enact their revenge. A slice of pepperoni pizza, a plate of liver and onions, and a tub of chocolate pudding all taunt the lunch lady with cruel words. A container of chop suey steps in and escalates the violence with a slap and a kick to the lunch lady's head, while the green beans and garlic bread cheer. The mob is placated only when sloppy joe, the lunch lady's friend and eventual husband, steps in to proclaim that the food would never even find its way to the kids' plates if it weren't for the lunch lady. They should be thanking her for giving them a purpose, sloppy joe tells the angry foods, not belittling her for their own shortcomings.

Indeed, Sandler's lunch lady serves reheated Salisbury steak with "a little slice of love."[9] In this way, his lyrics gesture, albeit crudely, to the care work involved in feeding schoolchildren. His lunch lady is both victim and villain. The only constants throughout the song are the laughable quality of school lunch and a cruel mocking of the lunch lady's appearance. The questionable status of Sandler's lunch lady as barely a woman—whose only marital prospect was a life-sized sandwich—was amplified in the *Saturday Night Live* version of the song when comedian Chris Farley played the role in drag, with red curly hair and a quarter-sized facial mole.[10]

Sandler's lunch lady is what the sociologist Ashley Vancil-Leap would call a witch, one of the two "controlling images" of lunch ladies in popular media."[11] The other, Vancil-Leap writes, is the mother. The witch is a scowling, crabby woman who cooks mystery meat and scoops gray-tinged slop on the tray of any kid who dares enter the cafeteria. The mother is a smiling, pleasant woman who lovingly dotes on children, dispensing hugs and serving tasty meals cooked with love. In these images, it seems perfectly natural for mothers to prepare tasty food—their innate womanly capabilities, rather than any skill or effort, make them successful. Witches, in contrast, seem personally deficient, even insufficiently womanly, just like Sandler's lunch lady.[12]

Children pick up on these codes. They learn to avoid the "witches" and seek out the "mothers" in the cafeteria. Consider Tommy Ramey's experience. He worked as the director of child nutrition programs for the entire state of Alabama before retiring in 2000. One day he walked into an elementary school cafeteria with two serving lines. Both lines offered the same menu choices, but one line had about fifty children in it and the other one had five. Ramey was perplexed, since most students hate to wait in line even a second longer than necessary. "Why are y'all over here in this long line when you can go over there?" he asked the kids. They pointed to the near-empty line and screamed, "Wilma the Witch works over there!"[13]

Witches have long been painted as hostile to children and to social reproduction. In fairy tales, old, ugly witches kill children, eat their bodies, or use them to make magical potions. And in the fifteenth through seventeenth centuries women who did not conform to their prescribed roles as unpaid reproductive laborers in the new capitalist economy were accused of witchcraft and killed in spectacular public hangings or burnings. These so-called witches were often community leaders, single mothers, and elderly women who fought to keep their power and self-determination. Persecuting and killing them made it easier for capitalism to plow ahead on the backs of women's unpaid labor. Centuries later, lunch ladies are similarly diminished as witchy impediments to the system.[14]

This has real consequences. Today, when lunch ladies are depicted as witches or even just witchlike, it disempowers workers and reinforces children's fear of the folks whose job is not to threaten them, but to care for them. These negative images perpetuate the idea that lunch ladies deserve their low social status—a perception that can, in turn, be used to justify their continued economic exploitation.[15] I watched this dynamic play out in the Comments section of a local newspaper back in 2010, when the New Haven, Connecticut, K–12 cafeteria workers were in a contract dispute with the board of education: "Apparently these food service employees are making much more than the average fast food worker makes in the private sector AND some qualify for a pension on top of that," one person commented. "Any idiot can cook in a cafeteria. Perhaps they don't want to deal with obnoxious school kids, but you're nothing special by being a school cook," fumed another. "Your union boss has blinded you into thinking you are an asset to the community and an irreplaceable part of the educational system.

The bad news is you're not. Take your pay, take your holidays off, and get to work." These readers, like many others, wrote in to express disbelief—outrage even—that "entitled" public sector employees wanted even more money and benefits in exchange for their "unskilled" labor. These naysayers were a self-selecting group that felt strongly enough about the issue to weigh in. Public opinion on the issue was far more nuanced, but the antiunion commenters presented a united front. By denying the public value of the NSLP, they box low-income cafeteria workers into a defensive corner, making it that much harder for them to organize a union, make strong demands at the bargaining table, or otherwise demand better.

Even real food advocates concerned with improving school lunch programs sometimes perpetuate the stereotype that school lunch workers are "witches." School foodservice directors and frontline lunch ladies are periodically portrayed as lazy, stubborn, ignorant adversaries who must be defeated in order to banish chicken nuggets, frozen pizza, and the like from school lunch trays.[16] British celebrity chef Jamie Oliver offers the highest profile example of this phenomenon. He crossed the Atlantic to bring his *Food Revolution* to American shores, only to find that public school freezers were "an Aladdin's cave of processed crap." But that's largely the fault of poorly crafted government policy and steadily diminished budgets, not individual workers. Instead of dissecting the ins and outs of NSLP policy in this way, however, the first season of *Jamie Oliver's Food Revolution* zeroed in on the lifeblood of reality television: interpersonal conflict. Oliver had pledged to bring his *Food Revolution* to Cabell County, West Virginia, where Rhonda McCoy was foodservice director. Some thirteen thousand students were enrolled in Cabell County's twenty-six public schools,[17] and Oliver wanted to help them. So did McCoy—otherwise she never would have agreed to be on the show.

Yet throughout the 2010 season, Oliver is portrayed as a heroic, benevolent, cosmopolitan outsider, while McCoy—who expresses doubts that her students will want to eat the food he suggests—comes off as uptight and unimaginative. This narrative made for decent television—*Jamie Oliver's Food Revolution* won an Emmy for the category of Outstanding Reality Program—but it didn't do much to improve public opinion about school lunch workers like McCoy and her staff. They've had to do that on their own. After *Food Revolution* wrapped, McCoy and her staff staged their own real food revolution. They began by adjusting Oliver's recipes to better align with the taste preferences and cultural expectations of West Virginians.[18]

Next, they secured money for new culinary equipment to make scratch cooking possible across the district, launched a farm-to-school initiative, and secured free lunches for all students, regardless of their family's incomes, through the NSLP's new Community Eligibility Provision, which allows low-income schools to offer free lunches and breakfasts to all children if at least 40 percent of students are directly certified for other means-tested federal antipoverty programs.[19]

Today, a team of sixteen Cabell County school cooks are taking their revolution on the road, teaching colleagues across the state of West Virginia the culinary techniques and real food recipes that made their own transition to scratch cooking so successful. The cameras are no longer running, but McCoy and her team of undervalued lunch ladies hope that other school districts will follow their lead.[20] They have made school lunch a site of living environmentalism, and in doing so they are redefining the economics, health, and culture of Cabell County.

For many people, worker-led transformations like this are surprising because we're not taught to expect much from working-class women workers, lunch ladies included. The tremendous amount of negative cultural baggage linked to lunch ladies is one of the reasons why many of the frontline workers, foodservice directors, and union organizers I interviewed reject the term as overly gendered, belittling, and too closely associated with unflattering stereotypes. *Lunch lady* doesn't sound like a breadwinner, but many of them are primary providers for their families and depend on earning a livable wage. Besides, the whole "lunch" part of the equation is outdated: the USDA runs parallel breakfast, snack, and dinner programs in thousands of communities nationwide, and school cafeteria workers make all these programs happen at the local level. The antiquated term *lunch lady* suggests their work is far more time-bound than it actually is, but alternatives like "food lady" and "meal lady" have never really caught on. In fact, some frontline workers continue to embrace the title of lunch lady as core to their professional identity. Instead of adopting a gender-neutral term like "school foodservice employee," they stick with lunch lady and jokingly call the men who join their ranks "lunch laddies."

In deference to the diversity of language that frontline workers use to describe themselves, I refer to school nutrition workers, cafeteria workers, and foodservice workers interchangeably and occasionally bring attention to specific roles like cashier or cook. At times, I even use the term *lunch lady,* especially when I find it helpful to underscore the gendered dimensions of the work or to remind readers of the cultural baggage that school cafeteria workers carry with them every day.

When I hear others use the term *lunch lady,* I often find myself returning to the memory of a conversation I had with Roxie, a cafeteria worker in Des Moines, Iowa, in the winter of 2016. She told me about how her relationship to her job and the term *lunch lady* had evolved over time. Back in 2003, when she first started working a three-and-a-half-hour shift in the cafeteria, she figured lunch ladies are the people who "serve kids and whatnot, but the kids don't remember [them]." Roxie's sixty-five-year-old mother gave her an earful when she heard her daughter describe lunch ladies as invisible, interchangeable workers—just cogs in a machine. Decades after she last interacted with her own lunch ladies, Roxie's mother still remembered how excited she had felt as a young girl when her small rural school first started offering hot lunch. "You'll touch kids' lives, and they'll remember you even when they get to be older adults," she told her daughter. This helped Roxie see lunch ladies in a new light, and over the years, she has found it to be true.

But when she heard her ten-year-old stepson tell some other kids, somewhat dismissively, "Yeah, my stepmom's a lunch lady," she started to wonder. So Roxie decided to ask him what he thought lunch ladies do. After all, she knew what the lunch ladies did at his school since she was one of them.

"Well, they just serve us food," he offered in response to her question.

"That's all they do?" she countered. "Who does the dishes? Who does the paperwork and stuff?"

He hesitated. "Oh, I don't know . . . maybe you're not a lunch lady?" he ventured. "Maybe you're a food worker."

Roxie's stepson didn't know it, but "food worker" is much closer to the official titles and job descriptions the School Nutrition Association (SNA) provides for frontline employees: School Foodservice Employee, School Nutrition Employee, Assistant, Technician, Cook, and Cashier. "School foodservice employees in an individual school are responsible for the preparation and serving of all menu items. Additional responsibilities include cleaning and dishwashing, as well as the care of some equipment," according to the SNA website. "Employees in cafeterias and kitchens include cooks, bakers, dishwashers and cashiers. School nutrition employees also may work at the district level as bookkeepers, secretaries, drivers and production/warehouse facility workers." Those with additional managerial responsibilities have different titles: School Foodservice Manager, School Nutrition Manager, Assistant Manager, Head Cook, or Lead. "Managers lead the day-to-day operations at an individual school or feeding site," according to the SNA job classification system. "Foodservice managers must ensure high standards for safety/sanitation and meal quality. In addition, they supervise site employees, place food/supply orders, account for meal service and à la carte sales and ensure adequate inventory is available."[21]

The SNA job descriptions account for part of the unseen labor that goes into running a child nutrition program, but—aside from the phrase "care of some equipment"—they do not mention care. In practice, however, frontline workers are expected to perform what sociologist Arlie Hochschild calls "emotional labor" by attending to the emotional state of the children they feed.[22] This expectation is highly gendered, unwritten, and unwaged. But bosses and workers know it's part of doing the job well.

Renée Hanks, a foodservice director in Albany, New York, makes sure her employees understand their responsibility to take note of and respond to children's emotional needs. She tells them that unlike the art teacher or the music teacher, who might see the kids once or twice a week, "you're one of the few people in the school that sees just about every student every day."[23] This, in Hanks's view, means that frontline cafeteria workers have a special responsibility to notice children's evolving emotional needs and to attend to them on a daily basis. Many of the frontline cafeteria workers I interviewed look forward to these regular interactions—so much so, in fact, that they don't see "customers" when they look out at the cafeteria tables. They see "their kids." But with hundreds or even thousands of kids to feed, making time for meaningful relationships is not always realistic. So, workers take shortcuts.

Marilyn Rylie, a foodservice director in Arkansas, tells her frontline workers to "always smile" at their child customers. "Smiles are free," she reminds her staff, "and you may be the only person who smiles at one of the students when they are having a bad day."[24] By smiling at children, frontline cafeteria workers can place themselves squarely in the "mother" camp—avoiding the fate of Wilma and other "witches"—and provide a friendly, nurturing face to children as they move through the cafeteria line.[25] What otherwise might be authentic expressions of care become increasingly routinized and transactional because of the need to keep the labor of lunch cheap. Fast, scripted commercial care might look great when viewed through the metric of meals per labor hour, but not when viewed in terms of the quality of care provided in school cafeterias.[26]

The difference becomes easier to see once we recognize that child-nutrition employees do more than just serve lunches. They are an integral part of a vast network of public and private care workers involved in the collective project of maintaining daily life and reproducing the next generation.[27] They support children's physical health and emotional well-being. They help create nourishing social worlds for communities to inhabit together. And they do so with knowledge, devotion, and skill, as school lunch manager Marge Evans makes clear in her 1968 poem "A Cafeteria Manager," which I found in a collection of documents at the Child Nutrition Archives.

> A Cafeteria Manager with smiling face,
> Takes care of the most loved of the human race.
> Mops their spills, dries their tears,
> Helps erase lost lunch fears.
> Gives praise and encouragement for a clean lunch tray,
> Hopes someday they'll all return that way.
> Listens to the phooeys, enjoys the yum yum,
> Has things in order when the supervisor comes.
> Counts every can at inventory time,
> For the ones she can't reach she has to climb.
> She tastes of this, she tastes of that,
> And worst of all, she gets fat.
> When the day's over she's kind of pooped,
> Besides tired feet her shoes full of soup.
>
> But it's all worth it, it's all worthwhile,
> Because what greater reward than a sweet child's smile.
> What greater reward than to know they care,
> For the one who's happy when their trays are bare.
> For the one who notices a new dress or shirt,
> Or comforts when a small one is hurt.
> She feeds their body needs and quenches their thirst,
> They know with her, they come first.
> Cafeteria Managers are very strange, indeed,
> Because last of all she tends to her needs.
> They represent love, responsibility, dedication so divine,
> I am so glad the title is mine.
> So glad God chose me children's lives to share,
> Thank you God for Cafeteria Managers everywhere.

Evans's tribute to cafeteria managers like herself doesn't just romanticize the labor of lunch—it also describes the physical and emotional costs of pushing oneself to always place children's needs above one's own. Yet all of these pains are overshadowed, at least in Evans's view, by the emotional rewards of providing for children and being valued in return. Indeed, cafeteria managers' seemingly innate willingness to make sacrifices for the good of the children transforms them into the "second mothers" Evans so admires. This midcentury portrait of cafeteria managers may seem overly sentimental or unrealistic, but I saw plenty of present-day examples of this type of care work in action during my fieldwork.

One day in early 2016, Kelley, a high school cook in St. Paul, Minnesota, described how frontline workers care both for and about the kids they feed as we sat in the cramped office at the back of her school's kitchen, ignoring the buzzing of oven timers and loudspeaker announcements all around us. "There's never a day you don't look out at the register and see there's kids standing there talking to their favorite lunch lady," she said. Kelley is a second-generation lunch lady, who takes pride in describing herself as such. The labor of lunch is in her blood. She's been doing it since elementary school, when she used to sneak into the kitchen to help her mom with little tasks before and after classes. Becoming a professional lunch lady was not a job of last resort for her; it was a calling. The food part is fine, but feeling connected to "her kids" is the part of the job Kelley likes the most. She feeds fifteen hundred students on a typical day. She doesn't always have a lot of time to chat, but she does her best to at least greet the students by name. "When I don't see them, I'm looking for them," she laughed. "I'm like, 'Where are they?' And then the next day they come in—I'm like, 'What happened? Why weren't you here yesterday? Is everything okay?'"

Such personalized concern is essential for children's well-being. In Alabama, Annie Drake—better known as "Miss Annie" in the small town where she was born, raised, and worked for twenty-five years as a school lunch worker—prided herself on being a "friend to the kids," and with good reason.[28] Miss Annie cared for some four hundred "babies," as she called them, at a time when racial tension pulsated through school cafeterias. In the 1960s and 1970s, as schools were desegregated, sometimes by court order and forced busing, Miss Annie did her best to keep the peace. As a black woman, she put herself on the line and spoke out whenever she observed white colleagues treating black students unfairly. "We had this young white girl that was going with a black guy on the ball team—and I had one of the cooks kind of mistreat him," Miss Annie recalled. The school cook whispered when they walked through the cafeteria and wasn't always as nice to the couple as Miss Annie would have liked. "That's when I decided I was going to get even closer to them, black or white, and they grew closer and closer to me—because that was hurting to me," she explained.[29] It was her way of protecting them from overt racism and the everyday microaggressions they might otherwise experience.

Miss Annie understood that stress could manifest and grow in children's bodies and psyches past the point of repair. This lesson really hit home years later when, during the summer break, one of her high school "babies" committed suicide. He was visibly stressed throughout the school year and, to Miss Annie's frustration, one of the frontline workers she supervised was "not as friendly" to him as she could have been. Miss Annie promised herself that she would never let something like that happen again; she would "always do something that would encourage them." In other words, if she couldn't force reluctant employees to act like second mothers, she could at least try to make up for their lack of care by doubling down on her own efforts to care well.

Returning to her hometown high school to work in the cafeteria was about the last thing Miss Annie would have thought she wanted to do when she graduated. But over time, she came to believe that God had led her back to the school for a reason: "To help these kids through their lives, teach them things, . . . let them know that segregation is nothing and together they can stand." She became a fixture in her community. Parents would stop her on the street and say, "Hey, Miss Annie, my kids talk about you night and day."[30] But years of hard work caring for other people's children never translated into much of a paycheck. Miss Annie held at least two jobs and sometimes as many as four jobs—working as a school janitor and cleaning local banks and office buildings—to provide for her own daughter. Despite her own economic hardship, Miss Annie often covered hungry kids' lunch fees out of her own pocket when they didn't have enough money.

Another school lunch worker, in Arizona, even bought food from outside the cafeteria, just to help a child eat. Karen Johnson, a former president of the SNA, told an oral history interviewer that the child had witnessed his father beat his mother to death.[31] Every day when the little boy came through the line, the cafeteria worker encouraged him to take a lunch. He would say, "I'm not very hungry" and move on. So one day she said, "Tell me what you like to eat. What's your favorite thing?" "A bean burrito from Del Taco and a chocolate shake," he answered. From then on, the cafeteria worker drove to the store during her morning break to get him his favorite meal. "He would come through the line and she'd say, 'I got something for you.' Oh, his eyes would light up," Johnson recalled. The cafeteria worker knew fast food wasn't the healthiest thing to feed the boy, but he was very thin and she just wanted to get calories in his body. Weeks later, she got busy and forgot to make her daily trip to Del Taco. The boy walked up to her serving station, and she apologized for not having his special lunch. "That's okay," he told her. "I like school lunch and I can eat this today."[32]

Thereafter the daily trip to Del Taco became weekly, and then finally, Johnson recalls, "she weaned him off the fast food burrito and the chocolate shake," and he ate school lunch every day. "He's probably a junior now in high school and those kids are doing just fine with Grandma and Grandpa," Johnson reported, "but it took a special lady, a special cafeteria lady, to recognize that her little boy wasn't eating, and whatever it took to get him to eat she was going to do."[33] "She went that extra mile like I know hundreds of ladies do every day," Johnson said. As a former SNA president, she heard stories from across the country about the heights to which some cafeteria workers went in their attempt to care well for "their children." I myself found dozens of such stories among the oral histories collected by staff at the Child Nutrition Archives.

The emotional and economic risks associated with striving to care well are typically downplayed in these heartwarming tales of cafeteria heroics. And while caring about children certainly brings deeper meaning to the labor of lunch, it can also drain frontline workers' limited emotional and financial reserves. Miss Annie and the Arizona cafeteria worker who made the daily trip to Del Taco used their own wages to perform their jobs well. No one reimbursed them. They held themselves to a higher standard of care than their coworkers—and they are certainly not alone in doing so. I interviewed dozens of frontline workers who were quick to tell me who in their kitchens and cafeterias really cared about the kids (the "mothers") and who should really find a job outside of school foodservice (the "witches").

THE STRUGGLE TO CARE WELL

The "mother" and "witch" imagery prevalent in popular culture representations of lunch ladies is grounded in reality. Both archetypes coexist in real-life school cafeterias. In my experience, few frontline workers are nasty to children, or "witchlike," because they enjoy being cruel or are simply aloof. Rather, these so-called witches of the school lunch world are generally quite caring people who have consciously or unconsciously settled on the strategy of shielding themselves emotionally by going through the motions of their jobs without performing the emotional labor typical of "second mothers."

Bearing witness to child hunger, homelessness, parental incarceration, and other injustices that affect young people—as well as dealing with kids who disrespect them—takes a toll on school cafeteria workers. Treating students as "customers" who need only the most basic service, instead of children who need holistic and personalized care, means cafeteria workers can clock out at the end of their shift without the weight of children's problems following them home or to their next part-time, low-wage job.

Frontline workers face challenging situations and tough judgement calls that add psychological stress to their jobs. Emily, a middle school cafeteria worker in Minneapolis, Minnesota, was surprised at the problems she encountered. "This is sixth, seventh, and eighth grade, and a couple girls are pregnant, a kid's on house arrest," she explained. When she notices kids who might be headed down a similar path, she takes the initiative to try get to know them so that she can talk with them about their behavior. "Man, you don't want that. What the heck! Look at how old you are," she tells them. Emily's not at all sure whether kids listen to her, but this doesn't stop her from trying to help them stay out of trouble. Theft is also a challenge. It's not always clear whether a child is intentionally stealing food or simply confused about the nuances of the NSLP payment system. Motive, too, can be difficult to tease out. The last time Emily caught a student stealing food, she asked why he'd done it. "For my little brother," he told her, "because there won't be anything when I get home." Child hunger motivated this particular student's theft, but others might be stealing to pocket their lunch money or just to rebel.

The fact that cafeteria workers may not be sufficiently embedded in the school community to know what is going on in a child's life or may not know how to handle problems within the constraints of the NSLP or district policy adds another layer of stress to their jobs. "If I yell at a child who's cutting, I'll get written up," one worker in Connecticut told me. She can't risk losing her job. So when the kids appeal to her to make things right, she shrugs it off and says, "I can only do so much, baby." She'd like to respond differently, but she feels trapped. Her coworker echoed this frustration: "Some of these kids don't even respect their parents, so what do you do? You can't touch them and you have to be careful with what you say." Such feelings of disempowerment are detectable at times on the faces and in the voices of frontline workers who struggle to keep their cool, especially when district policy forces them to restrict how and when they care about the kids.

"It breaks my heart . . . they don't have a choice—you know what I mean?" That's what Lydia, an elementary school cafeteria worker from Iowa, told me when I asked about the children at her school who experience homelessness and hunger. Lydia's mom and husband tell her that she "cares too much," but Lydia disagrees. In her view, there's no such thing as caring "too much" about kids, and she hates that her school resorts to lunch shaming to force parents to settle their debts.

"There's a little girl we had to feed [a] cheese sandwich yesterday," Lydia told me on the morning of my visit. "It's going to happen today too," she sighed. It didn't take much for me to realize that the prospect had already cast an emotional cloud over her day. Later, she admitted that she still felt terrible about inadvertently "making a spectacle" of the little girl during the previous day's lunch period. Lydia knows that kids with unpaid lunch debts aren't supposed to get anything besides a cheese sandwich, but the day before my visit she let this same little girl put a serving of fruit and a carton of milk on her tray, just like the rest of the students. Later, when the girl got to the cashier station, another cafeteria worker took the lunch tray and threw away everything except the cheese sandwich. The little girl was left crying in the middle of the cafeteria, attracting far more attention than she would have if Lydia had followed protocol and only given her the cheese sandwich of shame.

Why did Lydia break the rules? It's much easier to be the person sitting behind a desk writing policy and, as one child nutrition director put it, far "more difficult to be that cashier or that manager and look at a child in the face and take a tray away from them." She elaborated: "Sometimes that's what we tell them to do, and... that's not fair to them." "It's easy if you're not facing that person," she noted, acknowledging how much less emotionally draining it is to set policy from afar than to be the one tasked with enforcing it, especially when you know the children and their families are struggling.[34]

Lydia finds the whole business of enforcing lunch-shaming policies so distasteful and inhumane that she'd rather pay for children's lunches from her own pocket than allow them to be publicly shamed, but her district explicitly forbids cafeteria workers from settling children's lunch debts. "I've heard of lunch ladies being fired for doing that.... It happened just recently to somebody," she told me.

Subverting lunch-shaming rules is risky for Lydia and her coworkers, but following the rules isn't exactly risk-free either. They could be reprimanded or even fired, but still some choose to find creative ways to help out. Whether it is a simple act like letting children take food without paying, or a more complex effort to collect donations from the school or community, I've seen how lunch-shaming policies can motivate cafeteria workers to take extra measures to protect the dignity of poor children and working-class families. In most instances, schools don't lunch-shame until after they have sent notices to children's parents or called them to request that they pay down the school lunch balance. Children from families whose incomes slightly exceed the free and reduced-price eligibility threshold and qualifying children whose families haven't completed the proper paperwork are the ones who are most likely to fall into lunch debt and potentially be lunch shamed.

Lunch shaming is a widespread practice, but lunch debt is even more common. When the SNA surveyed close to one thousand school districts in 2015, about 75 percent reported having unpaid meal debt.[35] Forty-five percent of these districts served a cold sandwich to children with debt balances exceeding the approved threshold, while another 3 percent took the children's lunch tray and dumped it in the trash.[36] A slew of charitable efforts—some by nonprofits, others by individuals, GoFundMe pages, and even Casual-Friday fundraisers organized by cafeteria workers—are gathering money to help settle children's unpaid meal debt so that districts don't have to resort to lunch shaming.

One such initiative, "Philando Feeds the Children," was created in honor of Philando Castile, a thirty-two-year-old elementary school cafeteria manager in St. Paul, Minnesota, who was fatally shot by a police officer in July 2016 after being pulled over for a traffic stop in a nearby suburb. "Mr. Phil," as the students at J.J. Hill Montessori Magnet School knew him, spent his entire adult life (from age nineteen until his death) serving children in the city's schools.[37] "When a student couldn't pay for their lunch, a lot of times [Castile] actually paid for their lunch out of his own pocket," Stacy Koppen, the director of child nutrition programs for St. Paul Public Schools, told *Time* magazine.[38] "He just loved the kids, and he always made sure that they had what they needed," Anna Garnaas, a teacher at J.J. Hill, agreed. "He knew their names, he knew what they liked, he knew who had allergies. And they loved him."[39] When local college professor Pamela Fergus set up a YouCaring online fundraising page at the start of the 2017 school year to collect money to pay off unpaid lunch fees at J.J. Hill, she set the fundraising goal at $5,000. By March 2018, Philando Feeds the Children had far exceeded this goal and raised over $100,000—enough to erase the school lunch debt for all students in the St. Paul public schools.

Eliminating lunch shaming is an admirable cause to champion, but it would be a nonissue if the NSLP was a universally free program. But this isn't the solution that policymakers seem to be gravitating toward—yet. When lunch shaming became a topic of public debate in 2016, a handful of local and state policymakers introduced bills to outlaw lunch shaming.[40] At the federal level, a bipartisan group of lawmakers in the House and Senate introduced the Anti-Lunch Shaming Act of 2017, which would prevent schools from using a wristband or hand stamp to identify children with lunch debt, requiring them to perform chores or activities that are not required of all students, and disposing of food after it has already been served to a child. Such knee-jerk legislative responses restrict how schools are allowed to treat children but do nothing to make it easier for struggling families to afford school lunches. Such policy responses are wholly inadequate. Charitable campaigns like Philando Feeds the Children can help ease the strain on school lunch budgets and help families in need, but voluntary donations are no substitute for increased public investment.

This is certainly not the first time that the nonprofit school lunch movement has relied on charitable donations to feed children who cannot pay for their lunches. Millions of "needy" children were denied free lunches until the 1970s because schools didn't have enough money to feed them, which enabled administrators to decide which children were most "deserving" of assistance. This history teaches us that piecemeal financial plans rarely generate equitable outcomes for kids or workers. Then, just as now, frontline cafeteria staff bear the emotional cost of denying food to the children in their care. Some harden their hearts, dampen their emotions, and become "witchlike" in order to cope. Others do whatever they can to help prevent the standards of care from slipping even further. Both strategies—disassociating from the job and pushing themselves to be "a friend to the kids," as Miss Annie would put it—keep cafeteria workers in a state of individual and collective disempowerment.

Those like Lydia, whose family thinks she "cares too much" about the kids, are what feminist economist Nancy Folbre calls "prisoners of love."[41] The walls of the metaphorical prison of love become stronger as the givers and receivers of care become known to each other and relationships deepen over time. Those trapped inside the prison of love are unlikely to strike or make demands on their employers if they fear such actions might hurt the receivers of their care. Folbre's argument about the perils of relational care work helps explain why "motherly" cafeteria workers who develop emotional bonds with the children they feed tend to tolerate low pay and poor working conditions. I interviewed cafeteria workers who held two or even three jobs to supplement their school lunch earnings—doing this for years or even decades because they didn't want to leave "their kids." All the while, they were left with little time or energy to devote to collective struggles to improve the quality of care and jobs in the NSLP.

School cafeteria workers earned a median wage of $9,300 per year in 2008 (compared with $30,000 for workers across sectors).[42] Service sector unions UNITE HERE and SEIU and the public sector union AFSCME represent some of these workers, but union density remains quite low across the sector.[43] This drives down standards and makes it much more difficult for cafeteria workers to harness their collective power to push for policy changes at the state or federal level. Pushing back against injustices by targeting the district administrators who shape local policy can take workers only so far. The structural constraints of the NSLP, which push schools to rely on cheap food, cheap labor, and cheap care, place limitations on what kind of social changes seem feasible at the local level.

Frontline workers end up making great personal sacrifices just to do their jobs, shouldering the emotional costs of care work that policymakers and management companies have passed on in an effort to save money.[44] This is exactly what happened to Maria, the kitchen manager of a suburban Connecticut school, whose district decided to outsource the oversight of its lunch program to a multinational foodservice management company. Vacant positions in Maria's district are left unfilled for months or even years, which pushes the "prisoners of love" to work harder in order to protect the children in their care. "We have a lot of people that don't take breaks because they can't," she explained at the end of her shift on one of the days I observed her at work. I asked her why she didn't just hire new employees to fill the vacant positions—after all, she's a manager—but it turns out the foodservice management company does all the hiring. Sure, it can be hard for the management company to recruit people for extremely part-time, two- or three-hour positions, but this isn't the only factor at play. Another Local 217 shop, in nearby New Haven, had forty vacancies for several years, until workers built community power and used their contract negotiation to demand the district fill the vacancies.

School districts and foodservice management companies can save money by not hiring workers, so vacancies are, at least to some degree, a strategic decision to cut costs. This infuriates Maria. She knows it's unfair and hates asking her staff to work harder just to line the pockets of a for-profit company that is undermining their ability to care well. Maria encourages her staff to take their breaks and scolds workers who come in early or stay late to do unpaid work. If things fall apart, Maria tells them, upper management will have no choice but to finally fill the vacant positions. But her staff doesn't listen; they remain in the prison of love, exploiting themselves in a desperate attempt to care well. "Their main goal is to feed that child," as Maria put it, "so they continue to give up their breaks and no help comes." And why should it? The work is getting done and the prison of love is profitable. By regularly skipping their fifteen-minute breaks each day, each of Maria's staff will have gifted the management company two weeks of free labor by the end of the school year.[45]

According to Matt, one of the union organizers I interviewed, private management companies try to squeeze as much productivity as possible from workers at the lowest possible cost—even more so than school districts that manage their own nonprofit school lunch programs, since management companies have to find ways to generate a profit.[46] Selling cheap, factory-made entrées and popular brand-name snacks also helps management companies bring in more revenue, but the practice rubs some frontline cafeteria workers the wrong way. Number one, they don't like selling junk food to children, even if kids do seem to like buying pizza, nachos, cookies, and sugary drinks. Number two, setting up an à la carte line in addition to the federally reimbursable meal adds complexity and time to the labor of lunch. Sheri, a junior high school cafeteria manager in Connecticut who reports to one of the Big Three management companies—Aramark, Compass, and Sodexo—voiced these frustrations to me and Matt, her union representative, soon after the menu changes mandated by the Healthy, Hunger-Free Kids Act (HHFKA) had gone into effect.

Matt and I sat down with Sheri at the end of her shift. She seemed frazzled and apologized multiple times for needing to eat a snack while we talked. "Did you take your break?" Matt asked her. "No, of course not," she responded. Matt shook his head in exasperation. It was slightly past 2:00 pm and Sheri hadn't eaten anything or rested her feet since 5:30 am. "This school year has been especially rough," she said, exhausted and a bit demoralized. Like many workers around the country, Sheri was spending more time on paperwork, ensuring that the district had all of the documentation required to get the extra six-cent-per-meal reimbursement for meeting the HHFKA regulations. Ordering was also taking longer since the new regulations required schools to serve a wider variety of fruits and vegetables. Getting the correct portion sizes for the different grade levels and dealing with the kids who vociferously protested being "forced" to take a fruit or vegetable was another a new challenge.

On top of this, the management company created more work for Sheri and her staff to absorb without giving them any additional hours or part-time help. The company worried that sales would decline because of the switch to healthier fare and smaller portion sizes, so it increased the number of menu choices that cafeteria workers had to prepare for the reimbursable lunch and the à la carte line. Since Sheri is in a union, she could file a grievance against her employer and take collective action with her coworkers. Matt reminded her of this and told her to document each time she or any member of her staff worked through their break. "It's really pretty simple," Matt told her. "Management will be much more likely to respond to your complaints if the work isn't getting done." Sheri seemed to agree with Matt in principle, but she didn't commit to any course of action. Refusing to do extra work—leaving at the end of her shift, not coming in early, or even just taking her scheduled breaks—would cause standards of care to decline.

Sheri, like Maria's staff a few towns over, just wasn't willing to play that game of chicken with her employer. Children's well-being was at stake. But she was clearly upset and wanted change. "So, what's next?" I asked Matt. He didn't seem at all deflated by the conversation; in fact, he considered our one-on-one with Sheri to be a success since she had identified a shared struggle affecting cafeteria workers across the district. Taking the step of filing a formal grievance was, Matt hoped, just the first action in what might become a full-blown campaign to leverage their collective power as a union. It would have to start somewhere, and would likely be an uphill battle, but deep organizing has the power to make the NSLP better for workers and the children they feed.

THE NSLP'S LABOR CRISIS

The idea that school lunch workers should sacrifice themselves in order to serve children has deep roots. The municipal housekeepers of the early 1900s who helped experimental penny-lunch programs proliferate across American cities were typically middle-class, white women who could afford to volunteer. Many also hired working-class women to work in their school lunch programs, but they didn't cost much. The gendered nature of care work, coupled with women's exclusion from higher-paying labor markets, kept wages low. Despite home economists' lofty ideals—and their ability to make the labor of lunch a comparatively good job for working-class women and middle-class college-educated women—there is a pervasive assumption that "good" school lunch workers should be willing to work for love, not money. I encountered this sentiment repeatedly in the nearly two hundred oral histories collected by the Child Nutrition Archives. For example, Eleanor Pratt—who worked as a home economist in the USDA's Southeast Regional Office from 1960 to 1994—talked about the many workers she met over the years who were "very loyal to the program, very devoted, kind, and helpful to the children." Just like the "giants" of the Works Progress Administration community lunch program who "created a far-reaching vision" for the nonprofit school lunch movement, these workers gave their all to the labor of lunch despite "very low pay."[47]

In the early years of the NSLP, instructional pamphlets coached school foodservice directors to recruit women who might find cafeteria work amenable to their phase of life and personal economic situation: stay-at-home mothers, widows, and retirees who lived close to a school and might appreciate the supplemental income and social interaction. The strategy worked quite well. "Mothers wanted to come into the school lunch program and supplement their income," Pratt recalled. "It was sort of like they didn't have other opportunities in the early years to work anywhere except in the school food service program."[48] And once there, many of them chose to stay despite the low wages, because they knew they were "making such a contribution" to children's health and community well-being. That's how Pratt tells it, in any case. They did what she describes as "more than the minimum requirements of the job" out of altruism. Their moral character was unparalleled in Pratt's view. "These women had a dedication to feeding the children that was so genuine and so strong that they didn't mind working hard to prepare the food and to serve it," she recalled, a note of nostalgia in her voice.

Today's school foodservice directors draw from a much larger pool of workers and are not always so complimentary about their staff. "It has been growing increasingly hard to find good labor," Lyman Graham, the foodservice director of three New Mexico school districts, said in 2011. "It is hard work in a cafeteria, lots of hours standing on your feet and heavy lifting, so a lot of people are looking for jobs that they don't have to do that."[49] Likewise, Bertrand Weber, the foodservice director of the Minneapolis Public Schools, touched on his district's labor shortage during one of our conversations in 2015. "It used to be that within school, the lunch lady a lot of times used to be the mom that was a stay-at-home mom, and it was perfect because she

FIGURE 16. School lunch worker prepares muffins for 750 students in a Maryland high school through the new National School Lunch Program in February 1947. Records of the Office of the Secretary of Agriculture 1900–1959, Child Nutrition Archives.

could drop her kid to school, work a couple of hours, be back at home when the kid went home," Weber explained. "That doesn't happen anymore and I think that's one of the struggles managers face when struggling to staff the 11-am-to-1-pm serving shifts."[50] It is now difficult for directors like Weber to find workers who are able to forego a full-time position and work for just a few hours per day in a school cafeteria. It's a constant challenge to keep these positions filled and, even when they are filled, absenteeism is a problem. Prioritizing a two-hour shift in the middle of the day just isn't worth it, particularly for workers who have other employment options.

The NSLP faces much more competition from other low-wage employers than it once did. Staffing challenges, especially at the entry level, can be solved by improving job quality. The extremely part-time hours (as little as one or two hours per day), low pay, limited summer employment, and limited opportunities for advancement are to blame for the NSLP's labor woes. Yet some of the oral histories collected by the Child Nutrition Archives suggest that a generational difference is to blame.[51] For example, Mary Davis-Palms, an area manager who worked for over thirty-four years in Louisiana's schools, described the older generation of school cafeteria workers as "dedicated, hard-working, loyal, punctual, dependable, caring people," whose work ethic was far superior to that of the new employees, who "don't want to work hard."[52] In another oral history, Brenda Hawkins, a foodservice director from Tennessee, mentioned the new employees were different from the "dedicated ladies" who worked in the schools back when she started in 1971.[53]

Their dedication to the job helped the NSLP grow with limited resources and later withstand brutal budget cuts in the 1980s and a trend toward privatization in the 1990s and early 2000s. Like many of her contemporaries, Kathy Talley watched this dynamic play out during the nearly forty years that she worked in West Virginia's school lunch programs. "You just see that love for children with them and that still continues to be there despite many of the obstacles, cutbacks in labor, cutbacks in monies to purchase equipment, or even food products," she recalled.[54] Whether it was love for children or lack of other employment opportunities that allowed these "dedicated" cafeteria workers to persist when other people may have quit is rather beside the point.[55] Today's workers should not be expected to make emotional and economic sacrifices in order to subsidize and stabilize an underfunded public program. Casting them as bad, irresponsible, or "witchlike" misdirects criticism onto a group of workers (fig. 17)—many of them poor women of color—who cannot afford to be altruistic when neoliberal capitalism makes their lives and livelihoods so precarious.

The poor quality of entry-level jobs in the NSLP disproportionately affects women, who made up 93 percent of K–12 cafeteria workers in 2008, when women accounted for 48 percent of paid workers across the US economy.[56] Gender and motherhood both track women into paid care work, the labor of lunch included. In 2008, 63 percent of cafeteria workers had children under the age of eighteen at home,[57] while the same was true for only 44 percent of the US paid labor force. Even more cafeteria workers had young children when they first took a job in a school cafeteria and chose to stay in the position after their children graduated or left school. In most school cafeterias, frontline jobs are far from lucrative, yet women workers continue to fill these positions at a much higher rate than men.[58] Why? The labor of lunch fits gendered status obligations and the gender wage gap (which, in 2018, ranged from 58 cents to 85 cents per dollar payed to white, non-Hispanic men, depending on women's race and ethnicity) limits women's employment options and funnels far more of them into low-wage work.[59]

Many of the nearly two hundred oral histories I read and at least a dozen of the school foodservice directors, managers, and frontline workers I

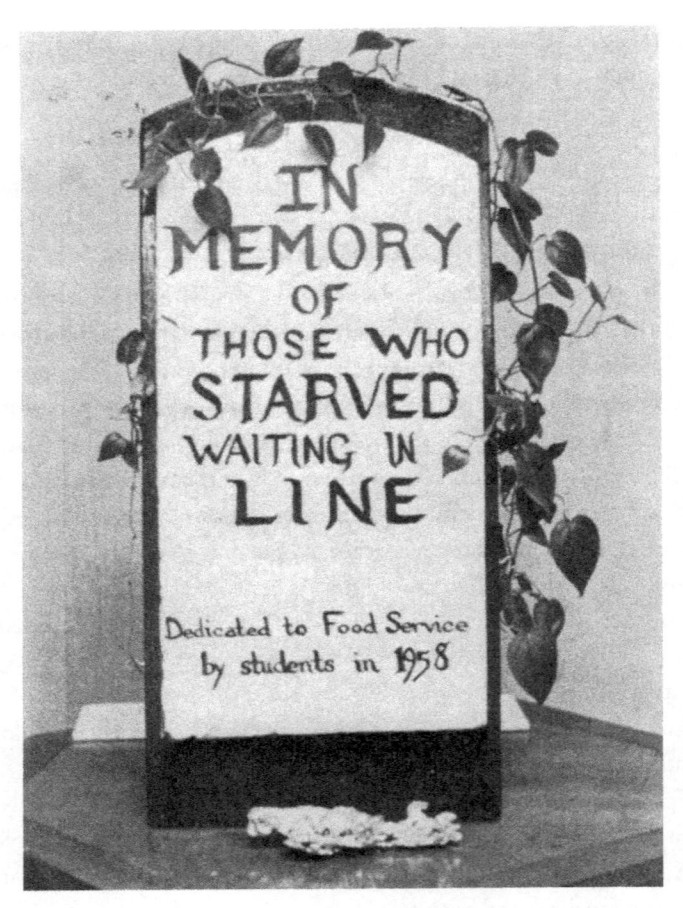

FIGURE 17. Sign from a student-led protest that dramatizes overcrowding in cafeterias and implicitly blames "lunch ladies" for slow service and long lines. Earnestine Camp Photo Collection, Child Nutrition Archives.

interviewed described working in the NSLP as the "perfect mom job." You don't have to send your kid to daycare or hire a babysitter. You can go to your children's activities and help them with their homework after school. And you'll always have the same holidays and vacations, they'd say.[60] This ability to carve out quality time for family life mattered to the workers I interviewed, but many of them get stuck in part-time jobs, working between two and six hours. Without full-time jobs, single parents and primary providers don't earn enough income and many not qualify for employer-provided health insurance through their jobs or their spouses. For those who don't, cobbling

158 · CAFETERIA WORKERS IN THE "PRISON OF LOVE"

together multiple part-time jobs is the new normal.[61] As one cafeteria worker I interviewed put it, "Mom can't hardly make it on this wage down here when it's part-time." Caring for their own kids—let alone the ones at school—is much harder when schools pay them to work only two or three hours per day.

In the summer, things get even harder for cafeteria workers. They get ten to eleven weeks of unpaid "vacation" in the form of summer break. Some cafeteria workers end up staying home with their kids because they can't afford to pay for childcare. Most cafeteria workers are eligible to collect unemployment benefits; however, this is only a small portion of their already meager salaries, so cafeteria workers must seek seasonal employment, shrink their expenses, or both. The USDA has a summer feeding program, but it is much smaller than the NSLP. Workers serve only 200 million federally subsidized lunches during the summer months, compared with 5 billion during the academic year.[62] Unlike the NSLP, the USDA's summer meals program is a bare-bones operation. The majority of shifts involve distributing plastic-wrapped meals and counting the number of kids who come to the schools, parks, and community centers where free summer meals are served. These serving positions are never full-time and often only two or three hours per day, since another set of food-chain workers prepares the lunches in district-owned central kitchens and industrial factories.

Economic circumstances have changed. It's much harder for today's school cafeteria workers to spend their entire careers in child nutrition than it was for previous generations of NSLP employees. Careers like Lova Jean Bullman's have become increasingly rare. She started as a part-time substitute cafeteria worker in the 1970s and eventually became not only the district's foodservice director but also the president of the South Carolina School Food Service Association. Over the years, labor got "so expensive with the fringe benefits and what have you" that the district began converting more and more school kitchen and cafeteria jobs to part-time so that it wouldn't have to pay for fringe benefits. When Bullman retired in 2002, the district was already facing a labor crisis. "It was hard to get people to come in who wanted to work four hours a day," she recalled. "If they came, they would work about a month or two or three months and they would say, 'This is too hard for what I'm bringing home, and get paid once a month, and then they're taking out all these taxes on it.... I've got to find something better.'"[63]

This labor crisis is not unique to school lunch. Scholars Eileen Boris and Jennifer Klein argue it is an artifact of how the low-wage care economy has evolved since the 1930s in the shadow of the welfare state. "The macroeconomic structuring of the occupation, as well as its interpersonal challenges, heighten the stresses of an already emotionally and psychologically intense and economically precarious job," they write. "Workers, family members, state administrators, and policy makers all wring their hands in frustration over the undependability of home healthcare services; for the former, there aren't enough steady hours; for the latter, there never seem to be enough trustworthy workers." Here they are writing specifically about home healthcare workers, but the same dynamic holds for school foodservice workers as well.[64] And it's not because the new generation of workers are less caring or otherwise inferior. Working conditions have worsened. The shorter hours and lack of "voice," or opportunity to contribute to what and how children are fed, impact how cafeteria workers feel about their jobs.[65]

Misidentifying the causes of the labor crisis divides cafeteria workers, pitting old against new. It also undercuts their ability to disrupt the system of cheap care and the many forms of structural oppression upon which the NSLP currently rests. Employees who have worked in child nutrition for decades can, at times, act standoffish, or even hostile, toward temporary workers and part-time employees who are relatively new to school foodservice. These "dedicated" older workers are operating from a place of loyalty to the NSLP as an institution. They don't want standards of care to slip.

This was certainly the case for Nicole, a senior cafeteria manager in Minnesota, whom I interviewed in 2016. Back in the 1990s, she refused to quit her foodservice job at a K–8 school, even when the district decided to cut labor costs by centralizing food production in a district-wide kitchen. What had once been a full-blown production kitchen at Nicole's school was converted into a "prepack" kitchen in a move that eliminated Nicole's eight-hour shift. She chose to take a part-time job in the same school at much lower pay because she worried about how her school and her kids would fare under the new model. "I was working three jobs. . . . I mean it was insane," she recalled during our interview. Quality time with her own family took a backseat to the needs of the children at her school. She worked evenings and weekends until she finally reached a breaking point about a decade later. Rather than leave the district, she applied for a job at another school that offered longer hours and slightly higher pay. She got the job and now juggles two part-time positions instead of three.

Newer employees, in contrast, are more likely to quit when they experience poor working conditions, rather than fight within, and for, the NSLP.[66] How new employees feel about their jobs—and whether they stay in school foodservice long enough to become trusted figures in children's social worlds—matters for the quality of care that kids receive.[67] Stewart Eidel from the Maryland State Department of Education blames the "whole financial structure of the organization."[68] To him, relying on "a lot of those four- or five-hour employees" to balance the budget is a dangerous strategy because it hurts employee morale and dedication. According to Eidel, these positions proliferated when schools "moved away from producing food that actually starts from scratch and then is served, to producing food that has already been manufactured or prepared in some way." Part-time employees think of their jobs in child nutrition as something they "do on the side" and "don't buy into it with their heart," Eidel says. Exceptions to this lack of engagement certainly exist, but Eidel's generalization rings true: the closer school cafeteria workers get to full-time work, the greater percentage of their time, energy, and professional identity is wrapped up in the labor of lunch.

Job detachment and high turnover rates impact part-time entry level positions the most, which is a shame since part-time workers fill front-of-house positions—on the serving line and at cashier stations—that put them in daily contact with students. The need to keep food, labor, and care cheap by outsourcing the work of cooking creates part-time jobs with little autonomy or voice. The basic structure of the NSLP's cheap food economy creates the conditions for frontline workers to disengage and ultimately leave the labor of lunch. This in turn makes it hard for schools to maintain a high quality of care, which depends on the ability of workers and children to form meaningful relationships over an extended period of time. There's a simple fix: longer hours.[69]

"When they used to have all full-time positions, they had no turnover—everybody kept their jobs," Veronica, a school cook in Des Moines, Iowa, told me when I visited her school in 2016. "We just had a lady that retired from here last year that had forty-some years in," she noted. Back when most jobs were full-time, Veronica felt like she was part of a "family" united by a common concern for "the kids and what they got to eat." These feelings faded after the district built a central kitchen in an effort to improve food safety and cut costs. Since the early days of the New England Kitchen in the 1890s, school districts have relied on central kitchens to prepare and distribute food to multiple buildings on the cheap. But this division of labor alienates frontline cafeteria workers from their jobs. They interact with the kids, but they're not serving food they're investing in having prepared.

Central kitchens do not have to contribute to deskilling and the proliferation of "bad" jobs in the NSLP. Some real food champions are reimagining central kitchens, not as minifactories designed to pump out premade school lunches but as food hubs designed to receive, minimally process, and package clean, locally grown, and other real foods into forms that are easier for schools to use given their time constraints and lack of kitchen infrastructure. That said, central kitchens divide K–12 foodservice workers into two camps: at one extreme are relational care workers who come face-to-face with children every day but do little, if any, food preparation and at the other are production workers who prepare and package lunches without ever seeing the children they feed. This split can lead to distrust, disrespect, and even hostility among K–12 foodservice workers, which weakens workers' ability to build the solidarity necessary to fight for real food and real jobs in their schools.

Debbie, a central kitchen worker in the Midwest once told me, "The people in the schools think that they work harder than we do here." Frontline workers at the schools in her district perform emotional labor in addition to physical and mental labor, unlike central-kitchen workers who do not interact with the kids. The extra layer of emotional labor and the interactive nature of their work made some people in the schools think they were working harder and for less pay in part-time jobs than the full-time staff at the central kitchen. Simply put, Debbie's district values "production" work more than interactive care work—a reality that is all too common given the critical role that frontline workers play in children's school lunch experience and the need for high-quality jobs in communities across the country. Frontline workers picked up on this, but their frustration led to infighting instead of solidarity.

Across the board, frontline workers' reactions to deskilling—whether at the hands of a central kitchen or Big Food corporations—are far from uniform. They typically respond much more favorably to "built-in" labor when it doesn't seem to threaten the quality of their jobs or the quality of the care they can provide. For example, Arlene Colston—a high school kitchen manager in Alabama—commented in a 2012 oral history that the introduction of precooked factory-made foods made her job "much better."[70] The ability to reheat precooked items made her job far less stressful. She no longer had to predict exactly how many portions of each menu item to cook from scratch. If she ran out of an item, she could run to the freezer, quickly grab more pallets of pizza or bags of chicken nuggets and warm them on an as-needed basis before the next wave of hungry children entered the cafeteria doors. Irma Maye, now retired after decades of work in an Alabama school kitchen, also appreciated how school lunches became far easier and faster to prepare after she started her job in the 1970s. "A long time ago we had to make rolls from scratch," she

FIGURE 18. Workers preparing lunch in a Hyattsville, MD, high school in February 1947. Records of the Office of the Secretary of Agriculture 1900–1959, Child Nutrition Archives.

recalled in a 2012 oral history. This required what she described as "a lot of preparation" and it was tricky: "You've got to have your yeast just right."[71]

Preparing fresh food required advanced planning and preparation (fig. 18). "We used to do greens. We had to wash those," Irma Maye explained. "We used to do dried beans—pinto beans, black-eyed peas, even lima beans. We used to have to pick through them and wash them." It may have been repetitive, mundane, and time-consuming, but doing this level of processing in house meant longer hours for Maye and her coworkers. Buying commercially baked bread, shelf-stable processed foods, and frozen convenience foods made the work of cooking easier. "I really like the frozen better, because it's close to fresh," Irma Maye explained. "And it's time-saving; really it is."[72] For her and the vast majority of workers I interviewed, fresh preparation is still the gold standard for the NSLP, but shortcuts like "built-in" labor are necessary in order to keep school lunch fast and cheap.

What counts as "scratch" cooking has changed over time, just like the ingredients school cooks use to prepare recipes from scratch. "The carrots come in cleaned and washed, sliced and packaged. So does the lettuce," noted Paul McElwain, the former director of Nutrition Services for the State of

Kentucky, in his 2004 oral history.[73] Even schools with the culinary capacity to prepare lunches from scratch began to expect, and ultimately rely on, commercial processors who could make whole foods easier and faster to cook. From there, it's a slippery slope to full-blown convenience cooking, which Big Food manufacturers, food brokers, and product representatives bill as both safer and cheaper than scratch cooking. If a school can reheat and serve a chicken ring (imagine an onion ring, but the inside is chopped-and-formed chicken) and have it count as both a serving of protein and a serving of grains, why devote time to preparing baked chicken thighs? As Donna Matsufuru, who spent thirty-five years working in the child nutrition profession in Hawaii, put it in her 2007 oral history: "Most of the managers don't want a whole bird . . . where you roast the turkey and you get the bones and you boil the bones and you make your own stock for your gravy."[74]

No foodservice manager or school food administrator wants to risk sickening a child. The precooked option is the safe option, the thinking goes. Even with mandatory trainings, workers might not always follow food safety protocol. There are reasons, too, why school cooks and cafeteria workers may prefer to remain "mixers" and "reheaters," as they often referred to themselves during my fieldwork in districts that didn't do much in the way of scratch cooking. First, they worry about not having the culinary skills to cook and bake using minimally processed ingredients. Second is the possibility that the labor of lunch might become harder—at least temporarily—without an increase in workers' hourly wages or hiring more staff to absorb the extra work. Third, some workers worry that kids won't like the food they make from scratch. The ubiquity of factory-made foods in school lunches, kids' meals at fast food and family restaurants, and the frozen foods aisles of supermarkets and convenience stores reinforces the idea that "real" food is for adults, not children.

The deskilling of home cooks is part of a broader gendered transformation that has occurred within the American food system over the past century.[75] As multinational food and agriculture corporations have gained ever greater power over domestic food policy and markets, women—the people who continue to do the majority of both unpaid and paid food work—have increasingly been taught to judge food quality on price, taste, and nutrition alone. The industrial diet that Big Food companies dish up looks much worse when the discussion of quality is broadened to incorporate food purity, animal welfare, labor standards, and environmental impact. That said, we are not yet at the point when home cooking has been reduced to "doing the microwave," as one now-retired school foodservice director tried to persuade me.

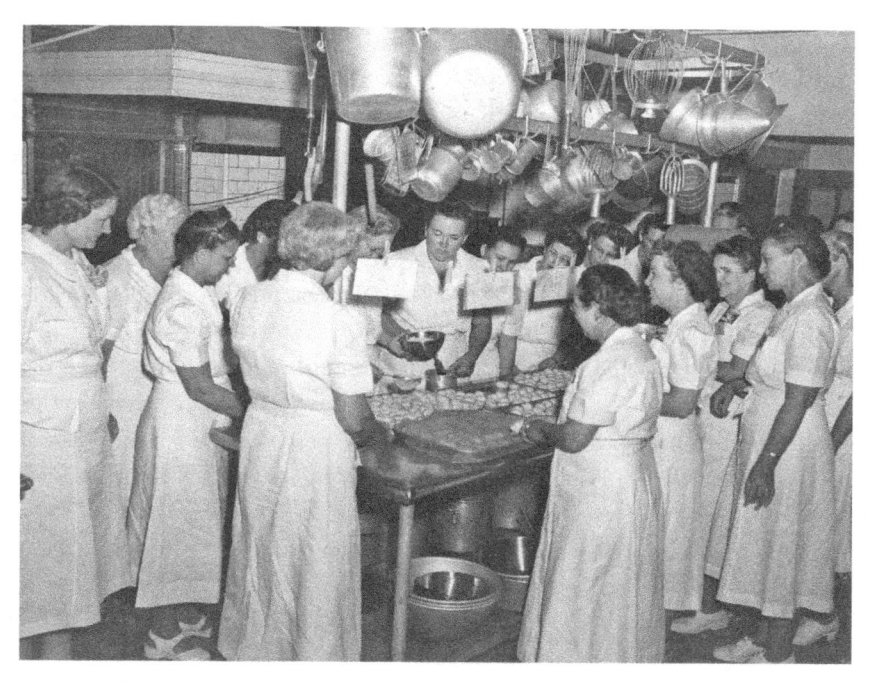

FIGURE 19. Arkansas school lunch managers learning bread-making techniques during a summer workshop in 1948. Earnestine Camp Photo Collection, Child Nutrition Archives.

Americans still cook at home and many folks are taking a newfound interest in changing the food system.[76]

But even if home cooking had been deskilled to the point where stoves and ovens were obsolete, why should schools be expected to follow suit? The answer, in part, has to do with the NSLP's reliance on the unpaid, highly gendered peripheries of the capitalist economy to equip potential recruits with at least some rudimentary culinary skills that could be harnessed for use in public school lunch programs (fig. 19).[77] Even women who were dismissively labeled as "unskilled housewives" were expected to know how to cook during the first few decades of the NSLP. To be sure, preparing a meal for a family of five or even a dinner party of twenty-five is quite different from preparing a meal for five hundred or five thousand children, but local administrators, school boards, and policymakers didn't always recognize the difference. They conflated the ability to cook for a small group of children in the home with the ability to cook for a far larger group of children at school.

The leaders of the nonprofit school lunch movement understood that the public work of feeding children required different, specialized skills. They lobbied the federal government to create professional standards and asked for money to train workers in key topics like nutrition, sanitation, ordering, menu planning, bulk food production, and service techniques. This was back in the 1940s. It took another seventy years—until 2015—for the federal government to actually create professional standards and training requirements for school foodservice directors and frontline employees as part of the Healthy, Hunger-Free Kids Act of 2010. Until then, it was up to individual states, local school boards, and the School Nutrition Association (formerly ASFSA) to set their own professional standards and training requirements. Some states, including Louisiana, took this seriously. Extra funding from the state made a huge difference, according to Louise Lapeze, an area supervisor from Baton Rouge, Louisiana. So, too, did the presence of a strong regional food culture. We "still had moms coming in who had been trained in food service at their mothers' knees," she explained. "They learned food safety and brought that knowledge with them.... They also had food preparation skills." This wasn't unique to Baton Rouge. "Almost every school in Louisiana made homemade rolls every day [and] just prepared food from scratch," recalled Lapeze in her 2009 oral history.[78]

Sylvia Grabert, the retired foodservice director of rural Iberia Parish, Louisiana, told a similar story. She and her staff were committed to serving what she called "real" food: simple lunches made from scratch using standardized recipes and donated USDA commodities. Every once in a while, they even managed to treat the children to costlier, more labor-intensive regional specialties like fried catfish, crawfish étouffée, and chicken gumbo.[79] Back in the 1970s, people used to joke that it was easy to identify Iberia's school cafeteria workers even outside of school when they weren't wearing uniforms. One simply had to look for the women with "the biggest muscles and most scars." It wasn't easy work and accidents happened. Chopping bushels of fresh vegetables, hoisting huge pots of bubbling soup, and ferrying tray after tray of fresh-baked rolls from ovens to cooling racks took a toll on workers' bodies. The coastal Louisiana humidity meant only the toughest women could withstand the sweltering heat of Iberia's high school kitchen, which was outfitted with six twelve-burner stoves and had no air conditioning.

Despite the tough working conditions and national trends, Iberia's school lunch workers were able to make continuous improvements to the quality of their lunch program under Sylvia Grabert's leadership. When she first arrived in 1970, only 32 percent of Iberia's students participated in the NSLP. By the time she retired in 1998, that number had grown to over 80 percent. In her first year on the job, Grabert convinced the school superintendent to invest in her plan to improve the quality of school lunches and expand the district's free and reduced-price lunch program, which would provide guaranteed federal reimbursement for qualifying students. The school lunch program had been operating at a deficit for years, and the district was eager to see it become self-sustaining. The superintendent gave Grabert one month to test out her ideas. It was all she needed. Paying "customers" liked the revamped school lunches. So, too, did the poor children who participated in ever greater numbers after the NSLP's free lunch provision went into effect.

Over the years, Iberia's school lunch staff kept their participation numbers high by making sure each cafeteria was "a very social gathering place" for students and teachers alike. This required a fair amount of emotional labor, especially during times of crisis, like the early 1980s, when Texaco closed down an oil refinery and employees were transferred away from the parish. Unemployment rates rose, families moved, and school enrollment declined, but Sylvia Grabert and her team did their best to care well for the Iberia community. Every day, they served made-from-scratch entrées, homemade bread, fresh vegetables, and salads. When pricing school lunches, Grabert always kept in mind the families who were "near poor" but not poor enough to qualify for free and reduced-price lunch subsidies. By the time she retired in 1998, the cost of a "full-price" lunch was still just sixty cents. A bargain in most people's estimation.

Some foodservice directors, including Sylvia Grabert, kept costs low and quality high by investing in culinary capacity. This involved not only a commitment to training, mentorship, and oversight, but also the strategic use of work simplification tools and techniques. June Crews, a program supervisor in Charlottesville, Virginia, visited her schools every week. "We made all of our breads, all of our hamburger buns, hotdog buns, rolls, pies, anything, we made from scratch," she recalled. "We had neat cutters for the hamburger rolls and the hotdog buns [and] . . . recipes to pass out if we needed those."[80] This was back in the 1960s, before the NSLP came to rely almost exclusively on "built-in" labor. "We used to teach lots and lots of classes about basic skills of food preparation: how to bake bread, how to work with raw meat products—even butchering skills, and desserts, all kinds of 'from scratch' products, and fruit and vegetable preparation," Marilyn Briggs, a foodservice director from California explained in her 2004 oral history. The introduction of new systems of production changed the type of training that new hires needed in order to become school lunch workers. "With central kitchens it's a whole

FIGURE 20. Cooks preparing lunch at a small-town Wisconsin school in 1954. Arthur M. Vinje Collection, Wisconsin Historical Society.

different way of operating, a whole different set of skills," she noted. "With reheating, even fewer skills are required."[81]

By time the Healthy, Hunger-Free Kids Act was being debated in the early 2000s, any training cafeteria workers received was much more likely to consist of topics like food safety, sanitation, and branding than baking skills or recipe simplification.[82] Briggs, among others, is saddened by this. "It seems to me that [scratch production] was just more interesting and more exciting in terms of skills that were learned and ability to use them in lots of places," she explained. Scratch cooking was, in her view, "very rewarding" for frontline cafeteria workers. They had "a product at the end of [their] hard work" and were able to "feel creative" by adding their own touches to recipes (fig. 20). They even had a hand in developing and testing new recipes until they'd found the perfect formula. It was "very exciting," Briggs recalls.[83]

Now it is far more common for districts to invite frontline cafeteria workers to do product testing of premade foods—but deciding which frozen pizza is best just doesn't have the same effect on worker morale. People tend to gain more satisfaction from work tasks that challenge them, so long as they feel supported in making decisions and tackling the challenges that arise.[84] The lack of job autonomy can be crushing for frontline workers, especially during times when they feel frustrated or embarrassed by the quality of the food. "One time the sloppy joes looked like cat food," Lydia, an elementary school lunch server in New Haven, Connecticut, told me during my fieldwork in 2014. She apologized over and over to the kids as they made their way through the lunch line, consciously defying her manager's instructions to encourage the kids to take school lunch no matter what.

During my visits to Lydia's cafeteria, a group of sixth-grade girls used the words *chalk, poop, nasty, plastic,* and *disgusting* to describe the school lunches. A table of boys sitting nearby flagged me over to complain about the grilled cheese sandwiches, which were served in plastic bags that had melted and adhered to the outsides of the bread, forming an inedible cheese-plastic mixture. The kids even considered the fresh foods to be subpar and pointed to the raw carrots on their plates that looked "like they had been freeze dried" as evidence. These kids, who came from more affluent families than most students in the district, had more flexibility to choose whether to participate in the NSLP on a given day. Most didn't. The food quality just wasn't high enough, and there seemed to be a cultural assumption that school lunch was gross, even on days when the meals and salad bar looked better than the contents of an average lunch box.

"If you can get the home-lunch kids to eat this food, it would be a miracle," Lydia told me one day. She'd love to try to make this happen, but her school didn't make anything on site. All the food was delivered premade from the district's central kitchen, so Lydia felt there wasn't much she could do to improve the quality of the food or shift the cafeteria culture. "If we had a say, if we had a choice, ... we would be floored to cook for these kids," one of her coworkers explained. "These are our kids, our grandkids, our coworkers' nieces, nephews."

For New Haven's school cafeteria workers, the issue of food quality is deeply personal. Back in 2008, UNITE HERE Local 217, the labor union representing New Haven's K–12 cafeteria workers, built a labor-community coalition including workers, parents, and activists to kick out Aramark, a for-profit management company, from New Haven Public Schools. Their efforts were bolstered by a national tour of unionized Aramark workers and a joint campaign between UNITE HERE and the Service Employees International Union (SEIU) to boot Aramark from the nation's private and public cafeterias.[85]

ORGANIZING FOR CHANGE

The national anti-Aramark activism in 2008 was a tipping point for Local 217, but workers had organized for years, demanding that the city of New Haven create a new economy of care that met the needs of children and families. They issued a fourteen-page report, *Putting Kids First?*, and called for public hearings to investigate whether the "rebates and discounts Aramark received for food purchases may have influenced the buying of less nutritious food for New Haven's kids."[86] UNITE HERE Local 35, which includes unionized members of Yale University's dining services, custodial, and maintenance staff, waged a simultaneous campaign. The workers in New Haven's two largest educational institutions united across workplaces to force a public conversation about the merits of returning to what is known in the industry as "self-operation" or "self-op."

At a February 2008 rally, Bruce Raynor and John Wilhelm, two of the UNITE HERE national leaders, stressed the need for a nationwide campaign to end outsourcing to private management companies. "This is wonderful coming together here in New Haven with all of these unions and all these community groups, but it's just as important to join with people in Philadelphia and New York and Detroit and all over the world because we are dealing with a worldwide company," Wilhelm said. There's always a risk that administrators will outsource their nutrition programs to private management companies at the first sign of a budgetary shortfall. Private management companies promise cost-savings—and a self-sustaining school lunch program—but do not always deliver the expected results. Under Aramark management, New Haven's child nutrition department was running at a $1 million deficit. "They produce deficits for schools and profits for themselves," said Raynor at the February 2008 rally.[87] Later that year, the New Haven Board of Education voted not to renew Aramark's contract and to instead bring management back in-house.

But campaign victories don't always have tidy endings. By the time I started doing fieldwork in New Haven in 2011, the cafeteria workers had been without a contract for over a year. Self-operation hadn't led to the improvements in food and job quality that children and cafeteria workers needed. All the while, the city's local food movement was gaining strength. Farmers markets and community-supported agriculture programs were popping up in urban parks and nearby farms. This movement made its way to schools in 2008, when the district hired Tim Cipriano, a chef turned school lunch director who calls himself the "local food dude." "We want to stop being experts at the can opener and start being experts on cooking," the district's chief administrative officer told the local newspaper.[88]

As New Haven Public Schools began sourcing more local food and serving "real" food, administrators continued to rely on built-in labor to keep school lunch cheap. The district eliminated full-time positions at the schools and shifted as much food preparation as possible to its central kitchen. There, a team of workers, many of whom had higher seniority than the school-based workers, prepared lunches that were shipped out to the school kitchens to be reheated by part-time general workers (the foodservice department's lowest-level permanent position).

When I first met Chef Tim, about two and a half years into his tenure as New Haven's school foodservice director, he had already garnered national acclaim for the city's real food transition. He was written up in the *New York Times*, recognized as a champion school lunch reformer by the White House and First Lady Michelle Obama's Let's Move campaign, and selected for multiple industry awards. He became a sought-after consultant for companies that were interested in manufacturing clean-label products for schools. "We need to work with manufacturers to make products that mirror what we can create [from scratch]," he often said. For a brief period, Cipriano was an advisor to ConAgra Foods, a Fortune 500 food company that sells highly processed foods to schools. An avid networker, Chef Tim brought new resources to the district to bolster its farm-to-school efforts and secured new resources like salad bars and a food truck to make fresh food more accessible to children. But the day-to-day management of such a large district left him with little time for his family or the antihunger and local food advocacy work he pursued in his free time, so he resigned at the start of the 2012 school year and moved first to a smaller, more affluent Connecticut school district and then to private industry.

It fell to the workers to continue the push for real food in New Haven public schools. But unlike the top-down approach to school lunch reform instituted by the board of education under Chef Tim's leadership, members of UNITE HERE Local 217 wanted real food and real jobs. After booting Aramark from the city's schools, district officials looked for new ways to keep the labor of lunch cheap. One strategy involved instituting what the industry calls "split shifts" in order to avoid paying for healthcare benefits. According to Local 217 labor organizer Cristina Cruz-Uribe, an employee might "work an hour in the morning, then maybe switch schools and go work another two, two and a half, two and three quarters, all getting them to three hours and forty-five minutes, which is fifteen minutes short of what they need to qualify for affordable family health insurance." This strategy for cost cutting hurt entry-level employees with little or no seniority the most, but everyone in the city's school kitchens and cafeterias felt the impacts. As Cruz-Uribe explained: "It's not good for either kitchen to have people running in and out, and it doesn't create a team that would be capable of doing more complex recipes . . . more fresh cooking."

Local 217 workers of all seniority levels decided to stand in solidarity and launch a campaign for "real food, real jobs." They wanted to banish cheap food from school cafeterias, improve their working conditions, and care for students without becoming "prisoners of love." And they had a compelling case. My fieldwork gave me ample opportunity to visit the city's central kitchen, grade schools, junior highs, and high schools. Schools were serving more locally sourced produce, "on-the-bone" chicken, and whole grains, but the vast majority of frontline workers felt like they were still just reheating premade food. The only space for creativity was the salad bar, which they prepared on-site with fresh ingredients. Likewise, central kitchen workers often seemed perplexed when I asked about local food and scratch cooking. They referenced a few memorable recipes, but the majority of their time was still spent unboxing and mixing premade foods, like "speed scratch" but on a larger scale.

Real food lite won't solve the crisis of care in the NSLP, but real food prepared by workers with sufficient training, resources, and compensation could. Kids deserve high-quality care provided by people who are treated with respect and afforded the economic security to care for themselves and their families. Worker-leaders in UNITE HERE Local 217 understand this and are actively banding together to hold public actions, send delegations to key decision-makers, and enlist the help of parents to compel the city to "put kids first."[89] To do this, they must convince people to reject the idea that lunch ladies do not know how to cook, do not want to learn, and aren't worth teaching. It isn't just the decisions made by local school boards but also those made by state and federal governments that are part of the problem. Public sector employees deserve better and ignoring their needs has consequences not only for cafeteria workers' ability to care for themselves and their families but also for their level of commitment to the job and their capacity to fight for a new economy of care in American public schools (fig. 21).

If the real food movement hopes to build a more just, egalitarian, and sustainable future, it cannot continue to treat school cafeteria workers as

FIGURE 21. UNITE HERE Local 1 workers gather in protest in April 2012 to demand an end to frozen airline-type lunches in Chicago Public Schools. Courtesy UNITE HERE.

nothing more than a cost to minimize. Nor can it remain complicit in a system that tracks children into different food systems based on their economic class. Instead, activists must recognize that lunch ladies can be their greatest allies in building a new economy of care for people and the planet, beginning in the school cafeteria. When reformers, workers, students and officials come together to elevate, rather than degrade the labor of lunch, whole communities will benefit. As Minneapolis Public Schools foodservice director Bertrand Weber once told me, cafeteria workers need livable wages, and it isn't fair to pit job quality against food quality. What we need is a "much deeper conversation about what we want food in schools to be, and what we want it to be able to support." So let's have that conversation.

FIVE

Building a Real Food Economy

Empowering school kitchen and cafeteria workers to cook real food from scratch using locally sourced and school-grown ingredients can transform the entire culture of the National School Lunch Program (NSLP). I witnessed this in action and interviewed dozens of workers who spoke about how much the shift from a cheap food economy to a real food economy impacted their ability to care for students and for their own families. The real food movement, and the country as a whole, has much to gain from rethinking and ultimately reorganizing the labor of lunch to allow frontline cafeteria workers to do more than just reheat processed factory food.

Consider Randi, a middle school prep cook, who prides herself on being a real food ambassador for Minneapolis Public Schools (MPS). She's not one to sit back and stay silent when a student points to an unfamiliar entrée and proclaims, "Ew, that is nasty!"

"You ain't tried it," she'll lob back. "It's good!"

In fact, she told me when I interviewed her in 2016, these kids don't know how good they've got it. In the 1980s, when Randi was a K–12 student in MPS, the food was "always in plastic." Thousands of uniform, prepackaged airline-type lunches rolled off the assembly lines at the central nutrition center MPS had built in 1975, to be trucked to schools all over the city. Randi never ate a school lunch that wasn't reheated and served to her in a single-portion plastic container. Now, she serves MPS students what she describes as "real food instead of... microwave food."

It's a relatively recent change. Even in 2012, when Randi was first hired through a temporary staffing agency as a part-time elementary school food service assistant, MPS used the central nutrition center to manufacture pre-pack lunches for most of the city's schools. As a woman in her late thirties,

Randi wasn't exactly thrilled about taking a job reheating the plastic containers of her youth in a school cafeteria. Nor was she particularly comfortable with her assignment in an elementary school—interacting with little kids was not her strong suit. At least that's how she felt at first. She was no stranger to care work: she'd spent her entire adult life feeding the sick and elderly in hospitals and assisted living homes. But "crybaby kindergartners" posed a new challenge for her patience. Despite these initial misgivings, Randi quickly developed a knack for interacting with even the youngest students at her school, calling them by name and remembering their favorite meals. But when a prep cook position opened in 2015 at an MPS middle school slated to switch to on-site cooking, Randi jumped at the chance to work for more hours at a higher wage.

The middle school's switch to on-site cooking was part of a much broader set of changes afoot in MPS. Under the leadership of Bertrand Weber, who had become the foodservice director in 2012, the district committed to building and renovating kitchens across the district so that workers could cook on site. MPS has also begun to clean up its supply chain, partner with local farms to source ingredients, and nurture communities to learn about and celebrate the real food movement. Their work isn't done, but their progress is impressive and can serve as a model for how to improve the quality of food, care, and working conditions in other school districts.

These changes have been great for Randi, who is now a middle school prep cook. Instead of having a part-time job, she now has career pathway and a more satisfying workday. Her new job is by no means "perfect," and she still struggles to make ends meet as a single mother. But she is now eligible for a wider range of employer-provided benefits, and she has found a higher degree of intellectual stimulation and personal satisfaction. Randi likes the variety of cooking from scratch. Unboxing and reheating the same old precooked meals in their plastic containers day after day was monotonous. It was also disempowering. Now that she has the opportunity to cook school lunches from scratch—and give MPS students healthier, fresher food than she had as a kid—she takes a lot more pride in the work.

"This is what I did from scratch," Randi tells her middle school students as they peer across the lunch line into the serving wells to get a glimpse of what's for lunch. Their lunches aren't cooked in some anonymous Big Food factory, but rather by Randi and her team—real people the students can recognize and go to with suggestions for improvement, although they don't cook everything from scratch at the schools themselves. In what MPS calls "fast scratch," some items, like salad dressing, béchamel sauce, and marinara sauce, are prepared at the central kitchen in order to make recipes cheaper, faster, and easier to prepare at the schools. Randi likes this model much better than the previous one and tells her students the food is tasty because she "cooks with love." Now she eagerly invites even the most skeptical students to sample her cooking and offer feedback. Before, when she worked at the elementary school kitchen reheating and serving precooked, preplated school lunches, she dreaded hearing negative comments from students. There wasn't anything she could do as an individual to help improve the quality of their lunches. Now, at the middle school production kitchen, she feels empowered to use her skills and ingenuity to make the food as tasty, attractive, and healthy as she can. Negative comments, when they happen, don't sting so much since she knows the quality is much better than even a few years ago. Besides, if the kids' suggestions fit the USDA's nutritional requirements and the district's budget, Randi knows she might actually be able to use them.

Decentralizing production, by shifting away from a central nutrition facility to on-site school kitchens, has helped Randi and other MPS workers feel connected to a broader movement to serve children real food. One of her coworkers told me how wonderful it feels to "put real food on a real plate and hand it to [the kids], and have it be just this amazing, colorful, beautiful thing." Another chimed in to say, "We eat better here than we do at a lot of other places I've worked." She had spent decades working back-of-the-house in restaurant kitchens before becoming an MPS prep cook in 2014. Amy, another MPS cafeteria worker, known to her friends as a total foodie, tells people that her kids "would eat hot lunch every day at Minneapolis Public Schools," but they attend a suburban school that serves total "junk," so she packs a lunch for them every day. Like Randi, Amy is proud of the food they make from scratch, especially on days like Minnesota Thursday, when all ingredients are locally sourced. She even whipped out her phone to show me a picture of a Minnesota Thursday lunch that she'd shared on Facebook: a plate filled with baked chicken, kale salad with carrots and tomatoes, and a Minnesota apple that was "so good, so crunchy." Amy hopes such posts will generate more than Facebook Likes. She wants to ignite parents in her children's school district to fight for changes to the lunch program there.

As a parent of two MPS children, Randi is very grateful the food quality has improved so much in the few short years since she's been with the district. Back in 2012, the chicken her children ate at school was the most generic of precooked industrial chicken. Now, they get to eat roasted Smart Chicken (cage-free birds raised in the Midwest without the use of antibiotics) prepared fresh and served hot and crispy from the oven.[1] They also get to choose from an assortment of hot vegetable sides and a cold salad bar, both of which feature locally grown produce on most days. It always puts a smile on Randi's face to see her daughter walk through the lunch line at the middle school where she works, lunch tray loaded with healthy, freshly cooked food. Baked chicken, salad bar, and fresh fruit is Randi's youngest daughter's favorite school lunch.

Randi is even happier that her older daughter, a high schooler who suffers from chronic stomach problems, has the ability to eat real food that leaves her feeling far healthier and more energized than an airline-type lunch ever did. She's not alone: Parents from across the district seem to appreciate the switch to on-site cooking and local sourcing. The kids seem to approve as well. One of Randi's coworkers told me they started saying "thank you" to the cafeteria staff much more frequently now that they have scratch-cooked lunches. Another told me the kids are so excited to "see that the food is in front of them and that it's piping hot, and looks delicious, and smells delicious" that she constantly has to "wipe off the little nose marks" from the glass partition that protects the food from sneezes and curious hands.

When parents ask Randi her opinion about school lunch, she tells them it has really changed and encourages them to go eat lunch at their children's schools to see for themselves. Her opinion has credibility in the community: she's a mom, born and raised in Minneapolis, who interacts with an economically, racially, and ethnically diverse set of students every day. During the 2016–2017 school year, about 63 percent of the 36,000-plus students enrolled in MPS qualified for free or reduced-price school lunches and 7 percent of students experienced homelessness or lack of stable housing.[2] About 66 percent of students enrolled in MPS were students of color and 20 percent were English learners. These English learners speak nearly ninety different languages, the most prevalent of which are Spanish, Somali, Hmong, and Oromo. English learners qualify for free or reduced-price lunches at a much higher rate (about 90%) than the district as a whole.[3] For those parents and children who need help navigating the ins and outs of MPS's school lunch program, cafeteria workers like Randi act as important intermediaries both during the application process and when children walk through the cafeteria line.

Frontline workers in MPS play a vital role in building community support for the NSLP. They publicize the district's efforts to serve kids real food by sharing pictures and stories within their social networks of fellow parents, neighbors, churchgoers, and Facebook friends. Anna, an MPS area supervisor who quickly rose through the ranks from prep cook to management, summed up a sentiment that arose frequently in my discussions with frontline staff. "What we're doing, we're proud of. And we should be," she said. "A lot of these kids get TV dinner at home. A lot of them eat food out of a convenience store. Hot Cheetos and Takis are huge." That's why she finds it so personally rewarding to serve kids a lunch that looks like "a home-cooked meal on a plate," which their parents or other caretakers may not always have the time, energy, or income to prepare. At school, they can "try things that they wouldn't necessarily try on their own," like hummus and roasted brussels sprouts.

A NEW VISION FOR SCHOOL LUNCH

It was this dream of providing children with wholesome, scratch-cooked lunches that drew MPS Culinary and Wellness Services director Bertrand Weber to the labor of lunch back in 2003. He'd trained at École Hotelière de Genève in Switzerland and built a career cooking for people in country clubs, resorts, and hotels. The school cafeteria was a world away from his stomping grounds—that is, until his son, Eric, was diagnosed with type 1 diabetes at age seven. Weber became the "angry parent" at his son's school in Burnsville, Minnesota. "All the school was serving was refined carbohydrates and processed foods, which were the last things Eric needed," he later recalled.[4] So when the position of foodservice director became available in a nearby school district, in Hopkins, Minnesota, he quit his country club job to join the movement for real school food. He quickly became "fairly famous in school food circles," according to sociologist Janet Poppendieck, for his efforts to "fix" school lunch at the local level through scratch cooking and farm-to-school sourcing.[5]

The founder of the Homegrown Minneapolis Food Policy Council, who happened to be the mayor's wife, encouraged Weber to take over leadership of Minneapolis's school foodservice department after the longtime director retired in 2011. During his interview with the school district, Weber says he was "very straightforward": If they wanted someone to continue the status quo, he was not their man. If, on the other hand, they wanted to invest in substantive change, he'd sign the hiring paperwork on the spot.[6] MPS offered

Weber the job, and suddenly he found himself in charge of a minifactory. The central nutrition center produced about 43,000 prepackaged lunches each day and trucked them to seventy-three schools across the city. But over the years, cooking had been increasingly outsourced to Big Food, and the central kitchen had been stripped of the culinary production equipment it once had. It operated mostly as a receiving, packaging, and distribution center—much like a production facility for the airlines.

Weber had a dramatically different vision for school lunch, and so did a vocal group of parents. "People were appalled by the food service, and I told them I was just as appalled," he explained to a reporter from *Education Week*. "I told them some ideas we had for making things better, but I also was very upfront that this was going to take time. I couldn't just flip one switch and go from a food-packing plant to a real kitchen."[7] Converting to scratch cooking—whether at the central nutrition center or on-site kitchens—would take time and resources. It would also take sustained community support. History taught Weber as much. On one of his first days in his new office, he found a small stack of weathered newspaper clippings from 1975, when the central nutrition center was first opened. "There was an outcry that we would serve kids TV dinners at school and about the environmental impact of prepack," Weber noted. But the outcry quieted, and "nothing was ever done."[8]

Seven years in, Weber and his team have accomplished a lot. They've been praised by district administrators, professional organizations, national trade magazines, and even the US Department of Agriculture for their real food revolution.[9] That said, Weber is among the first to admit that their changes didn't always go according to plan, especially in 2012 when MPS first began investing in a district-wide kitchen renovation project. By December 2015, when I began spending time in MPS kitchens and interviewing frontline workers, the district had three different types of school lunch operations: prepack only, prepack plus salad bar, and on-site cooking plus salad bar. There was a definite learning curve. As the labor of lunch shifted from the central production facility into the schools, figuring out the appropriate staffing levels was particularly challenging for management. This transition was stressful, even scary, for workers who were afraid they might be replaced if they couldn't adapt to the new system quickly enough. "I really was very candid about the vision and got the staff excited initially, but moved so fast that maybe [I] left them behind," Weber acknowledged during one of my visits to the district in 2016, as we sat in his second-floor office overlooking the assembly lines on the central kitchen floor below.

During the first few years of MPS's transition, all parts of the system—food, infrastructure, and staffing—were in flux.[10] Some of the senior staff members were excited about the new opportunities scratch cooking had to offer; others were ambivalent or even resistant. There were some workers who "felt that they were maybe not heard or not respected or not appreciated for the twenty-plus years that they were here, because we were making so many changes," Weber admitted. Deborah, a high school cook, was one of them. She'd been with the district for twenty years and had a lot of local knowledge and expertise to offer the new managerial regime, but when she spoke up, she felt they didn't take her seriously because she wasn't *really* a cook. In other words, she hadn't been to culinary school or worked in restaurants—just school kitchens. When Weber chose to make strategic hires to bring more people with culinary skill into the school kitchens, he risked alienating existing staff like Deborah, who had served prepack meals to Minneapolis schoolchildren for years or even decades.

Rectifying missteps and mending relationships strained by rapid change and top-down decision-making took time and intentional collaboration with union stewards to create training programs and pathways for existing workers. Deborah is one of those union stewards. "As a whole, I don't think they respect any of us that have been here longer than them," she told me the first time we talked, noting that district management had swept in and started making changes without talking to the lunch ladies. Several months later, when I returned to MPS for another round of conversations, she was in better spirits. She'd been asked to join a planning committee to give input on the kitchen renovation plans for the district, so she knew her experience was being valued. She'd also undergone training to cook with fresh ingredients in a newly renovated on-site kitchen, before being promoted to a full-time position. Ultimately, Deborah decided to embrace the changes, but some of her older coworkers, she said, chose to retire or stay in prepack "warming kitchens" instead.

Deborah was conflicted by these outcomes. On the one hand, she felt Weber and his team weren't doing enough to promote from within: the new, higher-paid, full-time positions in schools with renovated production kitchens disproportionately went to outsiders who were joining school foodservice for the first time. This "leapfrogging" seemed unfair to the low-level employees—mostly women—who had spent years earning seniority while toughing it out on the bottom rungs of the school lunch job hierarchy. On the other hand, Deborah believed that hiring folks with strong culinary skills helped the transition to scratch cooking go much more smoothly than it otherwise would have. "The new people that are coming on have gone to culinary school, have been chefs at other restaurants or hotels or whatever and they are coming on board and joining us lunch ladies and teaching us some of their tricks too," she explained.

Anna, one of these new people hired in 2012, saw things a bit more optimistically. "There are many people that have been here for years that have adapted well," she observed. "They want their kids that go to school to be able to have access to those foods, especially with Minneapolis being as high free and reduced-rate, and our poverty level as high as it is." Those who wanted to be a part of the transition could undergo district-sponsored training if their culinary skills weren't up to par. Even before the HHFKA required districts to provide frontline school lunch workers with professional development opportunities, the district offered a variety of free classes, such as knife skills, food preparation, and food service management. The classes were designed to help cafeteria workers prepare better, healthier food for kids at school and in their own homes. MPS also offered classes to help frontline workers prepare for the ServSafe food handler examination, an optional certification that made them eligible for job advancement and an immediate pay increase. "It's unpaid and all that. It's out of your own time," Anna noted. "But you're welcome to come, and they will teach it. And I think that has helped quite a bit of people figure out where they belong in this crazy atmosphere."

The MPS Department of Culinary and Wellness Services improved its hiring packages for "reskilled" positions. Weber explained, "We offer a good wage. We offer a retirement plan. We offer vacation, sick pay, guaranteed holidays off, guaranteed weekends off, guaranteed nights off." This impacts the roughly 253 MPS Culinary and Wellness Services staff who are represented by Service Employees International Union (SEIU) Local 284, especially those in the bottom rungs of the school lunch hierarchy. The union negotiated a new contract several years into the district's real food transition, which guaranteed a minimum starting wage of $12.93 for entry-level food service assistants and $15.37 for prep cooks during the 2015–2016 school year.[11] The contract also guarantees that all kitchen and cafeteria workers employed for twenty hours or more per week are eligible for employer-provided health insurance. That's why securing longer hours matters so much to employees. So, even though most positions are ten-month contracts, the overall package is more than what for-profit restaurants typically offer.

FIGURE 22. Staff of a Minneapolis high school production kitchen. Courtesy Minneapolis Public Schools.

The uptick in job quality is bringing more men to the frontlines of the labor of lunch, along with more women who hold advanced degrees.[12] For Tim, who has an associate degree in culinary arts, the decision to pursue a career in the MPS Culinary and Wellness Department was, in part, an homage to his mother. She worked twenty-eight years for the department, including three as Tim's junior high lunch lady during the 1990s. School lunch was pretty much "prepackaged burritos, prepackaged pizzas . . . just like heat and eat, grab and go type of food" when he was an MPS student. For Weber, these foods are "carnival food, not school food," and in retrospect Tim would agree. "The less processed the food is, the better it is for us," he told me, so looking back the food was pretty terrible.

In early 2014, when Tim heard people talking about the district "starting this whole farm-to-school, greenhouse-to-cafeteria program," he asked his mom, who was still employed with the district, to tell him more. He knew she worried that he was working himself to the bone with "twelve-, fourteen-, sixteen-hour days" at a local catering company—and he was. If he could get a job at one of the MPS high schools, he would have a predictable eight-hour shift. He'd always be done at 2:00 pm. The pay would be a step up, and he'd be eligible for benefits that he didn't get at the catering company. He'd also be able to join a union for the first time in his culinary career. And he liked the idea of giving back.

Tim applied and was hired. It's "amazing," he told me in 2016, two years into his new life as a high school cook. He feels a sense of purpose now that the high school where he works is a full-blown production kitchen. "It used to be everything came in a package, and you just threw it in the oven and pulled it out when it was hot and served it," he commented. "But now, we're actually given a recipe, given the ingredients, and making something that these kids enjoy." It's not just the ability to give kids healthy, freshly cooked lunches that makes Tim feel like he's doing something valuable with his days. It's also the ability to care for and about them in multiple ways. "It's fun to watch them grow up. They'll come in as freshmen, like little small freshmen, and leave as grown young adults," he observed. "It's fun to be a part of that: to nourish them not only with food, but to talk to them like people." Tim loves interacting with the kids at school. What's more, he loves that his new position is such a great "dad job." When his eight-hour shift ends in the afternoon, he can enjoy family life with his wife and two small children.

Like Tim, Amy was drawn to MPS after hearing about the district's transition to scratch cooking. She lives in a small town about a thirty-minute drive away from the school; she doesn't love the commute, but she wanted to get experience at MPS after finishing her culinary degree. There aren't many jobs available in her town, and, as she put it, those that do exist "aren't awesome." Neither is the school food program. Amy almost always packs lunches for her two elementary school children. She's not a real food purist. "You can't be like, my child will never eat any sodium metabisulfite," she quipped during one of our conversations. "It's part of the world." However, she believes it is reasonable for parents to expect school cafeterias to serve real food that parents like her serve their kids at home. She takes pride in preparing high-quality lunches for kids who "maybe haven't eaten a minimally processed piece of chicken in their life."

Amy hopes that she can eventually use the skills and experience she is building at MPS to become the foodservice director in her hometown, ushering in a real food transition in her own community. She dreams of scheduling a meeting with the school board and telling them, "You need a dietitian; you need local food. This is how we can make that work budgetarily.... This is how we can have real jobs in this community." She treats her job as an apprenticeship, and so far, she has learned a lot—not so much about food preparation but about the need to be adaptive and find innovative ways to cope with short-staffing.

Amy started out at MPS as a "floater," who moves between different school kitchens to cover absences and temporary staffing needs. But at the beginning of the 2015 school year, she landed a permanent position as the coordinator of an elementary school kitchen that was scheduled to convert from prepack to on-site production. The kitchen renovation was behind schedule, so Amy served limited choices from a "construction menu" for her first month on the job. Being asked to make three hundred meals an hour was a welcome challenge. Amy says she's "not like a workaholic or anything," but she likes to push herself. That being said, the thing she least likes about her job is "getting harped on for not doing a good enough job in a short enough time."

Amy struggles to complete all of her work within the seven "bid hours" of her position. The number of bid hours is the district's expectation of how long a particular job should take, and exceeding those hours requires manager approval. So most days Amy has to email her supervisor to ask, "Can I please stay and do my work?" Her supervisor never says no, but the protocol makes Amy feel as if she's incompetent and somehow breaking an unwritten rule. "That makes me a little cranky," she admitted. "Part of me is like, 'Wow, so you can spend $1.7 million on a kitchen but you can't pony up 24 extra dollars so I can work overtime?'" She thinks that focused training could help her learn to do paperwork and ordering more efficiently, but her supervisor is too busy dealing with the part-time Food Service Assistants (FSAs) who fill critical posts as cashiers and servers. At the eighteen schools her supervisor oversees, FSAs are "just quitting everywhere."

Even though MPS has made major gains in improving job quality, those gains are not equally distributed. FSAs may feel a sense of pride in the job like Tim and Amy do but may not be able to afford to stay in their part-time jobs for very long. Amy's two FSAs, for example, are nowhere close to full-time: they help out during peak serving times, one for 3.25 hours, the other for 4 hours.[13] When I interviewed Amy in late November, she'd already lost three FSAs since the start of the school year. They either didn't like the work—it's more physically and emotionally draining than most people think—or needed to find a job with more hours. The challenges of high turnover, Amy explains, are part of why her seven bid hours often spill into nine on the job. They're also why she prefers the title Kitchen Manager over the colloquial "lunch lady." "I *manage* to make it through a day," she jokes. Besides, she is in her early thirties, and "you need to be forty-five to be called a *lady*."

Weber is well aware that recruitment and retention continue to be significant challenges, if not *the* most significant hurdles, for MPS and districts like it. Even after MPS's kitchen renovations are complete, the Department of Culinary and Wellness Services will still have some three-hour FSA positions and no clear pathway for converting them into full-time jobs. Weber hopes that the "carrot" of a career ladder will make these positions more desirable than they once were. But, he was quick to remind me, "MPS runs a $21 million business" and he has to balance the budget. Notably, Weber has ensured that his department stays "in the black," operating as a financially self-sustaining entity while taking concrete steps to build a real food economy.

Attracting members of the "missing millions" to participate in the NSLP would certainly help grow revenue and allow MPS to create more full-time jobs, but shifting the culture of school lunch takes time and can be hard to achieve in the midst of a labor crisis. Increasing the NSLP budget would give Weber more leeway to shift away from three-hour FSA positions and build capacity for more transformative changes that extend beyond Minneapolis schools into Minneapolis communities. Additional local and state funding would also help, but such contributions to school lunch budgets have a history of reproducing existing social inequalities within the NSLP.

The ongoing challenge of making nonprofit school lunch programs financially self-sustaining pushes foodservice directors across the country to keep the labor of lunch cheap. Too often, that means exploiting low-wage workers and the environment. To fund their real food transitions, some districts actively court public-private partnerships that can generate government commitment and alleviate financial pressures. Weber has been remarkably successful in attracting such support. For example, MPS was awarded a grant from the Life Time Foundation to eliminate what the nonprofit calls the "harmful seven" from its supply chains: trans fats and hydrogenated oils, high-fructose corn syrup, hormones and antibiotics, processed and artificial sweeteners, artificial colors and flavors, artificial preservatives, and bleached flour. Other nonprofits and corporate foundations have also contributed to MPS's real food transition, which involved both constructing and renovating kitchens. The district did, however, feel strongly about not accepting donations that would offset the cost of local or other real food. Accepting donations for salad bars and other small-scale equipment helped to build the infrastructure and capacity for scratch production, but relying on a temporary grant to bolster their farm-to-school sourcing might undercut the sustainability of the program if the subsidy were to suddenly disappear.

The MPS school board, for its part, committed $100 million toward the master plan to build production kitchens at forty school sites. Weber points out that the board of education announced this decision after the MPS school lunch transformation had already generated a fair amount of buzz in the local media and attracted more paying "customers" to the program. The board seemed to have waited for proof that a significant public capital investment really would raise the profile of MPS. Now, they have even more proof: MPS's new production kitchens have enabled the district to become a national leader in the real food movement.

When MPS had on-site production kitchens at only a handful of schools, Weber and his team did their best to identify "clean" precooked products that fit the constraints of the district's prepack assembly lines and central kitchen distribution model. They even partnered with manufacturers to formulate clean-label items that could be sold to MPS and the broader school lunch market. It was a step in the right direction, but not a final stopping place. Erin, the MPS dietitian tasked with screening each food item the district considers purchasing, is eager to move beyond real food lite. "I'm hoping the ingredients-of-concern list takes a back seat more and that we focus more on just cooking from scratch—more or less scratch," she told me in early 2016 as we sat in her cramped office, just off the main production lines in the district's central nutrition center. As a school dietitian, she knows that cooking from scratch gives schools much greater control over their supply chains and recipe formulations. It enables schools to accommodate seasonal variations in local produce availability and make adjustments based on students' dietary needs and taste preferences.

MPS got so focused on ensuring none of the items they purchased contained ingredients of concern that they nearly lost sight of the fact that it's "almost impossible" not to end up with a clean-label product when you're "actually cooking," Erin told me. And by "actually cooking" she means roasting local vegetables, baking chicken in the oven, and preparing composed salads using fresh ingredients. She's certainly not alone in this realization, but making the leap from reheating to cooking is far more challenging than most people realize. The NSLP's cumbersome regulations, copious paperwork, and limited budget can shock even the most ardent real food advocates into submission and subsequent acceptance of real food lite as the only practical way forward.

Veteran foodservice directors and administrators are well aware of these challenges, which helps explain why quick-scratch and clean-label industrial foods have found such a ready audience in the NSLP. Novices entering the complex world of school lunch face an even steeper learning curve. During my fieldwork, for example, I witnessed a vocal real food advocate from New England—a chef with an impressive background in the restaurant industry and strong connections to the local farm-to-table scene—struggle with the NSLP's many rules and regulations after becoming foodservice director of an urban school district.[14] His situation could have been much worse: before his arrival, the local board of education had invested in kitchen upgrades for older schools and included full-blown production kitchens in newly built schools. But the foodservice director still felt stymied by competing priorities and what he described as "red tape" that made even the smallest wins feel unnecessarily difficult, and he left within four years of taking the job.

Plenty of schools whose meal programs are led by enthusiastic proponents of real food simply don't have the capacity, staff, or knowledge to cook from scratch. They lack the kitchen infrastructure and equipment to do anything other than reheat clean-label prepared foods or perhaps do a bit of quick-scratch cooking. Back in the 1960s and 1970s, when the federal government devoted resources for poor urban school districts to purchase kitchen equipment, it encouraged them to invest in things like prepack machines and rethermalizing ovens. Then, in 1981, Congress stopped allocating funding for the USDA's Equipment Assistance Program, which had once offered at least some funding for school food service programs to purchase necessary equipment. This provision remained unfunded for nearly thirty years until a rising tide of public concern about child obesity motivated public health and child nutrition organizations to advocate for change. This, coupled with the Obama administration's efforts to stimulate economic growth after the 2008 financial crisis, pushed Congress to allocate $100 million for school kitchen infrastructure as part of the American Recovery and Reinvestment Act of 2009. Grant requests came pouring in from school districts, eventually totaling some $630 million, but Congress allocated only an additional $25 million in equipment assistance funding to the 2010 budget.

While a step in the right direction, the Obama-era investment is a drop in the bucket relative to what schools across the country actually need to cook real food from scratch. According to a December 2013 report from the Kids' Safe and Healthful Foods Project, a collaboration between the Pew Charitable Trusts and the Robert Wood Johnson Foundation, nearly 90 percent of school districts nationwide need at least one piece of new equipment in order to serve healthy meals that would meet the HHFKA standards more effectively. The HHFKA requires schools to serve an array of fresh fruits and vegetables, but many schools reported that they lacked tools as basic as knives and cutting boards. The most commonly expressed need was simply "more physical space," reflecting the nonprofit school lunch movement's long, uphill battle to secure adequate funding for kitchens and cafeterias.[15] All told, the Kids' Safe and Healthful Foods Project estimated that it would cost about $5 billion to ensure all schools participating in the NSLP have the equipment and infrastructure necessary to safely and efficiently meet the updated HHFKA requirements.

The USDA responded to this news by making an additional $25 million available to schools on a competitive grant basis. "We know that there is still a significant unmet need for kitchen equipment in schools, and outdated equipment can make it more difficult to prepare healthy meals," Secretary of Agriculture Tom Vilsack said in a press release. "With these grants, schools will be able to get the tools they need to make the healthy choice the easy choice for America's youngsters."[16] This increase in federal funding was another step in the right direction, but it is an insufficient investment in meeting the needs of "America's youngsters" and the schools that feed them.

Without adequate public investment for kitchen infrastructure, training, and equipment at the federal and state levels, what options do schools have? In June 2013, the Kids' Safe and Healthful Foods Project convened seventy-five leaders from thirty-one states to brainstorm. They came up with four distinctively neoliberal strategies. First, schools can pursue sponsorship from businesses, philanthropic organizations, or wealthy individuals by offering naming rights or invite community organizations to adopt the cause and "take the lead in building robust funding support."[17] Second, schools can seek investment in the form of low-interest loans from banks and credit unions, attract matching funds from donors, and ask local voters to pass municipal bond measures to finance capital improvements to school kitchen and cafeteria infrastructure. Third, those districts with sufficient culinary capacity can be entrepreneurs when it comes to identifying and capitalizing on revenue generation opportunities like renting out their space, catering school events, and using their facilities to prepare meals for other sites that provide care for young children and the elderly. Fourth, schools can partner across districts and with other sectors of institutional feeding (e.g., colleges and universities, hospitals, assisted living facilities, and prisons) to leverage their buying power and reduce the cost of food and equipment expenditures;[18] they can also form resource- and skill-sharing partnerships with local businesses and reach out to the culinary community to "help train and professionalize food service staff, revamp menus, generate excitement, and raise the profile of school lunches."[19] None of these recommendations mentioned confronting the federal government over its refusal to take responsibility for ensuring that all schools have the means to serve healthy meals to children.

If the history of the nonprofit school lunch movement teaches us anything, it is that taking piecemeal approaches to financing school lunch programs tends to breed injustice and diminish the educational potential of the NSLP. Many states and local school boards have established schemes to supplement the federal NSLP reimbursement. The policy innovation and precedent exists, as does a growing body of research documenting the multitude of benefits that investing in school lunch would generate, so why not push the federal government to step up? Unless we spend public tax dollars on building community-based culinary capacity in all schools, we will fail to create a culturally enriching, life-nourishing school lunch program for the twenty-first century as many other wealthy nations have done.

The evidence from MPS and dozens of other school districts with active farm-to-school programs makes clear that developing high levels of community-based culinary capacity can open the door to far more transformative changes. Building and staffing production kitchens is the most promising path for ending Big Food's colonization of school cafeterias and, eventually, the cheap food economy itself. But what about communities, particularly rural and low-income communities, without the community capital or support to make these types of transformational changes? How can the NSLP be used as a resource to create good jobs and build wealth in these communities?

INVESTING IN THE REAL FOOD ECONOMY

The National Farm to School Network is an information, advocacy, and networking hub launched in 2007 by a group of thirty civil society organizations and state agricultural partners. Since the 1990s, farm-to-school activists have made inroads into one facet of the real food movement: the relocalization of school lunch in communities all across America. "At its core, farm-to-school is teaching our kids the importance of REAL food. Food that is grown from the earth, not manufactured in a laboratory. Food with names that you can pronounce, food that's colorful, nutrient dense and delicious," wrote Emily Miller, the director of marketing and education for the Chef Ann Foundation in an October 2016 piece published by the National Farm to School Network. "The kind of food," she continued, "that provides the healthy fuel their minds need to learn and their bodies need to grow."[20] Unlike more generic real food supply chains that deliver clean-label industrial food to school kitchens, farm-to-school supply chains provide what some agrifood scholars call "food from somewhere," which allows people to feel more knowledgeable about and connected to the origins of their food. School foodservice professionals can more easily visit local farms, ranches, and fisheries to learn about environmental and labor conditions of this "food from somewhere" than when they purchase "food from nowhere" that travels through complex corporate supply chains.[21]

Farm-to-school programs have gained both public support and the blessings of Congress, the US Department of Agriculture (USDA), and the School Nutrition Association.[22] From a policy perspective, farm-to-school helps meet the multiple objectives of solving the so-called obesity crisis and advancing the USDA's goal of "helping to improve the economy and quality of life in rural America" by increasing market access and therefore the viability of farms and ranches.[23] The 2008 farm bill made it easier for schools participating in the NSLP to incorporate local food into their supply chains by allowing them to apply a "geographic preference" when soliciting bids from potential vendors, which let them define a preference for locally produced food rather than being forced to go with the cheapest bid.[24] The 2014 farm bill directed more money into farm-to-school supply chains by launching a pilot program giving select state distributing agencies the flexibility to source and distribute locally produced agricultural commodities to schools.[25] Since USDA commodity foods account for about 20 percent of the food served through the NSLP, a nationwide rollout of the program would funnel substantial public funding into local, more diversified agricultural systems, though some farm-to-school activists have concerns that the program privileges large farms rather than opening doors for small and mid-sized producers. In the meantime, the HHFKA earmarked $5 million per year to support the farm-to-school movement, which amounts to less than one-tenth of a percent of the total federal budget for school food. The USDA distributes that funding through a competitive grant program that privileges districts with the capacity, time, and expertise to apply. Demand for these grants far exceeds supply. However, the USDA hopes that grant funding will help leading districts like MPS develop model programs that can be replicated in other districts with the technical assistance of regional staff.[26]

In recent years, the public health sector, philanthropic foundations, corporate giving programs, and even state legislatures have created their own grant programs and made donations to further support farm-to-school programs. Donors understand that the projects they underwrite likely wouldn't occur without help from civil society.[27] Like their Progressive Era forebears, they aim to motivate institutionalization within the USDA's child nutrition programs by first demonstrating the positive effects that farm-to-school programs have on children's health, academic achievement, and food literacy. Co-benefits, especially local economic development and job creation, are another selling point.[28] But using farm-to-school programs to support local farm economies and sponsoring food- and garden-based education for kids requires an allocation of resources that some districts just don't have, which is a shame since holistic farm-to-school programs yield far better outcomes for students, food producers, and the communities that support them.[29]

Such civil society initiatives may have positive outcomes at the local level, but they risk creating highly unequal access to local food, school gardens, and related educational opportunities. Funding for farm-to-school programs is disproportionately channeled to school districts—and even individual schools within districts—based on their ability to submit compelling applications and their personal connections to philanthropists, wealthy corporations, and policymakers. As a result, children from more affluent schools, districts, and states tend to see the benefits, while poorer children continue to be served cheap "food from nowhere."[30] Settling for private funding streams—or even state and local government funding—lets the federal government off the hook, devolving the costs of farm-to-school programs onto communities that may not have the necessary fund balance or nonprofit infrastructure to afford them.

Critical food scholars Patricia Allen and Julie Guthman made this point in a 2006 article that ruffled feathers within the farm-to-school community. They accused movement activists of "producing neoliberal forms and practices afresh" by failing to prioritize social equity.[31] At the local level, school administrators, teachers, parents, youth, nonprofit organizations, farmers, and school foodservice directors all play a role in establishing new farm-to-school programs and ensuring their longevity and expansion. How are schools without dedicated staff-time and financial resources supposed to broker new connections with local farmers or develop seasonal recipes and educational materials as part of a comprehensive farm-to-school program that involves not only local sourcing but also school gardens and food education?[32] And even more importantly, how are they supposed to raise money to renovate their kitchens so they can actually prepare the fresh ingredients they secure? Might there be other pathways forward—ways for schools to use their existing infrastructure?

These are pressing questions for the farm-to-school and real food movements to address. The Minneapolis Public School District's farm-to-school program can provide some possible answers. When Weber first took the helm, there were still some schools in the district that could serve only what the central kitchen prepackaged for them. They didn't even have salad bars. This lack of culinary infrastructure restricted not only which farm-to-school products these schools could serve children but also how the dishes could be prepared. Andrea Northup, then MPS's farm-to-school coordinator (she left in 2017 to work as a regional farm-to-school coordinator for the USDA), explained that while root vegetables and other storage crops that are local food staples do "awesomely" when roasted, the MPS central nutrition center didn't have an oven—only "a giant kettle," "giant mixers," and semiautomated prepack assembly lines. So schools that depended upon prepack lunches had to settle for what the nutrition center could cook with its limited equipment: apple-kale salad, potato salad, and little, individually wrapped portions of fresh fruits and vegetables.

For schools without a kitchen of their own, Northup said, even the simple addition of a salad bar could make a world of difference. Farm-to-school produce could be delivered directly to the school and processed on site using knives, cutting boards, and small processing equipment. Still, many local farm-to-school veggies truly shine only in schools with "beautiful combi-ovens" and full-blown production kitchens. "We've done roasted beets, roasted carrots, red potatoes, potato wedges, butternut squash, Brussels sprouts—you name it," Northup said. All these items are storage crops that can be served long into the winter and spring months, which helps alleviate the challenges of limited seasonal availability of local produce.

Culinary capacity alone, however, doesn't mean that everything comes in straight from nearby fields. Some of the local foods MPS serves come from farms and companies located within 250 miles of the city that already sell to the conventional produce market. These larger farms are established partners of the major produce distributors and therefore are local "by default," just as in California a "local" grower by proximity alone may be the same one who supplies most of the country's spinach. This supply chain is important for increasing the total volume of local food served in Minneapolis school cafeterias, Northup says, but the district doesn't consider it true farm-to-school procurement. That comes when the district is "really working with those

FIGURE 23. Immigrant farmer and member of Shared Ground Farmers' Co-op, a marketing and distribution cooperative, who sells to the Minneapolis Public Schools farm-to-school program. Courtesy Minneapolis Public Schools.

smaller small- to medium-sized growers who are committed to the same values that we have about food."

Farm-to-school procurement reflects the values associated with local food economies, not just the geographic proximity. MPS has codified these priorities in its annual Request for Proposals (RFP), a competitive bid document that school districts use to identify and eventually contract with growers and manufacturers. In its RFP, MPS states that it is "particularly interested in partnering with small- to medium-sized farmers, beginning farmers, farms in which families own or control decision making on the farm, and farms owned or operated by minority and/or immigrant farmers" (fig. 23).[33] In Northup's words, ideal sourcing is "relationship-based and values-driven." Farmers like knowing in advance what they'll be growing and for whom. In a toolkit designed to help other school districts follow Minneapolis' model, Northup explained that the commitment from MPS "helps with farm planning, minimizes marketing costs, reduces the anxiety of not knowing if a product will sell, and leverages additional large buyers."[34] She encourages schools across the country to directly contract small and medium-sized growers in their local foodsheds. To this aim, the MPS farm-to-school team develops an RFP each winter, after they've forecast how much local food they plan to purchase during the next growing season. Next, they invite farmers to a meeting where they can learn more about the district's needs and requirements.[35] Already-participating farmers share their experiences with prospective farmer partners who have the opportunity to ask any questions that might help them decide whether to submit a proposal to MPS. Northup and her farm-to-school team are on hand to explain the ways in which the district is willing to support new farmer partners in meeting the district's purchasing requirements. The bottom line is that this forward-contracting model allows MPS to move beyond featuring a farmer for a single, heartwarming purchase into the realm of high-volume, repeat purchasing that can actually have a significant impact on farmers' livelihoods.

In order to expand its farm-to-school network, MPS offers technical assistance to ensure that farmers are meeting all the necessary food safety requirements. In addition, MPS facilitates new connections between local growers and the district's contracted produce-processing partner. This enables growers to preprocess their crops into a "value-added" product that better aligns with the time and infrastructure constraints of K–12 school foodservice. Instead of receiving crates of butternut squash directly from a farm, for example, MPS schools might receive farm-to-school butternut squash that has already been peeled, diced, and bagged into standardized quantities that are easy to pull from cold storage and spread across a roasting pan. This type of preprocessing makes the transition to farm-to-school sourcing relatively seamless for MPS kitchens that already do on-site cooking. In fact, one worker told me that "nothing changes" in terms of preparation time or difficulty on the days they use preprocessed farm-to-school produce. In her view, "taking a box of frozen vegetables out of the freezer and steaming them, or heating them, or whatever" is really no more challenging or time-consuming than "taking a box of fresh broccoli and laying it out on a pan, and oiling and salt and peppering it, and throwing it in the oven." Sure, she may have to follow a different series of steps, but this "really isn't any more labor or anything" and the end product is "ten times better."

At cafeterias across the country, other school foodservice workers have differing opinions about what the transition to serving real food means for their jobs. In a study of six school districts within the School Food Focus network, Amy Rosenthal and Christine Caruso found that values-based purchasing, including farm-to-school procurement, pushes workers to take on more complex and time-intensive tasks. Yet managers and foodservice directors do not necessarily increase wages or staffing levels accordingly.[36] MPS's model of contracting with third-party companies to preprocess and deliver produce can alleviate some of these labor challenges, while still allowing schools to cultivate values-based supply chains. Farm-to-school purists might criticize MPS for adding in a middle man, but it's part of what allows MPS to integrate farm-to-school products into its cycle menu instead of limiting local procurement to items like apples that can be served whole.[37] If MPS used its own unionized labor and far less specialized equipment to process all farm-to-school items at the district's central nutrition center or on-site kitchens, Northup says it would be "very expensive compared to a produce company that may have invested in a big piece of equipment."[38]

But as she points out, there are trade-offs to this approach. Outsourcing a portion of farm-to-school labor frees up more money to devote to improving food quality for the kids and creating more equitable supply chain relationships with local growers, but there's a "whole big conundrum" of weighing the social value of a "good-paying job versus outsourced machine work."[39] Her task is not as simple as choosing one priority over another. If MPS helps a small-scale farm that doesn't typically sell to institutional markets become an approved vendor at a local processing company, the local food economy is strengthened. The arrangement helps farm-to-school products become more available across the Minneapolis foodshed—which extends well beyond the boundaries of MPS—and links small-scale farms into a values-based supply chain that handles packaging, distribution, and other logistics. Northup considers it a "huge win" when an MPS grower is able to sell additional product to the produce company on top of what MPS has direct-contracted—proof that the district's farm-to-school mentorship made a difference for the grower, and particularly their bottom line.

Creating denser and more diverse local food networks for schools to tap into is valuable in and of itself. MPS takes this a step further by partnering with farmers and processing companies to purchase "seconds" that don't match the strict requirements of supermarkets and commercial foodservice operators. Ugly produce is fine for schools that are going to be cutting it up before serving it; so too are fruits and vegetables that don't meet the cosmetic or size requirements for supermarket retail. "Figuring out the specifications of products has been an iterative process of working with the produce company, the farmers, and with our team internally," Northup told me. It involved asking, "What's the variation that we can handle? What's the variation they can handle? And what works for the farmers?"

The ability to take imperfect, oddly shaped, and larger-than-average produce saves labor on the farms by speeding up picking and sorting. This, in turn, helps MPS get lower prices and gives the growers an outlet for selling produce that may not meet the standards of their commercial buyers, CSA (community-supported agriculture) members, or farmers market customers. And it goes beyond cosmetics. MPS uses creativity and communication to identify all sorts of cost-saving measures on the farm, which allows the district to stretch its local procurement dollars. Leaving stickers off squash, packing unbunched kale, and bulk-packing produce into big watermelon boxes are just a few of the ways MPS and farmers have worked together to save labor on the farm and keep prices low. Using this strategy, MPS has successfully broadened its local sourcing to incorporate costlier items like meat, poultry, and grains. In one such partnership, a local turkey producer sells dark meat and ground turkey to MPS, while the pricier turkey roasts go to co-op grocery stores and other more lucrative markets in the area.[40] In another such creative partnership, MPS purchases broken pieces of wild rice (an expensive, hand-harvested product with significant cultural ties to the region's Indigenous tribes) that producers aren't able to sell through other market outlets. All of this helps to decrease food waste, while generating new revenue streams for local producers in a community-based food economy.

Nationally, only a few large school districts—such as Oakland Unified School District in California—have integrated farm-to-school procurement as successfully into their operations as MPS has. The district-wide rollout of scratch cooking and the ongoing effort to purchase food from small and mid-sized growers make MPS an inspirational model, especially for other urban school districts hoping to transform the NSLP. Unfortunately, most districts are lagging far behind. According to the 2015 USDA Farm to School Census, about 58 percent of school districts were not participating in any farm-to-school activities, let alone the kind of integrated initiatives MPS has developed.[41] While 16 percent of districts did say they plan to incorporate farm-to-school into their lunch programs in the future, it is unclear whether these programs will target specific students or school buildings. The district-level data contained in the USDA's Farm to School Census masks inequalities within districts: if even one school has a garden or classroom-based education to complement the local foods served in the cafeteria, the census gives the entire district credit for having these farm-to-school initiatives in place.

Establishing comprehensive farm-to-school programs that combine local food procurement, school gardening, and classroom education takes significant effort that is difficult to sustain with grant funding and personal donations. Even Berkeley, California, the ground zero for real school food, continues to struggle with this after years of community organizing, parent support, and foundation grants.[42] The situation is even tougher in large urban school districts, which are forced to "operate on efficiency and uniformity and simplicity" while serving large volumes of food at scale on tight federal reimbursements, according to MPS farm-to-school coordinator Andrea Northup. "That's one of the reasons why we need a dedicated person to navigate this... and work with the various people in our department and outside of our department to connect all the dots," she explained in a 2016 interview. Northup's position at MPS was initially funded as a contracted position and later converted into a permanent, district-funded position, paid for through a combination of district and grant funds. It was a full-time job with benefits focused entirely on farm-to-school, a rarity in the world of school lunch, yet one more reason why MPS was able to propel itself to the forefront of the national movement.

Continued reliance on grant funding puts farm-to-school programs in a precarious position. Debbie, one of the foodservice workers I interviewed in Iowa, told me why she was excited about her school's farm-to-school program: "It's real food. It's food that the kids can pronounce... and I think that's where we need to go." Her favorite part was the classroom-based education that encouraged kids to taste new fruits and vegetables and to think critically about the origins of their food. But this piece of the program was grant-funded, and after the grant period ended, the lessons "just fizzled out," Debbie said. "I don't think the classroom teachers kept up with it much, and [the foodservice department] didn't have the manpower to push it after a while." She was sad to see it disappear, particularly since the program had been really popular with the kids.

This type of experiential garden-and-food-based education was popularized by John Dewey during the Progressive Era and repopularized by famed chef and real food activist Alice Waters under the banner of the "edible schoolyard." In the past decade, the Whole Kids Foundation, the Edible Schoolyard Project, Big Green, and at least a dozen other private grantmakers have funded school gardens and cooking curricula. Among them is the Detroit School Garden Collaborative, a farm-to-school initiative led by Detroit resident Betti Wiggins, who got her start in child nutrition in the 1980s as a substitute worker "washing pots and pans, putting up stock, learning what school lunch is all about." Years later, after a stint in Washington, DC, she became foodservice director of Detroit Public Schools and began transforming the city's vacant lots into school gardens.

Wiggins knew the school system could not fund such changes alone. "Who do my partners need to be?" she asked herself. "I need a university if we're going to do research and grant writing; I need an extension service if we're going to learn to grow food; I need a healthcare provider if our emphasis is going to be on health; and I need a not-for-profit that's already out in the field."[43] She found them. By time she left Detroit in the spring of 2017 to become the foodservice director of Houston Independent School District, the Detroit School Garden Collaborative had created a successful garden program that "expands teachers' access to real-life laboratories to teach students about healthy eating, nutrition, and concepts around growing food while increasing schools' access to fresh fruits and vegetables."[44] The program continued to grow. In January 2018, Kimbal Musk announced that the nonprofit he cofounded, Big Green, would donate $5 million to build "learning gardens" in one hundred Detroit schools.[45] "Detroit is a resilient city with passionate and dedicated residents who care about the future of their kids and schools," Musk wrote in a press release. "There is inspiring work happening in urban agriculture, community gardening, and school gardens in Detroit; and we are proud to join this collective effort to impact even more kids."[46]

Evaluations of such real food "interventions" consistently find that children are more likely to eat fruits and vegetables when they help grow or cook them.[47] Marcie, one of the foodservice workers I interviewed in Des Moines, Iowa, saw this transformation firsthand at the elementary school where she works. The school has what Marcie calls a "huge, huge garden," complete with a chicken coop, and a small demonstration kitchen tucked in the corner of the cafeteria's seating area. The school is a FoodCorps site, which means it was staffed by one of the 225 full-time AmeriCorps service members employed by the national nonprofit during the 2017–2018 school year in 350 high-need schools spread across seventeen states and the District of Columbia.[48] Each Wednesday during Eco Hour, a FoodCorps member stationed in Marcie's school leads the children through a garden- or kitchen-based exploration. One day, when it was raining, a FoodCorps member went outside and brought in buckets of mud, dumped the dirt onto newspapers, and challenged the kids to start digging for signs of life. Anytime a kid found a bug or a worm, the class would stop to identify it and talk about what role it had in building healthy soil. "They had the best time doing that," Marcie recalled, even as they were learning "about gardening, nature, and all that kind of stuff."

Marcie's granddaughter, Lily, who attends the elementary school where she works, clearly enjoys the FoodCorps lessons too. When they vacationed together at a cabin on a nearby lake, Lily asked, "Grandma, when are you going to make that popcorn again that's made out of cauliflower?" She was referring to a FoodCorps recipe for cauliflower broken into little pieces and toasted in the oven until it takes on a texture similar to popcorn. On another occasion, Lily requested hummus, which surprised Marcie, because she herself had been a picky eater as a child and "would never serve hummus" to her family an adult. Lily's taste preferences and food knowledge are broadening as a result of the FoodCorps lessons, to her grandmother's delight. But the whole enterprise could fall apart if FoodCorps chooses to stop staffing Lily's school, or if FoodCorps can't attract sufficient corporate and private donations to supplement the federal funding it receives as part of the larger AmeriCorps service network.

Without full-time support from a service member or other staff, school gardens are notoriously difficult to keep up, particularly when the institutional commitment from teachers, school administration, and parents starts to waiver. The anticipation of future headaches makes some school administrators reluctant to allow gardens in the first place. Often, it all comes down to money. Minneapolis foodservice director Bertrand Weber summed up the dilemma: "The district is very supportive of school gardens, but there's no funding for school gardens." Even so, Weber has found ways to pursue innovative experiments, like using a portion of the school food budget to purchase produce grown in school gardens by MPS students. It began with four pilot sites during the 2015–2016 school year, each supported by a different type of "champion." A local nonprofit sponsored one, which includes a greenhouse and aquaponics lab for classroom-based education. An extremely enthusiastic parent spearheaded another, while two teachers from the district—a science teacher who managed a school-community garden and a special education teacher who ran a work-life skills program—each led a garden-to-classroom project.

The Garden to Cafeteria pilot program generated what Andrea Northup described as "really cool enthusiasm for the gardens" and a variety of "unintended positive impacts." It was a pleasure to see students at the four schools with production gardens really "taking ownership over what was on the salad bar and being ambassadors for the garden," Northup noted. This hyperlocalization of the school food supply chain—students stewarding the seeds that later became school lunch—was possible only because the "lunchroom staff really stepped up." Northup had expected them to feature a few items on the salad bar, but they were "doing beets and carrots and swiss chard and all this stuff" for both the hot vegetable choices and cold salad bar.

Despite the pilot program's success, school gardens remain a tough sell in many school districts, especially if they depend upon the volunteer leadership of parents, who can be unreliable. If their children switch schools or graduate, they're unlikely to continue helping with critical tasks like watering and weeding or assisting teachers with garden-based education. Mowing a flat patch of grass is much easier than coordinating garden maintenance, which is, according to Weber, why internal champions like principals and teachers are so important for the viability and longevity of school garden projects.

There is a rich literature on school gardens that highlights common models and local innovations for starting and maintaining school gardens.[49] At Lily's elementary school in Des Moines, for example, teachers take turns coming to the school on weekends to take care of the chickens at the FoodCorps garden. To help distribute the workload and maximize the public value of the school garden during the summer months, they host a weekly family night when people gather to help out with garden tasks and play outdoor games together. In rural areas with vocational agriculture classes and local chapters of organizations like Future Farmers of America (FFA) and 4-H, students can be employed to grow and harvest food.

In Arlington, Minnesota, a small agricultural town home to Sibley East High School, I spoke with teachers Tim Uhlenkamp and Jeff Eppen, who supervise roughly three hundred students who plant, tend, and harvest 3.5 acres of vegetables.[50] To ensure their garden program is financially self-sustaining, Sibley East runs a twenty-nine-member CSA program for community members. It generates enough revenue to pay three students to work as garden managers for fifteen to twenty hours per week during the summer months. This model allows the Sibley East student gardeners to grow, harvest, and donate about $12,000 of fresh produce to their school kitchen.

When I ate school lunch at Sibley East in May 2013, I had just missed the last of their preserved school-grown tomatoes and zucchini, but by that time they were already beginning to harvest early spring crops. Every single day during September through the beginning of November, their high school cafeteria serves vegetables they've grown. In winter, it's more like once or twice a week. The student gardeners grow spinach for the salad bar year-round under a high tunnel, but the rest of the season extension work falls to Joan Budahn, the Sibley East foodservice manager, and her staff. They are paid on an hourly basis during the summer to process tomatoes, carrots, cucumbers, beans, potatoes, pumpkins, and other vegetables. They can freeze and preserve hundreds, if not thousands, of pounds of produce during peak harvest so that the student-grown veggies can be served in the cafeteria throughout the academic year. Their kitchen equipment is antiquated—they still use a Hobart mixer purchased in 1958—but as Budahn once told a reporter, "We can work magic in this kitchen."[51]

MAKING REAL FOOD WORK FOR COMMUNITIES

The culinary skills of Sibley East's self-described "old farm ladies" enables students to eat from their gardens even in the long winters of the upper Midwest. Schools that work this type of magic in their kitchens have the ability to advance food justice on multiple levels. In addition to local sourcing and in-house processing, they can leverage the inherent flexibility of scratch production to be culturally responsive to community needs. This was true in the Progressive Era when New York City's network of school kitchens skillfully melded insights from nutrition science with attentiveness to ethnic foodways.[52] And it remains true today, which presents both a challenge and an opportunity for real food activists.

Consider the case of a Boston-area high school with a high concentration of children of Caribbean heritage that launched a pilot program focused on comprehensive nutrition education. This included hiring a chef and developing recipes in compliance with the HHFKA. The scratch-cooked recipes didn't go over well initially: kids and parents found the dishes lacking in flavor. "Can't we just have some Sazón?," the kids asked, longing for a spice blend commonly used in Latin American cuisine.[53] Goya, the most popular commercial brand of Sazón, lists monosodium glutamate and salt as the first two ingredients. It also contains Yellow #5 and Red #40. Should reducing children's sodium intake and minimizing their consumption of ingredients of concern be prioritized over cultural preferences? A school with limited culinary capacity would have no choice but to treat this question as some sort of either-or dichotomy, whereas a school with the capacity to work magic in its kitchen could make its own healthier version of Sazón using a mix of coriander, cumin, annatto seeds, garlic powder, salt, oregano, and black pepper. I'm not sure what the Boston school cooks ended up doing, but the ability to cook from scratch at least gave them options for how to balance health priorities and cultural relevance.

Being responsive to children's taste preferences and allowing them to customize their own dishes can make the difference between children pitching a tray full of picked-over food in the garbage and actually consuming a nutritious, balanced lunch. "Flavor stations," with their delightfully Willy Wonkaesque name, are becoming increasingly popular, especially as schools have begun to reduce the amount of sodium in the foods they serve. These cafeteria stations provide a DIY lab for students to experiment with adjusting the flavor profile of their lunches with herbs, seasonings, and clean-label, low-sodium hot sauces. Getting kids to simply try the food is paramount. It can take five or ten "exposures" to observe a noticeable difference in a child's acceptance of a new or disliked food.[54] Sometimes parents give up much sooner. They may think taste is immutable and not want to cause unnecessary headaches.

Low-income parents have less money to spend on food their children might reject, so they often buy foods that their children already like.[55] School cafeterias can absorb some of the financial risk and emotional strain that is disproportionately placed on low-income mothers. Inviting children to try new foods in a nonthreatening way—in a comfortable environment and without fear of going hungry or being reprimanded for not liking the food—is a good strategy for expanding their palates beyond the innate liking for salt, fat, and sugar that Big Food reinforces through its carefully engineered product formulations.[56] Research shows that providing information about the nutritional value of foods (e.g., "It's good for you.") has negligible effect on children's willingness to try new foods. Force-feeding them (e.g., "Only clean plates allowed!") doesn't work either.[57] It can even backfire.[58]

Getting kids to eat, and eventually crave, real food requires what Michael Carolan calls "retuning" their tastes, which have typically been "tuned" to crave the flattened tastes and textures of industrial food.[59] While folks on the frontlines of school foodservice might not use his exact terminology, they grapple with this tuning and retuning daily. For example, Erin, the dietitian at Minneapolis Public Schools, says that kids who are accustomed to the high salt content of canned foods, savory snacks, and other packaged items, can get "really upset" and reject low-sodium foods served in their school cafeterias. In Iowa, a foodservice director told me she had been "so excited" to put a whole-muscle, clean-label chicken breast on the menu, only to feel crestfallen when an employee called her to say, "This is terrible! This is the worst product ever." Without all the fillers, flavor enhancers, and artificial coloring that children were used to, the chicken breast seemed bland, the texture seemed off, and the color looked pale and "nasty."

"If kids are used to a spongy chicken rather than a chicken that you have to chew, there are some acceptability factors," she explained. These acceptability factors are an example of what Carolan calls "affective barriers," which are not about physical or economic access to alternative, or real, food, but rather about learned taste preferences and cultural expectations that require sustained social interaction to overcome.[60] By encouraging children to try new foods—especially fruits, vegetables, legumes, and whole grains—cafeteria workers provide an important public service.[61] "We get a lot of feedback from parents and it's pretty cool," a cafeteria worker in Connecticut told me. Parents call her to say, "I can't believe you got my kid to eat that! What did you say? What did you do?"

Two of the most common tactics cafeteria workers use are offering low-risk "tastes" and encouraging kids to eat more fruits and vegetables. Some lunch workers, especially those at elementary schools, make up little songs or games. Adding different spices—a dash of vanilla extract, a pinch of ground cinnamon, or a sprinkle of nutmeg— to her oatmeal and then asking the kids to guess the "secret ingredient" is a favorite trick of Annie Drake, better known as "Miss Annie."[62] Through this simple interactive game, she gets the kids to taste, and maybe even eat, a whole-grain breakfast. At the same time, they also slow down, use their senses, and think about how combinations of food yield different flavors. Through this simple act of care, Miss Annie develops children's food agency, retuning their bodies to allow them to become coproducers of real food and not just customers of Big Food.

Minneapolis Public Schools does something similar on a much larger scale through its True Food Taste Tests, which are designed to "encourage students to be adventurous eaters" and to "think critically about food beyond LIKE VS. DISLIKE."[63] At the taste tests, students across the district sample recipes developed through the collective efforts of the MPS Culinary and Wellness Services staff, the creative talents of the kids they feed, and a network of chefs, farmers, and workers from other parts of the school food chain who partner with MPS to support scratch cooking, food integrity, local food, and healthy eating, or what the district refers to as "True Food." Andrea Northup, tasked with developing such experiential learning opportunities for MPS's farm-to-school and True Food programs, hopes the taste tests will empower students to see food as more than just an "add-on or a little side necessity to the day."

On True Food days, MPS students participate in a community-wide effort to bring real food to their schools by tasting dishes like Green Lava Kale Salad, Tic Tac Taco Salad, and Far Out Farro Salad and thinking up creative names for the dishes. Over fifteen thousand students at twenty-nine schools participated in the True Food Taste Test for a dish that was later named the Red Rice EXPLOSION! Salad by an elementary school student who won the naming contest. More than fifty community-based volunteers helped with the logistics of the taste test. They encouraged kids to use their senses to experience the texture, color, and flavor of the dish instead of simply classifying the dish as "nasty" or "not nasty," while teachers led thematic lessons designed to maximize the educational impact of the event.

True Food taste tests happen three times a year, and when they do, MPS teachers are invited to use lesson plans for math, science, English, and social studies that connect the cafeteria to the classroom.[64] While this type of formal engagement is admittedly infrequent, the switch to fresh cooking and farm-to-school sourcing has created other opportunities for ongoing engagement. Teachers who once eschewed the school cafeteria are standing in line alongside their students and developing relationships with cafeteria staff—a huge win for the school's food culture. Convincing teachers to eat school lunch is a "big thing," as one of the MPS workers I interviewed put it, especially in schools where airline-type lunches were the norm for most of, if not all, their tenure as educators. Improving the quality of ingredients and recipes—offering more fresh options—helps a lot. Teachers' school lunches aren't free, but they are generally a more convenient and cheaper option than packing a similar-quality lunch from home or buying something off campus.

The teachers rarely, if ever, ate the prepack meals at Jessica's school before it was converted to on-site preparation. As an MPS prep cook, she's witnessed the change in teachers' attitudes toward school food and, by extension, the labor of lunch. Now, postconversion, she notices teachers "come down a lot... just salivating at the mouth." They say the food is "really good," that it has changed. On certain days, like taco bowl day, Jessica and her coworkers make extra servings because they know all the teachers will come to eat. "It's like Chipotle," they tell her, as they pile their choice of chicken, brown rice, black beans, shredded lettuce, chipotle mayo, jalapeños, and other fresh and flavorful toppings into a taco bowl. Jessica and her coworkers bring leftovers to the teacher's lounge on days when they prepare more complex recipes like made-from-scratch lasagna or, Jessica's favorite, wild rice meatloaf, made with Minnesota-grown wild rice, cranberries, and locally sourced ground turkey. The teachers' appreciation means a lot to Jessica. She feels like a respected member of the school community, not just an invisible lunch lady, when she overhears teachers bragging about the quality of the food to their families and friends as a perk of the job.

It's worth noting that partway through MPS's real food transition, the Child Nutrition department rebranded itself as the Department of Culinary and Wellness Services. The new name suggests a focus on care for all members of the school community—teachers and children alike—and a recognition that they are whole people, not just mouths to feed. It also reflects Weber's holistic approach to school lunch reform as a cultural shift. MPS educates workers to be part of that change, something that is far too rare—as I learned when visiting other school districts involved in farm-to-school and other real food initiatives. In other districts, frontline workers are often told only the bare minimum of what they need to do their jobs and not given formal training on topics related to the real food movement.

Take Sophie, for example. As a cook at a district-wide central kitchen in Iowa, she handles ingredients every day and even participates in taste testing new products. She was friendly and talkative in response to many of my questions, but when I asked her what the district was doing to eliminate ingredients of concern or to source local food, she was unusually quiet. Eventually, she told me that she had heard a dietitian and foodservice director use the term "clean label" during a taste test but didn't know what the term meant and hadn't spoken up. She said she just figured, "Okay, I don't need to worry about what a clean label actually is; that's the dietitian's job." When I pressed Sophie to tell me more about why she never followed up, even after the event, her answer was rather dismissive: "It comes to us and we know it's gone through the checkpoints." Likewise, when I asked her to tell me about why the district had made it a point to bulk-produce its own clean-label sauces and stews in the central kitchen, she repeated a stock phrase about the food being "healthy" but couldn't really elaborate on that. I don't bring this up to shame Sophie or any other workers who don't know what a clean label is, but rather to highlight the need to include all workers in conversations about the mission, vision, and values of the real food movement.

In contrast, many of the workers I interviewed in Minneapolis were fluent in the lexicon of real food. Nearly every person I spoke with shared a story about tasting a new food, trying out an unfamiliar culinary technique, or even altering their diet based on what they learned while on the job at MPS. "It's like I read labels constantly now, because what it says on the front doesn't necessarily translate to the back and it should," said Erin, the MPS dietitian in charge of screening products. "It's just kind of almost obsessive-compulsive. I'm at a friend's house and I go, 'What's in this? Not eating that,'" she said with a laugh. Given the hundreds if not thousands of hours she has spent screening labels at work, her newfound dogmatism isn't surprising, but MPS's decision to enlist workers in helping to screen product labels is—at least in comparison with other districts. During regular staff meetings, Erin teaches frontline workers about the MPS list of ingredients of concern, including why each ingredient is on the list and why it was used in industrial food production in the first place. She has also explained what clean labels are and encouraged frontline employees to help her make sure that all the foods they serve are in compliance with district policy.

MPS leadership was clear about its goals and transparent about hitting roadblocks when it came to sourcing clean-label versions of some products at the price point and packaging volume the district requires. Pickles, for example, typically include artificial yellow dye, an ingredient of concern. It's really hard to source a clean-label alternative for pickles, and district management explains these limitations to frontline workers, framing the service of such foods as an exception, not the rule in the city's cafeterias. May, an MPS school cook, told me that she and her coworkers were encouraged to "let them know if we saw something in the label that we thought we shouldn't." And they did. Empowered frontline workers caught mistakes made by district procurement specialists and delivery companies. One day, for example, May called the district's dietitian after receiving a new delivery. "Look at this label," she said. "Why are we buying this? It's got high-fructose corn syrup in it. We're not supposed to be serving that." To her satisfaction, MPS switched to a clean-label alternative for the next order, which made her feel more inclined to speak up in the future.

May and her coworkers have the opportunity to learn not only about ingredients of concern but also the farm-to-school side of the district's real food reforms. Farm-to-school coordinator Andrea Northup asks farmers to speak at district-wide meetings, creates promotional materials like signs and farmer trading cards (like baseball cards, but with pictures of farmers and their farm statistics), and shares videos and pictures from local farm visits in order to help K–12 staff understand what farm-to-school is and why it matters. "I had a carrot farmer come and speak about his farm, and his philosophy, and his land, and his family, and how our farm-to-school program has made a difference for his family. And we served his carrots there at the training and talked about the quality and the freshness and the sweetness of those carrots compared to conventional carrots," Northup told me when I asked her to describe the most recent staff training event. In her view, it's these types of personal connections that resonate with the MPS staff. "And with a lot of the staff teams," she noted,

FIGURE 24. The owners of Open Hands Farm, a local carrot vendor for the Minneapolis Public Schools farm-to-school program, participate in a back-to-school celebration with their daughter. Courtesy Minneapolis Public Schools.

"you'll find someone whose parents were farmers or who comes from a farming family, or who has a garden, who will be the spokesperson" for farm-to-school and why it matters for kids and community.

In the farm-to-school community, staff trainings are sometimes discussed as a means to a very concrete end: getting frontline workers to communicate excitement—not indifference, confusion, or revulsion—for the farm-to-school foods that may be unfamiliar for students. But in Minneapolis something far more profound seems to be happening as workers who don't come from agricultural backgrounds hear firsthand from local farm owners. "I had no idea that in order to be an organic farm, you had to be chemical-free for three years. I didn't know that," Anna, an MPS high school cafeteria manager, told me after one such farmer visit. Seeing pictures from farms, storage warehouses, and processing facilities has helped Anna visualize how the district's farm-to-school supply chain works and given her a sense of appreciation for the magnitude of the enterprise. "The tens of thousands of carrots that you see in a picture—it helps put things into perspective," she noted. "You see how much actually goes into this program, and the local support and local businesses . . . all the way through you too, and your involvement, and then all the way to the kids." In her job at MPS, Anna learned to place her work within a larger context—within a sustainable food movement—in a way she never had during culinary school. Hearing directly from farmers about their role in the labor of lunch made all the difference.

Having grown up on a nearby farm, Paul, the warehouse manager at the MPS central nutrition center, appreciates that the district is "actually using local farmers" to source ingredients for its menus. The switch to scratch cooking and local procurement has also made his job a lot more interesting. He used to feel like a "boring mouse on the wheel, running for no reason." The menus were so repetitive that he could correctly rattle off the district menu for any day of the week. Now, instead of just saying, "Oh, here's a frozen box of ravioli and some sauce and Cheez-Its," as Paul put it, he is shipping "fresh stuff" to the schools. The timing, volume, and variety of food flowing through the central nutrition center is much different now—and for Paul that's a good thing.[65] "It's a little better mentally, not knowing exactly what you're doing," he explained. "It speeds the day up . . . with a little bit of confusion and actually having to think."

Like many other MPS workers, Paul is especially fond of Minnesota Thursday, a monthly celebration of locally produced foods. The goal of Minnesota Thursday is to support the local food economy, while simultaneously raising the visibility of the farm-to-school program and attracting new "customers" by serving fresh, seasonal meals.[66] It seems to work: immediately following Minnesota Thursdays, traffic spikes on the website where MPS shares recipes for scaled-down, "family-size" versions of the specialty dishes served for Minnesota Thursday and its True Food taste tests. Kids talk to their parents about something they've had at school, and MPS makes it easy for them to learn more. However, the logistics of pulling off complex events like Minnesota Thursdays can create challenges for Paul and other MPS staff. "We have special farmers bringing in stuff we've never ordered before . . . that we're only going to use one or two times a year, so we have to find special spots for it in the freezer, in the warehouse," Paul explained. Minnesota Thursdays can be a bit hectic for school cooks as well. They have to make new recipes with ingredients that may not yet be part of the district's regular offerings, without the luxury of practice or additional staffing.

Weber hopes that serving a special meal of all locally sourced real food on Minnesota Thursdays will bring positive attention to the district and nudge parents and children who have opted out of the NSLP to give it a try. MPS continues to work on other ways to increase participation, especially among kids who don't qualify for free or reduced-price lunches. To this end, MPS

FIGURE 25. District-owned food truck at a back-to-school barbecue celebrating the Minneapolis Public Schools farm-to-school program. Courtesy Minneapolis Public Schools.

hosts a back-to-school barbecue so that the families in the district get a taste of what the city's schoolchildren eat for lunch (fig. 25). "We really target families, but we also involve dozens of partner organizations and everyone just for an interactive evening of farm-to-school fun and delicious food," Andrea Northup, the district's former farm-to-school coordinator, explained. And importantly, as Erin, the MPS dietitian, noted, these community events are not "preachy." Instead, they focus on creating "happy community events" that feature real food and the farmers who grow it in a celebratory way instead of lecturing people to "eat this, not that."

This philosophy that real food should be enjoyable helps win over staff who might otherwise be skeptical. "I think one of Bertrand's real big messages is that food that tastes good is what people like to eat, and so we have really tried to wow our staff with awesome tasting food," Northup explained, especially since "many of them have not tried a lot of the things that we're serving" before. I heard as much from the frontline workers I interviewed. One worker told me about her first experience eating a watermelon radish, also known as a "beauty heart" radish because of its bright pink interior. She was preparing it for the salad bar and decided to give it a quick taste. "When I bit into it, it was just fresh. It had the right amount of crispness to it. Does that make sense?" she asked, laughing as she recalled the experience. It made such an impression on her that she told a representative from one of the farm-to-school partner organizations about how much she loved the beauty heart radishes. He told her that if she liked the radishes raw, she'd love them on top of thinly sliced, toasted sourdough bread with butter and a sprinkle of salt and pepper. He was right: radish toast became a new favorite thanks to her experience at school.

Another MPS worker told me about how she shares school recipes with her friends and makes them for her own family: "Like today we're barbecuing, so I made a potato salad like what we had here, and I did—it's called a cowboy caviar. It's black beans, pinto beans, jalapenos, onions, and corn, and a little bit of olive oil, and vinaigrette or something. So, it's like I'm making things that I see here that I like." Jessica, a prep cook who spent years working in quick service restaurants before joining the MPS team, has a similar story. She's gleaned ideas from the farm-to-school program that help her accommodate her children's evolving dietary needs. "My oldest son is fifteen and he decided to become a vegan," Jessica said. It was "really hard," but MPS taught her how to feed him. "Working here has shown me options like the salad bar and the red rice and apple salad. . . . It's opened my mind. You don't have to eat meat with every meal." Instead she can make her own version of an MPS specialty, UnBEETable Hummus. Jessica was emphatic, telling me, "It's *so* pink," because they mix puréed roasted beets in with the chickpeas, tahini, and lemon juice. "The things that you can make are just endless."

MPS also pushed her to dig deeper and explore ways that she can participate in alternative food systems. Prior to working at MPS, she thought alternative food systems existed only in "hip grocery stores and farmers markets." She had supported the movement in theory but never quite felt like local food was for her. Then an MPS farmer told her about all the farmers in the area participating in CSAs during the Minnesota growing season, which picks up in late spring, peaks in late summer, and ends as the leaves are beginning to drop and the weather turns cold. "They have these programs where during the summer, if you want, you spend $500 and you can go out to the farm and do a little bit of work one week in a month, or whatever. Then you get all these different kinds of vegetables," she told me. Suddenly she saw a way for herself to support local growers and offset the cost of healthy, fresh food for her family. "I'm doing a little more homework and I like learning about it," she explained. Working for MPS had made her feel like local food could be for her, and other forms of alternative agriculture could be too: "I'm checking into more around organic homegrown, or what is it called: no cage, free range, or whatever?"

Jessica's real food terminology might not be perfect, but her enthusiasm is palpable. Andrea Northup says that such authentic curiosity about alternative food systems is a relatively new phenomenon. "Now, I think you could ask every staff in our district what farm-to-school is and they could explain to you what it is and what it's all about or why we're doing it. And they could maybe a name a farmer or something like that, whereas that was not the case even last year," she explained during a 2016 interview. "It's been a long road of both figuring out how to do it and communicating with staff," she continued. "It's taken videos and emails and presentations and showing up at their sites and taste tests and just a lot of barraging them with this concept."

Initially, Northup was hesitant to do much publicity about the district's farm-to-school program until her team figured out how to handle procurement challenges. Direct contracting with small and medium-sized producers is less predictable than awarding a bid to a large produce distribution company that can source from different farms or regions if weather, insects, disease, or some other factor decreases forecasted crop yields. So her first strategy to create visibility for local food initiatives involved building a vegetable and herb garden in the green space in front of the MPS central kitchen facility. Issuing a press release about farm-to-school sourcing or even just advertising local food on the lunch menus the department posted online would have created expectations that Northup and her team weren't sure they could meet. If local farmers couldn't actually grow enough food for MPS, they'd have to use conventional, nonlocal substitutes or change the menus altogether, which might be upsetting for some students and parents and leave the district vulnerable to criticism. Planting a garden in front of the district's central kitchen, in contrast, offered nothing but potential gains. It brought life to the grim exterior of the building, served as a symbol for where MPS was headed, and provided a direct service to the folks who lived nearby and worked inside the building.

Paul, the warehouse manager, takes advantage of the garden's bounty on a regular basis. "They have everything. They have the peppers and onions and tomatoes and cucumbers and pumpkins and flowers and kale and everything," he noted with some excitement in his voice. He'll be leaving work and say to himself, "Oh, I'll have this cucumber for dinner. There's a pepper; I'll take the pepper for dinner." It's a community garden—free to anyone who wants fresh, locally grown, organic produce. "They'll pick it when it's ripe. They'll put it up on the table up here and everyone can take it—all the employees," Paul explained, "and a lot of times people just come up off the street and start picking it, which—it's community food, so it's not a big deal. They're not trashing it or anything, so it's nice."

Blurring the boundaries between school and community, treating them as if they are one and the same, allows districts like MPS to contribute to the larger project of making the real food movement accessible and inclusive. Public schools in Minneapolis and its twin city, St. Paul, are actively redesigning their menus to be more culturally responsive and reflective of the families they serve. Parent advisory councils provide input to St. Paul's school foodservice department, and community members are invited to submit recipes for consideration.[67] In February 2016, the St. Paul school foodservice department collaborated with the African American Parent Advisory Committee to put together a menu for African American Parent Involvement Day featuring a red-beans-and-rice recipe that one of the parents contributed. Two community-sourced recipes—Hmong beef fried rice and Somali chicken suqaar—were already part of the district's repertoire. But one of the menu planners for the St. Paul public schools told me these dishes aren't particularly popular with the kids. "You can make a Hmong beef fried rice for twenty-five thousand people, and it doesn't taste like the Hmong beef fried rice your mom makes. So it's not necessarily that popular with Hmong kids," she explained. "So, we're really torn."[68] Partly, the issue is the scale of production. Centralized culinary capacity is not at all the same as distributed culinary capacity.

Like St. Paul, Minneapolis has a multimillion-dollar central kitchen. Now that MPS has built a distributed network of on-site production kitchens, its central kitchen is mostly used to prepare items for "fast-scratch" cooking at the schools. Bertrand Weber is eager to use the flexibility of on-site cooking to develop a culturally responsive school lunch program at the level of individual schools. "Three years ago the district, because of the concern over the Somalian population, went pork-free entirely," Weber told me. Yet, he explained, "I know my Hispanic population . . . and pork is a big part of their diet." Rather than pitting dietary constraints of one minority group against the staples of another, Weber crafted a new policy allowing any school to serve pork as long as it has the ability to serve more than one hot lunch option. He sees this policy as a way to "be respectful of cultural difference and expose all our kids to different options," while making sure that they also have the ability to opt out if need be.

The longer-term goal—after workers at on-site kitchens have a full year or two of production experience behind them—is to give them autonomy to serve culturally specific meals once or twice a month. The culinary traditions school cooks might tap into are more obvious for some schools than others. The Anishinabe Academy enrolls urban Indigenous students from diverse Native cultures. The student body at the Hmong Academy is 90 percent Hmong. About 90 percent of the students at the three Spanish immersion schools are of Latin American heritage. Weber hopes to partner with chefs from these ethnic communities to develop recipes for the schools that allow students to see multiple aspects of their own cultural traditions reflected in the shared experience of school lunch. For schools with a greater mix of ethnic and racial diversity, it will be up to the students, teachers, parents, cafeteria workers, and other interested parties to define unique food cultures reflective of their communities.

Minneapolis is at the vanguard of the real food movement, and its progress over the past decade is cause for celebration. Workers and administrators find purpose and pride in the transition to real food, which has often come with better wages and hours. Children are eating healthier foods. Local farmers are benefitting. And entire communities are feeling more connected. But there are limits to this type of district-level change. Even though Weber has secured corporate donations, government grants, and increased investment from the Minneapolis Board of Education to support the renovation and construction of the city's school kitchens and cafeterias, MPS is still constrained by the NSLP's conflation of cheapness with public value.

The NSLP still prioritizes cheap food and cheap care above all else. Schools across the country are forced to pinch pennies, which keeps the focus on cutting costs instead of investing in values-based food systems. Despite the many steps it has taken to reimagine school lunch, the MPS Department of Culinary and Wellness Services still faces tremendous pressure to maximize meals per labor hour in order to afford higher-quality food, while keeping the budget balanced. Simply put, the district's real food transition moves the NSLP in the right direction, but it only partially embodies the values and characteristics of a truly alternative approach to the labor of lunch.[69] Much of the decision-making remains centralized and top-down instead of participatory and inclusive. And not all of the food is cooked from scratch or sourced in ways that advance food justice or workers' rights. The department still outsources certain facets of the labor of lunch to companies that employ nonunion labor in order to cut costs, which is one of the reasons why the district still has some very part-time, low-skill positions at the schools.

There are limits to working for change within the system. For MPS and any other district tethered to the NSLP, advancing a revolutionary politics of sustainability will remain an elusive goal at best. Luckily, this isn't where the story ends. The NSLP is a public program. And we, the public, can reimagine and ultimately transform it into an engine for positive social and economic change.

Conclusion

ORGANIZING A NEW ECONOMY OF CARE

Big Food companies scored a major win in late 2018, when the Trump administration took strides to make school lunch "great again" by rolling back the nutritional upgrades contained in the Healthy, Hunger-Free Kids Act of 2010 (HHFKA). This reversal of federal policy was foolhardy: it sacrificed children's health and well-being for political gain and funneled school lunch dollars to Big Food companies that sell cheap, processed foods instead of using public dollars to support diverse community food economies. Further entrenching the National School Lunch Program (NSLP) into a cheap food economy that prevents lunch ladies from cooking healthy, fresh food for America's children is not the way to make school lunch great.

There are high-road alternatives to both the cheap food economy and to real food lite that offer a pathway toward a new economy of care in American public schools. Accessing this high road depends foremost on revaluing the labor of lunch. We must invest in professionalizing school cafeteria workers and recognize them for the multiple forms of care they already provide to the nation's children. I want to move beyond this foundational argument, however, to propose a more expansive vision of what food systems could look like if we focus our collective efforts on transforming the NSLP into a hub for food justice—real food and real jobs—in every community across the rural-urban divide.

First, let me acknowledge that I agree with political theorist Joan Tronto when she asserts: "The key to living well, for all people, is to live a care-filled life, a life in which one is well cared for by others when one needs it, cares well for oneself, and has room to provide for the caring—for other people, animals, institutions, and ideas—that gives one's life its particular meaning."[1] If we are to take seriously this premise of what it takes to live well, there is little alternative but to invest in new and existing forms of public infrastructure that support us in caring with each other.

It would be presumptuous, and not altogether helpful, for me to offer detailed policy prescriptions when my hope is to open up space for a collective reimagining of the NSLP in ways that respect and celebrate local context. With that caveat in mind, as a starting point for a much-needed national conversation, I'll suggest some directions that I believe are desirable, viable, and ultimately achievable in the years to come.[2]

INVEST IN UNIVERSAL CARE

The Community Eligibility Provision (CEP) included in the HHFKA offers an important way station on the road toward the ultimate goal of a universally free NSLP. The provision allows low-income schools to offer free lunches and breakfasts to all children if at least 40 percent of students are directly certified based on their household's participation in other means-tested federal antipoverty programs and/or their status as migrant, highly mobile, or without permanent housing. The rollout was gradual. Illinois, Kentucky, and Michigan piloted the CEP during the 2011–2012 school year. It was then expanded to the District of Columbia, New York, Ohio, and West Virginia in the 2012–2013 school year; to Maryland, Massachusetts, Florida, and Georgia in the 2013–2014 school year; and finally to all states in the 2014–2015 school year.

Momentum is building in communities across the country. Several of the nation's largest school districts have already converted their programs to a "free-for-all" model thanks to the CEP. In September 2013, Boston became one of the first major cities whose public schools began serving free breakfasts and lunches to *all* students, regardless of family income.[3] In September 2014, Chicago Public Schools, the nation's third largest school district, with 400,000 students, followed suit.[4] Then, in September 2017, the City School District of the City of New York, the nation's largest district, with 1.1 million students, announced that it too would serve breakfast and lunch free for all.[5] It took about 120 years to achieve the ideal of a universally free school lunch program in these major cities, but doing so at all wouldn't have been possible if Ellen Swallow Richards and Mary Hinman Abel hadn't envisioned and taken steps to create a new economy of care in Boston's public schools back in 1894.

Just as they were in the early 1900s, local outreach and organizing efforts are key to getting additional communities to opt in to a new way of providing care for children. Nearly 21,000 schools in over 3,500 districts opted in to the CEP free-for-all model during the 2016–2017 school year—a tremendous step in the right direction, but a far cry from the nearly 100,000 schools that currently participate in the NSLP.[6] Ensuring that *all* schools provide universal free lunches would be especially helpful for the many students in families that are not technically eligible for free or reduced-price meals but who cannot afford to purchase full-price lunches. The federal government's eligibility thresholds for free and reduced-price lunches are uniform nationally, but the cost of living is not. Families in high-cost-of-living areas who are just above the cutoff line but not well enough off to make ends meet would benefit the most from rejecting this model in favor of universal free school lunch. However, everyone stands to benefit. When school lunch programs are universal, lunch is for everyone and integration with the curriculum becomes a more realistic possibility.

EMBRACE SOLUTIONS THAT WORK FOR EVERYONE

The social organization of care—inside and outside school cafeterias—is a whole-family issue, but it affects children and women the most since care work remains heavily gendered. It's time to reclaim school lunch as a feminist issue, as one piece of a broader agenda to reorganize the economy and social policy to support care (e.g., paid parental leave and universal childcare). Continuously reminding upper- and middle-class parents of their immediate self-interest may help generate political traction to not only universalize the NSLP but also bump up the quality of public school lunches.[7]

A high-quality public school lunch program that meets the care standards of the "missing millions" who currently opt out of the NSLP would relieve the time burden linked to the labor of lunch, freeing up time for caregivers to do other things if they choose. On average, mothers still have less leisure time than fathers in two-parent heterosexual households and spend more of their time at home engaged in multitasking.[8] Planning and packing school lunches for the kids adds to the mental load of keeping track of everything that needs to be done to meet the care needs of the family. Shifting this labor out of home kitchens and into school kitchens by collectivizing the labor of lunch is one relatively easy way to reduce the time stress that families face when juggling the demands of unpaid care work and one or more paid jobs outside the home.

Rectifying the care imbalances that exist within the current realm of school lunch provisioning is itself a way station on the road to advancing worker justice across the food chain. When all children have access to free school lunches, participation rates increase. The same is true when food quality improves. In an ideal world, we'd be able to flip a switch and convert the NSLP into a universal free program that protects the health and well-being of children, workers, and the environment. Unfortunately, there are no shortcuts. Maximizing the potential of the NSLP as a force for public good will require members of the missing millions to temporarily set aside their own personal interests to invest in a shared future that is better for everyone.

There's only so much schools can do as long as millions of families are opting out of the NSLP and politicians are underinvesting in the program. The Minneapolis school district, for all it has managed to accomplish in a few short years, is still constrained by lack of money. The low federal reimbursement rate (a maximum of $3.46 for a free lunch served in the 2017–2018 school year and only $0.45 for a full-price lunch) puts pressure on the district to continue cutting costs at the point of labor—whether it be the part-time foodservice assistants it struggles to recruit and retain or the many factory and farm workers further down the supply chain, whose labor and environmental practices are more difficult for the school district to directly mediate. Higher reimbursement rates and explicit national policies would allow the NSLP to become a catalyst for real food and real jobs in Minneapolis and every other community across the country.

In 2010, Janet Poppendieck estimated that increasing reimbursement rates and converting the national school lunch and breakfast programs into a universally free model would add $12–$16 billion to the existing budget for school breakfast and lunch.[9] This may seem like a steep price tag, but families are already spending time and money shopping at farmers markets, grocery stores, corner stores, and quick-service restaurants in order to feed the 20 million children who currently opt out of the NSLP. Likewise, the parents of the roughly 10 million children who purchase full-price and reduced-price school lunches are also spending money on school lunches. What's more, there are the hidden costs of not investing in real food and real jobs. These include welfare benefits for low-paid lunch ladies and other food-chain workers, obesity-related healthcare costs (estimated at $147 billion each year), and the untold cost of industrial agriculture to planetary sustainability and global social justice.

There is tremendous power in the NSLP as an already existing network from which to advance a revolutionary politics of sustainability that organizes around and mobilizes through capitalism's dependence on cheap wage labor, unpaid care work, and the "free" work of nature itself.[10] Such a shift at the national scale is not unthinkable. Episodes of intense political pressure, economic depression, and war led to tremendous changes in federal school lunch policy at earlier points in US history. Finland has had a universal free school lunch program since 1948—the first in the world. The United States could learn a lot from the way Finnish schools cultivate care through their school lunch program, from the way the food is sourced and served to the centrality of food education and the emphasis on the meal as a joyful, restorative community event. Far more recently, in 2010, a coalition of over 2,100 civic groups and social organizations in South Korea successfully demanded that their government provide universally free school lunches made with local and organic ingredients through programs managed by school districts, not private companies.[11] Democratizing caregiving responsibilities in this way is an inherently feminist project—one that I hope school food activists in the United States will embrace in the coming years.

Moreover, as the backbone of a new economy of care, schools across the country could open their cafeteria doors to allow the elderly and other vulnerable populations to eat lunch alongside children and youth. This would reduce social isolation and teach children of all genders to be both givers and receivers of care—a step in the right direction for producing caring democratic citizens.[12] The idea may sound outlandish to some, or like a diversion from the main points of this book, but some schools successfully experimented with this model at earlier points in school lunch history. It may not work for all communities, but it's worth keeping in mind as a way to make efficient use of public infrastructure and help multiple populations currently served by the USDA's nutrition assistance programs.

LET YOUTH LEAD

Youth can play a key role in transforming not only school lunch but also the economic and ecological systems they will inherit as adults. They have agency to organize at the local level and to use social media to stage mass actions that force policy change at state and national levels. Already, Rooted In Community (RIC), a national grassroots network that empowers young people as community leaders, is pointing the way forward with the Youth Food Bill of Rights developed at its 2013 national summit.[13] It claims the right to culturally affirming, sustainable, organic, poison-free, local, and fair food, just as it claims the right to nutrition education, healthy food at school, and an environment filled with genetic diversity and functioning ecosystems. Perhaps most remarkably, it claims the right to good food subsidies and the right to support farmers through direct market transactions, which suggests a sophisticated understanding of the political economy of cheap food. And in the name of food sovereignty and community self-determination, it claims the right to save seeds and cultivate unused land.

Like Jean Fairfax, the NAACP staff member who coordinated the community-based research project that fueled the right-to-lunch movement in the late 1960s and later drafted a legal framework for children's nutritional rights in 1971, the RIC activists detailed a bill of rights that is fundamentally about what *care* should look like. The two are complementary: where Fairfax mainly focused on articulating the public responsibility to meet children's nutritional needs, the RIC youth activists draw on the environmental justice and sustainable food movements to expand the boundaries of care. In other words—and as number seventeen, the right to leadership education, in the Youth Food Bill of Rights suggests—care is relational and youth want to organize together to shape the world around them for the benefit of current and future generations. They must claim a seat at the table and demand that the NSLP reflect the diverse food cultures of American youth and their vision for food justice.

TURN SCHOOLS INTO GOOD-FOOD HUBS

The vast network of school kitchens and cafeterias in the United States could be reimagined, and ultimately reconfigured, to develop a culinary skill base of adults trained to prepare healthy, sustainable, culturally relevant foods and a "taste base" of children who have learned to accept or even desire foods that differ from the flattened-out tastes and expectations of the industrial food system.[14] To this end, children should be offered the opportunity to participate in the process of growing, preparing, and serving their own school lunches through the intentional design and delivery of inclusive and holistic programs that allow children to care for themselves, each other, and the environment. It is crucial that students be the beneficiaries of their collective labor and that such programs be designed to dismantle rather than reproduce systems of oppression. Asking students to play a role in the shared labor of lunch stands not only to provide them with hands-on education related to food and nutrition but also to advance the feminist goal of breaking down the gendered, classed, and racialized distribution of caring responsibilities.

Throughout this book I have made the case that culinary capacity is a way station for self-determination within food systems. Certainly, it is important to allow space for schools to serve high-quality industrially prepared foods (e.g., nutrient-dense, plant-based foods) that lower the environmental impact of the food system. But there is no substitute for investing in community-based culinary capacity. When schools have the ability to cook with raw and minimally processed ingredients, they are able to be more discerning about how public dollars are spent. Instead of lining the pockets of Big Food executives and shareholders, they can invest in providing the culturally affirming, sustainable, healthy, local, fair food that the Rooted In Community youth activists demand in their Youth Food Bill of Rights. Likewise, schools with high culinary capacity can support genetic diversity by serving a much wider range of agricultural foods and varietals. They can also support farmers through direct market transactions and accept irregular and misshapen produce that does not meet the strict aesthetic demands of retail at farmers markets and grocery stores. Moreover, schools participating in the NSLP can become an active lobbying base for changes to congressional agricultural subsidies: What if the donated commodity foods that schools receive were actually grown by new and beginning farmers (and older farmers willing to transition their production practices) who received federal subsidies for raising crops, poultry, and livestock according to organic principles? What if they got a premium for fair labor standards—an idea the Coalition of Immokalee Workers popularized with its Penny per Pound campaign for fair food? Or what if fair labor standards were a precondition for supplying food to the NSLP?

There is tremendous value to be gained by reimagining the role of the NSLP in the food system, but the project becomes exponentially harder when culinary capacity is constrained in privately owned factories beholden to the economic logic of cheap food. That said, large school districts with varying degrees of culinary capacity are already taking steps to use their collective purchasing power to direct public funding to "good-food" producers through the adoption and implementation of the Good Food Purchasing Program (GFPP).[15] The GFPP is a voluntary program coordinated by the nonprofit Center for Good Food Purchasing, which works with national partners and local grassroots coalitions in cities across the United States to support public school districts and other major institutions in purchasing food that supports local economies, a valued workforce, public health, animal welfare, and environmental sustainability. Los Angeles Unified School District, Chicago Public Schools, Boulder Valley School District, San Francisco Unified School District, and Oakland Unified School District have all adopted good-food purchasing policies. In June 2018, active campaigns were also under way in Austin, Chicago, Cincinnati, Madison, Minneapolis–St. Paul, and New York City.[16]

All this activity furthers the Center for Good Food Purchasing's agenda for nationally networked adoption and implementation of the GFPP. Market-based mechanisms may be able to effectively reorganize school lunch to promote care and sustainability if the procurement criteria encompass a holistic range of quality metrics, like those included in the GFPP.[17] It's important to remember, however, that the GFPP is a *voluntary* policy standard and schools participating in the GFPP have to do so on their existing budgets; they don't get any sort of incentive from the federal government for rewarding "good" producers with their business. In the absence of federal or state incentives for good-food purchasing, the GFPP offers a useful strategic intervention that could serve as a way station for the eventual creation of a mandatory federal standard built into the legal and financial structure of the NSLP. Federal legislation in Brazil's Home Grown School Food program, for example, mandates that 70 percent of food served in schools is fresh or minimally processed and 30 percent is sourced from local family farmers.[18] The United States would be wise to make a similar investment in the lives and livelihoods of rural communities and to provide schools with the funding necessary to turn K–12 cafeterias into good-food hubs.[19]

BUILD SCHOOL-COMMUNITY KITCHENS

Ultimately, public schools are a form of care infrastructure. There is ample space to reimagine who schools might serve—not just kids, but anyone with a need for collectivized care, just as Emma Smedley, Congressman William Clay, and other visionaries within the nonprofit school lunch movement saw as the future of school lunch. Imagine if full-time, well-paid workers used the culinary capacity of school kitchens to prepare affordable, nutritious, ethically sourced speed-scratch meal kits and ready-to-heat-and-eat meals that caregivers, the elderly, and folks with limited culinary capacity at home could purchase. This would help families, especially women, manage competing care responsibilities for children, the elderly, and others in need of care. It would also make efficient use of school-based infrastructure that is frequently unused in the afternoons, evenings, and weekends.

The nonprofit Center for Ecoliteracy is already doing the work of envisioning school-community kitchens through a collaboration with Oakland Unified School District. "A school-community kitchen presents a new kind of social contract: a public school kitchen, used by both the school and the community as a resource for educational, vocational, and production purposes," according to a white paper the center published in 2012. What school-community kitchens look like depends on the needs and existing assets of local communities. For instance, the Center for Ecoliteracy staff envisions a fully developed school-community kitchen in Oakland Unified School District as (1) a public space where employees, students, staff, parents, and community can access culinary education; (2) a culinary space connected to school gardens and/or district-wide farm gardens, (3) a public gathering area for community events and education, (4) a public kitchen community groups can use for food processing and preparation, (5) rentable joint-use space for food-based for-profit enterprises, and (6) a center for emergency preparedness, should the need arise.[20]

The Boulder Valley School District (BVSD) offers another compelling model for imagining school-owned kitchen infrastructure as a community asset. The vision Ann Cooper, the district's foodservice director, and her team laid out in their planning document for the Central Nutrition Center (CNC) is a true source of inspiration and worth reading in full. Here's a taste:

> BVSD's food program will be on the leading edge of school food in the country, hosting seminars, special events, cooking classes, boot camps and conferences to assist school district staff and advocates in segueing schools across the country from highly processed to scratch cooked food. Food literacy for the students, faculty, staff, and community of BVSD will be a major component of the program. The Center's gardens, outdoor eating area, and Café will serve as a community gathering place and as an educational facility for school field trips and student education. The CNC will host community cooking classes, seminars as well as food production and sustainability forums and events. The events will include a Harvest Festival as well as classes in chicken

and duck husbandry, greenhouse gardening, raised bed gardening, and cultured food production....

The Center, considered a Food Hub, will partner with local farmers and producers to assist in value added production and will service BVSD students as well as other schools, school districts and community organizations such as Meals on Wheels and Community Food Share....

As our students are seeing graduation on the horizon, they will take with them from the BVSD experience a true sense of real food, a sense of seasons, of flavors, of the deliciousness of what's on their plates, the balance between what they eat, how it's grown, and the sustainability of life itself.[21]

This vision of school lunch seems to me like the future Emma Smedley and Congressman Clay hoped for. So let's make it a reality. Now is the time to build a political movement capable of transforming school lunch as we know it. Doing so would bring quality public jobs to communities in rural, suburban, and urban America and help defray the future financial strain of healthcare costs by reorienting the "standard American diet."

INVEST IN SCHOOL-BASED COMMUNITY ORGANIZING

School kitchens and cafeterias can and should become hubs for community-based organizing around a wide range of food justice issues. Schools are already focal points of social activity within communities, and a growing number of schools (over 7,500 as of 2017) are pioneering a new model for converting public and private schools into "community schools," which act as hubs for educators, families, and community partners to work together to address the unique local needs of children and families. These community schools are part of a new open-access care infrastructure that creates an intentional public space for children, families, community members, and organizations to care for and with each other.[22] "Caring with" means constantly working to create a joyful, just, egalitarian, ecologically sustainable world and rejecting the short-term illusion of cheapness as a means for maximizing public value. Shifting the paradigm to a new economy of care in American public schools will not be easy, but it won't happen at all if we don't invest energy in community organizing.

So what do I mean by *organizing* exactly? In her book *No Shortcuts: Organizing for Power in the New Gilded Age*, scholar and organizer Jane McAlevey makes a critical distinction between advocacy, mobilizing, and organizing.[23] Advocacy is the professionalized wing of social change work that typically involves closed-door politics and strategic decision-making by elites—much like the School Nutrition Association's "Stop the Block" efforts to prevent Congress from converting federal entitlement funding for the NSLP to a block-grant formula of state-level appropriations. Mobilizing brings large numbers of people to the fight, but usually these are the same activists or organizations (e.g., the anti-hunger coalition forged in the 1960s that still continues to shape federal and state policy); the people most affected by the issues often have no real part in developing the strategy or goals pursued on their behalf. And in today's landscape of social-media activism, massive numbers of people might be "mobilized" to express their support or opposition to a particular policy proposal—like Bettina Elias Siegel's Change.org petition asking the USDA to remove "pink slime" from its commodity meat—but these moments of plug-in/plug-out engagement with an issue do little to cultivate the sustained power necessary to achieve structural change. Organizing, on the other hand, builds grassroots power within communities and allows for a much greater degree of self-determination when it comes to developing and enacting strategy.

Feminist economist Nancy Folbre has articulated several high-priority strategies for workers and consumers to work together to build a high road in the care sector that improves outcomes for both the givers and receivers of care:

1. Build links among care sector workers.
2. Emphasize the common interests of care providers and care recipients.
3. Challenge the claims that "care should not pay."
4. Promote unionization.
5. Reconceptualize the role of the public sector.
6. Publicize and encourage "best practices" management.[24]

Each of these recommendations should be part of an organizing platform for the labor of lunch. In addition, school foodservice workers should build strategic alliances with the teachers' movement and with workers and consumers across the food chain.

UNITE HERE, one of the unions that represents K–12 cafeteria workers, is already a member of the Food Chain Workers Alliance, a national organization that seeks to improve wages and working conditions for all workers along the food chain. UNITE HERE has organized some of the most visible worker-led campaigns for real food and real jobs in Chicago (Local 1), New Haven (Local 217), and Philadelphia (Local 634).[25] They have built community coalitions to both protect their standards of care and advance the type of high-road reforms Folbre suggests.

The value of school support staff was a subject of intense debate in Philadelphia, where UNITE HERE represents school cafeteria workers and student safety staff who help mitigate conflicts and keep children safe during mealtimes and between classes. In early June 2013, the School District of Philadelphia (SDP) announced the layoff of over 1,200 of these noontime aides. The frontline workers in school cafeterias across the district worried that such a drastic reduction in the number of dedicated school safety staff would make the schools more dangerous for the children. Along with a coalition of parents, clergy, SDP students, and, eventually, over fifteen elected officials, UNITE HERE workers lobbied the district to maintain care standards. They staged a series of demonstrations and a hunger strike during the summer of 2013 that drew national attention to the central role that school support staff play in keeping children physically and emotionally safe. Their activism proved successful when the district rehired nearly all of the laid-off school safety staff for the 2013–2014 school year.

Doing the sustained work of organizing is necessary but also taxing, and it can be hard to keep momentum once a contract negotiation is over or crisis like Philadelphia's mass layoffs subsides. The challenges are many, as Cristina Cruz-Uribe, an organizer with UNITE HERE Local 217, told me in June 2016 when I asked her about the progress of New Haven's real-food, real-jobs campaign: "Workers in New Haven work two jobs, three jobs, while raising multiple kids. We have a lot of single parents and it can be very difficult to bring forward leaders who would say, 'Oh, yeah, sure, I'd love to be there. Yes, that sounds like a great idea. I'd love to go visit the mayor and talk about how my kids need fresh food, but I have three jobs. I need to be in three places. I don't have childcare.'" Nearly three-quarters of the Local 217 members who were surveyed in 2013 as part of the union's real-food, real-jobs campaign were primary providers for their families. As Jasanea Hernandez, a middle school cafeteria worker and union leader, put it: "We're busy moms and dads, and we're all over the place at any given time. So it's difficult to kind of key into that after-work type of environment and have everybody motivated."

Cafeteria workers' economic struggles make it difficult to carve out time for anything but earning a wage and attending to their own household's needs. However, as I learned from Cruz-Uribe, their care responsibilities are also a source of strength and inspiration for building a high road for the care sector. She summarized it this way: "As mothers and oftentimes the primary breadwinner, disciplinarian, and organizer in their household, our school cafeteria workers are leaders. They know what the children in their homes and schools would love to eat and should be eating at school," she continued, "but oftentimes these same workers are spending time making those lunches for their kids to bring into school because they don't feel like they're able to do that kind of quality work in their school cafeteria."[26]

My fieldwork in school kitchens and cafeterias across the country told a similar story. However, the tremendous leadership potential within the ranks of K–12 school cafeteria workers is muted by the time demands of their paid and unpaid care work. I met many workers of all genders who were "organic leaders," meaning they may not hold a job title assigning them "leadership" over others or even self-identify as leaders, yet the way others in their workplace respond to them illustrates their tremendous capacity as leaders.[27]

School lunch activists would be well served to identify these organic leaders and support them by amplifying their voices. "Leaders that step up to help lead our campaign, to cook fresh food, are often doing that because they are parents or because they are grandparents," Cruz-Uribe told me. This was the case with Jasanea, a mother of two children who attend New Haven Public Schools, yet even she had doubts about her leadership capabilities when Cruz-Uribe first identified her as an organic leader and asked her to take on a larger role in the union's work. "Well, I am only one person. Why are you talking to me?" she asked herself. "What difference can I actually make when we really have no choice?" These questions and self-doubts began to break down as Jasanea talked to Cruz-Uribe and her coworkers. "I understood that it had to begin somewhere," she explained when I interviewed her in June 2016. "Being hopeful, I think I was like, 'You know what? It is time for a change. How can we make that happen?'"

Jasanea and her coworkers in the union developed a script to use during community presentations about their campaign. "We want New Haven Public Schools to develop a model school food program that embodies the principles of food justice. We want to be an engine for reviving a healthy local food economy and for maximizing the health of our children," the script begins. "We believe that investing in cafeteria workers will improve the quality of food served in New Haven schools and begin addressing the job crisis in New Haven." After this initial opening, the worker-presenter explains that the campaign's first priority is to address the acute issue of child hunger and food insecurity in New Haven by expanding school meal service. Members of Local 217 want to live in a city where children have access to healthy, freshly cooked school meals three times a day, 365 days a year. Their second campaign priority is to phase out heat-and-serve foods and institute a scratch-cooking model that provides all school cafeteria workers with full-time work and benefits. This will, they argue, help to solve the city's job crisis by enabling more New Haven residents, especially people of color, to have full-time union jobs that provide benefits, pathways to advancement, and the ability to have a say in the direction of their school lunch programs.

A powerful vision like this demonstrates that K–12 kitchen and cafeteria workers like Jasanea have situated knowledge that is too valuable for anyone who cares about children or the future of the food system to ignore.[28] Whether it be a contribution of time, money, or skills, those of us who aren't on the frontlines of school foodservice can step in to support worker-led campaigns that build power for realizing a new economy of care and a fair food system.[29] The history of the NSLP tells us that a national, networked, community-based research project aimed at uncovering injustice and challenging existing power structures can bring about change. The opportunity is there, but it will require confronting powerful politicians and corporations with a vested interest in maintaining the existing system of cheap government, cheap food, cheap care, cheap nature, cheap labor, and cheap lives.

It's up to us to change the paradigm. Cheapness is not synonymous with public value. Progressive Era reformers and right-to-lunch activists knew this, but they were never able to escape the powerful forces of patriarchy and racism that blunted the radical potential of their visions for the nonprofit school lunch movement. Their efforts should not be read as impartial or somehow misguided—as if they gave up too easily or too soon—but rather as bright spots of collective action that left behind important way stations for the work ahead. The NSLP in its present form is certainly not an ideal form of public care, but it offers a platform for nationally coordinated, locally specific forms of joint labor-community organizing rooted in a revolutionary politics of sustainability. Maximizing the public value of the NSLP rests on our ability to reclaim school kitchens and cafeterias as a home base for the crucial and challenging work of organizing community economies that enable us all to care well for ourselves, for each other, and for the planet. This is the *labor of lunch,* and it's on all of us, not just the lunch ladies, to make it happen.

NOTES

INTRODUCTION

1. Any direct quotations not otherwise attributed are from interviews I conducted. I use pseudonyms for all interviewees except foodservice directors, union organizers, and farm-to-school coordinators. In most cases, I do not mention age, race, or ethnicity of workers interviewed due to concerns about protecting their identity.

2. UNITE HERE is the largest and arguably most progressive labor union representing foodservice workers in North America. Local 217 has one of the strongest union contracts of any K–12 cafeteria employees, but even this isn't enough to ensure that cafeteria workers earn enough to support their families without working two or even three jobs. While it is home to Yale University, New Haven is a far from affluent school district—about 80 percent of the children enrolled in the city's schools qualify for free or reduced-price lunch.

3. MacMillan, "Union Blasts School Lunches"; Appel, "Aramark on the Way Out"; Appel, "Aramark Booted"; Appel, "School Snares 'Food Dude.'"

4. Feminist economist Nancy Folbre argues for this type of "high road" organizing in the care sector. Folbre, "Demanding Quality."

5. For more on the problems associated with the political economy of "cheap" goods and services, see Patel and Moore, *History of the World*. See also Simon, *Hamlet Fire*. For an analysis specific to cheap food, see Carolan, *Real Cost*.

6. Winson, *Industrial Diet*.

7. USDA FNS, "National School Lunch Program." For more on economic value and conflicts over how it is defined, see Collins, *Politics of Value*.

8. Families earning less than 130 percent of the federal poverty level ($31,960 per year for a family of four) qualified for free lunches in the 2017–2018 school year, while families with incomes between 130 and 185 percent of the federal poverty level (up to $45,510 per year for a family of four) qualified for reduced-price lunches. The federal government also chips in to offset the cost of full-price "paid" lunches for children whose families earn above this threshold. USDA FNS, "Child Nutrition Programs: Income Eligibility Guidelines."

9. Ralston et al., "National School Lunch Program." For more on how women's labor-market participation impacts children's participation in the NSLP, see Datar and Nicosia, "Outsourcing Meals," 565–93.

10. Poor food quality, limited menu options, short lunch hours, long lines, unpleasant cafeteria atmosphere, stigma, inability to pay, and wide availability of alternatives are some factors contributing to their nonparticipation. Poppendieck, *Free for All*, 133–60. For more on youth perceptions of school lunch, see Best, *Fast-Food Kids*, 54–121.

11. USDA FNS, "NSLP, SMP, SBP National Average Payments/Maximum Reimbursement Rates."

12. Food Chain Workers Alliance, *No Piece of the Pie*.

13. Hislop, "Reaping Equity," 19.

14. "Food is the single strongest lever to optimize human health and environmental sustainability on Earth," according to the EAT-Lancet Commission's 2019 report. Willett et al., "Food in the Anthropocene." Promoting diets rich in plant-based foods will help the United States reduce greenhouse gas emissions.

15. During the 2016–2017 school year, 73.6 percent of school lunches served through the NSLP were either free or reduced-price. USDA FNS, "NSLP: Participation and Lunches Served."

16. Scholarship on maternal foodwork illustrates the challenges and alienation that women face when trying to manage the risks posed to their children's health by the industrial food system—and who is systematically advantaged and disadvantaged—by the social expectation that "good" mothers engage in such practices through their shopping and food preparation routines. Brenton, "The Limits of Intensive Feeding."

17. Best, *Fast-Food Kids*, 155.

18. Fisher and Tronto, "Toward a Feminist Theory," 40.

19. The social organization of school lunch programs varies both within and across countries. Robert and Weaver-Hightower, *School Food Politics*. For a comparative analysis of the origins of public school lunch programs, see Rutledge, *Feeding the Future*. For a discussion of school lunch as sustainable development, see Morgan and Sonnino, *School Food Revolution*. See also Oostindjer et al., "Cross-National Comparative Perspective."

20. Laslett and Brenner, "Gender and Social Reproduction," 383.

21. Jacobs and Graham-Squire, "Labor Standards," 447–58. School cafeteria workers bear an economic penalty characteristic of caring occupations. Even after controlling for the education and employment of workers, there is a net penalty of 5–10 percent for working in an occupation involving care. See England, Budig, and Folbre, "Wages of Virtue."

22. For more on the new professional standards rule, see USDA FNS, *Guide to Professional Standards*.

23. Jacobs and Graham-Squire, "Labor Standards," 450.

24. Ibid., 449–50.

25. I looked for robust national statistics detailing the demographic breakdown of cafeteria workers by position type but was unable to find more detailed data.

I even contacted the SNA to see if it collects this type of data, but it didn't as of 2016. However, a wide body of scholarship documents the gendered and racialized occupational segregation of reproductive labor. See Duffy, "Reproducing Labor Inequalities," 71–73. For data on the food system specifically, see Allen and Sachs, "Women and Food Chains"; and Sachs et al., "Front and Back," 3–17.

26. Jacobs and Graham-Squire, "Labor Standards." This is all too common across the food chain—just one of the many hidden public costs of cheapness. See Allegretto et al., *Fast Food*.

27. In April 2019, the USDA issued the first nationally representative, comprehensive assessment of the NSLP since the enactment of the HHFKA. The report shows that nutrition rollbacks were unnecessary: the HHKFA has not contributed to an increase in plate waste, and children's participation in the NSLP was highest in schools that served the healthiest food. Schools need more money to operate their lunch programs, not looser nutritional standards. USDA FNS, *School Nutrition and Meal Cost Study*.

28. For more on the role that cooks and other foodservice workers in public settings can play in advancing public health and other food movement goals, see Tsui, "Pan de Yuca and Brown Rice." See also Tsui et al., "Missed Opportunities for Improving Nutrition."

29. Yoder, "Real Food, Real Jobs."

30. My discussion of care work in the NSLP draws on Glenn's three categories of care—direct care, maintenance of the caring environment, and community mothering—which occur at scales extending from the individual body to the immediate surroundings to the larger social world of a child. Glenn, *Forced to Care*, 5.

31. Ibid. For more on the history of community mothering, especially in African American women's activism, see Greene, *Our Separate Ways*; Levenstein, *Movement without Marches*; and Naples, *Grassroots Warriors*.

32. Katz, "Vagabond Capitalism," 711.

33. Tronto, *Caring Democracy*, 139.

34. The research for this book project followed the extended case method, beginning with immersion into the lives of those under study through ethnographic research in New Haven. The extended case method pushes scholars to expand the temporal and spatial horizons of their work and to think critically about how empirical research relates to existing theory. Burawoy, "Extended Case Method," 4–33.

35. Levine, *School Lunch Politics*; and Poppendieck, *Free for All*.

36. Focus merged with FoodCorps in 2018.

37. For more on community economies, see Gibson-Graham, Cameron, and Healy, *Take Back the Economy*; and Gibson-Graham, *Postcapitalist Politics*.

38. Wright, "Guidelines for Envisioning."

39. Raj Patel and Jason Moore use the term "revolutionary politics of sustainability" to refer to the process of organizing around and mobilizing through capitalism's dependence on cheap wage-labor, unpaid care work, and the "free" work of nature itself. Patel and Moore, *History of the World*, 110.

40. Gaddis and Cruz-Uribe, *Healthy Kids First*.

1. THE RADICAL ROOTS OF SCHOOL LUNCH

1. Smedley, *School Lunch*, 191–92.
2. Edible Schoolyard, "Our Pledge."
3. Ibid.
4. Di Chiro, "Living Environmentalisms," 281.
5. The Children's Aid Society of New York City, a charitable organization, started the first school lunch program in the United States in 1853, but the precursor to the NSLP, which relies on a mixture of public and private funding, emerged in the 1890s.
6. Koven and Michel, "Introduction: 'Mother Worlds,'" 2–6.
7. Ibid., 2.
8. Hayden, *Grand Domestic Revolution*.
9. Home economists frequently adopted what historian Susan Levine has called "a moralistic, if not proselytizing tone" when telling others what to eat. Levine, *School Lunch Politics*, 10–38, 54–70. For a broader discussion of reform projects designed to make non-elite women's caring practices fit elite domestic ideals and an examination of attempts to "Americanize" immigrant and indigenous women, see Glenn, *Forced to Care*, 42–87.
10. Hayden, *Grand Domestic Revolution*, 151–62. See also Levenstein, *Revolution at the Table*, 109–12.
11. Bryan, *School Cafeteria*, 4.
12. Boris, "Power of Motherhood," 229–32. The second generation of women progressives, born in the 1870s and 1880s, took a distinctly different tack and found less resonance with the maternalist discourse and strategy of the first generation. DuBois, "Harriot Stanton Blatch," 163.
13. Talbot, *Education of Women*, 32.
14. Dye, "Introduction," 5.
15. Likewise, between 1890 and 1930, secondary school enrollment virtually doubled every decade, which prepared an increasing number of middle-class students for college and professional careers. Gard and Pluim, *Schools and Public Health*, 65.
16. Zelizer, *Pricing the Priceless Child*.
17. Ruis, *Eating to Learn*, 29.
18. Founded in 1890, the General Federation of Women's Clubs provided a platform for middle-class women to push for social change from within civil society. In addition to addressing issues affecting their own families directly, they prioritized the need to improve labor conditions—especially by ending the exploitation of women and children—and dedicated time and resources to ensuring that existing labor laws were being enforced within their own cities and states. For more on this, see Sklar, "Historical Foundations of Women's Power."
19. MacKendrick, *Better Safe Than Sorry*.
20. Quoted in Ruis, *Eating to Learn*, 24.
21. Ibid. For more on the discourse of "perfect motherhood" during the Progressive Era, see Apple, *Perfect Motherhood*.

22. Ruis, *Eating to Learn*, 24. In particular, the caring practices of working-class women were scrutinized by upper- and middle-class women, the US government, and practitioners at health clinics, schools, and other municipal institutions. Glenn, *Forced to Care*, 42–87.

23. There were differences among racial and ethnic groups' attitudes toward mothers and children working outside the home. Glenn, *Forced to Care*, 24. See also Boris, "Power of Motherhood," 213–45.

24. Hunt, "School Lunches."

25. Ibid.

26. Mary Swartz Rose, quoted in Bryan, *School Cafeteria*, vii.

27. Although several states passed laws declaring women eligible to serve on school boards as early as the 1870s, the majority of positions nationwide were filled by men and influenced by city politics and fiscal conservatism. Ruis, *Eating to Learn*, 17.

28. Levine, *School Lunch Politics*, 58–59.

29. Folbre, "Unproductive Housewife," 464.

30. Megan Elias raises an important contradiction when she writes, "This created a dynamic paradox that the movement was never fully able to reconcile: if women's work was innately valuable, why attempt to replace so much of it with new technologies or for-hire services?" Elias, *Stir It Up*, 8.

31. Apple and Coleman, "'Members of the Social Whole,'" 104–26.

32. Home economists didn't have much interest in making their courses coeducational when the field was first established in the early 1900s, partly to protect the discipline and the knowledge it produced as a space of uniquely female authority. Elias, *Stir It Up*.

33. Hunt, "More Conscience for the Consumer."

34. Hunt, "Housekeeper," 77.

35. Sklar, "Historical Foundations of Women's Power," 63–64. While connected to key leaders from the settlement house movement who advocated racial justice, the federation refused to include black women as recognized members at their conventions. Boris, "Power of Motherhood," 218–19.

36. For more on women's efforts to make the federal government more caring, see Muncy, *Creating a Female Dominion*.

37. Bryan, "Sixty Years' Growth," 54–59, 98–104.

38. Boston Home and School Association, *Unique Function*.

39. Bryan, *School Cafeteria*, 4.

40. Smedley, *School Lunch*.

41. Ibid., 191.

42. Ibid., 25–26.

43. Ibid., 62.

44. Ibid., 56–57.

45. Ibid., 81.

46. Ibid., 67–82.

47. Ibid., 65.

48. Ibid., 66.

49. Dewey and Dewey, *Schools of To-morrow*.
50. Gunderson, "National School Lunch Program."
51. Ruis, *Eating to Learn*, 75.
52. "Restaurant Keeping in the Public Schools," *Modern Priscilla*.
53. Ruis, *Eating to Learn*, 79.
54. Ibid., 60–61.
55. Urban schools saw a dramatic influx of students from a wide range of cultural backgrounds with varying levels of English-language proficiency. Assimilating these immigrants into Anglo-Saxon norms through "Americanization" programs became a widespread, though not uncontroversial, practice in public schools.
56. Quoted in Ruis, *Eating to Learn*, 71.
57. For more on the SLC, see Ruis, *Eating to Learn*, 59–86.
58. Boris, "Power of Motherhood," 215. See also Gordon, "Black and White Visions."
59. White women benefitted from their familial ties to enfranchised white male voters, from the government's gifting of "public" lands to white settlers and state institutions after the forced removal of Native Americans, and from increased access to educational institutions.
60. For more on how women sought to build their collective power, see Freedman, "Separatism as Strategy," 512–29. See also Sklar, "Hull House," 658–77.
61. Boris, "Power of Motherhood," 229–32.
62. Harley, "Work Is Not Who You Are," 44–46. These numbers look different when accounting for nonmarried women. About 70 percent of black women earned wages at some point in the year, often as domestics caring for white women's children. Boris, "Power of Motherhood," 216.
63. Scott, "Most Invisible of All," 5.
64. Ibid., 17.
65. Sklar, "Historical Foundations of Women's Power," 68.
66. Hayden, *Grand Domestic Revolution*, 280–290.
67. Hayden-Smith, "'Soldiers of the Soil,'" 19–29.
68. Apple, *Perfect Motherhood*, 40–41.
69. Apple and Coleman, "'Members of the Social Whole,'" 104–26.
70. Hunt, "School Lunches."
71. Levine, *School Lunch Politics*, 37–38.
72. Ruis, *Eating to Learn*, 111–33.
73. Bryan, *School Cafeteria*, xv.
74. Ibid., 9.
75. For more on these systems, see Ruis, *Eating to Learn*, 97–100; and Bryan, *School Cafeteria*, 295–305.
76. Bryan, *School Cafeteria*, viii–x.
77. Ibid., 117.
78. Ibid., 34.
79. For more on the evolution of women's paid labor over course of the twentieth century, see Weiner, *Working Girl to Working Mother*.

80. Bryan, *School Cafeteria*, 66.
81. Ibid., 66–67.
82. Bryan's 1936 articulation of the educational value of nonprofit school lunch programs reflects a philosophy quite similar to Smedley's. Bryan, *School Cafeteria*, 15.
83. Twarog, *Politics of the Pantry*, 4.
84. Kent, "Nutrition Education."
85. Bryan, *School Cafeteria*, 17.
86. The New Deal included a series of federal programs and projects designed to stabilize the economy, create jobs, invest in public works, and lift the spirits of the American public by using public funds to create the foundation for a more caring society.
87. Poppendieck, *Breadlines Knee-Deep in Wheat*, xv–xvii.
88. A minority group of dissenters emerged almost as soon as it began, accusing the federal government of "commodities dumping" and questioning the logic of shipping food across the country when farms within their own communities also grew food and needed economic support. Levine, *School Lunch Politics*, 48; and Ruis, *Eating to Learn*, 128–30.
89. War Food Administration, "School Lunch Program."
90. Gunderson, "National School Lunch Program."
91. Woodward, "Hot Lunches."
92. The Federal Emergency Relief Administration first authorized states to use federal money to hire unemployed women to prepare and serve school lunches in 1933.
93. The WPA's school lunch projects were originally intended to serve only children whose families were on public relief. However, the agency soon learned that children weren't always getting the "proper kind of diet" even in homes where finances weren't quite as dire. Many communities opted to serve a hot lunch to any child who wanted one, with the expectation that the child's parents might contribute food or other supplies to the program if their financial circumstances allowed. Gunderson, "National School Lunch Program."
94. Ruis, *Eating to Learn*, 123.
95. DeBona, "Educational Program."
96. Ruis, *Eating to Learn*, 128–30.
97. Ibid., 131.
98. Gunderson, "National School Lunch Program."
99. War Food Administration, "School Lunch Program."
100. McDonald, *Food Power*, 26.
101. McMillin, "Victory Gardens."
102. Smedley, *School Lunch*, 194.
103. Ruis, *Eating to Learn*, 132.
104. McDonald, *Food Power*, 26.
105. Ruis, *Eating to Learn*, 136–37.
106. Levine, *School Lunch Politics*, 58–59.

107. For an overview of racial discrepancies in relief efforts and public health investment at this time, see Ruis, *Eating to Learn*, 149–52; and Levine, *School Lunch Politics*, 44–45.
108. Reynolds, *Maintaining Segregation*, 63–65.
109. "School Lunch Information for Citizens' Committee Report."
110. Flanagan, "What's New in Lunchroom Management."
111. Martin and Oakley, *Managing Child Nutrition Programs*, 73.
112. Poppendieck, *Free for All*, 50.
113. Levine, *School Lunch Politics*, 50–53, 57.
114. For a detailed discussion of these two bills, see Ruis, *Eating to Learn*, 141–57.
115. Richard B. Russell National School Lunch Act, § 2.
116. Levine, *School Lunch Politics*, 76–87; and Ruis, *Eating to Learn*, 147–56. War alone would not have provided sufficient justification to create a permanent national program; agricultural interests and the infrastructure established during the Great Depression made the material resources available and brought a powerful group of political actors to the table. Rutledge, *Feeding the Future*, 74.
117. Ruis, *Eating to Learn*, 143–45.
118. Levine, *School Lunch Politics*, 74.
119. Quoted in Martin and Oakley, *Managing Child Nutrition Programs*, 74.
120. Truman, "Statement by the President."

2. THE FIGHT FOR FOOD JUSTICE

1. Bard, *School Lunchroom*, 9–10.
2. Nicolaides and Wiese, "Suburbanization."
3. Bard, *School Lunchroom*, 15.
4. States received a share of these funds based on the number of children enrolled in school and the state's average per capita income (the allocation formula favored poor states with high participation). State agencies were expected to distribute these funds to individual school districts based on the number and type of meals served the previous year. Levine, *School Lunch Politics*, 99.
5. Martin and Oakley, *Managing Child Nutrition Programs*, 79.
6. Quoted in Steiner and Milius, *Children's Cause*, 180.
7. Levine, *School Lunch Politics*, 98–103.
8. "School Lunch Information," in Flanagan Papers, Child Nutrition Archives.
9. Levine, *School Lunch Politics*, 101.
10. Bard, *School Lunchroom*, 5.
11. For a full accounting of the range of practices put in place to decide who qualified for school meals and what they must do to receive them, see Levine, *School Lunch Politics*, 118–19, 124–25.
12. Gunderson, "National School Lunch Program."
13. Levine, *School Lunch Politics*, 117–18.

14. Johnson's Great Society initiative was designed to eliminate poverty and inequality, improve education, reverse environmental degradation, and break down omnipresent forms of structural racism (though some policies, including federal funding for invasive family planning practices like forced sterilization, reproduced existing injustices).

15. Martin and Oakley, *Managing Child Nutrition Programs*, 113.
16. "Palestine District Lunch Setup," *Arkansas Gazette*.
17. Levine, *School Lunch Politics*, 130–36.
18. Committee on School Lunch Participation, *Their Daily Bread*.
19. Beavers, interview.
20. Nix, interview.
21. Levine, *School Lunch Politics*, 110–11.
22. Ibid., 31.
23. Ibid., 90.
24. Ibid., 91.
25. Ibid., 138–39.
26. Perryman, "Log," September 1976, 12–14. Dr. John Perryman served as the executive director of ASFSA from 1955 until his retirement nearly twenty-two years later. ASFSA presidents, on the other hand, served only one-year terms.
27. Kennedy, "Proclamation 3499."
28. "Set Lunch Boycott," *New York Amsterdam News*. For other examples of local activism, see "Join in School Lunch Law Suits," *Bay State Banner;* and "Deprive Poor Kids," *Chicago Daily Defender*.
29. Povitz, "Hunger Doesn't Take a Vacation," 15–35.
30. Ibid., 15.
31. Triece, *Tell It Like It Is,* 100.
32. Ibid., 118.
33. "Protests Registered," *Chicago Tribune*.
34. Levine, *School Lunch Politics*, 142–50.
35. Heynen, "Bending the Bars of Empire," 412.
36. Ibid., 407–14.
37. Ibid., 412–14.
38. Ibid., 414.
39. Broad, *More Than Just Food*, 136.
40. The BPP intended revolution, but it, like the material feminists of the Progressive Era, was constrained by the paradoxical need to function within a capitalist economy while attempting to create noncapitalist alternatives. Broad, *More Than Just Food,* 137–38.
41. Ibid., 137.
42. Levine, *School Lunch Politics*, 140.
43. Sandler, "Reframing the Politics of Urban Feeding," 34–45. See also Broad, *More Than Just Food,* 138.
44. Heynen, "Bending the Bars of Empire," 411.
45. Nixon, "Remarks."

46. Levine, *School Lunch Politics*, 153.
47. Fairfax, "Universal Symposium."
48. Clay, "Beautify America," 41–48.
49. Ibid.
50. This was part of ASFSA's strategic plan, the "Doctrine of Dearborn," which outlined the priorities for its advocacy work during the early and mid-1970s. Reprinted in Martin and Oakley, *Managing Child Nutrition Programs*, 100.
51. Perryman, "Open Letter to Lyng," 29.
52. Lyng, "Comments to ASFSA."
53. Congressman Carl Perkins (D-Kentucky), then chairman of the Committee on Education and Labor, introduced this bill to the House of Representatives in March 1971. While H.R. 5291 was the first, it was not the only attempt; at least four bills for a universal school foodservice program were introduced in both the House and Senate between 1971 and 1974.
54. Perryman, "Log," September 1971.
55. Tronto, *Caring Democracy*, 100–106.
56. Perryman, "Log," June 1974.
57. Poppendieck, *Free for All*, 64–65.
58. "Dr. John Perryman," *School Foodservice Journal*, 30–31.
59. Ibid.
60. The September 1971 and November-December 1974 issues of the *School Foodservice Journal* profiled elderly feeding programs administered by school foodservice departments.
61. ASFSA strongly opposed these changes. Perryman, "Log," November-December 1968.
62. "School Lunch Program Opens to Commercial Contractors," *Volume Feeding Management*.
63. "USDA Considers Allowing Caterers," *Volume Feeding Management*.
64. Perryman, "Log," March 1970.
65. For more about privatization and industry involvement, see Levine, *School Lunch Politics*, 156–63.
66. For more on the relationship between women consumers and Big Food, see Shapiro, *Something from the Oven*; and Deutsch, *Housewife's Paradise*.
67. Perryman, "Log," March 1970.
68. Camp, "Cost of Convenience."
69. Camp, "Glamorizing Vegetables."
70. "Airline Lunch Is Really TV Dinners," *Bridgeport Post*.
71. Sheraton, "School Lunch Utopia?"
72. Sheraton, "Lunches for Pupils."
73. Ibid.
74. Although the USDA was slow to respond to accusations of fraud, it launched a nationwide probe into the use of private vendors and food management firms in the late 1970s. "Lunch Probe Imperils Funds," *Bridgeport Telegram*.
75. Sheraton, "Lunches for Pupils."

76. "Package Weight May Be Suspect," *Bridgeport Post*.

77. Lyng was the head of his family's California-based seed and bean processing company before joining the USDA. This, combined with Clifford Hardin's and Earl Butz's connections to Ralston Purina, helps explain the USDA's eagerness to approve substitute proteins.

78. Michalak, "City to Cut Back on Meat."

79. Perryman, "Log," January 1973.

80. "School Feeding Programs Criticized," *School Foodservice Journal*, 78–81.

81. Ibid.

82. Pollan, "Way We Live Now."

83. Risser, "Why They Love Earl Butz."

84. Ibid.

85. Ibid.

86. Carlson, "Earl Butz."

87. For more on this political transformation as seen through the lens of reproductive politics, see Briggs, *Reproductive Politics*, 19–46.

88. Winson, "Bringing Political Economy into the Debate," 299–312.

89. Bard, *School Lunchroom*, 37.

90. Ibid., 39.

91. For more on New York City's commitment to the frozen food model, see Miller, *20 Million for Lunch*.

92. "Frozen Entrees," *Merchandising*.

93. Bard, *School Lunchroom*, 35–52.

94. Levine, *School Lunch Politics*, 113–15.

95. "Public Hearings on Child Nutrition Programs," Stan Garnett Collection.

96. Poppendieck, *Free for All*, 68.

97. Lachance, "Engineered Foods."

98. Levine, *School Lunch Politics*, 168–69.

99. Poppendieck, *Free for All*, 68.

100. Another controversial policy from this time, Public Law 94–105, Offer versus Serve (OVS), was passed in 1975 in response to reports of excessive food waste.

101. Perryman, "Letters from Washington," 21.

102. Crane, ASFSA President's Column.

103. For more on ASFSA's early ties to industry, see Levine, *School Lunch Politics*, 158–59.

104. Kellogg, "Exhibits Are Important."

105. Westfall, "Don't Miss It."

106. Maley, "President's Notes: Our Advertisers."

107. Ramsey, "New Food Products."

108. "Revolution in School Feeding," *History of ASFSA*, 145.

109. Bash, "Training and Recruitment of Personnel."

110. Ashby, "Sounding Board."

111. The September 1972 *SFJ* included a special feature dedicated to the virtues of convenience food systems (i.e., lower labor costs, ease, efficiency, and high quality).

112. "1965 Educational Seminar," *School Lunch Journal*.
113. Miller, *20 Million for Lunch*, 35.
114. Caton, *History of ASFSA*, 243.
115. Miller, *20 Million for Lunch*, 39.
116. Ponti, "Financing School Food," 30.
117. Lyng, "Comments to ASFSA," September 1969.
118. "High Nourishment at Low Cost," *Hartford Courant*.
119. *Productionism* has been defined as the "ideology and suite of associated practices that privileges agricultural productivity over other values or goals that might be associated with agricultural landscapes or communities." Finan, "Productionism," 358–61.
120. Lyng, "Comments to ASFSA," September 1969.
121. Lynes, "Nutrition Center," 40–43.
122. Chegwidden, "Put the Nutrition Back."
123. Ellis, "To Form a More Perfect Union."
124. Caton, *History of ASFSA*, 239.
125. Cutter, "For the Children."
126. Cutter, "Employment Status of School Lunch Personnel."
127. "Unions, Continued," *School Foodservice Journal*, 60.
128. Ibid.
129. Dehn, "More Unions," 16.
130. Ninemeier, "To Form a More Perfect Union," 79.
131. Burrows, "Forced-Fed," 49–50.
132. For more on how Americans came to judge the success of the public realm as a consumer product, see Cohen, *Consumers' Republic*.
133. Levenstein, *Paradox of Plenty*, 199.
134. Pulido and Peña, "Environmentalism and Positionality," 33–50.
135. Levenstein, *Paradox of Plenty*, 161.
136. Barnett, "Nutrition Advocates Speak Out," 91–103.
137. Jukes, "Down the Primrose Path," 52–61.
138. "Hyperactivity May Be Caused by Artificial Colors," *School Foodservice Journal*, 4.
139. Sheraton, "Lunches for Pupils."
140. Lynes, "In Oakland," 58–64.
141. "V is for Vegetable Garden," *School Foodservice Journal*.
142. "Farm Fresh Products," *School Foodservice Journal*.
143. Foreman, "Remarks for National PTA Convention."
144. Ibid.

3. FROM BIG FOOD TO REAL FOOD LITE

1. For a look at how real food advocates discuss pure maple syrup versus popular pancake syrup brands, see "What's the Problem with Aunt Jemima?," *Alternative Daily*.

2. Stuckler and Nestle, "Big Food," 2.
3. Otero et al., "Neoliberal Diet and Inequality."
4. Centers for Disease Control, *Human Exposure to Environmental Chemicals*.
5. Food allergies among US children increased by about 50 percent between 1997 and 2011. Jackson, Howie, and Akinbami, "Trends in Allergic Conditions." The need to purchase products and plan menu items that all children can eat, even if they have special diets, is a major driver of the movement for minimally processed foods and transparent ingredient labeling. So, too, is the increasing prevalence of young people whose cultural or religious beliefs may require them to eat vegetarian meals or to avoid taboo foods such as pork or shellfish.
6. Minneapolis Public Schools Culinary and Wellness Services, "Ingredients of Concern."
7. Guthman, *Weighing In*, 91–115.
8. Simon, *Hamlet Fire*, 233.
9. Bentley, "Ketchup as a Vegetable."
10. Karnes, interview.
11. Beavers, interview.
12. Bender, interview.
13. Jonen, interview.
14. Eighty USDA commodity products were available for commercial reprocessing in 2018. One hundred and ten companies held multistate or national contracts for commodity reprocessing.
15. Tyson has committed to offering only "clean-label" chicken products through the USDA commodity program in the 2018–2019 school year. Over seventy commodity chicken products will contain no artificial ingredients and be made from chicken raised with no antibiotics ever. Tyson Foods, "Real. Clean. Delicious."
16. Striffler, *Chicken*, 19.
17. Ibid., 8.
18. On washing chickens in chemical baths, see USDA Food Safety and Inspection Service, "Petition for Rulemaking." On poultry capitalism and assembly line processing rates, see Simon, *Hamlet Fire*, 87–88.
19. Levine, *School Lunch Politics*, 182.
20. Miller, *Building Nature's Market*.
21. Carolan, "Affective Sustainable Landscapes," 320–24.
22. Ibid., 323.
23. Sackin, interview.
24. MacKendrick, *Better Safe Than Sorry*, 16.
25. Guides like the Environmental Working Group's "Dirty Dozen" that simplify this information into rules or lists are popular for this reason.
26. Aubrey, "26-Ingredient School Lunch Burger."
27. Zimmerman, "What's Inside a School Lunch Burger?"
28. Andrews, "Processing Aids, Labeling."
29. For more on the FDA and its management of GRAS, see MacKendrick, *Better Safe Than Sorry*, 40–42.

30. Belasco, *Appetite for Change*, 135–36.
31. Miller, *Building Nature's Market*, 118.
32. Ibid., 118–19.
33. Wells, "New Food Report."
34. Burros, "Soda Pop Society."
35. For more on Marshall Matz, see Confessore, "School Lunch."
36. Nestle, *Food Politics*.
37. Wood-Wright, "New U.S. Dietary Guidelines."
38. Pew Charitable Trusts, *Fixing the Oversight of Chemicals*.
39. Flynn, "FDA Continues to Trust Industry."
40. Kullgren, "Ag Talking Points."
41. For more on processing aids, see USDA Food Safety and Inspection Service, "Compliance Guide." For more on why processing aids are not labeled, see Andrews, "Processing Aids, Labeling."
42. Bottemiller, "Slimegate."
43. Moss, "Safety of Beef Processing."
44. Siegel, "Tell USDA to Stop."
45. Associated Press, "Public Schools Can Opt Out."
46. The strategy of mobilizing around one ingredient at a time or one supplier at a time works to Big Food's advantage. See Clapp and Scrinis, "Big Food," 4.
47. Beef Products, Inc., "Beef Is Beef."
48. For more on the difference between neoliberal food activism and food activism that builds a politics of the possible, see Alkon and Guthman, *New Food Activism*, 1–20.
49. As of March 2018, the USFA was a coalition of eleven of the largest school districts in the United States and the nonprofit Alliance for a Healthier Generation. Focus operated at an even more expansive scale, encompassing forty-five urban districts in its network of regional "learning labs," though it merged with Food-Corps in early 2018.
50. Urban School Food Alliance, "Alliance of Alliances."
51. Focus engages in advocacy, particularly when Congress or the USDA is considering legislation related to school food.
52. School Food Focus, "Ingredient Guide for Better School Food."
53. For an example of this, see Hawkes and Harris, "Content of Food Industry Pledges."
54. Guthman uses the term "organic lite" to describe how the agribusiness industry's involvement in shaping the standards and discourse of organic agriculture restricted "the ability for even the most committed organic growers to farm in more sustainable ways." Guthman, "Trouble with 'Organic Lite,'" 307.
55. Watrous, "Q&A: Nestle USA."
56. Public concern about consuming "ultraprocessed" food is fueling industry efforts to provide minimally processed, local, organic, natural, clean, and real foods. Katz and Williams, "Cleaning Up Processed Foods."
57. Berenstein, "Clean Label's Dirty Little Secret."

58. Watrous, "Trend of Year: Clean Label." Millennials' preference for socially and environmentally responsible companies, coupled with the emergence of new technologies that enable product and supply chain transparency, is driving this trend. Winston, "Keeping Up."

59. Panera, "Panera Bread." See also Panera, "No No List."

60. "Papa John's Completes Removal," *BusinessWire*.

61. Ibid.

62. Campbell's, "What Is Real Food?"

63. Moss, "Science of Addictive Junk Food."

64. Ibid.

65. For a discussion of the challenges of cooking with limited resources, see Bowen, Elliott, and Brenton, "Joy of Cooking?," 20–25. For a broader discussion of home cooking in the contemporary United States, see Trubek, *Making Modern Meals*. And for a discussion of food, care, and women's sense of identity, see Cairns and Johnston, *Food and Femininity*.

66. Hochschild, *Time Bind*. For more on the work-spend cycle, see Schor, *Overworked American*.

67. Philip Morris (the cigarette company) acquired Kraft for $13.1 billion in 1988, in what was then the nation's largest non-oil merger.

68. Cairns, Johnston, and MacKendrick, "Feeding the 'Organic Child,'" 97–118. This dynamic exacerbates gender and class burdens in alternative food provisioning, see Castellano, "Gendered Act" and "Third Shift?"

69. Hamrick, "Americans Spend."

70. Tyson and Walske, "Revolution Foods," 125–41.

71. Hamrick, "Americans Spend."

72. MacKendrick, *Better Safe Than Sorry*, 13.

73. MacKendrick, "More Work for Mother," 705–28.

74. Campbell's, "Campbell's Real Food Philosophy."

75. Product reformulation may become faster and cheaper when clean-label chemistry matures. Until then, some Big Food companies diversify their portfolios by acquiring real food companies and brands that are already profitable. Others develop clean-label items as part of a smaller portfolio of premium offerings.

76. Berenstein, "Clean Label's Dirty Little Secret."

77. Mahlow, "Understanding Clean Label Trends."

78. Clapp and Scrinis, "Big Food," 10.

79. Perdue Foodservice, "Kings Delight®."

80. Stuckler and Nestle, "Big Food," 2–3.

81. Brownell and Warner, "Perils of Ignoring History," 259–94.

82. When schools have higher culinary capacity, they also have greater autonomy to purchase real food and leverage their collective purchasing power to drive reforms up the food chain. See, for example, Stanley, Colasanti, and Conner, "'Real Chicken' Revolution," 384–87.

83. For more on the conflict of interest and industry self-promotion through school health initiatives in the context of the NSLP and especially the Let's Move

Salad Bars to Schools initiative, see Gard and Pluim, *Schools and Public Health,* 181–203.

84. Shen, "Big Food Corporations."
85. Pollan, "Big Food Strikes Back."
86. For an extended discussion of how Big Food influences markets and public policy, see Clapp and Scrinis, "Big Food," 578–95. See also Nestle, *Food Politics.*
87. Confessore, "School Lunch."
88. Siegel, "Reagan Revisited."
89. Some foodservice directors were especially critical of the SNA's position. See, for instance, Cooper, "School Nutrition Annual Round-Up."
90. Blad, "Proposed School Lunch Waivers."
91. For more on the waiver debate, see Woo Baidal and Taveras, "Protecting Progress against Childhood Obesity," 1862–65.
92. Poppendieck describes a similar experience at the SNA exhibit hall. She argues that the relationships between buyers and sellers—especially the attention and respect afforded the child nutrition professionals—influence which foods end up on the menu. Poppendieck, *Free for All,* 108–10.
93. School Nutrition Association, "Do You Know."
94. A district purchasing agent could, for example, buy $140,000 worth of carrots from a local farmer after soliciting three price quotes from potential suppliers. If the district needed $150,000 worth of carrots, however, it would go through the formal bid process.
95. USDA FNS, *Food Buying Guide.*
96. Woldow, "Choicelunch Founder."
97. Chef Ann Foundation, "#RealSchoolFood: Future is Fresh."
98. Chef Ann Foundation, "#RealSchoolFood is Back!"
99. Ibid.
100. Collins, "Can Schools Save Kids' Palates?," 323–26.
101. Ten years after RevFoods sold its first preplated lunches to schools in California's Bay Area, the company had expanded to sixteen states and the District of Columbia. It now offers bulk "cafeteria-style" service and a retail line of convenience kits and prepackaged meals and snacks. Tyson and Walske, "Revolution Foods."
102. Revolution Foods, "Our Mission."
103. B Corps are for-profit companies certified by the nonprofit B Lab to meet criteria related to social and environmental performance, accountability, and transparency. B Corporation, "What Are B Corps?"
104. RevFoods has contracts in multiple cities. The largest is a $9 million contract to supply the 114 schools of the San Francisco Unified School District. Schwartz, "Revolution Foods in San Francisco."
105. Mcgray, "War Over America's Lunch."
106. Dreilinger, "Labor Leaders"; and Woldow, "Who Should Lead."
107. Miller, *Building Nature's Market,* 13.
108. For many school foodservice directors, legumes were the most difficult category of the new meal pattern to satisfy. Back in 2012, I overheard one vendor talk

about "carrying" the legume requirement with a slice of pizza. Modern food science can make this possible by reformulating recipes to include white bean flour in the crust and puree in the tomato sauce. This strategy, often referred to as "stealth health," is little more than the long-standing practice of nutrient fortification updated for the real food era. For more on stealth health, see "What Is 'Stealth Health?'," *Food Service Director*.

109. Wilking, *Copycat Snacks in Schools*.

110. Clapp and Scrinis, "Big Food," 4. There is a large body of scholarship on corporate co-optation of alternative food movements, including Jaffee and Howard, "Corporate Cooptation"; Johnston, Biro, and MacKendrick, "Lost in the Supermarket," 509–32; and Thompson and Coskuner-Balli, "Countervailing Market Responses," 135–52.

111. Real Food Challenge, "What Is Real Food?"

112. Poppendieck, *Free for All*, 292–96.

113. For more on the emergence of what Harriet Friedmann has called a "corporate-environmental food regime" and its characteristics, see Campbell, "Breaking New Ground," 309.

114. Bowen, Brenton, and Elliott, *Pressure Cooker*.

115. For more on how meals have been prepared in American homes and the changing labor landscape, see Trubek, *Making Modern Meals*. See also Laudan, "Plea for Culinary Modernism," 36–44.

116. Deutsch, "Memories of Mothers," 173–74.

117. Gibson and Dempsey, "Make Good Choices, Kid," 50.

4. CAFETERIA WORKERS IN THE "PRISON OF LOVE"

1. Jones, "Lunch Shaming."
2. Ibid.
3. Frontline care workers are disproportionately women without college degrees. Across the care sector, the dirtiest, most dangerous forms of intimate caregiving tend to fall on the shoulders of immigrant women and women of color. Glenn, "From Servitude to Service Work," 1–43.
4. Tronto, *Caring Democracy*, 103–5. For a discussion of devaluation theory, see England, "Emerging Theories of Care Work," 381–99.
5. Workers have varied experiences, but the oral histories, interviews, and participant observation I share in this chapter speak to broad trends within the NSLP.
6. Di Chiro, "Living Environmentalisms," 276–98.
7. Ibid., 280.
8. Daniels, "Invisible Work."
9. Sandler, "Lunchlady Land."
10. To see "Lunchlady Land" on *Saturday Night Live*, go to https://youtu.be/VY14zcUM9SI.
11. Vancil-Leap, "Gendered Representations of School Lunch Ladies," 67–85.

12. Ibid.

13. Ramey, interview. For more on how workers' attitudes affect children's reception of school lunch, see Best, *Fast-Food Kids*, 67–68. For more on the perception of lunch ladies, see Poppendieck, *Free for All*, 276–77. And for an ethnographic study of school cafeteria workers, see Byrd, "Serving amid Institutional Camouflage."

14. Federici, *Caliban and the Witch*.

15. Vancil-Leap, "Gendered Representations of School Lunch Ladies."

16. Gibson and Dempsey, "Make Good Choices, Kid" 44–58.

17. National Center for Education Statistics, "Cabell County Schools."

18. Black, "Revenge of the Lunch Lady."

19. Ibid.

20. Cabell County Schools, "Cabell Connection: Scratch Cooking."

21. School Nutrition Association, "School Nutrition Professionals."

22. As Arlie Hochschild shows in her study of "nicer than natural" airline stewardesses and "nastier than natural" bill collectors, emotional labor can be rationalized through recruitment and training. Despite being honed into concrete modes of interaction and expression through managerial techniques, these learned proclivities are unlikely to result in significant remuneration for the worker. Hochschild, *Managed Heart*.

23. Hanks, interview.

24. Rylie, interview.

25. The relationship between the providers and recipients of care matters; see Himmelweit, "Prospects for Caring," 583. See also Tronto, *Caring Democracy*, 22–23.

26. Average daily participation and meals per labor hour are two of the most widely used performance indicators in the NSLP. Rushing, "Essential KPIs." As Poppendieck notes, the NSLP overemphasizes easily measurable outputs (e.g., meals served) at the expense of less easily measurable outputs (e.g., quality care). Poppendieck, *Free for All*, 132.

27. All K-12 foodservice workers are part of the reproductive labor force, though only a subset of workers who have regular face-to-face interaction with the kids provide "nurturant" care. For a discussion of this distinction, see Duffy, "Reproducing Labor Inequalities," 73.

28. Drake, interview.

29. Ibid.

30. Ibid.

31. Johnson, interview.

32. Ibid.

33. Ibid.

34. Kavanaugh, interview.

35. School Nutrition Association, "Comments on School Lunch Shaming."

36. USDA FNS, *Special Nutrition Program Operations Study*.

37. Brown, "'He Knew the Kids.'"

38. Lang, "Fund Honors Philando Castile's Legacy."

39. Brown, "'He Knew the Kids.'"
40. Anti-Lunch Shaming Act of 2017, S. 1064.
41. Folbre, "Holding Hands at Midnight," 73–92.
42. Jacobs and Graham-Squire, "Labor Standards."
43. My own view of the "union difference" has been influenced by UNITE HERE Local 217, which prioritizes workplace democracy and labor-community alliances and uses its contract negotiations to bargain for the common good.
44. This type of self-exploitation has parallels across care industries, where "owners and managers often seem to depend on their workers' willingness to sacrifice for their clients." England, Folbre, and Leana, "Motivating Care," 33.
45. A typical K–12 cafeteria employee worked twenty-five hours a week for forty weeks in 2008. Since some weeks include school holidays, I round this down to 180 days. A daily fifteen minutes of unpaid extra work then equals forty-five hours of free work by the end of the school year.
46. Systematic research on the difference in wages and benefits for employees working in outsourced versus self-operated programs underscores the truth of this claim. Jacobs and Graham-Squire, "Labor Standards," 448–50. Outsourced cafeteria workers in New Jersey earned $4–$6 an hour less than those hired directly by school districts. McCain, "Serving Students."
47. Pratt, interview.
48. Ibid. Pratt never specified the class, race, or ethnic backgrounds of these women, but her statement reflects the norms of white middle-class motherhood. The postwar ideology of a family with a male breadwinner whose wife needed only "supplementary" income was racialized.
49. Graham, interview.
50. Foodservice directors I interviewed between 2012 and 2016 often struggled to recruit and retain workers for entry-level positions (two- to five-hour shifts). In some districts, retired school cooks fill the short-hour and substitute positions and may be satisfied with the limited hours, unlike younger workers who need more than "supplementary" earnings.
51. The race and ethnicity of these frontline cafeteria workers mirror that of their respective state populations and the total US workforce, yet the criticisms wielded against cafeteria workers are not only about generational differences but, at times, are racially coded.
52. Davis-Palms, interview.
53. Hawkins, interview.
54. Talley, interview.
55. Romanticizing care work as altruistic deflects attention away from inadequate compensation characteristic of such jobs. England, Folbre, and Leana, "Motivating Care."
56. Jacobs and Graham-Squire, "Labor Standards," 450.
57. This figure is consistent with a survey of Local 217 workers, which revealed that nearly three-quarters were primary providers for their families. Gaddis and Cruz-Uribe, *Healthy Kids First*.

58. Glenn argues such jobs are shaped by coercion, the "physical, economic, social, or moral pressure used to induce someone to do something." Glenn, *Forced to Care*, 6–7.

59. National Partnership for Women and Families, "America's Women and Wage Gap."

60. Cafeteria workers in New Jersey expressed similar motivations and experiences. McCain, "Serving Students," 6–7.

61. Many cafeteria workers hold second jobs, often in home care/cleaning or the service sector, especially restaurants, cafeterias, and assisted-living facilities.

62. USDA FNS, "Child Nutrition Tables."

63. Clark et al., interview.

64. Boris and Klein, *Caring for America*, 17.

65. Improving training, wages, and working conditions would likely decrease turnover and lead to better care. Folbre, *Invisible Heart*, 63. Recent scholarship also makes the case for improving training and job quality among public foodservice workers; see Tsui et al., "Missed Opportunities for Improving Nutrition," e14–e20.

66. Workers experience a loss of professional identity as their jobs become degraded and deskilled. Sennett, *Corrosion of Character*, 94.

67. Children are much likelier to thrive when they like and trust cafeteria workers and other adults in their social lives. Whitebook and Sakai, *By a Thread*, 13.

68. Watkins et al., interview.

69. Each additional hour that care workers add to their weekly paychecks (to reach full time) increases their odds of staying in the job by 2 percent. Howes, Leana, and Smith, "Paid Care Work," 78.

70. Colston, interview.

71. Maye, interview.

72. Ibid.

73. Elam and McElwain, interview.

74. Matsufuru, interview.

75. Jaffe and Gertler, "Victual Vicissitudes," 143–46.

76. Trubek, *Making Modern Meals*.

77. A similar dynamic exists in low-wage textile work. Collins, "Mapping a Global Labor Market," 921–40.

78. Lapeze, interview.

79. Grabert, interview.

80. Crews, interview.

81. Briggs, interview.

82. There are exceptions, but the overall trend is toward "heat-and-serve" preparation. For an overview of how culinary infrastructure has changed, see Poppendieck, *Free for All*, 88–98. For more on the status of kitchen infrastructure for scratch cooking, see Collins, "Can Schools Save Kids' Palates?," 323–26. See also Kids' Safe and Healthful Foods Project, *Serving Healthy School Meals*.

83. Briggs, interview.

84. Sennett, *Corrosion of Character*.

85. O'Donnell, "Aramark Workers."
86. Appel, "Custodians vs. Aramark."
87. King, "School Board."
88. Bass, "On the Menu: Baked Chicken."
89. Gaddis and Cruz-Uribe, *Healthy Kids First*.

5. BUILDING A REAL FOOD ECONOMY

1. Tyson Foods, the largest meatpacker in the United States, acquired Smart Chicken in June 2018.
2. Minneapolis Public Schools, "2016 Fact Sheet."
3. Minneapolis Public Schools, "Demographics."
4. Shilling, "Bertrand Weber."
5. Poppendieck, *Free for All*, 225–26.
6. Maxwell, "Minneapolis Leader."
7. Ibid.
8. Ibid.
9. In addition to serving in multiple leadership positions for the National Farm to School Network and the School Nutrition Association, Weber was named Foodservice Director of the Month in August 2014 by *Foodservice Director* magazine. Shilling, "Bertrand Weber."
10. Boss, "Facility Design Project."
11. Minneapolis Public Schools, *Agreement*.
12. Attracting more men to the public work of feeding—and to caring more generally—sends an important message to kids about who does care work. On the other hand, it could reproduce existing gender hierarchies and economic inequalities if men are hired for the best positions.
13. At least that's how long their bid hours say they should be working, but often the two FSAs end up working more like 4 hours and 5.5 hours because of understaffing.
14. A similar phenomenon occurred when celebrity chef Jamie Oliver attempted to reform school lunch in Huntington, West Virginia. Black, "Revenge of the Lunch Lady."
15. Kids' Safe and Healthful Foods Project, *Serving Healthy School Meals*.
16. USDA Office of Communications, "USDA Awards Grants."
17. When public entities and nonprofits are forced to turn to the private sector for support, it lets the government off the hook and reinforces the notion that the government is not capable of providing a safety net as effectively or efficiently as the private sector can. This erodes public confidence and gives lawmakers reason to make further cuts to the programs. It also compromises the mission, vision, and values of public sector organizations and nonprofits, which are at least partially beholden to the views and priorities of their donors, which can run counter to their efforts to solve the root causes of the issues they're trying to solve. Fisher, *Big Hunger*.

18. This proposal has unintended consequences. "When the buying power gets too big, you cut out the type of 'values based' and hyperlocal purchasing that schools are able to do on their own," explained Andrea Northup in an email exchange with the author in late 2018. It prioritizes cheapness over the direct community reinvestment and values of farm-to-school. Sharing resources, skills, and strategies is great, but pushing schools to scale up and aggregate purchasing should be approached with caution.
19. Kids' Safe and Healthful Foods Project, *Serving Healthy School Meals*, 25.
20. Miller, "Kids Need #realschoolfood."
21. Campbell, "Breaking New Ground."
22. For more on the evolution of farm-to-school, see Feenstra and Ohmart, "Evolution."
23. USDA Rural Development, "About RD."
24. For more on the bid process, see School Nutrition Association, *Solving the Procurement Puzzle*.
25. The pilot allows the California, Connecticut, Michigan, New York, Oregon, Virginia, Washington, and Wisconsin state agencies to apply geographic preference and form direct-contract relationships with farmers and produce companies when sourcing unprocessed fruits and vegetables for the federal government's commodity distribution program. USDA FNS, "Food Distribution."
26. Regional staff build farm-to-school capacity within the state agencies that administer NSLP funding to schools and within the state-level departments of agriculture and health that are integral to the work, which amplifies the reach of limited USDA funding.
27. Kloppenburg and Hassanein, "From Old School to Reform School?"
28. Christensen et al., *Economic Impacts of Farm to School*.
29. Rauzon et al., "Changing Students' Knowledge."
30. Lyson, "National Policy and State Dynamics."
31. Allen and Guthman, "From 'Old School' to 'Farm-to-School.'"
32. Regional USDA farm-to-school staff report that small rural districts find this especially challenging. Farm-to-school Census data show that small rural communities are less likely to have farm-to-school programs than urban schools. They lack the economy of scale necessary to hire a robust staff that can offer comprehensive farm-to-school programs.
33. Minneapolis Public Schools Culinary and Wellness Services, "Request for Proposal."
34. Northup, "MPS Farm to School Toolkit."
35. To work with Minneapolis Public Schools, farms must have a food safety plan, product liability insurance, and a recent water test, in addition to a farm visit from the farm-to-school coordinator and a University of Minnesota food safety expert.
36. Rosenthal and Caruso, "Bringing School Foodservice Staff Back."
37. In a similar vein, Minneapolis Public Schools secured grant funding to purchase an industrial apple slicer for its central nutrition center. This reduces prep time

for school-based staff, whose time can then, according to Weber, be reallocated toward cooking on site.

38. Small-scale equipment can make scratch cooking with farm-to-school ingredients much easier. Anna, a manager of a high school with an on-site kitchen, credits MPS's dual strategy of investing in small-scale equipment and outsourcing some of the farm-to-school processing to a produce company for making it relatively easy to prepare farm-to-school foods within the constraints of the NSLP.

39. A range of specialty companies, including Northern Girl in New England and Just Local in the upper Midwest, have stepped in to process local foods into forms that are more convenient for schools to use.

40. School foodservice director Doug Davis describes a similar dynamic in Burlington, Vermont. Davis, Robert, and Kang, "Going Local." Such collaborative efforts are also emerging at regional and even national scales; see Stanley, Colasanti, and Conner, "'Real Chicken' Revolution."

41. USDA FNS, "Overview: Farm to School Census."

42. Henry, "Berkeley's School Lunch Program."

43. Nargi, "School Food Hero Betti Wiggins."

44. Detroit Public Schools, "Office of School Nutrition."

45. Afana, "Brother of Elon Musk."

46. Ibid.

47. For more on the impact of cooking classes, see Hersch et al., "Impact of Cooking Classes." For a review of the impact of school gardens, see Ohly et al., "Systematic Review." And for "comprehensive" approaches, see Gatto et al., "LA Sprouts Randomized Controlled Nutrition."

48. FoodCorps (now merged with Focus) aims to create a "schoolwide culture of health" by working with parents, teachers, administrators, and school foodservice staff to provide children with hands-on cooking and gardening classes and encouragement to try healthy cafeteria foods. Siegel, "Why Is FoodCorps Merging?"

49. See, for instance, USDA FNS, "School Gardening."

50. When naming their partners, Uhlenkamp mentioned over fifteen, including statewide agencies, county organizations, and local branches of agricultural supply stores. Eppen and Uhlenkamp recommend that schools look for underutilized city property, privately owned local fields, school-owned property, and even county fairgrounds for land that can be used for free or leased for a small fee.

51. Community Blueprint, "Growing a Better School Lunch."

52. Ruis, *Eating to Learn*, 59–86.

53. Chatterjee et al., "'Can't We Just Have Some Sazón?'"

54. Birch, "Development of Food Preferences."

55. Low-income parents' risk aversion may restrict children's taste formation. Daniel, "Economic Constraints on Taste Formation."

56. Public health literature, particularly studies of the sociocultural determinants of taste, recommends such strategies. Birch, "Development of Food Preferences." Recent scholarship also speaks to the importance of "responsive feeding" in promoting a liking for new foods. Black and Aboud, "Responsive Feeding."

57. The HHFKA requires kids who participate in the NSLP to take half a cup of fruit or vegetables with their lunch, even if they don't plan on eating it. Some people take issue with this policy, including Sheila, an Iowa foodservice director, who told me: "Anyone who is a child-feeding expert would say 'You want to encourage kids to taste things' rather than 'You don't like this food, but put a half cup on your plate' because as soon as they are forced to do that, then it becomes 'I'm not going to eat *any* now that you made me do that.'"

58. Maimaran and Fishbach, "If It's Useful."

59. Carolan, "Affective Sustainable Landscapes."

60. Ibid.

61. Taste development is a process. Lakkakula et al., "Repeated Taste Exposure." The NSLP and the USDA's Fresh Fruit and Vegetable Program are two publicly funded mechanisms for exposing children to healthy fruits and vegetables on a repeated basis in order to develop increased liking.

62. Drake, interview.

63. Minneapolis Public Schools Culinary and Wellness Services, "True Food Taste Test."

64. See, for example, Minneapolis Public Schools Culinary and Wellness Services, "Red Rice Apple Salad Mini-Lesson Ideas" for social sciences and English and for science and math.

65. It can be challenging to find the space to store all the fresh ingredients. Paul says they're now dealing with anywhere between three to five times as much product on a given day, depending on the menu.

66. Minneapolis Public Schools Culinary and Wellness Services, "Minnesota Thursdays."

67. St. Paul's foodservice director Stacy Koppen pointed out that adapting community-sourced recipes—often produced through embodied knowledge (e.g., a handful of this and a pinch of that)—for an institutional foodservice environment takes time and effort.

68. When St. Paul public schools serve community-sourced dishes, they typically serve a popular alternate like chicken nuggets or corn dogs to offset an anticipated loss in participation, which results in lower participation for the ethnic meal.

69. Wright, "Guidelines for Envisioning," 38.

CONCLUSION

1. Tronto, *Caring Democracy,* 170.

2. The discussion of desirability, viability, and achievability comes from Wright, "Guidelines for Envisioning." Morgan and Sonnino articulate a new "moral economy" of school food based on three factors: a broad conception of care, public procurement as a tool for enhancing social justice and ecological sustainability, and active citizen participation in the design and delivery of school food programs. Morgan and Sonnino, *School Food Revolution.* My vision shares similarities but is

heavily influenced by adrienne maree brown's assertion that contemporary movements for social justice need to prioritize impacted leadership, privileged support, and feminist leadership. Brown, *Emergent Strategy*, 65–66. Some of the ideas presented in this conclusion were developed in an abbreviated form in Gaddis and Coplen, "Reorganizing School Lunch."

3. Boston Public Schools, "Boston Offers Universal Free Meals."
4. Chicago Public Schools, "Free Meals for All CPS Students."
5. New York City Department of Education, "Free School Lunch for All."
6. Food Research and Action Center, "Community Eligibility."
7. Folbre, Howes, and Leana, "Care Policy and Research Agenda."
8. Offer and Schneider, "Revisiting the Gender Gap."
9. Poppendieck, *Free for All*, 290.
10. Patel and Moore, *History of the World*, 110.
11. Kang, "Organic School Lunch Programs."
12. Tronto, *Caring Democracy*.
13. Rooted In Community, "Youth Food Bill of Rights."
14. Carolan, "Affective Sustainable Landscapes," 317–29.
15. For more on the potential for the GFPP to advance both worker justice and sustainable food systems, see Lo and Delwiche, "Good Food Purchasing Policy."
16. Center for Good Food Purchasing, Good Food Purchasing Program (website).
17. Morgan and Sonnino, *School Food Revolution*, 65–88.
18. Otsuki, "Sustainable Partnerships."
19. Kleine and Brightwell, "Repoliticising and Scaling-up Ethical Consumption."
20. Center for Ecoliteracy, *School-Community Kitchens*.
21. Chef Ann Foundation, "Boulder Valley School District."
22. Coalition for Community Schools, "What Is a Community School?"
23. McAlevey, *No Shortcuts*.
24. Folbre, "Demanding Quality," 10.
25. Gaddis, "Mobilizing."
26. Cruz-Uribe, interview; Hernandez, interview.
27. McAlevey, *No Shortcuts*, 34–37.
28. For more on situated knowledges, see "Feminist Epistemology," Stanford Encyclopedia of Philosophy.
29. For models of recent academic-activist collaborations, see Alkon and Guthman, *New Food Activism*. See also Levkoe et al., "Forging Links."

BIBLIOGRAPHY

Sources frequently cited may be identified by the following abbreviations:

ASFSA	American School Food Service Association (now SNA)
CNA, ICN	Child Nutrition Archives, Institute of Child Nutrition, University of Mississippi, Oxford, MS
FNS	Food and Nutrition Service (agency of the USDA)
MPS	Minneapolis Public Schools
SNA	School Nutrition Association (formerly ASFSA)
USDA	United States Department of Agriculture

Afana, Dana. "Brother of Elon Musk to Bring $5M Food Initiative to Michigan Schools." MLive, January 17, 2018. www.mlive.com/news/detroit/index.ssf/2018/01/brother_of_elon_musk_to_bring.html.

"Airline Lunch Is Really TV Dinners." *Bridgeport (Connecticut) Post,* August 11, 1972. Thomas Carroll personal collection.

Alkon, Alison, and Julie Guthman, eds. *The New Food Activism: Opposition, Cooperation, and Collective Action.* Oakland: University of California Press, 2017.

Allegretto, Sylvia A., Marc Doussard, Dave Graham-Squire, Ken Jacobs, Dan Thompson, and Jeremy Thompson. *Fast Food, Poverty Wages: The Public Cost of Low-Wage Jobs in the Fast-Food Industry.* Berkeley, CA: UC Berkeley Labor Center, 2013. http://laborcenter.berkeley.edu/fast-food-poverty-wages-the-public-cost-of-low-wage-jobs-in-the-fast-food-industry/.

Allen, Patricia, and Julie Guthman. "From 'Old School' to 'Farm-to-School': Neoliberalization from the Ground Up." *Agriculture and Human Values* 23, no. 4 (2006): 401–15.

Allen, Patricia, and Carolyn Sachs. "Women and Food Chains: The Gendered Politics of Food." *International Journal of Sociology* 15, no. 1 (2007): 1–23.

Andrews, James. "Processing Aids, Labeling and 'Pink Slime': What Doesn't Have to Be Labeled and Why?" *Food Safety News*, March 26, 2012. www.foodsafetynews.com/2012/03/processing-aids-labeling-and-pink-slime/#.WS3E3RPysWo.

———. "Processing Aids: What's Not on the Label, and Why?" *Food Safety News*, June 10, 2013. www.foodsafetynews.com/2013/06/processing-aids-whats-not-on-the-label-and-why/#.WS3K3BPysWo.

Anti-Lunch Shaming Act of 2017, S. 1064. 115th Congress. www.govtrack.us/congress/bills/115/s1064.

Appel, Allen. "Aramark Booted, Once Again." *New Haven Independent*. June 24, 2008. www.newhavenindependent.org/index.php/archives/entry/aramark_booted_yet_again/.

———. "Aramark on the Way Out." *New Haven Independent*, April 29, 2008. www.newhavenindependent.org/index.php/archives/entry/aramark_on_the_way_out/.

———. "Custodians vs. Aramark: Round 2." *New Haven Independent*, February 28, 2008. www.newhavenindependent.org/index.php/archives/entry/custodians_vs._aramark_round_2.

———. "School Snares 'Food Dude.'" *New Haven Independent*, July 11, 2008. www.newhavenindependent.org/archives/2008/07/board_of_ed_sna.php.

Apple, Rima Dombrow. *Perfect Motherhood: Science and Childrearing in America*. New Brunswick, NJ: Rutgers University Press, 2006.

Apple, Rima Dombrow, and Joyce Coleman. "'As Members of the Social Whole': A History of Social Reform as a Focus of Home Economics, 1895–1940." *Family and Consumer Sciences Research Journal* 32, no. 2 (2003): 104–26.

Ashby, Rodney A. "Sounding Board." *School Lunch Journal*, April 1961.

Associated Press. "Public Schools Can Opt Out of 'Pink Slime' Beef: USDA; More Meat Options for National School Lunch Program." *Daily News*, March 15, 2012. www.nydailynews.com/life-style/health/public-schools-opt-pink-slime-beef-usda-meat-options-national-school-lunch-program-article-1.1039871.

Aubrey, Allison. "What's Inside the 26-Ingredient School Lunch Burger?" National Public Radio, April 2, 2012. www.npr.org/sections/thesalt/2012/04/02/149717358/whats-inside-the-26-ingredient-school-lunch-burger.

B Corporation. "What Are B Corps?" www.bcorporation.net/what-are-b-corps.

Bard, Bernard. *The School Lunchroom: Time of Trial*. Hoboken, NJ: Wiley, 1968.

Barnett, Lucille. "Nutrition Advocates Speak Out." *School Foodservice Journal*, September 1973.

Bash, Wade. "Training and Recruitment of Personnel." *School Lunch Journal*, April 1963.

Bass, Paul. "On the Menu: Baked Chicken." *New Haven Independent*, March 25, 2009.

Beavers, Elizabeth. Interview by Sandy Sadler, August 3, 2006. Transcript. Oral History Project, CNA, ICN. http://archives.theicn.org/oral-history-project/elizabeth-beavers.

Beef Products, Inc. "Beef Is Beef: The Facts on Lean Finely Textured Beef." n.d. Accessed May 30, 2017. http://beefisbeef.com.

Belasco, Warren J. *Appetite for Change: How the Counterculture Took on the Food Industry.* Ithaca, NY: Cornell University Press, 2014.

Bender, Betty. Interview by Meredith Johnston, December 2, 2004. Transcript. Oral History Project, CNA, ICN. http://archives.theicn.org/oral-history-project/betty-bender/.

Bentley, Amy. "Ketchup as a Vegetable: Condiments, Culture, and the Politics of School Lunch in Reagan's America." In *Sauces and Identity in the Western World*, edited by Deirdre Murphy, Beth Forrest, and Andrew Donnelly. New York: Oxford University Press, forthcoming.

Berenstein, Nadia. "Clean Label's Dirty Little Secret." *New Food Economy*, February 1, 2018. https://newfoodeconomy.org/clean-label-dirty-little-secret/.

Best, Amy. *Fast-Food Kids: French Fries, Lunch Lines, and Social Ties.* New York: New York University Press, 2017.

Birch, Leann. "Development of Food Preferences." *Annual Review of Nutrition* 19 (1999): 41–62.

Black, Jane. "Revenge of the Lunch Lady: How an Unassuming Bureaucrat Outsmarted Jamie Oliver and Pulled Off an Honest-to-God Miracle in One of America's Unhealthiest Cities." *Huffington Post*, February 9, 2017.

Black, Maureen, and Frances Aboud. "Responsive Feeding Is Embedded in a Theoretical Framework of Responsive Parenting." *Journal of Nutrition* 141, no. 3 (2011): 490–94.

Blad, Evie. "Proposed School Lunch Waivers Prompt Debate." *Education Week* 33, no. 33 (May 30, 2014): 10–11. www.edweek.org/ew/articles/2014/06/04/33foodfight.h33.html.

Boris, Eileen. "The Power of Motherhood: Black and White Activist Women Redefine the 'Political.'" In *Mothers of a New World: Maternalist Politics and the Origins of Welfare States*, edited by Seth Koven and Sonya Michel. London: Routledge, 1993.

Boris, Eileen, and Jennifer Klein. *Caring for America: Home Health Workers in the Shadow of the Welfare State.* New York: Oxford University Press, 2015.

Boss, Donna. "Facility Design Project of the Month: Minneapolis Public Schools." *Foodservice Equipment and Supplies*, August 1, 2016.

Boston Home and School Association. *The Unique Function of the Boston Home and School Association.* Boston: Boston Home and School Association, November 1909. https://archive.org/details/uniquefunctionofoobost.

Boston Public Schools Communications. "Boston Offers Universal Free Meals for Every Child." Press release, December 2013. www.bostonpublicschools.org/Page/110.

Bottemiller, Helena. "Slimegate: Should USDA Require Labeling for LFTB?" *Food Safety News*, April 3, 2012. www.foodsafetynews.com/2012/04/slimegate-should-usda-require-labeling-for-lftb/#.WL9KFxLyuRt.

Bowen, Sarah, Joslyn Brenton, and Sinikka Elliott. *Pressure Cooker: Why Home Cooking Won't Solve Our Problems and What We Can Do about It.* New York: Oxford University Press, 2019.

Bowen, Sarah, Sinikka Elliott, and Joslyn Brenton. "The Joy of Cooking?" *Contexts* 13, no. 3 (2014): 20–25.

Brenton, Joslyn. "The Limits of Intensive Feeding: Maternal Foodwork at the Intersections of Race, Class, and Gender." *Sociology of Health and Illness* 39, no. 6 (2017): 863–77.

Briggs, Laura. *How All Politics Became Reproductive Politics: From Welfare Reform to Foreclosure to Trump*. Oakland: University of California Press, 2018.

Briggs, Marilyn. Interview by Beth King, July 8, 2004. Transcript. Oral History Project CNA, ICN. http://archives.theicn.org/oral-history-project/marilyn-briggs/.

Broad, Garrett. *More Than Just Food: Food Justice and Community Change*. Oakland: University of California Press, 2016.

brown, adrienne maree. *Emergent Strategy: Shaping Change, Changing Worlds*. Chico, CA: AK Press, 2017.

Brown, Emma. "'He Knew the Kids and They Loved Him': Minn. Shooting Victim Was an Adored School Cafeteria Manager." *Washington Post*, July 7, 2016.

Brownell, Kelly, and Kenneth Warner. "The Perils of Ignoring History: Big Tobacco Played Dirty and Millions Died. How Similar Is Big Food?" *Milbank Quarterly* 87, no. 1 (2009): 259–94.

Bryan, Mary de Garmo. *The School Cafeteria*. New York: F. S. Crofts, 1936.

———. "Sixty Years' Growth of School Feeding as a Half Billion Dollar Enterprise." *The Nation's Schools* (1955).

Burawoy, Michael. "The Extended Case Method." *Sociological Theory* 16, no. 1 (March 1998): 4–33. https://doi.org/10.1111/0735-2751.00040.

Burros, Marian. "In the Soda Pop Society." *New York Times*, September 28, 1978.

Burrows, Frances. "Forced-Fed." *School Foodservice Journal*, July-August 1973.

Byrd, Janette. "Serving amid Institutional Camouflage: The Invisibility of School Food Service Workers." Master's thesis, Oregon State University, 2016.

Cabell County Schools. "Cabell Connection: Scratch Cooking." YouTube. Published July 2, 2018. https://youtu.be/2HjuB9Vol2I.

Cairns, Kate, and Josée Johnston. *Food and Femininity*. London: Bloomsbury, 2015.

Cairns, Kate, Josée Johnston, and Norah MacKendrick. "Feeding the 'Organic Child': Mothering through Ethical Consumption." *Journal of Consumer Culture* 13, no. 2 (2013): 97–118.

Camp, Earnestine. "Glamorizing Vegetables," speaking notes to accompany slideshow. Box 9.10. Earnestine Camp Collection, CNA, ICN.

———. "The Cost of Convenience," speaking notes. Box 9.8. Earnestine Camp Collection, CNA, ICN.

Campbell, Hugh. "Breaking New Ground in Food Regime Theory: Corporate Environmentalism, Ecological Feedbacks and the 'Food from Somewhere' Regime?" *Agriculture and Human Values* 26, no. 4 (2009): 309–19.

Campbell's. "Campbell's Real Food Philosophy." Accessed March 1, 2018. www.campbellsoupcompany.com/about-campbell/our-purpose/real-food-philosophy/.

———. "What Is Real Food?" Last updated July 21, 2016. Accessed May 29, 2017. www.campbellsoupcompany.com/newsroom/news/2016/07/21/what-is-real-food.

———. "What's in My Food?" Accessed May 29, 2017. www.whatsinmyfood.com.

Carlson, Michael. "Earl Butz: US Politician Brought Down by Racist Remark." *Guardian,* February 4, 2008. www.theguardian.com/world/2008/feb/04/usa.obituaries.

Carolan, Michael. "Affective Sustainable Landscapes and Care Ecologies: Getting a Real Feel for Alternative Food Communities." *Sustainability Science* 10, no. 2 (2015): 317–29.

———. *The Real Cost of Cheap Food.* London: Earthscan, 2011.

Castellano, Rebecca L. Som. "Alternative Food Networks and Food Provisioning as a Gendered Act." *Agriculture and Human Values* 32, no. 3 (2015): 461–74.

———. "Alternative Food Networks and the Labor of Food Provisioning: A Third Shift?" *Rural Sociology* 81, no. 3 (2016): 445–69.

Caton, Jay. *The History of the American School Food Service Association: A Pinch of Love.* Arlington, VA: School Nutrition Association, 1990.

Center for Ecoliteracy. *School-Community Kitchens: Resource Hubs Serving Students and Surrounding Communities.* Rethinking School Lunch. 2012. www.ecoliteracy.org/sites/default/files/uploads/shared_files/CEL-School-Community-Kitchens.pdf.

Center for Good Food Purchasing. Good Food Purchasing Program (website). Accessed June 14, 2018. https://goodfoodpurchasing.org.

Centers for Disease Control. *Fourth National Report on Human Exposure to Environmental Chemicals.* 2009. www.cdc.gov/exposurereport/pdf/fourthreport.pdf.

Chatterjee, Avik, Genevieve Daftary, Matthew W. Gillman, and Meg Campbell. "'Can't We Just Have Some Sazón?' Student, Family, and Staff Perspectives on a New School Food Program at a Boston High School." *Journal of School Health* 86, no. 4 (2016): 273–80.

Chef Ann Foundation. "Boulder Valley School District Central Kitchen Vision Statement." n.d. Accessed June 14, 2018. www.chefannfoundation.org/assets/uploads/documents/BVSD_CK_Vision_Statement.pdf.

———. "#RealSchoolFood: The Future Is Fresh." October 7, 2015. www.chefannfoundation.org/news-media/the-lunch-line-blog/RealSchoolFood/.

———. "#RealSchoolFood Is Back! Join the Fight to Help Save School Lunches." September 26, 2016. www.chefannfoundation.org/news-media/the-lunch-line-blog/realschoolfood-is-back/.

Chegwidden, Gwen. "Put the Nutrition Back in Child Nutrition Programs." *School Foodservice Journal,* April 1974.

Chicago Public Schools. "Free Meals for All CPS Students under New Federal Program." Accessed June 15, 2018. http://cps.edu/News/Press_releases/Pages/PR1_09_02_2014.aspx.

Christensen, Libby, Becca Jablonski, Lacy Stephens, and Anupama Joshi. *Economic Impacts of Farm to School: Case Studies and Assessment Tools.* National Farm to

School Network. September 2017. www.farmtoschool.org/Resources/EconomicImpactReport.pdf.

Clapp, Jennifer, and Gyorgy Scrinis. "Big Food, Nutritionism, and Corporate Power." *Globalizations* 14, no. 4 (2017): 578–95.

Clark, Bernice, Mary Thompson, Betty Werner, Jean Watts, Joan Bickley, Gertice Rister, Pauline Ballentine, Lova Jean Bullman, Pat Holstein, Susan Cassels, and Marcella Clark. Interview by Virginia Webb and Meredith Johnston, September 21, 2004. Transcript. Oral History Project, CNA, ICN. http://archives.theicn.org/oral-history-project/group-discussion-bernice-clark-mary-thompson/.

Clay, William L. "If You Want to Beautify America, Feed a Child." *School Lunch Journal,* February 1970: 41–48.

Coalition for Community Schools. "What Is a Community School?" Accessed June 14, 2018. www.communityschools.org/aboutschools/what_is_a_community_school.aspx.

Cohen, Lizabeth. *A Consumers' Republic: The Politics of Mass Consumption in Postwar America.* New York: Vintage Books, 2004.

Collins, Beth. "Can Schools Save Kids' Palates? Cooking from Scratch in Schools—the Greatest Food Service Challenge of Our Time." *Childhood Obesity* 8, no. 4 (2012): 323–26.

Collins, Jane L. "Mapping a Global Labor Market: Gender and Skill in the Globalizing Garment Industry." *Gender and Society* 16, no. 6 (2002): 921–40.

———. *The Politics of Value: Three Movements to Change How We Think about the Economy.* Chicago: University of Chicago Press, 2017.

Colston, Arlene. Interview by Linda Godfrey, January 27, 2012. Transcript. Oral History Project, CNA, ICN. http://archives.theicn.org/oral-history-project/arlene-colston/.

Committee on School Lunch Participation. *Their Daily Bread: A Study of the National School Lunch Program.* Atlanta: McNelley-Rudd Printing Service, 1968.

Community Blueprint. "Growing a Better School Lunch." Accessed March 8, 2018. http://communityblueprint.com/portfolio/growing-a-better-school-lunch/.

Confessore, Nicholas. "How School Lunch Became the Latest Political Battleground." *New York Times Magazine,* October 7, 2014.

Cooper, Ann. "School Nutrition Annual Round-Up." *U.S. News and World Report,* July 22, 2015. https://health.usnews.com/health-news/blogs/eat-run/2015/07/22/school-nutrition-annual-round-up.

Crane, Helen. ASFSA President's Column. *School Lunch Journal,* January 1951.

Crews, June. Interview by Meredith Johnston. March 3, 2004. Transcript. Oral History Project, CNA, ICN. http://archives.theicn.org/oral-history-project/june-crews/

Cruz-Uribe, Cristina (Labor organizer, UNITE HERE Local 217), interview with the author, June 2016.

Cutter, Ruth. "Employment Status of School Lunch Personnel." *School Lunch Journal,* June 1961.

———. "For the Children." *School Lunch Journal,* December 1959.

Daniel, Caitlin. "Economic Constraints on Taste Formation and the True Cost of Healthy Eating." *Social Science and Medicine* 148 (2016): 34–41.

Daniels, Arlene Kaplan. "Invisible Work." *Social Problems* 34, no. 5 (1987): 403–15.

Datar, Ashlesha, and Nancy Nicosia, "Outsourcing Meals: Effects of Maternal Work on Children's School Meal Participation." *Social Service Review* 86, no.4 (December 2012): 565–93.

Davis, Doug, Sarah A. Robert, and Mi Ok Kang. "Going Local: Burlington, Vermont's Farm-to-School Program." In *School Food Politics: The Complex Ecology of Hunger and Feeding in Schools Around the World,* edited by Sarah A. Robert and Marcus B. Weaver-Hightower, 162–82. New York: Peter Lang, 2011.

Davis-Palms, Mary. Interview by Melba Hollingsworth, November 12, 2008. Transcript. Oral History Project, CNA, ICN. http://archives.theicn.org/oral-history-project/mary-davis-palms/.

DeBona, Merle. "An Educational Program." *Practical Home Economics.* (October 1942): 354–58.

Dehn, Virginia. "More Unions—Speak Up!" *School Foodservice Journal,* May 1973.

"Deprive Poor Kids in Suburbs of Free Lunch." *Chicago Daily Defender,* December 16, 1972. ProQuest Historical Newspapers (1965–1979).

Detroit Public Schools Community District. "Office of School Nutrition." Accessed March 14, 2018. http://detroitk12.org/content/school-nutrition/.

Deutsch, Tracey. *Building a Housewife's Paradise: Gender, Politics, and American Grocery Stores in the Twentieth Century.* Chapel Hill: University of North Carolina Press, 2010.

———. "Memories of Mothers in the Kitchen: Local Foods, History, and Women's Work." *Radical History Review* 101 (2011): 167–77.

Dewey, John, and Evelyn Dewey. *Schools of To-morrow.* Boston: E. P. Dutton, 1915.

Di Chiro, Giovanna. "Living Environmentalisms: Coalition Politics, Social Reproduction, and Environmental Justice." *Environmental Politics* 17, no. 2 (2008): 276–98.

"Dr. John Perryman: A 21-Year Legacy." *School Foodservice Journal,* November-December 1976.

Drake, Annie. Interview by Linda Godfrey, January 26, 2012. Transcript. Oral History Project, CNA, ICN. http://archives.theicn.org/oral-history-project/annie-drake/.

Dreilinger, Danielle. "Labor Leaders Claim New Orleans School Lunch Provider Is Illegally Pressuring Workers to Keep Union Out." *Times-Picayune,* December 18, 2012.

DuBois, Ellen Carol. "Harriot Stanton Blatch and the Transformation of Class Relations among Woman Suffragists." In *Gender, Class, Race and Reform in the Progressive Era,* edited by Noralee Frankel and Nancy S. Dye. Lexington: University Press of Kentucky, 1991.

Duffy, Mignon. "Reproducing Labor Inequalities: Challenges for Feminists Conceptualizing Care at the Intersections of Gender, Race and Class." *Gender and Society* 19, no. 1 (2005): 66–82.

Dye, Nancy S. "Introduction." In *Gender, Class, Race and Reform in the Progressive Era,* edited by Noralee Frankel and Nancy S. Dye. Lexington: University Press of Kentucky, 1991.

Edible Schoolyard. "Our Pledge to Children and Farmers." Accessed November 1, 2018. https://edibleschoolyard.org/.

Elam, Sylvia, and Paul McElwain. Interview by Meredith Johnston, December 2, 2004. Transcript. Oral History Project, CNA, ICN. http://archives.theicn.org/oral-history-project/sylvia-elam-and-paul-mcelwain/.

Elias, Megan J. *Stir It Up: Home Economics in American Culture.* Philadelphia: University of Pennsylvania Press, 2010.

Ellis, Marjorie. "To Form a More Perfect Union," letter to the editor. *School Foodservice Journal,* November-December 1972.

England, Paula. "Emerging Theories of Care Work." *Annual Reviews of Sociology* 31 (2005): 381–99.

England, Paula, Michelle Budig, and Nancy Folbre. "Wages of Virtue: The Relative Pay of Care Work." *Social Problems* 49, no. 4 (November 2002): 455–73.

England, Paula, Nancy Folbre, and Carrie Leana. "Motivating Care." In *For Love and Money: Care Provision in the United States,* edited by Nancy Folbre. New York: Russell Sage Foundation, 2012.

Environmental Working Group. "EWG's Dirty Dozen Guide to Food Additives." November 12, 2014. Accessed February 15, 2017. www.ewg.org/research/ewg-s-dirty-dozen-guide-food-additives.

Fairfax, Jean. "Universal Symposium: Each Child's Right," *School Foodservice Journal,* October 1971.

"Farm Fresh Products from Field to Plate." *School Foodservice Journal,* April 1976.

Federici, Silvia. *Caliban and the Witch.* New York: Autonomedia, 2004.

Feenstra, Gail, and Jeri Ohmart. "The Evolution of the School Food and Farm to School Movement in the United States: Connecting Childhood Health, Farms, and Communities." *Childhood Obesity* 8, no. 4 (2012): 280–89.

"Feminist Epistemology and Philosophy of Science." Stanford Encyclopedia of Philosophy. August 5, 2015. Accessed on June 14, 2018. https://plato.stanford.edu/entries/feminism-epistemology.

Finan, Ann. "Productionism." In *Green Food: An A-to-Z Guide,* edited by Dustin Mulvaney and Paul Robbins. Thousand Oaks, CA: Sage, 2011.

Fisher, Andrew. *Big Hunger: The Unholy Alliance between Corporate America and Anti-hunger Groups.* Cambridge, MA: MIT Press, 2017.

Fisher, Bernice, and Joan C. Tronto. "Toward a Feminist Theory of Caring." In *Circles of Care,* edited by E. Abel and M. Nelson. Albany: SUNY Press, 1990, 36–54.

Flanagan, Thelma. "What's New in Lunchroom Management." *What's New in Home Economics,* January 1945. Box 1.5, Thelma G. Flanagan Papers, CNA, ICN.

Flynn, Dan. "FDA Continues to Trust Industry under GRAS Substance Rule." *Food Safety News.* August 16, 2016. Accessed January 4, 2017. www.foodsafetynews.com/2016/08/fda-continues-to-trust-industry-under-gras-substance-rule/#.WMF05RIrKRs.

Folbre, Nancy. "Demanding Quality: Worker/Consumer Coalitions and 'High Road' Strategies in the Care Sector." *Politics and Society* 34, no. 1 (March 2006): 1–21.

———. "Holding Hands at Midnight: The Paradox of Caring Labor." *Feminist Economics* 1, no. 1 (1995): 73–92.

———. *The Invisible Heart: Economics and Family Values.* New York: New Press, 2001.

———. "The Unproductive Housewife: Her Evolution in Nineteenth-Century Economic Thought." *Signs: Journal of Women in Culture and Society* 16, no. 3 (1991): 463–84.

Folbre, Nancy, Candace Howes, and Carrie Leana. "A Care Policy and Research Agenda." In *For Love and Money: Care Provision in the United States,* edited by Nancy Folbre, 183–204. New York: Russell Sage Foundation, 2012.

Food Chain Workers Alliance and Solidarity Research Cooperative. *No Piece of the Pie: U.S. Food Workers in 2016.* Los Angeles: Food Chain Workers Alliance, 2016.

Food Research and Action Center. "Community Eligibility." n.d. Accessed June 14, 2018. http://frac.org/community-eligibility.

Foreman, Carol Tucker, "Remarks for National PTA Convention, Milwaukee, Wisconsin, June 11, 1979." Box 5.14, Stan Garnett Collection, CNA, ICN.

Freedman, Estell. "Separatism as Strategy: Female Institution Building and American Feminism, 1870–1930." *Feminist Studies* 5, no. 3 (1979): 512–29.

"Frozen Entrees Chalk Up Big Breakthrough in NYC Schools." *Merchandising,* November 1968. Thomas Carroll personal collection.

Gaddis, Jennifer E. "Mobilizing to Re-value and Re-skill Foodservice Labor in US School Lunchrooms: A Pathway to Community-Level Food Sovereignty?" *Radical Teacher* 98, (2014): 15–21.

Gaddis, Jennifer, and Amy K. Coplen. "Reorganizing School Lunch for a More Just and Sustainable Food System in the US." *Feminist Economics* 24, no. 3 (2018): 89–112.

Gaddis, Jennifer, and Cristina Cruz-Uribe. *Healthy Kids First: Why Cafeteria Workers Want to Cook Fresh Meals in New Haven Public Schools.* New Haven, CT: UNITE HERE, May 8, 2013. Accessed April 28, 2017. www.realfoodrealjobs.org/wp-content/uploads/NH-Cafeteria-Report-for-web.pdf.

Gard, Michael, and Carolyn Pluim. *Schools and Public Health: Past, Present, Future.* Lanham, MD: Lexington Books, 2014.

Gatto, Nicole M., Lauren C. Martinez, Donna Spruijt-Metz, and Jaimie N. Davis. "LA Sprouts Randomized Controlled Nutrition: Cooking and Gardening Program Reduces Obesity and Metabolic Risk in Hispanic/Latino Youth." *Pediatric Obesity* 12, no. 1 (2017): 28–37.

Gibson, Kristina E., and Sarah E. Dempsey. "Make Good Choices, Kid: Biopolitics of Children's Bodies and School Lunch Reform in Jamie Oliver's Food Revolution." *Children's Geographies* 13, no. 1 (2015): 44–58.

Gibson-Graham, J. K. *A Postcapitalist Politics.* Minneapolis: University of Minnesota Press, 2006.

Gibson-Graham, J. K., Jenny Cameron, and Stephen Healy. *Take Back the Economy: An Ethical Guide for Transforming Our Communities.* Minneapolis: University of Minnesota Press, 2013.

Glenn, Evelyn Nakano. *Forced to Care: Coercion and Caregiving in America.* Cambridge, MA: Harvard University Press, 2012.

———. "From Servitude to Service Work: Historical Continuities in the Racial Division of Paid Reproductive Labor." *Signs: Journal of Women in Culture and Society* 18, no. 1 (1992): 1–43.

Gordon, Linda. "Black and White Visions of Welfare: Women's Welfare Activism, 1890–1945." *Journal of American History* 78, no. 2 (1991): 559–90.

Grabert, Sylvia. Interview by Melba Hollingsworth, November 11, 2008. Transcript. Oral History Project, CNA, ICN. http://archives.theicn.org/oral-history-project/sylvia-grabert.

Graham, Lyman. Interview by Jeffrey Boyce, March 6, 2011. Transcript. Oral History Project, CNA, ICN. http://archives.theicn.org/oral-history-project/lyman-graham/.

Greene, Christina. *Our Separate Ways: Women and the Black Freedom Movement in Durham, North Carolina.* Chapel Hill: University of North Carolina Press, 2005.

Gunderson, Gordon. "National School Lunch Program (NSLP): Background and Development." USDA, 1971. Last updated June 17, 2014. Accessed July 1, 2015. www.fns.usda.gov/nslp/history.

Guthman, Julie. "The Trouble with 'Organic Lite' in California: A Rejoinder to the 'Conventionalisation' Debate." *Sociologia Ruralis* 44, no. 3 (2004): 301–16.

———. *Weighing In: Obesity, Food Justice, and the Limits of Capitalism.* Berkeley: University of California Press, 2011.

Hamrick, Karen. "Americans Spend an Average of 37 Minutes a Day Preparing and Serving Food and Cleaning Up." *Amber Waves,* November 7, 2016. www.ers.usda.gov/amber-waves/2016/november/americans-spend-an-average-of-37-minutes-a-day-preparing-and-serving-food-and-cleaning-up.

Hanks, Renee. Interview by Jeffrey Boyce, March 6, 2011. Transcript. Oral History Project CNA, ICN. http://archives.theicn.org/oral-history-project/renee-a-hanks/.

Harley, Sharon. "When Your Work Is Not Who You Are: The Development of a Working-Class Consciousness among Afro-American Women." In *Gender, Class, Race and Reform in the Progressive Era,* edited by Noralee Frankel and Nancy S. Dye. Lexington: University Press of Kentucky, 1991.

Hawkes, Corinna, and Jennifer Harris. "An Analysis of the Content of Food Industry Pledges on Marketing to Children." *Public Health Nutrition* 14 (2011): 1403–14.

Hawkins, Brenda. Interview by Meredith Johnston, December 4, 2004. Transcript. Oral History Project, CNA, ICN. http://archives.theicn.org/oral-history-project/brenda-hawkins/.

Hayden, Dolores. *The Grand Domestic Revolution: A History of Feminist Designs for American Homes, Neighborhoods, and Cities.* Cambridge, MA: MIT Press, 1982.

Hayden-Smith, Rose. "'Soldiers of the Soil': The Work of the United States School Garden Army during World War I." *Applied Environmental Education and Communication* 6, no. 1 (2007): 19–29.

Henry, Sara. "Berkeley's School Lunch Program Is Flawed, Say Insiders." *Berkeleyside,* February 14, 2011.

Hernandez, Jasanea (worker-leader, UNITE HERE Local 217). Interview with the author, June 2016.

Hersch, Derek, Laura Perdue, Theresa Ambroz, and Jackie L. Boucher. "The Impact of Cooking Classes on Food-Related Preferences, Attitudes, and Behaviors of School-Aged Children: A Systematic Review of the Evidence, 2003–2014." *Preventing Chronic Disease* 11 (2014).

Heynen, Nik. "Bending the Bars of Empire from Every Ghetto for Survival: The Black Panther Party's Radical Antihunger Politics of Social Reproduction and Scale." *Annals of the Association of American Geographers* 99, no. 2 (2009): 406–22.

"High Nourishment at Low Cost." *Hartford Courant,* November 1, 1970. Thomas Carroll personal collection.

Himmelweit, Susan. "The Prospects for Caring: Economic Theory and Policy Analysis." *Cambridge Journal of Economics* 31, no. 4 (2007): 581–99.

Hislop, Rasheed Salaam. "Reaping Equity across the USA: FJ Organizations Observed at the National Scale." Master's thesis, University of California, Davis. 2014.

Hochschild, Arlie Russell. *The Managed Heart: Commercialization of Human Feeling.* Berkeley: University of California Press, 1983.

———. *The Time Bind: When Work Becomes Home and Home Becomes Work.* New York: Metropolitan Books, 1997.

Howes, Candace, Carrie Leana, and Kristin Smith. "Paid Care Work." In *For Love and Money: Care Provision in the United States,* edited by Nancy Folbre, 65–91. New York: Russell Sage Foundation, 2012.

Hunt, Caroline L. "The Housekeeper and Those Who Make What She Buys." *Life and Labor* 1 (March 1911).

———. "More Conscience for the Consumer." Reprinted in Caroline L. Hunt, *Home Problems from a New Standpoint.* 2nd ed. Boston: Whitcomb & Barrows, 1913.

———. "School Lunches." *Farmers Bulletin* 712. Washington, DC: USDA, March 1916, rev. June 1922 and May 1924, photocopy. 22 pages. Box 2.10, Gene White Collection. CNA, ICN.

"Hyperactivity May Be Caused by Artificial Colors and Flavors." *School Foodservice Journal,* January 1974.

Jackson, Kristen D., LaJeana D. Howie, and Lara J. Akinbami. "Trends in Allergic Conditions among Children: United States, 1997–2011." *NCHS Data Brief* 121, no. 121 (2013): 1–8.

Jacobs, Ken, and Dave Graham-Squire. "Labor Standards for School Cafeteria Workers: Turnover and Public Program Utilization" *Berkeley Journal of Employment and Labor Law* 31, no. 2 (September 2010): 447–58.

Jaffe, JoAnn, and Michael Gertler. "Victual Vicissitudes: Consumer Deskilling and the (Gendered) Transformation of Food Systems." *Agriculture and Human Values* 23 (2006): 143–62.

Jaffee, Daniel, and Philip Howard. "Corporate Cooptation of Organic and Fair Trade Standards." *Agriculture and Human Values* 27, no. 4 (2010): 387–99.

Johnson, Karen. Interview by Beverly Lowe, April 19, 2006. Transcript. Oral History Project, CNA, ICN. http://archives.theicn.org/oral-history-project/karen-johnson/.

Johnston, Josée, Andrew Biro, and Norah MacKendrick. "Lost in the Supermarket: The Corporate-Organic Foodscape and the Struggle for Food Democracy." *Antipode* 41, no. 3 (2009): 509–32.

"Join in School Lunch Law Suits." *Bay State Banner,* August 31, 1972. ProQuest Historical Newspapers (1965–1979).

Jonen, Ruth. Interview by Jeffrey Boyce, September 11, 2007. Transcript. Oral History Project, CNA, ICN. http://archives.theicn.org/oral-history-project/ruth-jonen/.

Jones, Clay. "Lunch Shaming." Editorial cartoon. Claytoonz.com (blog). May 30, 2017. https://claytoonz.com/2017/05/30/lunch-shaming.

Jukes, Thomas. "Down the Primrose Path with "Organic" Foods." *School Foodservice Journal,* October 1974.

Kang, Mi Ok. "Organic School Lunch Programs in South Korea." In *School Food Politics: The Complex Ecology of Hunger and Feeding in Schools around the World,* edited by Sarah A. Robert and Marcus B. Weaver-Hightower, 120–40. New York: Peter Lang, 2011.

Karnes, Offie. Interview by Jeffrey Boyce, June 26, 2007. Transcript. Oral History Project, CNA, ICN. http://archives.theicn.org/oral-history-project/Offie-Karnes/.

Katz, Barbara, and Lu Ann Williams. "Cleaning Up Processed Foods." *Food Technology* 65, no. 12 (2011): 32–38.

Katz, Cindi. "Vagabond Capitalism and the Necessity of Social Reproduction." *Antipode* 33, no. 4 (2001): 709–78.

Kavanaugh, Gail S. Interview by Jeffrey Boyce, October 7, 2010. Transcript. Oral History Project, CNA, ICN. http://archives.theicn.org/oral-history-project/gail-s-kavanaugh/.

Kellogg, Lydia M. "Exhibits Are Important to the Members." *American School Food Service News,* October 1952.

Kennedy, John F. "Proclamation 3499: National School Lunch Week, 1962." October 9, 1962. www.govinfo.gov/content/pkg/STATUTE-76/pdf/STATUTE-76-Pg1507.pdf.

Kent, Druzilla. "Nutrition Education and the School Lunch Program." *School Life* 26, no. 8 (1941): 232.

Kids' Safe and Healthful Foods Project. *Serving Healthy School Meals: U.S. Schools Need Updated Kitchen Equipment.* Pew Charitable Trusts and Robert Wood Johnson Foundation, December 2013. www.pewtrusts.org/~/media/assets/2013/12/kits_equipment_report.pdf.

King, Rachel Scarborough. "School Board to Seek New Food, Facilities Pacts as Unions Rally against Aramark." *New Haven Register,* February 2, 2008. http://rachaelsking.blogspot.com/2008/02/school-board-to-seek-new-food.html.

Kleine, Dorothea, and Maria das Graças Brightwell. "Repoliticising and Scaling-up Ethical Consumption: Lessons from Public Procurement for School Meals in Brazil." *Geoforum* 67 (2015): 135–47.

Kloppenburg, Jack, and Neva Hassanein. "From Old School to Reform School?" *Agriculture and Human Values* 23, no. 4 (December 2006): 417–21.

Koven, Seth, and Sonya Michel. "Introduction: 'Mother Worlds.'" In *Mothers of a New World: Maternalist Politics and the Origins of Welfare States,* edited by Seth Koven and Sonya Michel. London: Routledge, 1993.

Kullgren, Ian. "Trump Team's Ag Talking Points." *Politico,* November 14, 2016. www.politico.com/tipsheets/morning-agriculture/2016/11/trump-teams-ag-talking-points-217390.

Lachance, Paul. "Engineered Foods." *School Foodservice Journal,* January 1974.

Lakkakula, Anantha, James Geaghan, Michael Zanovec, Sarah Pierce, and Georgianna Tuuri. "Repeated Taste Exposure Increases Liking for Vegetables by Low-Income Elementary School Children." *Appetite* 55, no. 2 (2010): 226–31.

Lang, Cady. "This Fund Honors Philando Castile's Legacy by Paying for Students' Lunches." *Time,* September 1, 2017.

Lapeze, Louise. Interview by Melba Hollingsworth, January 27, 2009. Transcript. Oral History Project, CNA, ICN. http://archives.theicn.org/oral-history-project/louise-lapeze/.

Laslett, Barbara, and Johanna Brenner. "Gender and Social Reproduction: Historical Perspective." *Annual Review of Sociology* 15 (1989): 381–404.

Laudan, Rachel. "A Plea for Culinary Modernism: Why We Should Love New, Fast, Processed Food." *Gastronomica* 1, no. 1 (2001): 36–44.

Levenstein, Harvey. *Paradox of Plenty: A Social History of Eating in Modern America.* Berkeley: University of California Press, 2003.

———. *Revolution at the Table: The Transformation of the American Diet.* Berkeley: University of California Press, 2003.

Levenstein, Lisa. *A Movement without Marches: African American Women and the Politics of Poverty in Postwar Philadelphia.* Chapel Hill: University of North Carolina Press, 2010.

Levine, Susan. *School Lunch Politics: The Surprising History of America's Favorite Welfare Program.* Princeton, NJ: Princeton University Press, 2010.

Levkoe, Charles Z., Nathan McClintock, Laura-Anne Minkoff-Zern, Amy K. Coplen, Jennifer Gaddis, Joann Lo, Felipe Tendick-Matesanz, and Anelyse M. Weiler. "Forging Links between Food Chain Labor Activists and Academics." *Journal of Agriculture, Food Systems, and Community Development* 6, no. 2 (2016): 129–42.

Lo, Joann, and Alexa Delwiche. "The Good Food Purchasing Policy: A Tool to Intertwine Worker Justice with a Sustainable Food System." *Journal of Agriculture, Food Systems, and Community Development* 6, no. 2 (2016): 185–94.

"Lunch Probe Imperils Funds." *Bridgeport Telegram*. March 30, 1979. Thomas Carroll personal collection.

Lynes, Jack. "In Oakland It's Makin', Bakin', and Educatin'." *School Foodservice Journal,* March 1976.

———. "Nutrition Center Highlights Minneapolis Foodservice Operation." *School Foodservice Journal,* February 1976.

Lyng, Richard. "Comments to ASFSA." *School Lunch (Foodservice) Journal,* September 1969 and October 1971.

Lyson, Helena C. "National Policy and State Dynamics: A State-Level Analysis of the Factors Influencing the Prevalence of Farm to School Programs in the United States." *Food Policy* 63 (2016): 23–35.

MacKendrick, Norah. *Better Safe Than Sorry: How Consumers Navigate Exposure to Everyday Toxics.* Oakland: University of California Press, 2018.

———. "More Work for Mother: Chemical Body Burdens as a Maternal Responsibility." *Gender and Society* 28, no. 5 (2014): 705–28.

MacMillan, Thomas. "Union Blasts School Lunches." *New Haven Independent,* November 14, 2007. www.newhavenindependent.org/archives/2007/11/union_unhappy_w.php.

Mahlow, Karen. "Understanding Clean Label Trends." Paper presented at Annual National Conference, School Nutrition Association, San Antonio, TX, July 8–13, 2016.

Maimaran, Michael, and Ayelet Fishbach. "If It's Useful and You Know It, Do You Eat? Preschoolers Refrain from Instrumental Food." *Journal of Consumer Research* 41, no. 3 (2014): 642–55.

Maley, Anne W. "President's Notes: Our Advertisers . . ." *School Lunch Journal,* April 1959.

Martin, Josephine, and Charlotte Beckett Oakley. *Managing Child Nutrition Programs: Leadership for Excellence.* Burlington, MA: Jones and Bartlett, 2008.

Matsufuru, Donna. Interview by Dr. Josephine Martin, March 15, 2007. Transcript. Oral History Project, CNA, ICN. http://archives.theicn.org/oral-history-project/donna-matsufuru/.

Maye, Irma. Interview by Linda Godfrey, January 27, 2012. Transcript. Oral History Project, CNA, ICN. http://archives.theicn.org/oral-history-project/irma-maye/.

Maxwell, Lesli A. "Minneapolis Leader Turns School Cafeterias into 'Real Kitchens.'" *Education Week,* March 3, 2014.

McAlevey, Jane F. *No Shortcuts: Organizing for Power in the New Gilded Age.* New York: Oxford University Press, 2016.

McCain, Mary. "Serving Students: A Survey of Contracted Food Service Work in New Jersey's K–12 Public Schools." Rutgers Center for Women and Work. May 2009. www.inthepublicinterest.org/wp-content/uploads/2009-McCain-Serving-Students.pdf.

McDonald, Bryan L. *Food Power: The Rise and Fall of the Postwar American Food System.* New York: Oxford University Press, 2016.

Mcgray, Douglas. "The War over America's Lunch." *Time,* April 26, 2010.

McMillin, Martha. "Victory Gardens for School Cafeterias." *Practical Home Economics,* April 1943: 143–46.

Michalak, Joseph. "City to Cut Back on Meat in Public-School Lunches." *New York Times,* August 20, 1973.

Miller, Emily. "Kids Need #realschoolfood—and Farm to School Is Making It Happen." National Farm to School Network. October 11, 2016. www.farmtoschool.org/news-and-articles/kids-need-realschoolfood-and-farm-to-school-is-making-it-happen.

Miller, Laura J. *Building Nature's Market: The Business and Politics of Natural Foods.* Chicago: University of Chicago Press, 2017.

Miller, William O'Donnell. *20 Million for Lunch.* Report No. TR-NO-3. New York: Educational Facilities Laboratories, 1968.

Minneapolis Public Schools (MPS). *Agreement between Special School District No. 1 MPS and Service Employees International Union Local No. 284.* Approved June 24, 2016. http://humanresources.mpls.k12.mn.us/uploads/food_service_2015-2017_contract_final.pdf.

———. "Demographics." Multilingual Department. n.d. Accessed November 1, 2018. http://multilingual.mpls.k12.mn.us/demographics.

———. "2016 Fact Sheet." Last updated August 2016. www.mpls.k12.mn.us/by_the_numbers.

Minneapolis Public Schools Culinary and Wellness Services. "Ingredients of Concern." Last updated June 2018. Accessed May 1, 2019. http://nutritionservices.mpls.k12.mn.us/ingredients_of_concern.html.

———. "Minnesota Thursdays." Last updated March 1, 2018. http://nutritionservices.mpls.k12.mn.us/minnesota_thursdays.

———. "Red Rice Apple Salad Mini-Lesson Ideas: English and Social Studies." Taste Test Archive, MPS. Accessed April 10, 2017. http://nutritionservices.mpls.k12.mn.us/uploads/red_rice_apple_salad_mini_lessons_-_english_social_studies.docx.

———. "Red Rice Apple Salad Mini-Lesson Ideas: Science and Math." Taste Test Archive, MPS. Accessed April 10, 2017. http://nutritionservices.mpls.k12.mn.us/uploads/red_rice_apple_salad_mini_lessons_-_science_math.docx.

———. "Red Rice EXPLOSION! Salad." Taste Test Archive, MPS. Accessed April 10, 2017. http://nutritionservices.mpls.k12.mn.us/tftt_red_rice_explosion_archive.

———. "Request for Proposal for Farm to School Fresh Produce, RFP 16-2." Last updated February 1, 2016. http://nutritionservices.mpls.k12.mn.us/uploads/appendix_5_-_farm_to_school_rfp_fresh_produce.pdf.

———. "True Food Taste Test." n.d. Accessed May 12, 2017. http://nutritionservices.mpls.k12.mn.us/uploads/true_food_taste_test_one_pager.pdf.

Morgan, Kevin, and Roberta Sonnino. *The School Food Revolution: Public Food and the Challenge of Sustainable Development.* London: Routledge, 2016.

Moss, Michael. "The Extraordinary Science of Addictive Junk Food." *New York Times Magazine.* February 20, 2013. www.nytimes.com/2013/02/24/magazine/the-extraordinary-science-of-junk-food.html.

———. "Safety of Beef Processing Method Is Questioned." *New York Times*. December 30, 2009. www.nytimes.com /2009/12/31/us/31meat.html.

Muncy, Robyn. *Creating a Female Dominion in American Reform 1890–1935*. New York: Oxford University Press, 1991.

Naples, Nancy A. *Grassroots Warriors: Activist Mothering, Community Work, and the War on Poverty*. London: Routledge, 1998.

Nargi, Lela. "School Food Hero Betti Wiggins Takes on Houston's Public Schools." *Civil Eats*, October 9, 2017. https://civileats.com/2017/10/09/food-hero-betti-wiggins-takes-on-houstons-public-schools/.

National Center for Education Statistics. "Cabell County Schools." n.d. https://nces.ed.gov/ccd/districtsearch/district_detail.asp?start=0&ID2=5400180.

National Partnership for Women and Families. "America's Women and the Wage Gap." April 2019. Accessed May 8, 2019. www.nationalpartnership.org/research-library/workplace-fairness/fair-pay/americas-women-and-the-wage-gap.pdf.

Nestle, Marion. *Food Politics: How the Food Industry Influences Nutrition and Health*. Rev. and expanded 10th anniversary ed. Oakland: University of California Press, 2013. First published 2002 by University of California Press.

New York City Department of Education. "Chancellor Fariña Announces Free School Lunch for All." September 6, 2017. Accessed June 15, 2018. www.schools.nyc.gov/about-us/news/announcements/contentdetails/2017/09/06/chancellor-fari%C3%B1a-announces-free-school-lunch-for-all.

Nicolaides, Becky and Andrew Wiese. "Suburbanization in the United States after 1945." In *Oxford Research Encyclopedia of American History*. Published online April 2017. http://dx.doi.org/10.1093/acrefore/9780199329175.013.64.

Ninemeier, Jack. "To Form a More Perfect Union," letter to the editor. *School Foodservice Journal*, November-December 1972.

"The 1965 Educational Seminar." *School Lunch Journal*, April 1965.

Nix, Mary. Interview by Virginia Webb. September 2, 2004. Transcript. Oral History Project, CNA, ICN. http://archives.theicn.org/oral-history-project/mary-nix/.

Nixon, Richard. "Remarks of President Richard Nixon at the Opening Plenary Session of the White House Conference on Food, Nutrition, and Health." December 2, 1969. Box 5.F52 Stan Garnett Collection, CNA, ICN.

Northup, Andrea (farm-to-school coordinator, Minneapolis Public Schools). Interviews with the author, November 2015 and May 2016.

———. "Minneapolis Public Schools Farm to School Toolkit." May 2016. http://nutritionservices.mpls.k12.mn.us/uploads/2016_mps_farm_to_school_toolkit.pdf.

O'Donnell, Kevin. "Aramark Workers Launch National Tour." Press release, UNITE HERE, April 3, 2008. https://unitehere.org/press-releases/aramark-workers-launch-national-tour-2.

Offer, Shira, and Barbara Schneider. "Revisiting the Gender Gap in Time-Use Patterns: Multitasking and Well-Being among Mothers and Fathers in Dual-Earner Families." *American Sociological Review* 76, no. 6 (2011): 809–33.

Ohly, Heather, Sarah Gentry, Rachel Wigglesworth, Alison Bethel, Rebecca Lovell, and Ruth Garside. "A Systematic Review of the Health and Well-Being Impacts of School Gardening: Synthesis of Quantitative and Qualitative Evidence." *BMC Public Health* 16, no. 1 (2016): 286.

Oostindjer, Marije, Jessica Aschemann-Witzel, Qing Wang, Silje Elisabeth Skuland, Bjørg Egelandsdal, Gro V. Amdam, Alexander Schjøll, Mark C. Pachucki, Paul Rozin, Jarrett Stein, Valerie Lengard Almli, and Ellen van Kleef. "Are School Meals a Viable and Sustainable Tool to Improve the Healthiness and Sustainability of Children's Diet and Food Consumption? A Cross-National Comparative Perspective." *Critical Reviews in Food Science and Nutrition* 57, no. 18 (2017): 3942–58.

Otero, Gerardo, Gabriela Pechlaner, Giselle Liberman, and Efe Gürcan. "The Neoliberal Diet and Inequality in the United States." *Social Science and Medicine* 142 (2015): 47–55.

Otsuki, Kei. "Sustainable Partnerships for a Green Economy: A Case Study of Public Procurement for Home-Grown School Feeding." *Natural Resources Forum* 35, no. 3 (2011): 213–22.

"Package Weight May Be Suspect—School Meals Audited in Stratford by U.S." *Bridgeport Post,* March 29, 1979.

"Palestine District Lunch Setup Hit; Probe Demanded." *Arkansas Gazette,* April 22, 1967.

Panera Bread. "The No No List." Last updated March 14, 2017. Accessed May 5, 2017. www.panerabread.com/panerabread/documents/panera-no-no-list-05-2015.pdf.

———. "Panera Bread Becomes First National Restaurant Company to Share List of Unacceptable Ingredients." Press release, May 5, 2015. Accessed December 10, 2016. www.panerabread.com/panerabread/documents/press/2015/no-no-list-release%205-5-15.pdf.

"Papa John's Completes Removal of 14 Unwanted Ingredients." *BusinessWire,* October 4, 2016. Accessed December 12, 2016. www.businesswire.com/news/home/20161004005478/en.

Patel, Raj, and Jason W. Moore. *A History of the World in Seven Cheap Things: A Guide to Capitalism, Nature, and the Future of the Planet.* Oakland: University of California Press, 2017.

Perdue Foodservice. "Kings Delight®." n.d. Accessed May 30, 2017. www.perduefoodservice.com/products/brands/kings-delight/.

Perryman, John. "Letters from Washington." *School Foodservice Journal,* November-December 1972.

———. "Log of the Executive Director." *School Foodservice Journal,* November-December 1968; March 1970; September 1971; January 1973; June 1974; and September 1976.

———. "An Open Letter to the Honorable Richard E. Lyng." *School Foodservice Journal,* October 1971.

Pew Charitable Trusts. *Fixing the Oversight of Chemicals Added to Our Food: Findings and Recommendations of Pew's Assessment of the U.S. Food Additives Program.*

November 2013. www.pewtrusts.org/~/media/legacy/uploadedfiles/phg/content_level_pages/reports/foodadditivescapstonereportpdf.pdf.

Pollan, Michael. "Big Food Strikes Back: Why Did the Obamas Fail to Take on Corporate Agriculture?" *New York Times Magazine,* October 5, 2016.

———. "The Way We Live Now: The (Agri)Cultural Contradictions of Obesity." *New York Times Magazine,* October 12, 2003.

Ponti, Irene Y. *A Guide for Financing School Food and Nutrition Services.* Chicago: American School Food Service Association and Association of School Business Officials, 1970.

Poppendieck, Janet. *Breadlines Knee-Deep in Wheat: Food Assistance in the Great Depression.* Updated and expanded ed. Berkeley: University of California Press, 2014.

———. *Free for All: Fixing School Food in America.* Berkeley: University of California Press, 2011.

Povitz, Lana Dee. "Hunger Doesn't Take a Vacation: The Food Activism of United Bronx Parents." In *Women's Activism and "Second Wave" Feminism: Transnational Histories,* edited by Barbara Molony and Jennifer Nelson. London: Bloomsbury, 2017.

Pratt, Eleanor. Interview by Meredith Johnston, September 24, 2004. Transcript. Oral History Project, CNA, ICN. http://archives.theicn.org/oral-history-project/eleanor-pratt/.

"Protests Registered on School Lunch System." *Chicago Tribune,* April 10, 1969.

"Public Hearings on Child Nutrition Programs: National Summary." 1977. Box 5F.14. Stan Garnett Collection. CNA, ICN.

Pulido, Laura, and Devon Peña. "Environmentalism and Positionality: The Early Pesticide Campaign of the United Farm Workers' Organizing Committee, 1965–71." *Race, Gender and Class* (1998): 33–50.

Ralston, Katherine, Constance Newman, Annette Clauson, Joanne Guthrie, and Jean Buzby. "National School Lunch Program: Background, Trends, Issues." *USDA ERS Reports,* July 2008. www.ers.usda.gov/webdocs/publications/46043/12050_err61_reportsummary_1_.pdf?v=0.

Ramey, Tommy. Interviewed by Beverly Cross, March 4, 2010. Transcript. Oral History Project, CNA, ICN. http://archives.theicn.org/oral-history-project/tommy-ramey/.

Ramsey, Gerald. "New Food Products Are Real Time Savers." *School Lunch Journal,* June 1958.

Rauzon, Suzanne, May Wang, Natalie Studer, and Pat Crawford. *Changing Students' Knowledge, Attitudes and Behavior in Relation to Food: An Evaluation of the School Lunch Initiative.* Berkeley, CA: Dr. Robert C. and Veronica Atkins Center for Weight and Health, University of California at Berkeley, September 2010.

Real Food Challenge. "What Is Real Food?" n.d. Accessed May 29, 2017. www.realfoodchallenge.org/what-real-food/.

"Restaurant Keeping in the Public Schools: What It Is Doing for Child Welfare." *Modern Priscilla,* May 1914. Box 2.12. Gene White Collection. CNA, ICN. (Sent to Gene White by Barry Sackin, August 20, 1999.)

Revolution Foods. "Our Mission." n.d. Accessed May 25, 2017. http://revolutionfoods.com/about.

"Revolution in School Feeding." *Volume Feeding Management,* November 1959. Quoted in Jay Caton, *The History of the American School Food Service Association: A Pinch of Love.* Arlington, VA: School Nutrition Association, 1990.

Reynolds, LeeAnn G. *Maintaining Segregation: Children and Racial Instruction in the South, 1920–1955.* Baton Rouge: Louisiana State University Press, 2017.

Risser, James. "Why They Love Earl Butz." *New York Times,* June 13, 1976.

Robert, Sarah A., and Marcus B. Weaver-Hightower, eds. *School Food Politics: The Complex Ecology of Hunger and Feeding in Schools around the World.* Global Studies in Education, vol. 6. New York: Peter Lang, 2011.

Rooted In Community. "Youth Food Bill of Rights." n.d. Accessed June 14, 2018. www.youthfoodbillofrights.com/index.html.

Rosenthal, Amy, and Christine C. Caruso. "Bringing School Foodservice Staff Back In: Accounting for Changes in Workloads and Mindsets in K–12 Values-Based Procurement." In *Institutions as Conscious Food Consumers,* edited by Sapna E. Thottathil and Annelies M. Goger, 261–83. Cambridge, MA: Academic Press, 2019.

Ruis, Andrew R. *Eating to Learn, Learning to Eat: The Origins of School Lunch in the United States.* New Brunswick, NJ: Rutgers University Press, 2017.

Rushing, Keith. "Essential KPIs for School Nutrition Program Success." *Journal of Child Nutrition and Management* 42, no. 2 (2017).

Rutledge, Jennifer Geist. *Feeding the Future: School Lunch Programs as Global Social Policy.* New Brunswick, NJ: Rutgers University Press, 2016.

Rylie, Marilyn. Interview by Jeffrey Boyce, July 23, 2008. Transcript. Oral History Project, CNA, ICN. http://archives.theicn.org/oral-history-project/marilyn-rylie/.

Sachs, Carolyn, Patricia Allen, A. Rachel Terman, Jennifer Hayden and Christina Hatcher. "Front and Back of the House: Socio-spatial Inequalities in Food Work." *Agriculture and Human Values* 31, no. 1 (2014): 3–17.

Sackin, Barry. Interview by Jeffrey Boyce, January 21, 2011. Transcript. Oral History Project, CNA, ICN. http://archives.theicn.org/oral-history-project/barry-sackin/.

Sandler, Adam. "Lunchlady Land." *They're All Going to Laugh at You,* album. 1993. AZLyrics. www.azlyrics.com/lyrics/adamsandler/lunchladyland.html.

———. "Lunchlady Land." *Saturday Night Live.* January 1, 1994. YouTube. https://youtu.be/VY14zcUM9SI.

Sandler, Jen. "Reframing the Politics of Urban Feeding in U.S. Public Schools: Parents, Programs, Activists, and the State." In *School Food Politics: The Complex Ecology of Hunger and Feeding in Schools around the World,* edited by Sarah A. Robert and Marcus B. Weaver-Hightower. New York: Peter Lang, 2011.

"School Feeding Programs Criticized in Panel Report." *School Foodservice Journal,* September 1974.

School Food Focus. "Ingredient Guide for Better School Food Purchasing." Accessed May 1, 2017. www.schoolfoodfocus.org/wp-content/uploads/2016/07/Ingredient-Guide-for-Better-School-Food-Purchasing.pdf.

"School Lunch Information for Citizens' Committee Report." January 15, 1947. Box 2.12. Thelma G. Flanagan Papers, CNA, ICN.

"School Lunch Program Opens to Commercial Contractors." *Volume Feeding Management,* March 1970. Thomas Carroll personal collection.

School Nutrition Association (SNA). "Do You Know How to Increase Your Priority Points?" n.d. Accessed May 30, 2017. https://schoolnutrition.org/uploadedFiles/2_Meetings_and_Events/ANC_2017/Pages/ANC2017-PriorityPoints.pdf.

———. "School Nutrition Professionals: Roles and Responsibilities." About School Meals. n.d. Accessed April 10, 2017. https://schoolnutrition.org/AboutSchoolMeals/SNPRolesResponsibilities/.

———. "SNA Comments on School Lunch Shaming." Press release, April 11, 2017. https://schoolnutrition.org/news-publications/press-releases/sna-comments-on-school-lunch-shaming.

———. *Solving the Procurement Puzzle: Managing the Complexities of Doing Business in K-12 School Foodservice.* A White Paper Report from the SNA. 2016. https://schoolnutrition.org/uploadedFiles/Resources_and_Research/Operations/WhitePaper-SolvingtheProcurementPuzzle.pdf.

Schor, Juliet. *The Overworked American: The Unexpected Decline of Leisure.* New York: Basic Books, 1993.

Schwartz, Carly. "Revolution Foods in San Francisco: Public School Students to Receive Healthier Meals." *Huffington Post,* January 7, 2013. www.huffingtonpost.com/2013/01/07/revolution-foods-in-san-francisco_n_2422958.html.

Scott, Anne Firor. "Most Invisible of All: Black Women's Voluntary Associations." *Journal of Southern History* 56, no. 1 (1990): 3–22.

Sennett, Richard. *The Corrosion of Character: The Personal Consequences of Work in the New Capitalism.* New York: W. W. Norton, 1998.

"Set Lunch Boycott to Reduce Prices." *New York Amsterdam News,* August 30, 1969. ProQuest Historical Newspapers (1962–1993).

Shapiro, Laura. *Something from the Oven: Reinventing Dinner in 1950s America.* Waterville, ME: Thorndike Press, 2004.

Shen, Aviva. "How Big Food Corporations Watered Down Michelle Obama's 'Let's Move' Campaign." *Think Progress,* February 28, 2013.

Sheraton, Mimi. "Lunches for Pupils Given Poor Marks as Unappetizing and Low in Nutrition." *New York Times,* May 19, 1976.

———. "School Lunch Utopia? No Impossible Dream." *New York Times,* May 20, 1976.

Shilling, Becky. "Bertrand Weber: Game On." *Food Service Director,* August 14, 2014.

Siegel, Bettina Elias. "Reagan Revisited: Should Pizza Count as a School Vegetable?" *Lunch Tray,* November 15, 2011. www.thelunchtray.com/tag/coalition-for-sustainable-school-meal-programs/.

———. "Tell USDA to Stop Using Pink Slime in School Food!" Petition, Change.org, March 6, 2012. www.change.org/p/tell-usda-to-stop-using-pink-slime-in-school-food.

———. "Why Is FoodCorps Merging with School Food Focus—And How Will Kids Benefit?" Interview with Cecily Upton. *Lunch Tray,* February 28, 2018. www.thelunchtray.com/tag/cecily-upton.

Simon, Bryant. *The Hamlet Fire: A Tragic Story of Cheap Food, Cheap Government, and Cheap Lives.* New York: New Press, 2017.

Sklar, Kathryn Kish. "The Historical Foundations of Women's Power in the Creation of the American Welfare State, 1830–1930." In *Mothers of a New World: Maternalist Politics and the Origins of Welfare States,* edited by Seth Koven and Sonya Michel. London: Routledge, 1993.

———. "Hull House in the 1890s: A Community of Women Reformers." *Signs: Journal of Women in Culture and Society* 10, no. 4 (1985): 658–77.

Smedley, E. *The School Lunch: Its Organization and Management in Philadelphia.* 2nd ed. Media, PA: self-published, c. 1930.

Stanley, Laura, Kathryn J. A. Colasanti, and David S. Conner. "A 'Real Chicken' Revolution: How Two Large Districts Are Shifting the School Poultry Paradigm with Scratch Cooking." *Childhood Obesity* 8, no. 4 (2012): 384–87.

Steiner, Gilbert Y., and Pauline H. Milius. *The Children's Cause.* Washington, DC: Brookings Institution, 1976.

Striffler, Steve. *Chicken: The Dangerous Transformation of America's Favorite Food.* New Haven, CT: Yale University Press, 2005.

Stuckler, David, and Marion Nestle. "Big Food, Food Systems, and Global Health." *PLoS Med* 9, no. 6 (2012): e1001242.

Talbot, Marion. *The Education of Women.* Chicago: University of Chicago Press, 1910.

Talley, Kathy. Interview by Jeffrey Boyce, July 22, 2008. Transcript. Oral History Project, CNA, ICN. http://archives.theicn.org/oral-history-project/kathy-talley/.

Thompson, Craig, and Gokcen Coskuner-Balli. "Countervailing Market Responses to Corporate Co-optation and the Ideological Recruitment of Consumption Communities." *Journal of Consumer Research* 34, no. 2 (2007): 135–52.

Triece, Mary Eleanor. *Tell It Like It Is: Women in the National Welfare Rights Movement.* Columbia: University of South Carolina Press, 2013.

Tronto, Joan. *Caring Democracy: Markets, Equality, and Justice.* New York: New York University Press, 2013.

Trubek, Amy B. *Making Modern Meals: How Americans Cook Today.* Oakland: University of California Press, 2017.

Truman, Harry S. "Statement by the President upon Signing the National School Lunch Act." June 4, 1946. www.presidency.ucsb.edu/node/231847.

Tsui, Emma K. "Pan de Yuca and Brown Rice: The Meanings of 'Good' Food for Cooks Working in Publicly Funded Foodservice." *Food, Culture and Society* 19, no. 2 (2016): 273–95.

Tsui, Emma, Jonathan Deutsch, Stefania Patinella, and Nicholas Freudenberg. "Missed Opportunities for Improving Nutrition through Institutional Food: The Case for Food Worker Training." *American Journal of Public Health* 103, no. 9 (2013): e14-e20.

Twarog, Emily. *Politics of the Pantry: Housewives, Food, and Consumer Protest in Twentieth-Century America*. New York: Oxford University Press, 2017.

Tyson Foods. "Real. Clean. Delicious." 2018. www.tysonfoodservice.com/k-12-NAE/NAI.

Tyson, Laura, and Jennifer Walske. "Revolution Foods: Expansion into the CPG Market." *California Management Review* 58, no. 3 (2016): 125–41.

"Unions, Continued." *School Foodservice Journal*, April 1973.

Urban School Food Alliance. "An Alliance of Alliances." October 21, 2015. Accessed May 15, 2017. www.urbanschoolfoodalliance.org/an-alliance-of-alliances.

"USDA Considers Allowing Caterers in School Lunch Program." *Volume Feeding Management*, 1969. Thomas Carroll personal collection.

USDA Food and Nutrition Service (FNS). "Child Nutrition Programs: Income Eligibility Guidelines (July 1, 2017–June 30, 2018)." April 10, 2017, www.govinfo.gov/content/pkg/FR-2017-04-10/pdf/2017-07043.pdf.

———. "Child Nutrition Tables." Last updated May 9, 2017. Accessed June 1, 2017. www.fns.usda.gov/pd/child-nutrition-tables.

———. *Food Buying Guide for Child Nutrition Programs*. n.d. Accessed March 1, 2017. www.fns.usda.gov/tn/foodbuying-guide-child-nutrition-programs.

———. "Food Distribution: Pilot Project for Procurement of Unprocessed Fruits and Vegetables." Last modified June 20, 2017. www.fns.usda.gov/fdd/pilot-project-procurement-unprocessed-fruits-and-vegetables.

———. *Guide to Professional Standards for School Nutrition Programs*. FNS 303. January 2016. https://fns-prod.azureedge.net/sites/default/files/tn/ps_guide.pdf.

———. "National School Lunch Program." Last modified October 2, 2017. www.fns.usda.gov/nslp/history_8.

———. "National School Lunch Program: Participation and Lunches Served." Last updated May 3, 2019. https://fns-prod.azureedge.net/sites/default/files/resource-files/slsummar-4.pdf.

———. "NSLP, SMP, SBP National Average Payments/Maximum Reimbursement Rates." July 19, 2018. www.federalregister.gov/documents/2018/07/19/2018-15465/national-school-lunch-special-milk-and-school-breakfast-programs-national-average-paymentsmaximum.

———. "Overview: Farm to School Census 2105." Last updated January 11, 2017. https://farmtoschoolcensus.fns.usda.gov/overview-farm-school-census-2015.

———. Richard B. Russell National School Lunch Act of 1946. P. L. 79–396, 60 Stat. 230. June 4, 1946. www.fns.usda.gov/richard-b-russell-national-school-lunch-act.

———. "School Gardening." Community Food Systems. Last updated March 15, 2018. www.fns.usda.gov/farmtoschool/farm-school-resources#School Gardening.

———. *School Nutrition and Meal Cost Study*. April 23, 2019. www.fns.usda.gov/school-nutrition-and-meal-cost-study.

———. *Special Nutrition Program Operations Study: State and School Food Authority Policies and Practices for School Meals Programs School Year 2011–12*. Nutrition Assistance Program Report, March 2014. www.fns.usda.gov/sites/default/files/SNOPSYear1.pdf.

USDA Food Safety and Inspection Service. "Compliance Guide on the Determination of Processing Aids." April 8, 2008. www.fsis.usda.gov/wps/wcm/connect/9a34e8d9-997a-4c58-bd5e-d87cc371ecda/Determination_of_Processing_Aids.pdf?MOD=AJPERES.

———. "Petition for Rulemaking Addendum: In re: Fecal Contamination of Poultry and Meat." Petition No. 13–02. May 6, 2013. www.fsis.usda.gov/wps/wcm/connect/1a42fae1-775b-45f1-bafc-f242054ebe2d/Petition_Adendum_Physican_Committee.pdf?MOD=AJPERES.

USDA Office of Communications. "USDA Awards Grants for New School Food Service Equipment to Help Schools Dish Up Healthy Meals." Release No. 0065.14. April 18, 2014. https://content.govdelivery.com/accounts/USDAOC/bulletins/b21254.

USDA Rural Development. "About RD." n.d. Accessed March 1, 2018. www.rd.usda.gov/about-rd.

Vancil-Leap, Ashley. "Resistance and Adherence to the Gendered Representations of School Lunch Ladies." *Gender Issues* 34, no. 1 (2017): 67–85.

"V is for Vegetable Garden." *School Foodservice Journal*, March 1974.

War Food Administration. "The School Lunch Program: Facts for Women's Groups." May 1945. Box 10.5TD. Thelma Flanagan Papers, CNA, ICN.

Watkins, Shirley, Dorothy Pannell-Martin, Anita Ellis, and Stewart Eidel. Interview by Beth King, June 23, 2004. Transcript. Oral History Project, CNA, ICN. http://archives.theicn.org/oral-history-project/group-discussion-watkins-ellis-eidel-panne/.

Watrous, Monica. "Q&A: Nestle USA Putting a Fresh Spin on Frozen." *Food Business News*, July 24, 2015. www.foodbusinessnews.net/articles/6449-q-a-nestle-usa-putting-a-fresh-spin-on-frozen?v=preview.

———. "Trend of the Year: Clean Label." *Food Business News*, 2015. http://features.foodbusinessnews.net/corporateprofiles/2015/trend-index.html.

Weber, Bertrand (director of Culinary and Wellness Services, Minneapolis Public Schools). Interviews with the author, November 2015 and May 2016.

Weiner, Lynn. *From Working Girl to Working Mother: The Female Labor Force in the United States, 1820–1980*. Chapel Hill: University of North Carolina Press, 2016.

Wells, Patricia. "New Food Report Provides a Taste of U.S. Policy Fight." *New York Times*, May 30, 1978.

Westfall, Eleanor. "Don't Miss It . . . The Line-up for the Convention Is Getting Mighty Impressive." *American School Food Service News*, October 1953.

"What Is 'Stealth Health'?" *Food Service Director,* November 25, 2012. www
.foodservicedirector.com/research/big-picture/articles/what-stealth-health.

"What's the Problem with Aunt Jemima?" *Alternative Daily,* n.d. Accessed May 30, 2017. www.thealternativedaily.com/whats-problem-aunt-jemima.

Whitebook, Marcy, and Laura Sakai. *By a Thread: How Child Care Centers Hold On to Teachers, How Teachers Build Lasting Careers.* Kalamazoo, MI: W. E. Upjohn Institute for Employment Research, 2004.

Wilking, Cara. *Copycat Snacks in Schools.* Public Health Advocacy Institute. May 2014. www.phaionline.org/wp-content/uploads/2014/05/PHAI-Copy-Cat-Snacks-Issue-Brief-FINAL.pdf.

Willett, Walter, Johan Rockström, Brent Loken, Marco Springmann, Tim Lang, Sonja Vermeulen, Tara Garnett, et al. "Food in the Anthropocene: The EAT–Lancet Commission on Healthy Diets from Sustainable Food Systems." *Lancet,* January 16, 2019. https://doi.org/10.1016/S0140-6736(18)31788-4.

Winson, Anthony. "Bringing Political Economy into the Debate on the Obesity Epidemic." *Agriculture and Human Values* 21, no. 4 (2004): 299–312.

———. *The Industrial Diet: The Degradation of Food and the Struggle for Healthy Eating.* New York: New York University Press, 2013.

Winston, Andrew. "Keeping Up with the 'Clean Label' Movement." *Harvard Business Review,* October 30, 2015. https://hbr.org/2015/10/keeping-up-with-the-clean-label-movement.

Woldow, Dana. "Choicelunch Founder Explains New USDA School Lunch Rules." Choicelunch News and Updates: From the CEO's Desk. August 8, 2012. www.choicelunch.com/blog/justins-interview-on-the-new-usda-school-lunch-rules.

———. "Who Should Lead SFUSD's School Meal Program?" *BeyondChron,* August 9, 2016.

Woo Baidal, Jennifer, and Elsie M. Taveras. "Protecting Progress against Childhood Obesity—the National School Lunch Program." *New England Journal of Medicine* 371, no. 20 (2014): 1862–65.

Wood-Wright, Natalie. "New U.S. Dietary Guidelines Ignore Broad Support for Food Sustainability." Johns Hopkins University Hub. March 11, 2016. https://hub.jhu.edu/2016/03/11/dietary-guidelines-sustainability-survey/.

Woodward, Ellen S. "Hot Lunches for a Million School Children." Speech, 1935. WPA, Record Group 69, Series 737, Box 8. National Archives, Washington, DC.

Wright, Erik Olin. "Guidelines for Envisioning Real Utopias." *Soundings: A Journal of Politics and Culture* 36 (Summer 2007): 26–39.

Yoder, Sheldon. "Real Food, Real Jobs: An Interview with Chris Bohner." Worldwatch Institute. November 11, 2011. Accessed October 1, 2018. http://blogs.worldwatch.org/real-food-real-jobs-an-interview-with-chris-bohner.

Zelizer, Viviana A. *Pricing the Priceless Child: The Changing Social Value of Children.* Princeton, NJ: Princeton University Press, 1994.

Zimmerman, Jess. "What's Inside a School Lunch Burger? 26 Ingredients, and Only One is Meat." *Grist,* April 11, 2012. http://grist.org/school-lunches/whats-inside-a-school-lunch-burger-26-ingredients-and-only-one-is-meat/.

INDEX

Abel, Mary Hinman, 19–20, 24, 216
activism on school lunch programs, 7–15, 224–228; in 1960–1970s, 56–57; NSLA and, 18; real food movement, 104–113, 242n46; by youth leaders, 131–132, 219–220. *See also* community organizing; feminist food politics; protests; real food movement; right-to-lunch movement
Addams, Jane, 33
additives, 96–98, 103–114, 117–118, 185, 201. *See also* chemicals in food; "clean labels"
advocacy, defined, 224–225
affective barriers, 202–203
African American Parent Advisory Committee, 212
African Americans' rights, 34. *See also* racial (in)equity
AFSCME, 152
Agricultural Adjustment Act (1933), 42
agricultural chemicals, 91, 96–97, 110–112. *See also* chemicals in food
agriculture industry, 73–75, 109–110. *See also* food industry
airline-type lunches, 70 *fig.*, 71–72, 85, 86, 127
Allen, Patricia, 191
allergies to foods, 9, 64, 150, 241n5
alternative proteins, 72–73, 129
altruism and self-sacrifice, 6–7, 79, 144–145, 152, 154–157, 247n44, 247n55
American Dietetic Association, 80

American Home Economics Association, 80
Americanization, 19–20, 33, 69–71, 232n9, 234n55
American Recovery and Reinvestment Act (2009), 187
American School Food Service Association (ASFSA): on economic efficiency, 79, 84, 87; on factory *vs.* whole food diets, 92; on foodservice workers, 87–90; leadership terms in, 237n26; on NSLP, 55; on privatization, 69, 71, 77–78, 80, 238n61; *School Foodservice Journal,* 71, 86, 88, 92, 93, 239n111; *School Lunch Journal,* 71, 80–81, 88; on universal school lunch program, 59, 65–68. *See also* School Nutrition Association (SNA)
AmeriCorps. *See* FoodCorps
ammonia, 111. *See also* LFTB
Anishinabe Academy, 213
antihunger movement, 58–59, 75, 171, 225
Applegate, 115
Aramark, 1, 2, 135, 153, 169–171
Arby's, 104
Archer-Daniels-Midland, 72–73
Arkansas, 56, 58, 71, 79 *fig.*, 102 *fig.*, 165 *fig.*
Arlington, Minnesota, 200–201
artificial colors, 96, 97. *See also* chemicals in food
Ashby, Rodney, 83
Association of School Business Officials, 84

279

Aubrey, Allison, 106
Aunt Jemima, 96

Back to the Roots company, 129
Banquet Frozen Foods, 77
Bard, Bernard, 52
Bash, Wade, 81
B Corporations, 127, 244n103
Beavers, Elizabeth, 99
Beef Products, Inc. (BPI), 112
Bender, Betty, 99–100
Berenstein, Nadia, 113, 118
Berkeley, California, 196–197
Best, Amy, 5
Beyond Meat, 129
Big Agriculture. *See* agriculture industry
Big Food. *See* food industry
Big Green project, 197
bisphenol A (BPA), 97, 107
bite tax, 54
The Bitter Cry of the Children (Spargo), 23
Bittman, Mark, 132
Black Panther Party (BPP), 61–63, 237n40
Blimpie, 104
body burden, as term, 96–97
Boris, Eileen, 159–160
Boston, Massachusetts, 19, 27 *fig.*, 201, 216
Boston Committee on Hygiene of the Home and School Association, 26
Boulder, Colorado, 222, 223–224
Bragg, Paul, 92
branding: of cafeteria food, 75–79, 104, 129–130; of "real" food products, 114–118, 125–130. *See also* food industry; labeling
Brazil, 222
Bridgeport, Connecticut, 70 *fig.*, 72, 82 *fig.*, 85–86
Bridgeport Post, 71–72
Briggs, Marilyn, 167–168
Brownell, Kelly, 119
Brown v. Board of Education, 53
Bryan, Mary de Garmo, 37–38, 39, 40 *fig.*, 235n82
Budahn, Joan, 200–201
"built-in" labor, 81, 84–86, 126, 162–163, 167. *See also* foodservice workers
Bullman, Lova Jean, 159

bullying, 134–136
burgers, 72, 78, 106, 110–111
Burrows, Frances, 90
Butz, Earl, 73–75

"A Cafeteria Manager" (Evans), 144
cafeteria workers. *See* foodservice workers
Califano, Joseph, 58
California, 43 *fig.*, 46, 196–197, 222, 223
Camp, Earnestine, 71
Campbell's, 114, 116
cancer, 96, 97, 107–108, 119
canning. *See* preservation, food
capitalism. *See* cheap-food economies; food industry; patriarchal capitalism
care. *See* economy of care
Cargill, 72–73
Carnegie, Andrew, 31
Carolan, Michael, 105, 202, 203
Carroll, Thomas, 72, 82 *fig.*, 85
carrots, 163, 169, 206, 207 *fig.*, 244n94
Carson, Rachel, 91, 94
cartoon, 135–136
Caruso, Christine, 194
Castile, Philando, 150
Center for Ecoliteracy, 223
Center for Food Safety, 110
Center for Good Food Purchasing, 221–222
Center for Science in the Public Interest, 74, 110
central kitchen model, 26, 161–162, 179. *See also* group kitchen model; satellite kitchen model
Central Soya, 73
charitable gifts, 54–55, 76, 150–151
Chavez, Cesar, 91
cheap-food economies, 2–4; NSLP development and, 69–74, 84–87, 90–91, 98–104; social premise of, 17–18. *See also* convenience foods; economic models; food industry; privatization; values-based food economy
Chef Ann Foundation, 123, 189
Chegwidden, Gwen, 86
chemicals in food, 96–98, 103–114, 117–118, 185, 201. *See also* cheap-food economies; "clean labels"

Chicago, Illinois, 9 *fig.*, 31, 173 *fig.*, 216, 222, 226
chicken, as food, 101–103, 118, 125, 176–177, 241n14
chickens in school gardens, 198, 200
Chick-fil-A, 103, 104
Child Nutrition Act (1966), 56
Child Nutrition Archives, 11, 144, 147, 155, 156
child obesity, 119, 120, 187, 190
Children's Aid Society of New York City, 232n5
Children's Bureau, 26, 35
Children's Foundation, 56
children's rights, 21, 60–61, 64, 219–220
Choicelunch, 123
Church Women United, 57
Cipriano, Tim, 170–171
civil rights movement, 58–59
class (in)equity: care practices and, 232n9, 233nn22–23; cooperative food preservation and, 46; food preferences and, 251n55; real food and, 116, 131–133; in school lunch programs, 33, 90. *See also* intersectionality of school lunch programs issues; racial (in)equity
classifications of foodservice workers, 142–143
Clay, William, 65, 94, 222
"clean labels," 13, 205, 241n14, 243n58. *See also* labeling; organic food; real food movement
CN (Child Nutrition) certification and labeling, 123, 125
Coalition for Sustainable School Meals Program, 120
Coalition of Immokalee Workers, 221
Coca-Cola, 79 *fig.*
collective action. *See* community organizing; unions
college food programs, 131
Colston, Arlene, 162
commercialization of cafeteria food, 75–79, 104, 129–130. *See also* branding; food industry; vending machines
Committee on School Lunch Participation (CSLP), 57–59

commodity foods, 42–45, 98–101, 190, 235n88. *See also* cheap-food economies
communism, 49
community-based culinary capacity. *See* culinary capacity
community benefits of real food, 201–214. *See also* real food movement
Community Eligibility Provision (CEP), 141, 216–217
community gardens, 211–212. *See also* Victory Gardens
community kitchens, 19–20, 222–224. *See also* school-community kitchens
Community Lunch Program (WFA), 46–48
Community Nutrition Institute, 56
community organizing, 20–21, 25, 224–228, 229n4. *See also* activism on school lunch programs; right-to-lunch movement; unions
community-supported agriculture (CSA) programs, 109, 170, 210
Compass, 153
ConAgra Foods, 120, 171
Connecticut: agriculture industry and, 250n25; farm-to-school programs in, 93, 171, 203; foodservice workers in, 1–2, 72, 82 *fig.*, 139, 148; multinational foodservice companies in, 152, 153, 169–171; school lunch programs in, 1–2, 169
consumer purchasing power, 110, 114. *See also* "clean labels"; real food movement
Consumer's Union, 110
consumer veil, 105, 132
convenience foods, 69–73, 76–78, 115, 239n111. *See also* cheap-food economies
Cooper, Ann, 123, 124, 223–224
Coordinating Committee on School Lunches (CCSL), 48
corn syrup, 96, 130, 185, 206
corporate food industry. *See* food industry
Crane, Helen, 79
Crawford, Joe, 93
Creole meals, 125–126, 166
Crews, June, 167
Cronon, Marion, 84
Cruz-Uribe, Cristina, 171–172, 226–227

CSA (community-supported) agriculture programs, 109, 170, 210
culinary capacity: of central kitchen programs, 99–100, 212; development of community-based, 188–189, 221–223; of early USDA programs, 44; food policy reform and, 243n82; of real food programs, 124, 128, 192–194, 201; of scratch cooking programs, 164, 167–168. *See also* kitchen infrastructure; scratch cooking
cultural food preferences, 125–126, 166, 201, 212–213, 241n5. *See also* Americanization
Cutter, Ruth, 88

Davis, Doug, 251n39
Davis-Palms, Mary, 156–157
day care program, 68
debt. *See* lunch debt
decentralized kitchen model, 26, 175–176
Dehn, Virginia, 89
Des Moines, Iowa, 142, 161, 198–199, 200
Detroit, Michigan, 170, 197–198
Dewey, John, 30, 197
Di Chiro, Giovanna, 17, 137
Dietary Guidelines for Americans (DGA), 108–110
dietary restrictions, 9, 64, 150, 241n5
Diet for a Small Planet (Lappé), 91
distrust of federal oversight, 105–107, 111, 119, 132
domestic science, as field of study, 30
Domino's Pizza, 104
Drake, Annie, 145–146, 203
Drane, Bob, 114
drying. *See* preservation, food

Eco Hour, 198
E. coli, 103, 111
economic models: of real food, 174–178, 189–201; values-based, 131, 193–195, 213, 250n18. *See also* cheap-food economies; economy of care
Economic Opportunity Act (1964), 56
economic segregation of school lunch programs, 5, 17, 61, 66, 134–136, 173, 216–217, 229n8. *See also* lunch debt; lunch shaming
economy of care: on altruism and sacrifice, 6–7, 79, 144–145, 152, 154–157, 247n44, 247n55; BPP on, 61–63; economic efficiency *vs.*, 79–80, 87–88; emotional labor of foodservice workers, 88, 143–148, 162, 167, 246n22; gender and, 5–7, 66, 83, 132, 249n12; Progressive Era politics on, 17–24, 232n12; proposed vision for, 215–228; wage penalty in, 230n21. *See also* economic models; foodservice workers; reproductive labor
edible schoolyard. *See* farm-to-school programs; school gardens
Edible Schoolyard Project, 197
education: for foodservice workers, 83, 164–168, 181, 211; garden-based, 30, 197, 198–200; on nutrition, 64–65, 110, 251n48
Educational Facilities Laboratories, 76
efficiency foods. *See* convenience foods
Eidel, Stewart, 161
elderly feeding programs, 56, 68, 188, 219, 238n60
Elderly Nutrition Program, 68
Elementary and Secondary Education Act (1965), 56, 58
Elias, Megan, 233n30
Ellis, Marjorie, 87
emotional labor of foodservice workers, 88, 143–148, 162, 167, 246n22. *See also* economy of care
empathy gap, 67. *See also* patriarchal capitalism
Environmental Defense Fund, 110
environmental justice movement, 8, 91, 220. *See also* food justice; sustainable food movement
environmental toxins, 96–97, 107
Environmental Working Group, 110, 241n25
Eppen, Jeff, 200
ethnic communities. *See* cultural food preferences
Evans, Marge, 144–145
Everything Added to Food in the United States (EAFUS) list, 107

Fairfax, Jean, 57, 64–65, 94, 220
fair labor standards, 83, 221
Fair Labor Standards Act (1966), 83
Farley, Chris, 138
Farley, Thomas, 72, 93
farmers markets, 109, 170, 218
Farm-to-School Census (USDA), 196
farm-to-school programs, 189–192; experimental initiatives in, 197–198; in Minneapolis, 182, 192–197, 203–213; in New Haven, 171; rural *vs.* urban, 93, 189, 250n32; school gardens, 2, 30, 93–94, 197–201; of USDA, 128, 190. *See also* real food movement; school gardens; school lunch programs; scratch-cooking programs
fast-food industry and school lunch, 77, 83–84, 104
fast scratch foods. *See* speed-scratch foods
FBI (Federal Bureau of Investigation), 62
FDA. *See* US Food and Drug Administration (FDA)
Federal Emergency Relief Administration, 235n92
federal-state partnerships: in national school lunch programs, 46–49, 54–55; in nonprofit school lunch programs, 35–36, 37, 41–42
Federal Surplus Relief Corporation, 42
feminist food politics, 18–24, 33–34, 50, 217–219, 221. *See also* activism on school lunch programs; food justice
Fergus, Pamela, 150
Finland, 219
Fisher, Berenice, 5
Flanagan, Thelma, 47, 87
flavor stations, 202
Florida, 47
Focus. *See* School Food Focus
Folbre, Nancy, 151, 225, 229n4
food allergies, 9, 64, 150, 241n5
food assistance programs, federal, 42–43, 68
Food Business News, 113
Food Chain Workers Alliance, 225
FoodCorps, 198–199, 251n48
food industry: on alternative diets, 91–92; cheap-food economy of, 2–3, 17, 69–71, 98–104; on consumer veil, 105; defined, 51; *DGA* and, 109–110; public-private partnerships of, 54–55, 75–78, 112–113, 249n17; "real food" by, 123–133; response to real food activism, 112–123, 243n75; single-ingredient campaigns against, 110–112, 242n46; USDA's support of, 73–75, 98–99. *See also* privatization of school lunch programs
food intolerance, 9, 64, 150, 241n5
food justice, 3–5; in Georgia, 52–53; protest campaigns for, 8, 9 *fig.*, 131, 134, 169–173; real food movement and, 131–133; solutions for, 201–214; suburbanization and, 53–54. *See also* activism on school lunch programs; economy of care; intersectionality of school lunch programs issues
food preferences. *See* taste preferences
Food Research and Action Center, 56, 73
food safety, 21–22, 99, 105–107, 164. *See also* chemicals in food
foodservice management companies, 1–2, 135, 152–153, 169–171
foodservice workers: altruism and sacrifice of, 6–7, 79, 136–138, 144–145, 152, 154–157, 247n44, 247n55; *vs.* "built-in labor," 81, 84–86, 126, 162–163, 167; cartoon about, 135–136; classifications of, 142–143; on corporate management, 2–3; emotional and financial struggles of, 147–154, 160–161; emotional labor by, 88, 143–148, 162, 167, 246n22; gender and, 5–7, 81–83, 154–158; labor crisis and, 152–169, 235n92, 247n50; lunch lady, as term for, 141–142, 184; lunch shaming and, 134–136, 149–151; mother caricature of, 138–139, 143; New Deal programs for, 43–45; performance indicators and, 83, 85–86, 143, 184, 213, 246n26; poem about, 144–145; protest campaigns by, 8, 9 *fig.*, 131, 173 *fig.*; race and, 7; relationships with kids of, 145–147, 246n25; of RevFoods, 127–128; schedule of, 40 *fig.*; skills and training of, 7, 83, 164–168, 181, 206–208, 252n67; song about, 138; students as, 30, 43, 53, 58, 220–221;

foodservice workers *(continued)*
    turnover of, 83, 137, 160–161, 184,
    248n65; unions of, 88–90, 94, 139–140,
    153–154, 225–228; wages and benefits
    of, 3, 7, 30, 83, 151–152, 154–159, 230n21,
    234n62, 247n46; witch caricature of,
    138–139, 147. *See also* economy of care;
    school lunch programs
Food Stamp Act (1964), 56
food stamp program, 56, 68
food waste: LFTB and, 112; NSLP and,
    77, 86, 239n100; real food movement
    and, 126, 196; studies on, 14, 231n27
Ford Foundation, 76, 84
Foreman, Carol Tucker, 93–94
for-profit food vendors, 18, 31, 38–39,
    75–79, 104, 129–130. *See also* outsourcing food programs
fortification of foods, nutritional, 77–78,
    244n108. *See also* vitamins
4-H, 200
Frederick, Len, 78
Free Breakfast for Children Program
    (FBCP), 61–62
free breakfast programs, 61–63
Free for All (Poppendieck), 132
free lunch program, 32, 43, 58, 63, 84, 90.
    See also school lunch programs
Freeman, Orville, 73
free public education, 20–21
frozen foods, 69–72, 76–78
fruit and vegetable requirements, 123, 129,
    153, 187–188, 252n57, 252n61
Future Farmers of America (FFA), 200

Gagnon, Justin, 123
games, food, 203–204
gardens: community gardens, 211–212;
    school garden army, 35, 36 *fig.;* school
    gardens, 2, 30, 93–94, 197–201; Victory
    Gardens, 45–46, 94. *See also* farm-to-school programs; real food movement
Garnaas, Anna, 150
gender: economy of care and, 5–7, 66, 83,
    132, 249n12; of foodservice workers, 5,
    6–7, 81–83, 154–158; women's rights,
    20, 24, 60–61. *See also* feminist food
    politics; reproductive labor

General Federation of Women's Clubs, 22,
    26, 34, 232n18
General Foods, 114
General Mills, 73
Georgia, 46, 52–53
Good Food Purchasing Program (GFPP),
    221–222
Grabert, Sylvia, 166–167
Graham, Lyman, 155
GRAS (generally recognized as safe) list,
    107–108, 110
Great Society programs, 56, 59, 62, 237n14
Griffith Laboratories, 73
Grist (online publication), 106
Grocery Manufacturers Association, 120
ground beef, 110–111
group kitchen model, 32. *See also* central
    kitchen model; satellite kitchen model
*A Guide for Financing School Food and
    Nutrition Services* report, 84
*Guidelines for Food Purchasing in the
    United States*, 109
Guthman, Julie, 113, 191, 242n54

hamburgers. *See* burgers
Hamilton, Jeff, 113
Hanks, Renée, 143
Hardin, Clifford, 73–74
Harpers' Bazaar, 22
Hartford Courant, 85
Hawkins, Brenda, 157
Hayden, Dolores, 19
health risks of food chemicals, 96–98
Healthy, Hunger-Free Kids Act (2010): Big
    Food and, 119–120, 122; debates on,
    168; grants for farm-to-school programs, 190; nutritional requirements
    of, 121–123, 129, 153–154, 187–188, 215,
    231n27, 244n108, 252n57, 252n61;
    Smart Snack rule, 130; on staff requirements, 7, 166; taste development and,
    252n57
Hernandez, Jasanea, 226, 227
high-fructose corn syrup, 96, 130, 185, 206
Hilliard, David, 62
Hislop, Rasheed, 3–4
Hispanic food preferences, 212
Hmong Academy, 213

Hmong food preferences, 212
Hochschild, Arlie, 143, 246n22
home economics, as field of study, 19, 24–25, 30, 35, 37, 232n9, 233n32
Homegrown Minneapolis Food Policy Council, 178
Home Grown School Food program, 222
home healthcare work, 6, 160, 248n61
Hoover, J. Edgar, 62
Hoover administration, 41–42
housekeeping, 20, 24–26
Houston, Texas, 198
H.R. 5291 (proposed), 66, 238n53
Huerta, Dolores, 91
Hull House, 33
Hult, Eugene, 76
Humane Society, 129
hummus, 178, 199, 210
hunger, 23, 52–53, 63, 146, 148–149. *See also* food justice; malnutrition
Hunt, Caroline, 24–25, 33, 37

Illinois, 61
industrial pollution, 25
ingredients of concern, 96–97, 105–106, 110–112, 113, 115, 117. *See also* chemicals in food
injustice. *See* food justice
institutional racism, 55
Intercontinental Foods Industries, 72
intersectionality of school lunch programs issues, 5–7, 17–18, 33, 60, 131–133, 245n3. *See also* class (in)equity; racial (in)equity
Iowa, 142, 161, 198–199, 200

Jennie-O Turkey Store, 117–118
Johnson, Karen, 146–147
Johnson administration, 56, 62. *See also* Great Society programs
Jonen, Ruth, 100
Jones, Clayton, 135–136
Jukes, Thomas, 92
The Jungle (Sinclair), 21
Just Local, 251n39

Karnes, Offie, 99
Kelley, Florence, 33–34

Kellogg, John Harvey, 104
Kennedy, John F., 59
Kent, Druzilla, 41
ketchup, 98
Kids' Safe and Healthful Foods Project, 187, 188–189
King, Martin Luther, Jr., 60
kitchen infrastructure: for nonprofit school lunch programs, 27, 37, 47; for NSLP, 49, 76, 77, 86, 141; for scratch cooking, 185, 186–188, 251n38. *See also* culinary capacity
Kittredge, Mabel Hyde, 31, 33, 38, 39
Klein, Jennifer, 159–160
Koppen, Stacy, 150, 252n67
Kraft, 115, 243n67
Kramer, John, 59–60
Krimmel, Gary, 86

labeling, 21, 113, 116, 117, 123. *See also* branding; "clean labels"
labor crisis, 152–169, 235n92, 247n50. *See also* foodservice workers
Lachance, Paul, 78
lamb, 99
Lapeze, Louise, 166
Lappé, Frances Moore, 91, 94
Las Vegas, 78
learning and malnutrition, correlation of, 23
legumes, 122, 203, 244n108
Let's Move campaign, 119, 171
Levine, Susan, 59
LFTB, 110–112
Life Time Foundation, 185
like-scratch foods, 125–127
Little Caesars, 104
living environmentalism, 137
Local 217. *See* UNITE HERE
local food procurement, 186, 192, 206–208, 250n18, 250n25, 252n68. *See also* real food movement
Los Angeles, California, 222
Louisiana, 125, 127, 134–135, 156, 166–167
Lunchables, 115
lunch debt, 134–136, 149–151. *See also* economic segregation of school lunch programs

lunch lady, as term, 141–142, 184. *See also* foodservice workers
"Lunchlady Land" (Sandler), 138
lunch shaming, 135–136, 149–151. *See also* economic segregation of school lunch programs
Lyng, Richard, 65–66, 84, 86

MacKendrick, Norah, 22, 115
macrobiotic diet, 91
Maley, Anne, 81
malnutrition, 23, 35, 43. *See also* Healthy, Hunger-Free Kids Act (2010); hunger
Markey, Ed, 110
Maryland, 156 *fig.*, 163 *fig.*
Mass Feeding, 72
material feminism. *See* feminist food politics
maternal caricature, 138–139, 143. *See also* economy of care; emotional labor
Matsufuru, Donna, 164
Matz, Marshall, 109
Maye, Irma, 163
McAlevey, Jane, 224–225
McCoy, Rhonda, 140–141
McDonald's, 83, 101–102, 104
McElwain, Paul, 163–164
McGlone, Frances, 93
McGovern, George, 74
meals-per-labor hour performance indicators, 83, 85–86, 143, 184, 213, 246n26
meat, 72–73, 99, 101–102, 106, 117–118; substitutes, 72–73, 129
Merchandising (publication), 76
Michigan, 170, 197–198
Miles Laboratories, 73
military draft and malnutrition, 35, 43
Miller, Emily, 189
Miller, Laura J., 108, 128
Milwaukee, Wisconsin, 31, 72, 92, 93
Minneapolis, Minnesota, 58, 86, 174–187, 192–197, 203–213, 218
Missouri, 42
The Modern Priscilla (periodical), 32
Morgan, J. P., 32
Morris, Philip, 243n67
Morton Frozen Foods, 70 *fig.*, 72
Moss, Michael, 114

mother caricature, 138–139, 143. *See also* economy of care; emotional labor
Mottern, Nick, 109
muffins, 156 *fig.*
Musk, Kimbal, 198

NAACP (National Association for the Advancement of Colored People), 34, 56, 57, 64
naming contests, food, 203–204
National Association of Colored Women, 34
National Council of Catholic Women, 57
National Council of Jewish Women, 57
National Council of Negro Women, 57
National Council on Hunger and Malnutrition, 56, 59
National Farm to School Network, 189–190
nationalization of school lunch programs, 41–51
National Portion Control, 72
National Restaurant Association, 69, 83
National School Lunch Act (1946), 18, 48–49, 69
National School Lunch Program (NSLP), 2–4; Big Food's control of, 98–104, 110, 119–121; block-grant formula of, 225; Community Eligibility Provision, 141, 216–217; economic efficiency priorities of, 73–74, 84–85, 87, 90–91, 98–104, 213–214; establishment and management of, 18, 48–50, 55–56, 110, 186–187, 236n116, 250n26; funding of, 3, 49, 52–55, 63, 68, 236n4; HHFKA on, 119–123; labor crisis of, 152–169; lunch shaming policies of, 135–136, 149–151; nationwide survey of, 57–58; nonprofit origins of, 18–41; nutritional standards of, 7–8; participation in, 55, 67, 86–87, 208–209, 230n10; performance indicators in, 83, 85–86, 143, 213, 246n26; privatization of, 5, 57, 69–91, 238n74; proposed reform for, 16–17, 50–51, 215–228; staff wage increase and, 83–84; use of frozen foods, 69–72, 76–78. *See also* school lunch programs; US Department of Agriculture (USDA)

National School Lunch Week (October 12–17), 59, 65
National Soft Drink Association, 78
National Welfare Rights Organization (NWRO), 60–61
National Youth Association, 43
natural foods, 104, 108, 114, 118–120, 130. *See also* organic foods; real food movement
neoliberal federal food policies, 4, 51, 75, 96, 120, 188
neoliberal food activism, 191, 242n48. *See also* activism on school lunch programs
Nestle, Marion, 109
New Deal programs, 41–45, 47, 235n86
New England Kitchen, 19–20, 24, 26–28
New Haven, Connecticut, 1, 2, 13–14, 131, 139, 169–171, 226, 229n2
new school construction, 53–54
New York City, New York, 31–33, 60, 76, 201, 216, 232n5
New York Times, 72, 73, 74, 92, 109, 111, 171
Ninemeier, Jack, 89–90
Nixon administration, 63–64, 67
"No More Frozen Food" protest (2012), 173 *fig.*
nonprofit school lunch programs, 16–18; in Boston, 19–20, 24, 26, 27 *fig.*; in Chicago, 31; federal-state partnerships, 35–36, 37, 41–42, 46–49; on for-profit food vendors, 18, 38–39; on malnutrition and learning, 23; in New York City, 31–33; in Philadelphia, 27–31; public-private partnerships in, 36–37; Richards in, 19; of WEIU, 26. *See also* school lunch programs
Northern Girl, 251n39
Northrup, Andrea, 197, 203, 206, 209
Northup, Andrea, 192–195, 199
No Shortcuts (McAlevey), 224–225
NPR (National Public Radio), 106
NSLA. *See* National School Lunch Act (1946)
NSLP. *See* National School Lunch Program (NSLP)
nutrition: federal programs on, 68, 72, 98–99, 107–110, 219; fortification, 77–78, 244n108; in frozen foods, 72–73, 78; school education on, 64–65, 119. *See also* real food movement
Nutrition Reviews, 108

Oakland, California, 61, 93, 196, 222, 223
Obama, Michelle, 2, 119–120, 171
Obama administration, 120–121, 187
obesity, 96, 119, 120, 187, 190, 218
Office of Home Economics, 23, 25, 26. *See also* US Bureau of Home Economics
Older Americans Act (1965), 56
Oliver, Jamie, 2, 123, 140, 249n14
Omnibus Budget Reconciliation Act (1981), 98
Open Hands Farm, 207 *fig.*
organic foods: 1960s demand for, 91, 92; "organic lite," 113, 242n54; public support of, 104, 220, 221, 242n56, 243n68; regulation of, 207; USDA on, 74, 113–114. *See also* "clean labels"; real food movement
Oscar Mayer, 114–115
outsourcing food programs: in farm-to-school programs, 195, 251n38; to food-service management companies, 1–2, 135, 152–153, 169–171, 213; in nonprofit lunch programs, 22, 31, 38–39, 47; NSLA on, 69; prevalence of, 7, 179; unions on, 170; workers' compensation in, 247n46. *See also* for-profit food vendors

Panera Bread, 113
Papa John's Pizza, 113
Parent Teacher Association, 80, 93
patriarchal capitalism, 5–6, 11, 24, 50, 62, 66–67, 139, 228. *See also* economic models; women's rights
penny lunch program, 18, 31, 33, 36, 66, 154
Perdue, 103, 118
Perkins, Carl, 238n53
Perryman, John, 59, 65–66, 68, 71, 73, 78, 237n26. *See also* American School Food Service Association (ASFSA)
pesticides, 91, 97. *See also* agricultural chemicals
Pew Charitable Trusts, 110, 187

Pfizer, 73
Philadelphia, Pennsylvania, 27–29, 226
"Philando Feeds the Children" initiative, 150
phthalates, 97
"pink slime," 110–112
pizza, 120, 124 *fig.*
Pizza Hut, 104
Pollack, Ronald, 73, 75
Pollan, Michael, 74, 132
Poor People's Campaign (PPC), 60
Poppendieck, Janet, 132, 178, 218, 244n92
population boom, 54
poultry, 101–103. *See also* chicken, as food
poverty. *See* economic segregation of school lunch programs
Povitz, Lana Dee, 60
Pratt, Eleanor, 155
prepack lunches, 4 *fig.*, 85 *fig. See also* airline-type lunches
preservation, food, 30, 45, 46
President's Organization on Unemployment Relief, 41–42
prison food programs, 103, 111, 188
privatization of school lunch programs, 5, 57, 69–91, 238n74, 249n17. *See also* food industry; outsourcing food programs; public-private partnerships
productionism, as term and concept, 80, 240n119
Progressive Era politics, 17–24, 25, 232n12
protests: community organizing, 224–228; in right-to-lunch movement, 58–61; signs of, 158 *fig.*; UNITE HERE, 8, 9 *fig.*, 131, 169–170, 171–172, 173 *fig. See also* activism on school lunch programs
public-private partnerships, 36–37, 54–55, 75–78, 112–113, 249n17
Public Voice, 56
Pure Food and Drug Act (1906), 22
Putting Kids First? report, 170

racial (in)equity: care work attitudes and, 233n23; fear of, 49; federal-state partnerships and, 47; foodservice workers and, 7, 157, 247n51; history of federal policies and, 234n59, 237n14; in nonprofit school lunch programs, 33, 34; in

NSLA and NSLP, 49–50, 55, 56–57, 74–75; real food and, 131–133; in settlement house movement, 233n35; wages and, 234n62, 247n48. *See also* class (in)equity; intersectionality of school lunch programs issues
Ralston Purina Corporation, 73, 74, 100
Ramey, Tommy, 139
Raymond, Richard, 107
Raynor, Bruce, 170
Reagan administration, 63, 98
Real Food, Real Kids organization, 106
Real Food Challenge campaign, 131–132
real food lite, 113, 116, 123–133
real food movement: Big Food's response to, 112–123, 243n75; celebrity advocates in, 2, 123, 140, 249n14; community benefits of, 201–214; development and successes of, 104–113; economic model of, 174–178, 189–201; intersectionality and, 116, 131–133, 245n3; local procurement in, 186, 192, 206–208, 250n18, 250n25, 252n68; in Minneapolis, 174–187, 192–197, 203–213, 218; in New Haven, 169–171; public concern and, 242n56; *vs.* "real" factory food, 123–131. *See also* activism on school lunch programs; farm-to-school programs; organic foods; sustainable food movement
#RealSchoolFood campaign, 123–124
reproductive labor, 17, 114–115, 132, 217, 230n16. *See also* economy of care; feminist food politics; gender
RevFoods (Revolutionary Foods), 115, 126–128, 244n101, 244n104
Richards, Ellen Swallow, 19–20, 24, 216
right-to-lunch movement, 58–61
Robert Wood Johnson Foundation, 187
Rockefeller, John D., 31
Rolling Stone, 74
Roosevelt administration, 42. *See also* New Deal programs
Rooted in Community (RIC), 219–220, 221
Rose, Mary Swartz, 23
Rosenthal, Amy, 194
Ruis, Andrew, 22, 32

Russell, Richard, 49
Rylie, Marilyn, 143

Sackin, Barry, 105
salmonella, 111
Sanders, Beulah, 61
Sanders, Frances, 93
Sandler, Adam, 138
San Francisco, California, 222
satellite kitchen model, 32. *See also* central kitchen model; group kitchen model
Saturday Night Live, 138
savior complex, 33
Sazón, 201
Schmidt, Leah, 121
school breakfast programs, 63–64, 141, 216. *See also* free breakfast programs
The School Cafeteria (Bryan), 37–38, 40 *fig.*
school-community kitchens, 219, 222–224. *See also* community benefits of real food; community kitchens
school dinner programs, 141
School Food Focus, 112–113, 128, 194, 242n49, 242n51, 251n48
school foodservice employees. *See* foodservice workers
School Foodservice Journal (publication), 71, 86, 88, 92, 93, 239n111. *See also* *School Lunch Journal* (publication)
school garden army, 35, 36 *fig.*
School Garden Collaborative, 197–198
school gardens, 2, 30, 93–94, 197–201. *See also* farm-to-school programs; real food movement
School Life (periodical), 41
The School Lunch (Smedley), 27, 28
School Lunch Committee (NYC), 31–33
School Lunch Journal (publication), 71, 80–81, 88. See also *School Foodservice Journal* (publication)
school lunch programs: alternative visions for, 91–95, 178–189; convenience foods in, 69–73, 76–78, 115, 239n111; economic segregation of, 5, 17, 61, 66, 134–136, 173, 216–217, 229n8; funding for, 3, 49, 52–55, 63, 68, 236n4; gardens for, 2, 30, 93–94, 197–201; nationalization of, 41–51; penny lunch, 18, 31, 33, 36, 66, 154; statistics on, 3, 37, 44, 46, 230n15; surplus commodities program for, 42–45, 98–99, 235n88, 241n14; teachers' support of, 204; as universal and free, 58–59, 65–68, 150–151, 216–217, 235n93, 238n53; of WFA and Victory Gardens, 45–47. *See also* farm-to-school programs; National School Lunch Program (NSLP); nonprofit school lunch programs
The School Lunchroom (Bard), 52
School Nutrition Association (SNA): advocacy campaigns of, 225; conferences of, 12, 105, 117–118, 120–122, 128; on farm-to-school programs, 190; on job classifications, 142–143; as organization, 7, 11; on processed foods, 105. *See also* American School Food Service Association (ASFSA)
school snack programs, 141
Schwan's Company, 120
scratch cooking: rural examples of, 200–201
scratch-cooking programs, 123–133, 163–168; kitchen equipment for, 89, 251n38; speed-scratch foods, 124–125, 172, 175–176, 212; urban examples of, 92, 140–141, 178–187. *See also* culinary capacity; farm-to-school programs; kitchen infrastructure; real food movement
Seale, Bobby, 62
seed saving, 220
SEIU (Service Employees International Union), 152, 169, 181
Senate Select Committee on Nutrition and Human Needs, 73, 74, 109
senior food programs, 56, 68, 188, 219, 238n60
settlement house movement, 33, 35, 233n35
Shared Ground Farmers' Co-op, 193 *fig.*
Sheraton, Mimi, 72, 92
Siegel, Bettina Elias, 111
Silent Spring (Carson), 91
Simon, Bryant, 103
single-ingredient campaigns, 110–112, 242n46
Smart Snack rule, 130

Smedley, Emma, 16, 18, 27–31, 222
Smith-Lever Act (1914), 30–31
Smucker's, 129–130
snack industry, 98, 104, 129–130
socialism, 23, 35
social reproduction, 17, 61–63. *See also* economy of care; reproductive labor
soda industry, 75, 78, 79 *fig.*, 104
Sodexo, 153
sodium erthorbate, 117
sodium nitrite, 117
Somali food preferences, 212
sorbates, 97
South Carolina, 58
Southern Christian Leadership Conference, 60
South Korea, 219
Spargo, John, 23
special dietary needs, 9, 64, 150, 241n5
Special Supplemental Food Program for Women, Infants, and Children (WIC), 68
speed-scratch foods, 124–125, 124 *fig.*, 172, 175–176, 186–187, 212. *See also* scratch-cooking programs
spices, 71, 201–202, 203
split-shift staffing, 171–172
stagflation, 67
Stare, Frederick J., 108
stealth health strategy, 244n108
stigmatization of foodservice workers, 134–138
student activists, 131–132, 219–220
student workers, 30, 43, 53, 58, 220–221
suburbanization, 53–54
Subway, 104
summer food program, 60, 68, 159, 210
surplus food distribution, 42–45, 98–99, 235n88
sustainable food movement, 110, 137, 172, 207–208, 220, 230n14, 231n39, 252n2. *See also* environmental justice movement; real food movement
Swift Chemical, 73

Taco Bell, 104
Talley, Kathy, 157

taste preferences: class and, 251n55; culture and, 125–126, 166, 201, 212–213, 241n5; development of, 199, 203–204, 220, 252n57, 252n61
taste tests, 203–204
Texas, 198
TGI Fridays, 130–131
theft, 148
Their Daily Bread report, 57–59
Time (publication), 127, 150
tobacco industry, 118–119
toxins. *See* agricultural chemicals; chemicals in food
Tronto, Joan, 5, 67, 136, 215
True Food Taste Tests, 203–204
Truman administration, 50
Trump administration, 110, 215
turkey, 100, 101 *fig.*, 117–118, 196, 204
turnover, 83, 137, 160–161, 184, 248n65
20 Million for Lunch report, 84
Tyson Foods, 101–102, 103, 125, 241n15

Uhlenkamp, Tim, 200, 251n50
unions, 88–90, 91, 94, 139–140, 153–154, 181, 225–228. *See also* community organizing; UNITE HERE
United Bronx Parents, 60
United Farm Workers, 91
UNITE HERE, 229n2; community organizing of, 225–226, 247n43; failure of, 90; protest campaigns of, 8, 9 *fig.*, 131, 134, 169–170, 171–172, 173 *fig.*; union members of, 1, 152, 247n57. *See also* unions
universal free school lunch programs, 58–59, 65–68, 150–151, 216–217, 235n93, 238n53
university food programs, 131
University of Wisconsin–Madison, 24–25
Urban School Food Alliance (USFA), 112–113, 242n49
US Bureau of Home Economics, 37. *See also* Office of Home Economics
US Department of Agriculture (USDA): ASFSA campaign against, 65–66; commodity program, 42–45, 98–101; Equipment Assistance Program, 187; Farm-to-School Census, 196; Farm-to-

School Program, 128, 190; free breakfast program by, 63; on labeling, 116, 130; on NSLA provisions, 55–56; nutrition assistance programs, 68, 219, 252n61; on privatization of NSLP, 69, 238n74; summer food program of, 68, 159; support of agriculture and food industry by, 72, 73–77, 84, 98–104. *See also* National School Lunch Program (NSLP)
US Department of Health, Education, and Welfare, 58
US Food and Drug Administration (FDA), 107–108, 110, 114, 179
US War Department, 35

values-based food economy, 131, 193–195, 250n18. *See also* real food movement; sustainable food movement
Vancil-Leap, Ashley, 138
vegan diet, 210
vegetables. *See* fruit and vegetable requirements
vegetarian diet, 91, 241n5
vending machines, 78, 104, 129, 130. *See also* commercialization of cafeteria food
Victory Gardens, 45–46, 94. *See also* community gardens
Vilsack, Tom, 120, 188
Virginia, 44 *fig.*
vitamins, 72, 106. *See also* fortification of foods, nutritional; nutrition
Volume Feeding Management (publication), 81

War Food Administration, 42–43, 45–48
Warner, Kenneth, 119

Washington DC, 6 *fig.*
Washington Post, 109
waste. *See* food waste
water pollution, 25
Waters, Alice, 2, 16–17, 123, 197
Weber, Bertrand: on food, 182, 185–186, 212–213; position of, 175, 178–179; on school gardens, 199; on staffing, 155–156, 173, 180, 181, 184–185. *See also* Minneapolis, Minnesota
welfare rights movement, 58–61, 66
Wells, Patricia, 109
West Virginia, 140–141, 249n14
white flight, 53
white privilege, 33–34, 234n59, 247n48. *See also* racial (in)equity
Whole Kids Foundation, 197
Wilhelm, John, 170
Winson, Anthony, 75
Wisconsin, 31, 92–93, 168 *fig.*
witch caricature, 138–139, 147
Women's City Club of Chicago, 31
Women's Educational and Industrial Union (WEIU), 26, 27 *fig.*
women's rights, 20, 24, 60–61. *See also* gender; patriarchal capitalism
Women's School Alliance of Wisconsin, 31
Woodward, Ellen, 43
workers. *See* foodservice workers; labor crisis; student workers
Works Progress Administration (WPA), 43–45, 235n93

Young Women's Christian Association, 57
Youth Food Bill of Rights, 220, 221
youth leaders, 131–132, 219–220

Zelizer, Viviana, 21

CALIFORNIA STUDIES IN FOOD AND CULTURE

Darra Goldstein, Editor

1. *Dangerous Tastes: The Story of Spices,* by Andrew Dalby
2. *Eating Right in the Renaissance,* by Ken Albala
3. *Food Politics: How the Food Industry Influences Nutrition and Health,* by Marion Nestle
4. *Camembert: A National Myth,* by Pierre Boisard
5. *Safe Food: The Politics of Food Safety,* by Marion Nestle
6. *Eating Apes,* by Dale Peterson
7. *Revolution at the Table: The Transformation of the American Diet,* by Harvey Levenstein
8. *Paradox of Plenty: A Social History of Eating in Modern America,* by Harvey Levenstein
9. *Encarnación's Kitchen: Mexican Recipes from Nineteenth-Century California: Selections from Encarnación Pinedo's* El cocinero español, by Encarnación Pinedo, edited and translated by Dan Strehl, with an essay by Victor Valle
10. *Zinfandel: A History of a Grape and Its Wine,* by Charles L. Sullivan, with a foreword by Paul Draper
11. *Tsukiji: The Fish Market at the Center of the World,* by Theodore C. Bestor
12. *Born Again Bodies: Flesh and Spirit in American Christianity,* by R. Marie Griffith
13. *Our Overweight Children: What Parents, Schools, and Communities Can Do to Control the Fatness Epidemic,* by Sharron Dalton
14. *The Art of Cooking: The First Modern Cookery Book,* by the Eminent Maestro Martino of Como, edited and with an introduction by Luigi Ballerini, translated and annotated by Jeremy Parzen, and with fifty modernized recipes by Stefania Barzini
15. *The Queen of Fats: Why Omega-3s Were Removed from the Western Diet and What We Can Do to Replace Them,* by Susan Allport
16. *Meals to Come: A History of the Future of Food,* by Warren Belasco
17. *The Spice Route: A History,* by John Keay

18. *Medieval Cuisine of the Islamic World: A Concise History with 174 Recipes,* by Lilia Zaouali, translated by M. B. DeBevoise, with a foreword by Charles Perry
19. *Arranging the Meal: A History of Table Service in France,* by Jean-Louis Flandrin, translated by Julie E. Johnson, with Sylvie and Antonio Roder; with a foreword to the English-language edition by Beatrice Fink
20. *The Taste of Place: A Cultural Journey into Terroir,* by Amy B. Trubek
21. *Food: The History of Taste,* edited by Paul Freedman
22. *M. F. K. Fisher among the Pots and Pans: Celebrating Her Kitchens,* by Joan Reardon, with a foreword by Amanda Hesser
23. *Cooking: The Quintessential Art,* by Hervé This and Pierre Gagnaire, translated by M. B. DeBevoise
24. *Perfection Salad: Women and Cooking at the Turn of the Century,* by Laura Shapiro
25. *Of Sugar and Snow: A History of Ice Cream Making,* by Jeri Quinzio
26. *Encyclopedia of Pasta,* by Oretta Zanini De Vita, translated by Maureen B. Fant, with a foreword by Carol Field
27. *Tastes and Temptations: Food and Art in Renaissance Italy,* by John Varriano
28. *Free for All: Fixing School Food in America,* by Janet Poppendieck
29. *Breaking Bread: Recipes and Stories from Immigrant Kitchens,* by Lynne Christy Anderson, with a foreword by Corby Kummer
30. *Culinary Ephemera: An Illustrated History,* by William Woys Weaver
31. *Eating Mud Crabs in Kandahar: Stories of Food during Wartime by the World's Leading Correspondents,* edited by Matt McAllester
32. *Weighing In: Obesity, Food Justice, and the Limits of Capitalism,* by Julie Guthman
33. *Why Calories Count: From Science to Politics,* by Marion Nestle and Malden Nesheim
34. *Curried Cultures: Globalization, Food, and South Asia,* edited by Krishnendu Ray and Tulasi Srinivas

35. *The Cookbook Library: Four Centuries of the Cooks, Writers, and Recipes That Made the Modern Cookbook,* by Anne Willan, with Mark Cherniavsky and Kyri Claflin
36. *Coffee Life in Japan,* by Merry White
37. *American Tuna: The Rise and Fall of an Improbable Food,* by Andrew F. Smith
38. *A Feast of Weeds: A Literary Guide to Foraging and Cooking Wild Edible Plants,* by Luigi Ballerini, translated by Gianpiero W. Doebler, with recipes by Ada De Santis and illustrations by Giuliano Della Casa
39. *The Philosophy of Food,* by David M. Kaplan
40. *Beyond Hummus and Falafel: Social and Political Aspects of Palestinian Food in Israel,* by Liora Gvion, translated by David Wesley and Elana Wesley
41. *The Life of Cheese: Crafting Food and Value in America,* by Heather Paxson
42. *Popes, Peasants, and Shepherds: Recipes and Lore from Rome and Lazio,* by Oretta Zanini De Vita, translated by Maureen B. Fant, foreword by Ernesto Di Renzo
43. *Cuisine and Empire: Cooking in World History,* by Rachel Laudan
44. *Inside the California Food Revolution: Thirty Years That Changed Our Culinary Consciousness,* by Joyce Goldstein, with Dore Brown
45. *Cumin, Camels, and Caravans: A Spice Odyssey,* by Gary Paul Nabhan
46. *Balancing on a Planet: The Future of Food and Agriculture,* by David A. Cleveland
47. *The Darjeeling Distinction: Labor and Justice on Fair-Trade Tea Plantations in India,* by Sarah Besky
48. *How the Other Half Ate: A History of Working-Class Meals at the Turn of the Century,* by Katherine Leonard Turner
49. *The Untold History of Ramen: How Political Crisis in Japan Spawned a Global Food Craze,* by George Solt
50. *Word of Mouth: What We Talk About When We Talk About Food,* by Priscilla Parkhurst Ferguson
51. *Inventing Baby Food: Taste, Health, and the Industrialization of the American Diet,* by Amy Bentley

52. *Secrets from the Greek Kitchen: Cooking, Skill, and Everyday Life on an Aegean Island,* by David E. Sutton
53. *Breadlines Knee-Deep in Wheat: Food Assistance in the Great Depression,* by Janet Poppendieck
54. *Tasting French Terroir: The History of an Idea,* by Thomas Parker
55. *Becoming Salmon: Aquaculture and the Domestication of a Fish,* by Marianne Elisabeth Lien
56. *Divided Spirits: Tequila, Mezcal, and the Politics of Production,* by Sarah Bowen
57. *The Weight of Obesity: Hunger and Global Health in Postwar Guatemala,* by Emily Yates-Doerr
58. *Dangerous Digestion: The Politics of American Dietary Advice,* by E. Melanie duPuis
59. *A Taste of Power: Food and American Identities,* by Katharina Vester
60. *More Than Just Food: Food Justice and Community Change,* by Garrett M. Broad
61. *Hoptopia: A World of Agriculture and Beer in Oregon's Willamette Valley,* by Peter A. Kopp
62. *A Geography of Digestion: Biotechnology and the Kellogg Cereal Enterprise,* by Nicholas Bauch
63. *Bitter and Sweet: Food, Meaning, and Modernity in Rural China,* by Ellen Oxfeld
64. *A History of Cookbooks: From Kitchen to Page over Seven Centuries,* by Henry Notaker
65. *Reinventing the Wheel: Milk, Microbes, and the Fight for Real Cheese,* by Bronwen Percival and Francis Percival
66. *Making Modern Meals: How Americans Cook Today,* by Amy B. Trubek
67. *Food and Power: A Culinary Ethnography of Israel,* by Nir Avieli
68. *Canned: The Rise and Fall of Consumer Confidence in the American Food Industry,* by Anna Zeide
69. *Meat Planet: Artificial Flesh and the Future of Food,* by Benjamin Aldes Wurgaft
70. *The Labor of Lunch: Why We Need Real Food and Real Jobs in American Public Schools,* by Jennifer E. Gaddis

Founded in 1893,
UNIVERSITY OF CALIFORNIA PRESS
publishes bold, progressive books and journals
on topics in the arts, humanities, social sciences,
and natural sciences—with a focus on social
justice issues—that inspire thought and action
among readers worldwide.

The UC PRESS FOUNDATION
raises funds to uphold the press's vital role
as an independent, nonprofit publisher, and
receives philanthropic support from a wide
range of individuals and institutions—and from
committed readers like you. To learn more, visit
ucpress.edu/supportus.

CPSIA information can be obtained
at www.ICGtesting.com
Printed in the USA
FSHW021908081019
62814FS